SECOND EDITION

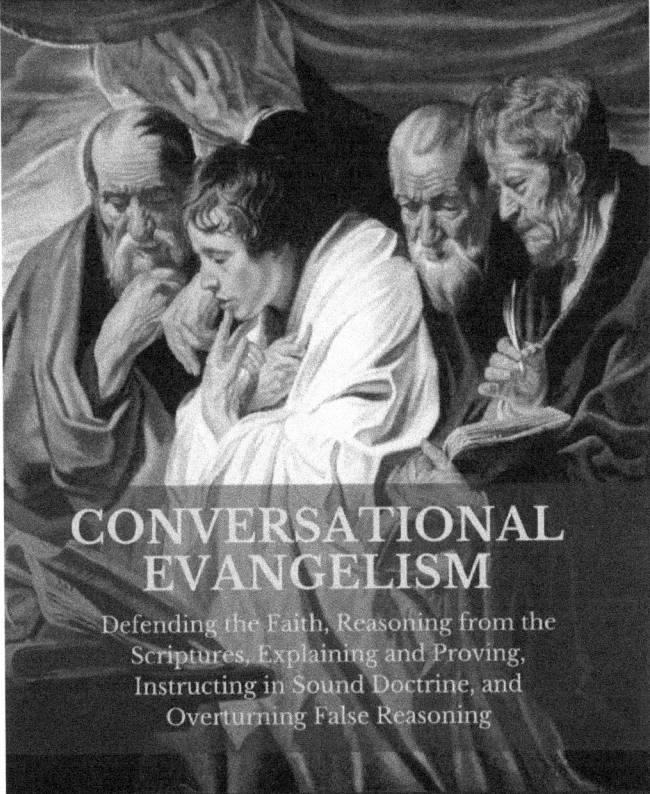

CONVERSATIONAL EVANGELISM

Defending the Faith, Reasoning from the
Scriptures, Explaining and Proving,
Instructing in Sound Doctrine, and
Overturning False Reasoning

Edward D. Andrews

CONVERSATIONAL EVANGELISM

Defending the Faith, Reasoning from the
Scriptures, Explaining and Proving,
Instructing in Sound Doctrine, and
Overturning False Reasoning

Edward D. Andrews

Christian Publishing House

Cambridge, Ohio

Unless otherwise stated, scripture quotations are from *The Holy Bible, Updated American Standard Version (UASV)®*, copyright © 2016 by Christian Publishing House, Professional Conservative Christian Publishing of the Good News!

CONVERSATIONAL EVANGELISM Defending the Faith, Reasoning from the Scriptures, Explaining and Proving, Instructing in Sound Doctrine, and Overturning False Reasoning

Publishing by Christian Publishing House

ISBN-13: 978-1-945757-37-2

ISBN-10: 1-945757-37-X

Table of Contents

PREFACE How This Book Works

Evangelism is the work of a Christian evangelist, of which all true Christians are obligated to partake to some extent, which seeks to persuade other people to become Christian, especially by sharing the basics of the Gospel, but also the deeper message of biblical truths. Today the Gospel is almost an unknown, so what does the Christian evangelist do? **Preevangelism** is laying a foundation for those who have no knowledge of the Gospel, giving them background information, so that they can grasp what they are hearing. The Christian evangelist is preparing their mind and heart so that they will be receptive to the biblical truths. In many ways, this is known as apologetics.

Christian apologetics [Greek: *apologia*, "verbal defense, speech in defense"] is a field of **Christian theology** which endeavors to offer a reasonable and sensible basis for the **Christian faith**, defending the faith against objections. It is reasoning from the Scriptures, explaining and proving, as one instructs in sound doctrine, many times having to overturn false reasoning before he can plant the seeds of truth. It can also be earnestly contending for the faith and saving one from losing their faith, as they have begun to doubt. Moreover, it can involve rebuking those who contradict the truth. It is being prepared to make a defense to anyone who asks the Christian evangelist for a reason for the hope that is in him or her. – Jude 1.3, 21-23; 1 Pet 3.15; Acts 17:2-3; Titus 1:9.

We Live In a New World

We are living a very secular humanistic, secularistic, relativistic, and nihilistic world, which is a philosophy or worldview that stresses human values without reference to religion or spirituality. In the 1950s, life was very simple and the vast majority of the populace, the world, accepted Christianity over. Almost all people living then were familiar with the Bible, generally accepting it as truth. Then, we could easily engage almost anyone in a lengthy Bible conversation, and evangelism, the sharing of the good news, was well received. Times have changed for the worst. The world today is full of skeptics and Bible critics, who are actually educating themselves with hundreds of books coming on the market, which is designed to undermine God, the Bible, and the faith.

The new atheist is not like the atheist of 1950. In those days, the atheist just did not believe in God, and he did not share those beliefs with others, it was live and let live atmosphere. Today we have an atheist, who is not content with keeping his views private. In fact, they are on an atheist revival like those the Christian revivals had in the 19th-and 18th-centuries (John Wesley, Charles Wesley and George Whitefield in England and the Great Awakening in America). This is an enormous increase in activity, from enraged persons, who have an interest in try to persuade Christians and non-Christians to their point of view, both nationally and globally. Even the agnostic[1] is in the crosshairs of the atheist, for the new atheist will not allow there to be doubt as to the existence of a god or creator.

Like most skillful turns of phrase, atheist comments about god or God all *sound* good. "Men never commit evil so fully and joyfully as when they do it for religious convictions." — Blaise Pascal "All thinking men are atheists." — Ernest Hemingway "Atheism is more than just the knowledge that gods do not exist, and that religion is either a mistake or a fraud. Atheism is an attitude, a frame of mind that looks at the world objectively, fearlessly, always trying to understand all things as a part of nature." — Emmett F. Fields "There is something infantile in the presumption that somebody else has a responsibility to give your life meaning and point... The truly adult view, by contrast, is that our life is as meaningful, as full and as wonderful as we choose to make it." — Richard Dawkins, *The God Delusion*

The greatest book to have ever been written is the inerrant, inspired Word of God. The greatest tool of the atheist in the 20th and 21st centuries has been their written words. We think of the internet's reach, the new devices like the Amazon Kindle and Barnes & Noble Nook, and the greatest force for influencing the mind for good or bad, the smartphone. Everything written, magazines, newspapers, blogs, and of course books are all read on these devices. The atheist book will become a bestselling book far sooner than any Christian book. Note these **titles by the atheists**. There is *The God Delusion* by Richard Dawkins (Jan 2011), *God Is Not Great: How Religion Poisons Everything* by Christopher Hitchens (May 2007), and *Why There Is No God: Simple Responses to 20 Common Arguments for the Existence of God* by Armin Navabi and Nicki Hise (Oct 2014). Now note these **titles by Christian apologists**. *On Guard: Defending Your Faith with Reason and Precision* by William Lane Craig and Lee Strobel (Mar 2010), *The Reason for God* by Timothy Keller (Feb 2008), and *I Don't Have Enough Faith to Be an Atheist* (Foreword by David Limbaugh by Norman L. Geisler and Frank Turek (Mar 2004). The atheist's books are # 1 bestsellers, while the top three Christian apologetic books are nowhere near being bestsellers. Christians who have little knowledge of God or his Word are buying these atheist books just to see

---

[1] Agnostics believe that it is impossible to know whether God exists.

what they say, which has resulted in tens of thousands losing their faith because of intense doubts, as they did not have all the facts.

The purpose of this book is to **Defend the Faith and God's Word.** This book is meant to serve as a training tool, to enable its readers to carry out 1 Peter 3:15. Therefore, the book is to be *studied* through not *read*. Sadly, almost all Christians are biblically uninformed as to what the Bible really teaches, so they are unable to teach others sound doctrine and defend those doctrines against attack. Therefore, our other purpose for this book is to help its readers to **Reasoning from the Scriptures.** This is done by skillfully using the Word of God to **explain and prove** the truth of God, his Word and that he has a people, i.e., Christians and all that entails. Reasoning from the Scriptures is also **instructing in sound doctrine**, not to mention **overturning false reasoning**, and helping our fellow brothers and sisters, **who have begun to doubt**. CONVERSATION EVANGELISM will also have a partner publication that will help with those, who are uninformed as to the foundational doctrines of the faith. It is *THE EVANGELISM STUDY TOOL: Basic Bible Doctrines of the Christian Faith.* It will be out sometime in 2016. It is also by the author of this book, Edward D. Andrews.

INTRODUCTION The Importance of Apologetic Evangelism

The Christian Evangelist

Before delving into our book on Conversational Evangelism, let us take a moment to listen to one of the world's leading authorities on Spiritual disciplines for our Christian life by Donald S. Whitney, who covers our obligation to evangelize very well,

Most of those reading this book will not need convincing that evangelism is expected of every Christian. All Christians are not expected to use the same methods of evangelism, but all Christians are expected to evangelize.

Before we go further, let's define our terms. What is evangelism? If we want to define it thoroughly, we could say that evangelism is to present Jesus Christ in the power of the Holy Spirit to sinful people, in order that they may come to put their trust in God through Him, to receive Him as their Savior, and serve Him as their King in the fellowship of His Church.[2] If we want to define it simply, we could say that New Testament evangelism is communicating the gospel. Anyone who faithfully relates the essential elements of God's salvation through Jesus Christ is evangelizing. This is true whether your words are spoken, written, or recorded, and whether they are delivered to one person or to a crowd.

Why is evangelism expected of us? The Lord Jesus Christ Himself has commanded us to witness. Consider His authority in the following:

"Therefore go and make disciples of all nations, baptizing them in the name of the Father and of the Son and of the Holy Spirit, and teaching them to obey everything I have commanded you. And surely I will be with you always, to the very end of the age" (Matt. 28: 19-20).

"He said to them, 'Go into all the world and preach the good news to all creation'" (Mark 16: 15).

---

[2] See J. I. Packer, Evangelism and the Sovereignty of God (Downers Grove, IL: InterVarsity Press, 1979), pages 37-57.

"And repentance and forgiveness of sins will be preached in his name to all nations, beginning at Jerusalem" (Luke 24: 47).

"Again Jesus said, 'Peace be with you! As the Father has sent me, I am sending you'" (John 20: 21).

"But you will receive power when the Holy Spirit comes on you; and you will be my witnesses in Jerusalem, and in all Judea and Samaria, and to the ends of the earth" (Acts 1: 8).

These commands weren't given to the apostles only. For example, the apostles never came to this nation. For the command of Jesus to be fulfilled and for America to hear about Christ, the gospel had to come here by other Christians. And the apostles will never come to your home, your neighborhood, or to the place where you work. For the Great Commission to be fulfilled there, for Christ to have a witness in that "remote part" of the earth, a Christian like you must discipline yourself to do it.

Some Christians believe that evangelism is a gift and the responsibility of only those with that gift. They appeal to Ephesians 4:11 for support: "It was he who gave some to be apostles, some to be prophets, some to be evangelists, and some to be pastors and teachers." While it is true that God gifts some for ministry as evangelists, He calls all believers to be His witnesses and provides them with both the power to witness and a powerful message. Every evangelist is called to be a witness, but only a few witnesses are called to the vocational ministry of an evangelist. Just as each Christian, regardless of spiritual gift or ministry, is to love others, so each believer is to evangelize whether or not his or her gift is that of evangelist.

Think of our responsibility for personal evangelism from the perspective of 1 Peter 2:9: "But you are a chosen people, a royal priesthood, a holy nation, a people belonging to God." Many Christians who are familiar with this part of the verse don't have a clue how the rest of it goes. It goes on to say that these privileges are yours, Christian, "that you may declare the praises of him who called you out of darkness into his wonderful light." We normally think of this verse as establishing the doctrine of the priesthood of all believers. But it is equally appropriate to say that it also exhorts us to a kind of prophet hood of all believers. God expects each of us to "declare the praises" of Jesus Christ.[3]

While this author agrees with Whitney's every word in the above, I would emphasize that we are to evangelize, so as to make disciples, which is more involved that simply sharing the Gospel. Paul summarizes the most basic elements of the gospel message, that is, the death, burial, resurrection, and appearances of the resurrected Christ. (1 Cor. 18:1-8) Therefore, the Gospel explained in detail or simply stated as Paul has put it, will not be enough to convert many unbelievers to the faith. Therefore, it is best to understand our responsibility as evangelist, in the sense of being able to proclaim or explain our Christian teachings both offensively and defensively: to **(1)** defend God's Word, **(2)** defend the faith, **(3)** pull some who doubt back from the fire, and **(4)** most importantly, to help the lost find salvation.

All Christians are to be Evangelizers

We live in the world today where Genesis 6:5 and 8:21 is magnified a thousand fold.

Genesis 6:5 Updated American Standard Version (UASV)

⁵ Jehovah saw that the wickedness of man was great in the earth, and that every inclination of the **thoughts of his heart was only evil continually**.

Imperfect humans are mentally bent toward evil, meaning that they lean toward wickedness.

Genesis 8:21 Updated American Standard Version (UASV)

²¹ And when Jehovah smelled the pleasing aroma, and Jehovah said in his heart, "I will never again curse the ground because of man, for the inclination of **man's heart is evil from his youth**. Neither will I ever again strike down every living thing as I have done.

Who teaches their children to lie? Who teaches their children to steal? Who teaches their children to be stingy? No normal parent would teach their child to do such things, but they will pick them up naturally if they are not taught to do otherwise. Imperfect human still has the conscience that God gave Adam and Eve, and even in its imperfect state, it will help us to determine what is good and what is bad. However, if it is ignored, it will grow callused, meaning that it will have no feelings

---

[3] Whitney, Donald S. (2012-01-05). Spiritual Disciplines for the Christian Life with Bonus Content (Pilgrimage Growth Guide) (p. 100-101). Navpress.

when it should be prompting us to avoid wrongdoing. On the other hand, if it is fed the Word of God, our conscience can enable us to avoid sin, to control our mental bent toward evil. This is just one facet of the good news that we are to share with all the nations, in all of the inhabited earth.

Matthew 24:14 Updated American Standard Version (UASV)

[14] And this gospel of the kingdom will be proclaimed **in all the inhabited earth**[4] as a testimony **to all the nations,** and then the end will come.

With much of what people see today, one wonders what the Goods News could be. We have Iran, a terrorist nation that seeks to use nuclear weapons against Israel and the United States and is the biggest sponsor of terrorism in the Middle East. We have Al Qaeda, radical Islam, who is seeking to establish Shariah Law in all the inhabited earth, which they are doing through torture and acts of terrorism. We have an, even more, extreme form of Islam, ISIS. They are slaughtering and raping little children by the thousands as the United States under President Obama had done very little. We have North Korea, a communist nation, which has its people starving to death while the leaders live a life of luxury. We have Russia, who seeks to establish its former self, i.e., the Soviet Union. We have mass murders, serial killers, rapists, child molesters, and the list could go on infinitely.

Isaiah 52:7 Updated American Standard Version (UASV)

[7] How beautiful upon the mountains
   are the feet of him who **brings good news,**
who publishes peace, who brings good news of happiness,
   who **proclaims salvation,**
   who says to Zion, "Your God has become king!"[5]

Nahum 1:15 Updated American Standard Version (UASV)

[15] Behold, upon the mountains, the feet of him
   who brings good news,
   who publishes peace!
Keep your feasts, O Judah;
   fulfill your vows,
for never again shall the worthless[6] pass through you;
   he is cut off completely.

---

[4] Or *in the whole world*

[5] Or *"Your God Reigns!"*

[6] Or *wicked*

Romans 10:14-15 Updated American Standard Version (UASV)

14 How then will they call on him in whom they have not believed? And how are they to believe in him of whom they have never heard? And how will they hear without someone to preach? **15** And how are they to preach unless they are sent? As it is written, "How beautiful are the feet of those who declare good news of good things!"[7]

Christianity today, has sadly, fallen away from the evangelism that they had been assigned, the preaching and teaching of the good news, the making of disciples. (Matt. 24:14; 28:19-20) The first-century Christians were very zealous when it came to sharing the good news and biblical truths with others. In fact, the new believers were taught the basics of the faith, before they were baptized. Once they were baptized, they were immediately involved in spreading these same biblical truths to others. This is why just ninety years after the sacrificial death of Jesus Christ; there were more than a million Christians spread all throughout the then known world of the Roman Empire. Christians today, should have this same zeal because Jesus gave only one command that was to be carried out after his departure, the making of disciples.

The good news is that this current evil age that we live in is not all that we have to look forward to, as all have the opportunity of gaining eternal life. Yes, the path of salvation is open to all. Therefore, Christians today should be in the work of being used by God to help as many as possible to find the path of salvation, before Christ's second coming. Some might argue that God already knows the ones who are his; therefore, they will find the truth themselves. Yes, he foreknows those that will accept the truth or find the truth because he can see ahead. What God has is a foreknowledge of people's free will. However, his foreknowledge does not determine what humans will do, but rather what humans freely choose to do that determines God's foreknowledge. It is better to understand it that God knows in advance what choice people will freely make. It is the free decisions of human beings that determine what foreknowledge God has of them, as opposed to the reverse. Foreknowledge is to know all that is going to happen based on the free willed decisions of humans. Foreordination is God interjecting himself, to bring about a desired outcome. God foreknows all that he foreordains but God does not foreordain all that he foreknows. To know something and to bring about something are entirely different. Therefore, what he sees in the future is his people taking the good news of the kingdom to the inhabited earth before the end can come, so the right-hearted ones can trust in Jesus and receive everlasting life.

---

[7] Romans 10:15 : Cited from Isa. 52:7; [Nah. 1:15; Eph. 6:15]

John 3:16 Updated American Standard Version (UASV)

[16] "For God so loved the world that he gave his only-begotten Son, in order that everyone trusting[8] in him will not be destroyed but have eternal life.

John 3:36 Updated American Standard Version (UASV)

[36] The one trusting[9] in the Son has eternal life, but the one who disobeys the Son will not see life, but the wrath of God remains on him.

Revelation 21:3-4 Updated American Standard Version (UASV)

[3] And I heard a loud voice from the throne, saying, "Behold, the tabernacle of God is among men, and he will dwell[10] among them, and they shall be his people,[11] and God himself will be among them,[12] [4] and he will wipe away every tear from their eyes, and death shall be no more, neither shall there be mourning, nor crying, nor pain anymore, for the former things have passed away."

An evangelizer is a proclaimer of the gospel or good news, i.e., a messenger of good. The Greek *euaggelistes* (evangelizer) is closely related to the word euaggelion, "good news" or "gospel."

All Christians are commissioned to be evangelizers. It should be understood the word is used in a special way at Ephesians 4:8, 11-12, where Paul describes "the gifts to men" that Christ gave to the congregation when he ascended on high. "And he gave some as apostles, and some as prophets, and some as **evangelists** and some as pastors and teachers ... It is the observation of this author that this is applying to the narrow sense of evangelizers who serve as missionaries.

However, in a broader sense of the word, all Christians are to be evangelizers. The only way that we are going to accomplish the Great Commission and the statement made by Jesus is, if all are working toward that goal, "This gospel of the kingdom shall be preached in the whole world as a testimony to all the nations, and then the end will come." (Matt 24:14) We have had missionaries since the days of Paul, and especially the last couple of centuries, and yet Christianity is not getting

---

[8] The grammatical construction of pisteuo "believe" followed by eis "into" plus the accusative causing a different shade of meaning, having faith into Jesus.

[9] The grammatical construction of pisteuo "believe" followed by eis "into" plus the accusative causing a different shade of meaning, having faith into Jesus.

[10] Lit *he will tabernacle*

[11] Some mss *peoples*

[12] One early ms and be *their God*

the work done. In fact, while the US and UK were the primary ones sending out the most missionaries, they are now receiving missionaries themselves from the very countries they had been sent missionaries to long ago.

Christians are under obligation to herald, or proclaim the Word of God and make disciples. The pastor and all Christians should view the sharing of God's Word, to win people to the faith, as full-time, all the time because faith involves all of life. We need always to be ready and alert in our faith, so as to participate willingly in proclaiming God's Word, whether it is convenient or not. If a police officer and a firefighter are on duty 24/7, to save lives, should we expect less of a Christian, who is saving souls? This is not to say that all Christians are to give up their lives, their ministries they were called to (e.g., preaching, teaching, etc.) and become a full-time evangelist. Rather, it just means that all Christians are capable of evangelizing when the opportunity presents itself (i.e., informal), and give of themselves a few hours a month in an official church evangelism program (phone, street, houses-to-house, internet, and the like). Otherwise, they are very much involved in church life, family life, and the ministry they were called to do.

What Is Specifically Meant by Obligated and Evangelism?

What do we mean by **obligated** and what we mean by **evangelism** are at the heart of the matter and are indeed related to each other.

EVANGELISM: Again, an evangelist is a proclaimer of the gospel or good news, as well as all biblical truths. There are levels of evangelism, which is pictured in first-century Christianity. All Christians evangelized in the first century, but a select few fit the role of a full-time evangelist (Ephesians 4:8, 11-12), as Philip and Timothy.

Both Philip and Timothy are specifically mentioned as evangelizers. (Ac 21:8; 2 Tim. 4:5) Philip was a full-time evangelist after Pentecost, who was sent to the city of Samaria, having great success. An angel even directed Philip to an Ethiopian Eunuch, to share the good news about Christ with him. Because of the Eunuch's already having knowledge of God by way of the Old Testament, Philip was able to help him understand that the Hebrew Scriptures pointed to Christ as the long-awaited Messiah. In the end, Philip baptized the Eunuch. After that, the Spirit again sent Philip on a mission, this time to Azotus and all the cities on the way to Caesarea. (Ac 8:5, 12, 14, 26-40) Paul evangelized in many lands, setting up one congregation after another. (2 Cor. 10:13-16) Timothy was an evangelizer or missionary, and Paul placed distinct importance on evangelizing when he gave his parting encouragement to Timothy. – 2 Timothy 4:5; 1 Timothy 1:3.

The office of apostle and evangelist seem to overlap in some areas but could be distinguished in that apostles traveled and set up congregations, which took evangelizing skills, but also developed the congregations after they were established. The full-time evangelists were more of a missionary, being stationed in certain areas to grow and develop congregations. In addition, if we look at all of the apostles and the evangelists, plus Paul's more than one hundred traveling companions, and it seems very unlikely that they could have had Christianity at over one million by the 125 C.E. This was accomplished because all Christians were obligated to carry out some level of evangelism.

OBLIGATED: In the broadest sense of the term for evangelizer, all Christians are obligated to play some role as an evangelist.

Basic Evangelism is planting seeds of truth and watering any seeds that have been planted. [In the basic sense of this word (*euaggelistes*), this would involve all Christians.] In some cases, it may be that one Christian planted the seeds, which were initially rejected, so he was left in a good way because the planter did not try to force the truth down his throat. However, some time later he faces something in life that moves him to reconsider those seeds and some other Christian waters what had already been planted. This evangelism can be carried out in all of the methods that are available: informal, house-to-house, street, phone, internet, and the like. What amount of time is invested in the evangelism work is up to each Christian to decide for themselves.

Making Disciples is having any role in the process of getting an unbeliever from his unbelief state to the point of accepting Christ as his Savior and being baptized. Once the unbeliever has become a believer, he is still developed until he has become strong. Any Christian could potentially carry this one person through all of the developmental stages. On the other hand, it may be that several have some part. It is like a person that specializes in a certain aspect of a job but is aware of all the other aspects, in case he is called on to carry out that aspect. Again, each Christian must decide for themselves what role they are to have, and how much of a role, but should be prepared to fill any role needed.

Part-Time or Full-Time Evangelist is one who sees this as their calling and chooses to be very involved as an evangelist in their local church and community. They may work part-time to supplement their work as an evangelist. They may be married with children, but they realize their gift is in the field of evangelism. If it were the wife, the husband would work toward supporting her work as an evangelist and vice-versa. If it were a single person, he or she would supplement their work by being employed part-time, but also the church would help as well. This person is well trained in every aspect of bringing one to Christ.

Congregation Evangelists should be very involved in evangelizing their communities and helping the church members play their role at the basic levels of evangelism. There is nothing to say that one church could not have many within, who have the calling of an evangelist, which would and should be cultivated.

Jesus Set the Example

Christians today should be seeking to walk in the steps of their exemplar, Jesus Christ. Yes, we have been called, so that we might follow in Jesus' steps.

1 Peter 2:21 Updated American Standard Version (UASV)

[21] For to this you were called, because Christ also suffered for you, leaving you an example, so that you should follow in his footsteps.

Luke 4:17-21 Updated American Standard Version (UASV)

[17] And the scroll of the prophet Isaiah was given to him. And he unrolled the scroll and found the place where it was written,

[18] "The Spirit of the Lord is upon me,
because he has anointed me
to **proclaim good news**[13] to the poor.
He has sent me to **proclaim release** to the captives
and recovering of sight to the blind,
to set free those who are oppressed,
[19] to **proclaim the favorable year of the Lord.**"

[20] And he rolled up the scroll and gave it back to the attendant and sat down; and the eyes of all in the synagogue were fixed on him. [21] And he began to say to them, "Today this Scripture has been fulfilled in your hearing."

A survey of the Gospels indicates that Jesus' publishing program—via his traveling throughout Galilee and Judea and proclaiming the good news of the kingdom—was extensive and effective. Thousands and thousands of people heard the word from Jesus himself. In ancient times, the method of oral publication was far more effective than written publication. Books were expensive to make, and many people did not read. Most relied on oral proclamation and aural reception to receive messages. Indeed, most education was based upon oral delivery and aural reception/memorization to transmit texts. Thus, Jesus

---

[13] Or the gospel

taught his disciples orally, and they committed his teachings to memory. When it came time, several years later, for the disciples to put these teachings into writing, they were aided by the Holy Spirit, who would remind the disciples of all that Jesus had taught them (John 14:26). Jesus' disciples, commissioned by him, continued the same publishing work after Jesus' death and resurrection. This publishing is known as the *kerygma* (Greek for "proclamation"). The word *kerygma* is taken straight from a well-known practice in ancient times. A king publicized his decrees throughout his empire by means of a *kerux* (a town crier or herald). This person, who often served as a close confidant of the king, would travel throughout the realm, announcing to the people whatever the king wished to make known. In English, we known him as a herald. Each New Testament disciple considered himself or herself to be like the *kerux*—a herald and publisher of the Good News.[14]

Yes, Jesus was an evangelizer, and he trained hundreds of evangelizers throughout his three and half years of ministry. "He went throughout all Galilee, teaching in their synagogues and proclaiming the gospel of the kingdom." (Matthew 4:23) Then he said to his disciples, "The harvest is plentiful, but the laborers are few; therefore pray earnestly to the Lord of the harvest to send out laborers into his harvest." (Matt. 9:37-38) The apostles set up Christian congregations, with every Christian following the footsteps of Christ, to be an evangelizer.

There is nothing, wrong with helping our neighbor deal with the social ills of the world, or taking some time to support a political candidate that we hope will implement laws that will allow for the greater work of evangelizing. However, Christianity on some levels has become a social institution, working night and day to save the world of humankind that is alienated from God, which has diverted them from the lifesaving work of being an evangelist. While we are citizens of this world, and of the country that we live in, our true Kingdom is the Kingdom of God in the person of Jesus Christ. Below we will quote the *Holman Illustrate Bible Dictionary* at length, to understand and appreciate what the Kingdom of God is.

The Kingdom of God

In the NT, the fullest revelation of God's divine rule is in the person of Jesus Christ. His birth was heralded as the birth of a king (Luke 1:32–33). The ministry of John the Baptist

---

[14] Philip Comfort, *Encountering the Manuscripts: An Introduction to New Testament Paleography & Textual Criticism* (Nashville, TN: Broadman & Holman, 2005), 2.

prepared for the coming of God's kingdom (Matt. 3:2). The crucifixion was perceived as the death of a king (Mark 15:26–32).

Jesus preached that God's kingdom was at hand (Matt. 11:12). His miracles, preaching, forgiving sins, and resurrection are an in-breaking of God's sovereign rule in this dark, evil age.

God's kingdom was manifested in the church. Jesus commissioned the making of disciples on the basis of His kingly authority (Matt. 28:18–20). Peter's sermon at Pentecost underscored that a descendent of David would occupy David's throne forever, a promise fulfilled in the resurrection of Christ (Acts 2:30–32). Believers are transferred from the dominion of darkness into the kingdom of the Son of God (Col. 1:13).

God's kingdom may be understood in terms of "reign" or "realm." Reign conveys the fact that God exerts His divine authority over His subjects/kingdom. Realm suggests location, and God's realm is universal. God's reign extends over all things. He is universally sovereign over the nations, humankind, the angels, the dominion of darkness and its inhabitants, and even the cosmos, individual believers, and the church.

In the OT, the kingdom of God encompasses the past, present, and future. The kingdom of God had implications in the theocratic state. The kingdom of God is "already" present but "not yet" fully completed, both a present and future reality. The kingdom was inaugurated in the incarnation, life, ministry, death, and resurrection of Jesus. God's kingdom blessings are in some measure possessed now. People presently find and enter God's kingdom. God is now manifesting His authoritative rule in the lives of His people. God's kingdom, however, awaits its complete realization. His people still endure sufferings and tribulations. When fully consummated, hardships will cease. Kingdom citizens currently dwell alongside inhabitants of the kingdom of darkness. God will eventually dispel all darkness. The final inheritance of the citizens of God's kingdom is yet to be fully realized. The resurrection body for life in the eschatological kingdom is a blessing awaiting culmination.

God's kingdom is soteriological in nature, expressed in the redemption of fallen persons. The reign of Christ instituted the destruction of all evil powers hostile to the will of God. Satan, the "god of this age," along with his demonic horde, seeks to hold the hearts of people captive in darkness. Christ has defeated Satan and the powers of darkness and delivers believers. Although Satan still is active in this present darkness, his ultimate conquest and destruction are assured through Christ's sacrificial death and resurrection. Sinners enter Christ's kingdom through regeneration.

Many of Jesus' parables emphasize the mysterious nature of God's kingdom. For example, an insignificant mustard seed will grow a tree, as God's kingdom will grow far beyond its inception (Matt. 13:31–32). The kingdom of God is like seed scattered on the ground. Some seed will fall on good soil, take root, and grow. Other seed, however, will fall on hard, rocky ground and will not grow. Likewise, the kingdom will take root in the hearts of some but will be rejected and unfruitful in others (Matt. 13:3–8). As wheat and tares grow side by side, indistinguishable from each other, so also the sons of the kingdom of God and the sons of the kingdom of darkness grow together in the world until ultimately separated by God (Matt. 13:24–30, 36–43).

Although closely related, the kingdom and the church are distinct. George Eldon Ladd identified four elements in the relationship of the kingdom of God to the church. The kingdom of God creates the church. God's redemptive rule is manifested over and through the church. The church is a "custodian" of the kingdom. The church also witnesses to God's divine rule.

The kingdom of God is the work of God, not produced by human ingenuity. God brought it into the world through Jesus Christ, and it presently works through the church. The church preaches the kingdom of God and anticipates the eventual consummation.[15]

The last sentence of our quote says in part, "the church preaches the kingdom of God." This has not been the case for almost 2,000 years. Today, the church preaches from the pulpit to those that are already Christian, as well as those, who happen into the church.

Romans 10:13-17 Updated American Standard Version (UASV)

[13] For "everyone who calls on the name of the Lord[16] will be saved.""

---

[15] Stan Norman with Gentry Peter, "Kingdom of God," ed. Chad Brand, *Holman Illustrated Bible Dictionary* (Nashville, TN: Holman Bible Publishers, 2003), 988–989.

[16] Quotation from Joel 2:32, which reads, "everyone who calls on the name of Jehovah shall be saved." In other words, Paul was referring to the Father not the Son.

14 How then will they call on him in whom they have not believed? And how are they to believe in him of whom they have never heard? And **how will they hear without someone to preach**? **15** And how are they to preach unless **they are sent**? As it is written, "How beautiful are the feet of **those who declare good news** of good things!"**17**

16 But they have not all obeyed the gospel. For Isaiah says, "Lord,**18** who has believed what he has heard from us?" **17** So **faith comes from hearing**, and hearing through **the word of Christ**.

10:14b. Faith requires hearing. **And how can they believe in the one of whom they have not heard?** More than anything else, this question is the crux of all missiological activity since the first century. God has ordained that people must hear (or read, or otherwise understand the content of) the word of God in order to be saved. One who knows the gospel must communicate it to one who does not know it.[19]

Yes, missionaries have been sent out throughout the last few centuries, but this is not the first-century way, it is the way of the last few centuries. However, over the last few decades, many trained in missions have come to realize the error of their ways. They have tried to grow the church by going outside of their community, to grow it back to their community. The other alternative was to grow from their community out to the rest of the world. The objective of sinking time, energy and finances into just a select few (missionaries), believing they were going to get the Great Commission accomplished. Of late, we hear much about having missionary churches that evangelize their own community, with their own members.

10:14c. Hearing requires preaching. **And how can they hear without someone preaching to them?** Since no other media except the human voice was of practical value in spreading the gospel in the first century, **preaching** is Paul's method of choice. And yet, in the media-rich day in which we minister, has anything replaced preaching as the most effective way to communicate the gospel? We thank God for the printed page, and even for cutting-edge presentations of the gospel circling the globe on the internet. But it is still the human voice that cracks with passion, the human eye that wells with tears of

---

[17] Quotation from Isa 52:7; Nah 1:15

[18] Quotation from Isaiah 53:1, which reads, "Who has believed our message? And to whom has the arm of Jehovah been revealed?"

[19] Kenneth Boa and William Kruidenier, *Romans*, vol. 6, Holman New Testament Commentary (Nashville, TN: Broadman & Holman Publishers, 2000), 314.

gratitude, and the human frame that shuffles to the podium, bent from a lifetime of service to the gospel, which reaches the needy human heart most readily. Hearing may not *require* **preaching** in person today, but it always benefits from it.[20]

This author agrees with the *Holman* commentary that modern technology is great, but there is but one-way to reach "the whole world as a testimony to all nations" (Matt. 24:14). Yes, it is the human voice, but not as the *Holman* Commentary suggests with one man walking to a podium to preach, but for hundreds of millions to take to their communities, trained to preach (herald, proclaim) the message, and to teach what they had been taught "to one who does not know it." Most will be a part-time evangelist, in that they have the skills to deal with opportunities that present themselves, but also spend a few hours a month being more officially involved with an evangelism church program. A smaller number, those called to be evangelists in the stricter sense of the word, should serve as full-time evangelists within their community.

First-Century Christians Evangelized

Evangelism is the work of a Christian evangelist (persuading people to become Christian), while **preevangelism** is laying a foundation for those who have no knowledge of the Gospel, giving them background information, so that they are able to grasp what they are hearing. The Christian evangelist is preparing their mind and heart so that they will be receptive to the biblical truths. In many ways, this is known as apologetics. **Christian apologetics** [Greek: *apologia*, "verbal defense, speech in defense"] is a field of **Christian theology** which endeavors to offer a reasonable and sensible basis for the **Christian faith** , defending the faith against objections. It is reasoning from the Scriptures, explaining and proving, as one instructs in sound doctrine, many times having to overturn false reasoning before he can plant the seeds of truth. However, some Christians feel that apologetics is not biblical. They say that our only obligation is to share the basic gospel (Jesus life and ministry, his ransom sacrificial death, his resurrection, and ascension) and leave the rest up to the Holy Spirit.

While that may sound like the easy route to take, we must entertain Jesus' words and take them to heart. He said, "Not everyone who says to me, 'Lord, Lord,' will enter the kingdom of heaven, but the one who does the will of my Father who is in heaven." (Matt 7:21) The key here is that our obligation as slaves of Christ is to do the "will of the Father."

---

[20] Ibid., 314.

What happens to those who felt like they were doing the "will of the Father" but were not? Jesus said in verse 23, "I declare to them, 'I never knew you; depart from me, you workers of lawlessness.'" The apostle John touched on this all-important point as well. He said, "The one who does the will of God lives forever." (1 John 2:17) Therefore, it might be beneficial to look at the example that Jesus and the apostles set.

Jesus did not just state what the good news of the kingdom and then sit back waiting for the Holy Spirit to do the rest. No, Jesus appealed to the Moses and prophets of old. By doing so, he was using apologetics, i.e., offering a reasonable and sensible basis for accepting him as the long-awaited Messiah. In essence, his offering such evidence would shut down any critics, and give reasons for hope to those with a receptive heart.

Luke 24:25-27 Updated American Standard Version (UASV)

25 And he said to them, "O foolish men, and slow of heart to believe all that the prophets have spoken! **26** Was it not necessary for the Christ to suffer these things and to enter into His glory?" **27** And beginning from Moses and all the Prophets, he interpreted to them in all the Scriptures the things concerning himself.

Jesus is doing apologetics in his sharing the good news. He is using the Hebrew Scriptures, as evidence of what he is saying is so. In other words, he is **reasoning** from the Scriptures.

John 14:10-11 Updated American Standard Version (RSV)

10 Do you not believe that I am in the Father and the Father is in me? The words that I say to you, I do not speak on my own authority, but the Father who dwells in me does his works. **11** Believe me that I am in the Father and the Father is in me; otherwise, believe on account of the works themselves.

Here, again, Jesus is carrying out apologetics, as opposed to just saying, 'I came to give my life as a ransom for many.' He is using the miracles as evidence that he is the long-awaited Messiah. Jesus was using evidences to establish something as true. He offered a reasonable and sensible basis for accepting the he had come to offer his life as a ransom, defending against objects to the contrary. This is reasoning, explaining, and proving, as he instructs them in the good news of the kingdom, having to overturn their false reasoning that the coming king would be like the one that the Jewish leaders described.

What about the apostles, did they also use apologetics? William Lane Craig says that we need to look at "Peter's sermon on the day of Pentecost recorded in the second chapter of Acts. In verse 22, he appeals to Jesus' miracles. In verses 25–31 he appeals to fulfilled prophecy. In verse 32, he appeals to Christ's resurrection. By means of these arguments the apostles sought to show their fellow Jews that Christianity is true."[21] Then, we have the apostle Paul, who set an example like no other.

Acts 17:1-4 Updated American Standard Version (UASV)

¹ Now when they had passed through Amphipolis and Apollonia, they came to Thessalonica, where there was a synagogue of the Jews. ² And according to Paul's custom, he went to them, and for three Sabbaths **reasoned with them from the Scriptures,** ³ **explaining** and **proving** that it was necessary that the Christ had to suffer and rise again from the dead, and saying, "This Jesus whom I am proclaiming to you is the Christ." ⁴ And **some of them were persuaded** and joined Paul and Silas, as did a great many of the devout Greeks and not a few of the leading women.

Clearly, when we consider the Gospels, all Jesus said therein comes to about a three to four-hour talk, and he quoted or referred to over 120 Scriptures. Of course, in a three and a half year ministry, Jesus said far more than that, but it gives us insight into how much the Son of God himself depended on Scripture. The apostle Paul is one of the greatest Christian teachers of all time. At a synagogue of the Jews in Thessalonica, "according to Paul's custom, he went to them, and for three Sabbaths **reasoned with them from the Scriptures, explaining and proving** that it was necessary that the Christ had to suffer and rise again from the dead, and saying, 'This Jesus whom I am proclaiming to you is the Christ.'" – Acts 17:1-3.

What was the result of Paul's "reasoned with them from the Scriptures, explaining and proving"? The account says, "Some of them were persuaded and joined Paul and Silas, as did a great many of the devout Greeks and not a few of the leading women." – Acts 17:4.

While we can proclaim and teach anything that is within the Scriptures, what should be our primary message? Since we are to follow in the footsteps of Jesus, we might consider his commission. On one occasion, Jesus "departed and went into a desolate place. And the people sought him and came to him, and they tried to keep him from going away from them. But he said to them, "I must **preach the kingdom of God** to the other cities also, for **I was sent for this purpose**." – Luke 4:43.

---

[21] Craig, William Lane (2010-03-01). *On Guard: Defending Your Faith with Reason and Precision* (Kindle Locations 175-177). David C. Cook. Kindle Edition.

In fact, in reference to the last days, Jesus said, "And this gospel of the kingdom will be proclaimed in all the inhabited earth[22] as a testimony to all the nations, and then the end will come." – Matthew 24:14.

Returning to the apostle Paul, we see this was an emphasis in his proclaiming and teaching. Here again, Paul "entered the synagogue and for three months **spoke boldly, reasoning** and **persuading** them **about the <u>kingdom of God</u>**. When Paul was in Rome, "they came to him at his lodging in greater numbers; and he **expounded** to them, **testifying about <u>the kingdom of God</u>** and **trying to persuade** them concerning Jesus both from the Law of Moses and from the Prophets, from morning till evening." For two whole years in Rome, Paul was "**proclaiming the <u>kingdom of God</u>** and **teaching** about the Lord Jesus Christ **with all boldness** and without hindrance." – Acts 19:8; 28:23, 31.

> [Jesus] reminded them in John 20:20 of his crucifixion: "He showed them his hands and side. The disciples were overjoyed when they saw the Lord." Then he reminded them again about his peace in verse 21. Jesus said, "Peace be with you!" Jesus proclaimed peace, reminded them of his crucifixion, pronounced peace again, and then told them, "As the Father has sent me, I am sending you" (John 20: 21). With that one command, Jesus announced two thousand years of direction for the church, still in effect for the churches of today, even your church. He proclaimed that we are sent. The church is, and you are individually, God's missionary to the world. Your church is God's instrument to reach the world, and it includes reaching your community. We are sent on mission by God. We are to be a missions-centered church by calling, nature, and choice. We are called to be on mission in our community. We have been sent to be on mission in our context, and we must accept that call, that directive to be on mission where God has placed us, not five, not fifty, not five hundred years ago and not thirty miles away, not three hundred miles away, not three thousand miles away. We are exhorted to be on mission where God has placed us now, and our job is to [evangelize] wherever we are.[23]

Yes, the Great Commission was an assignment given to all Christians, which starts right in our own backyard. We can effectively evangelize the world if we do it one community at a time, starting with our community.

---

[22] Or *in the whole world*

[23] Putman, David; Ed Stetzer (2006-05-01). Breaking the Missional Code: Your Church Can Become a Missionary in Your Community (pp. 30-31). B&H Publishing. Kindle Edition.

Matthew 28:19-20 Updated American Standard Version (UASV)

¹⁹ Go therefore and make disciples of **all nations** … teaching them … I am with you always, even to the end of the age."

In the Greek, the words for "all nations" are *panta ta ethnē*. We get our English word ethnic from the Greek word *ethnē*. When we hear (or read) Jesus' command to "go to all nations," we think countries. But when Jesus spoke those words, there were no countries as we understand them today. The nation-state is an invention of the modern era. In Jesus' day there were groups of people, and there were empires. Jesus' instructions mean that we must go to all the people groups in the world. The Jewish disciples of that day knew that Jesus was speaking about the Gentiles. The gospel was to go beyond the Jewish nation. But they also thought of Phoenicians, Macedonians, Greeks, Romans, and others Jesus did not use the word for empires like the Roman Empire, the Persian, or the Greek. Jesus used the word for peoples, and the Jews knew this meant all the different kinds of Gentiles. It meant to go to all the different kinds of people that existed. This is still God's plan today. In today's world, we have to remember that we are still sent … to all different kinds of peoples. The word peoples represents every ethno-linguistic people group around the world, all the different ethnicities present in our cities, and even the different generations that live in our communities.[24]

Who all were involved in the evangelism work of the first-century? The evidence is all too clear that Jesus set the example for the apostles. Jesus had said that they would do a work greater than his, meaning that his ministry would only last three and a half years, while theirs would run for decades. In the end, all Christians were evangelizing their communities, with a select few, taking the message everywhere. By the beginning of the first century, there were over one million Christians. One of the gifts of the Holy Spirit, i.e., the speaking in tongues, that is, a foreign language, accomplished this miraculous growth.

Acts 1:14 Updated American Standard Version (UASV)

¹⁴ All these with one mind were continually devoting themselves to prayer, together with the women and Mary the mother of Jesus, and his brothers.

---

[24] Putman, David; Ed Stetzer (2006-05-01). Breaking the Missional Code: Your Church Can Become a Missionary in Your Community (p. 34). B&H Publishing. Kindle Edition

Let us not why these disciples were gathered, "with one mind were continually devoting themselves to prayer." Christians gathering has been essential from the very beginning. Christians gather to be instructed and counseled, to encourage one another, and most importantly, to join together in our worship of the Father. Our prayers as a group are very pleasing to Him.

Acts 2:1, 4 Updated American Standard Version (UASV)

[1] When the day of Pentecost was being fulfilled, they were all together in one place. [4] And they were all filled with the Holy Spirit and began to speak with other tongues,[25] as the Spirit was giving them utterance.[26]

Here again, the Christian were "**all together** in one place," an upper room, and who were anointed with the Holy Spirit.

Acts 2:17 Updated American Standard Version (UASV)

[17] "'And it shall be in the last days, God says,
that I will pour out my Spirit on all flesh,
and your **sons** and your **daughters** shall prophesy,*
  and your young men shall see visions,
  and your old men shall dream dreams; (See Joel 2:28-29)

* The Greek behind the word "prophecy" here does not carry the meaning of "prediction," or "foretelling," (Gr., *propheteuo*), but literally means "a speaker out [Gr., pro, "before" or "in front of," and *phemi*, "say"]" and thus describes a proclaimer, one who proclaims messages of God. That is, namely "**to proclaim an inspired revelation, *prophesy* ... Acts 2:17f; John 3:1; 19:6; 21:9; 1 Cor, 11:4f ...; 13:9; 14:1, 3–5, 24, 31, 39; Rev. 11:3 ...**[27]

Therefore, prediction, or foretelling, is not the primary meaning conveyed by the root verbs in the original languages (Heb., *nava*; Gr., *propheteuo*). All, who proclaim the Word of God to another are prophesying, i.e., proclaiming the inspired, inerrant Word.

Thus, in the first century, both Christian men and women prophesied the good news of the kingdom, as well as other revealed biblical truths. Moreover, going into the second century, many would have the twenty New Testament books to share as well.

---

[25] Or *languages*

[26] Or *enable them to speak*

[27] William Arndt, Frederick W. Danker, and Walter Bauer, *A Greek-English Lexicon of the New Testament and Other Early Christian Literature* (Chicago: University of Chicago Press, 2000), 890.

Matthew 24:14 Updated American Standard Version (UASV)

¹⁴ And this gospel of the kingdom **will be proclaimed in all the inhabited earth**[28] as a testimony to all the nations, and then the end will come.

In reading dozens of books on missions and evangelism, I have seen focus on the proclaiming, but the bigger question has not received much attention. An important question that many are not asking is, "What gospel is going to be proclaimed in all the inhabited earth. There are 41,000 different Christian denominations, all of which hold different doctrinal views, some of which even contradictions others, and yes, even salvation doctrines, so, which is to be proclaimed?

Acts 1:8 Updated American Standard Version (UASV)

⁸ But you will receive power when the Holy Spirit has come upon you; and you will be my witnesses **in both Jerusalem** and in **all Judea** and **Samaria**, and to **the extremity of the earth**."

The prophecy of Jesus that the Good News would be "**proclaimed throughout the [then known] whole world** to all the nations [peoples], and then the end will come," was applicable to them, and was carried out. The "nations" (Gr., *ethnē*), means the same as it does at Matthew 28:19, where we are commanded to "make disciples of **all nations.**" The first-century Christians made disciples of **all nations** (the peoples), in all of **the then known world,**[29] before **the end came** for the natural nation of Israel, as the Romans destroyed Jerusalem in 70 C.E.,[30] killing over a million Jews, and taking hundreds of thousands captive. The apostle Paul wrote the Christians in Colossae about ten years earlier, 60 C.E, commenting on the spread of Christianity

Colossians 1:23 Updated American Standard Version (UASV)

²³ if indeed you continue in the faith firmly established and steadfast, and not moved away from the hope of the gospel that you have heard, **which was proclaimed in all creation under heaven**, and of which I, Paul, became a minister.

---

[28] Or *in the whole world*

[29] Christianity had spread from Jerusalem to Rome, Macedonia, Greece, Asia, Bithynia, Pontus, Galatia, Cappadocia, Pamphylia, Syria, Cyprus, Crete, Babylon, Persian Gulf, Spain, Italy, Malta, Illyricum, Media, Parthia, Elam Arabia, Cyrene, Libya, Egypt, and Ethiopia.

[30] Dates of events before the Common Era (Also known as AD) are marked by the abbreviation B.C.E. Dates of events during the Common Era are marked by the abbreviation C.E.

First-Century Christian Worship and the Truth

The early Christians met in congregations, which for many of them, were private homes, to take in the truth. (Rom. 16:3-5) The book of Hebrews tells us some of what happened at these meetings. They were there, in part, to "consider how to stir up one another to love and good works, not neglecting to meet together, as is the habit of some, but encouraging one another, and all the more as you see the Day drawing near." (Heb. 10:24-25) Tertullian of the late second, early third century (c.155–after 220 C.E.), wrote, "We meet to read the books of God ... In any case, with those holy words we feed our faith, we lift up our hope, we confirm our confidence."[31] In order to become a Christian, certain requirements had to be met, as we can see from the *Zondervan Handbook to the History of Christianity*,

> As before, people who converted to Christianity were baptized. First, however, the new believer would be properly instructed in the beliefs and practices of Christianity. These 'beginner' Christians were the 'catechumens' (from the Greek meaning 'oral handing down', that is, teaching by word of mouth) and the way in which they were instructed developed as time went on. In the First apology, published in the middle of the second century, the Christian writer Justin Martyr (c. 100-165) gives us a valuable insight into how people were admitted into the church in Rome:[32]

> As many as are persuaded and believe that what we teach and say is true, and undertake to be able to live accordingly, are instructed to pray and to entreat God with fasting, for the remission of their sins that are past, we praying and fasting with them. Then they are brought by us where there is water, and are regenerated in the same manner in which we were ourselves regenerated. For, in the name of God, the Father and Lord of the universe, and of our Saviour Jesus Christ, and of the Holy Spirit, they then receive the washing with water.[33]

Thus, there were clear requirements before someone could be baptized, such as education of basic doctrinal beliefs, praying, fasting, and

---

[31] Thomas C. Oden, Ministry Through Word and Sacrament, Classic Pastoral Care, 59 (New York: Crossroad, 1989).

[32] Jonathan Hill, *Zondervan Handbook to the History of Christianity*, 46 (Grand Rapids: Zondervan, 2006).

[33] Justin Martyr, "The First Apology of Justin", in The Ante-Nicene Fathers, Volume I: The Apostolic Fathers With Justin Martyr and Irenaeus, ed. Alexander Roberts, James Donaldson and A. Cleveland Coxe, 183 (Buffalo, NY: Christian Literature Company, 1885).

a commitment to live a moral life and an understanding of Christian beliefs. These new believers were discovered by taking the message into the community. Then, they were taught to become a disciple of Jesus Christ. They were then organized into Christian congregations. These same disciples (learners) were trained to make more disciples, in the same way, preaching the Good News, and sharing the basic doctrinal beliefs.

Note the introduction in Paul's counsel to the Corinthians,

2 Corinthians 1:1 Updated American Standard Version (UASV)

[1] Paul, an apostle of Christ Jesus by the will of God, and Timothy our brother,

To the church of God which is at Corinth with all the saints [holy ones] who are throughout Achaia:

Clearly, Paul is speaking to all Christians in Corinth and Achaia, not just those taking the lead within the Christian Congregation. All Christians are being addressed, which pertains to the evangelism of biblical truths, as Paul went on to write, "Therefore, since we have this ministry, as we received mercy, we do not lose heart ... Now all these things are from God, who reconciled us to Himself through Christ and gave us the ministry of reconciliation, namely, that God was in Christ reconciling the world to Himself, not counting their trespasses against them, and He has committed to us the word of reconciliation. Therefore, we are ambassadors for Christ, as though God were making an appeal through us; we beg you on behalf of Christ, be reconciled to God ... giving no cause for offense in anything, so that the ministry will not be discredited, but in everything commending ourselves as servants of God, in much endurance, in afflictions, in hardships, in distresses."– 2 Corinthians 4:1; 5:18-20; 6:3-4.

A ministry (*diakonia*) is a service to others on God's behalf. God had called Paul to be an instrument of **reconciliation;** his life was devoted to making peace between God and humanity through the preaching of the gospel ... Paul's role in the divine plan of reconciliation led him to a remarkable claim. He and his company were **Christ's ambassadors**. "Ambassadors" was a technical political term used in Paul's day that closely parallels our English word "ambassadors." An ambassador represented a nation or kingdom in communication with other nations. Paul had in mind his apostolic call to represent the kingdom of Christ to the nations of the earth. Ambassadors held positions of great honor in the ancient world because they represented the authority of the kings on whose behalf they spoke.

This was also true for Paul as the ambassador of Christ. When he spoke the message of reconciliation, it was **as though God were making his appeal through** him. Rather than speaking directly to the nations of earth, God ordained that human spokespersons would speak for him. As an apostle, Paul had authority to lead and guide the church (2 Cor. 13:3, 10). Yet, this description applies to all who bear the gospel of Christ to others—even to those who do not bear apostolic authority (1 Pet. 4:11). Though we may not present the gospel as perfectly as Paul did, we do speak on God's behalf when we bring the message of grace to others. But Paul and his company were to be received as mouthpieces of God in the most authoritative sense. (Pratt Jr 2000, pp. 359-60)

There is a reason why Christians are given the role of speaking on God's behalf. What reason would that be? The world of mankind is "being darkened in their understanding, excluded from the life of God because of the ignorance that is in them, because of the hardness of their heart." Eph. 4:18) Our ministry of reconciliation is to be a spokesperson on God's behalf offering a message of grace to those who have receptive hearts. We are giving them an opportunity to "have peace with God through our Lord Jesus Christ." We speak in behalf of God, so that they may also 'be declared righteous, obtaining access through Him by faith into this grace in which they stand, and they rejoice in the hope of the glory of God." (Rom. 5:1-2) Note the introduction in Paul's counsel to the Christians in Rome,

Romans 1:7-8 Updated American Standard Version (UASV)

7 to all those who are in Rome as beloved ones of God, called to be holy ones: Grace to you and peace from God our Father and the Lord Jesus Christ. 8 First, I thank my God through Jesus Christ concerning all of you, because your faith is being proclaimed in the whole world.

Clearly, Paul is speaking to all Christians in Rome, not just those taking the lead within the Christian Congregation. All Christians are being addressed, which pertains to the evangelism of biblical truths, as Paul went on to write,

Romans 10:8-10 Updated American Standard Version (UASV)

8 But what does it say? "The word is near you, in your mouth and in your heart," that is, the word of faith which we are proclaiming, 9 that[34] if you confess with your mouth that Jesus is Lord and believe in your heart that God raised him from the dead, you will be saved. 10 For with the

---

[34] Or *because*

37

heart one believes, resulting in righteousness,[35] and with the mouth one confesses, resulting in salvation.[36]

The privilege of preaching the word of faith is open to all. In fact, he reinforced his argument by adding,

Romans 10:14-15 Updated American Standard Version (UASV)

[14] How then will they call on him in whom they have not believed? And how are they to believe in him of whom they have never heard? And how will they hear without someone to preach? [15] And how are they to preach unless they are sent? As it is written, "How beautiful are the feet of those who declare good news of good things!"

"**The word of faith** is not a word in the literal sense but is a "message"—essentially a condensed summary of the gospel. It is the message that a person must receive in order to become a Christian." (Boa and Kruidenier 2000, p. 311) All Christians should find joy in the privilege of preaching the word of faith, resulting in salvation for some. While Paul is speaking of himself here, we should want to have that same mental disposition for whatever role we may play in speaking on God's behalf. Paul wrote, "For if I preach the gospel, I have nothing to boast of, for I am under compulsion; for woe is me if I do not preach the gospel." (1 Cor. 9:16, NASB) May we all have an active Christian ministry as spokesperson on God's behalf?

Exercise

At times, people will ask us questions, and we may not have an impromptu answer. Someone just asked you, were Adam and Eve not purely allegorical (fictional) persons? How would you respond? If you have no ready answer, research whether Adam and Eve were actual historical people, and then share the answer with at least one friend.

Review Questions

- What is evangelism?
- What is specifically meant by obligated and evangelism?
- How did Jesus set the example as to evangelism?
- What is the Kingdom of God?
- Who were all involved in the evangelism work of the first-century?

---

[35] Lit *into righteousness*

[36] Lit *into salvation*

CHAPTER 1 Using Persuasion to Reach the Heart of Our Listeners

Acts 19:8 Updated American Standard Version (UASV)

⁸ And he entered the synagogue and for three months **spoke boldly, reasoning** and **persuading** them about the kingdom of God.

In some ways, many might think that the word "persuasion" seems like a sneaky or devious kind of word. Some might think of the salesperson that sells cars, who comes across as pushy or those using deceptive language in a contract that someone wants us to sign. Maybe the word "persuasion" hits us as if it is simply manipulation. It is used in a similar vein by the apostle Paul when he writes of Christians in Galatia, "You were running well. Who hindered you from obeying the truth? This **persuasion** is not from him who calls you." (Gal. 5:7-8) The Greek word used here *peismone* has the sense of 'persuasion, i.e., communication intended to induce belief or action.'[37] Paul also told the Colossians, "I say this so that no one will delude you with **persuasive** argument." (Col 2:4) The Greek word use here *pithanologia* has the sense of 'persuasive speech, namely, using language effectively to please or persuade.'[38] When persuasion is used in this way, it does have somewhat of a negative connotation, as it hinges on crafty arguments built on false details. However, the sense of the two words is very similar.

Nevertheless, we have the apostle Paul using the art of persuasion or convincing with a different implication. In his second letter to Timothy Paul writes, "You, however, continue in the things you have learned and were **persuaded** to believe, knowing from whom you have learned them." (2 Tim. 3:14, UASV) The NASB renders the verse this way, "Continue in the things you have learned and become **convinced** of." (The ESV, HCSB and LEB render it similarly.) The Greek word here Pistoo[39] has the sense of 'being convinced, or being persuaded or sure of the truthfulness or validity of something.'[40] When Paul was speaking of what Timothy had been persuaded or convinced to believe, it was used in a different connotation from the above Greek words, while still having the same sense as the other two Greek words. In the above verses to the Galatians and Colossians it was a manipulation of the truth that was being

---

[37] Bible sense Lexicon by Logos Bible Software

[38] IBID

[39] The Greek word e**pisto**thes in the New Testament is identified as a New Testament hapax legomenon, a word of which there is only one recorded use.

[40] Bible sense Lexicon by Logos Bible Software

used to persuade, while here Timothy's mother and his grandmother were persuading or convincing Timothy to believe based on the truth itself.– 2 Timothy 1:5.

When Paul was under house arrest in Rome, he effectively witnessed to many. The account reads, "When they had appointed a day for him, they came to him at his lodging in greater numbers; and he expounded to them, testifying about the kingdom of God and trying to **persuade** them concerning Jesus both from the Law of Moses and from the Prophets, from morning till evening." The Greek word *peitho* has the sense persuading, causing someone to adopt a certain position, belief, or course of action.'[41] Was the apostle Paul manipulating truth to deceive those to whom he was witnessing? No, he was persuading them to believe about Jesus Christ based on truth. Therefore, the art of persuasion can be used for good or for bad. Christians use persuasion to help others adopt a certain position, belief about the Father and the Son, and the Word of God. As teachers, evangelists, proclaimers we can use sound logical reasoning, as we explain, persuade and convince, convicting others of Bible truth. (2 Tim. 2:15) Clearly, one of the most skilled persuaders in the history of Christianity was the apostle Paul. Demetrius, the "silversmith in Ephesus who incited a riot directed against Paul because he feared that the apostle's preaching would threaten the sale of silver shrines of Diana, the patron goddess of Ephesus." He said of Paul, "And you see and hear that not only in Ephesus but in almost all of Asia this Paul has persuaded and turned away a great many people, saying that gods made with hands are not gods."–Acts 19:26

Using Persuasion in Our Evangelism

Jesus commanded all Christians, "Go therefore and make disciples of all nations, baptizing them in the name of the Father and of the Son and of the Holy Spirit, teaching them to observe all that I have commanded you. And behold, I am with you always, to the end of the age." Christianity has been sending missionaries for centuries and it has been very productive in that Christian congregations are now found throughout the entire world. The last forty years or so, many missionaries have come to believe that evangelism is needed to enter a new era of all Christians effective evangelizing in their own communities.

A *Part-Time or Full-Time Evangelist* is one who sees this as their calling and chooses to be very involved as an evangelist in their local church and community. They may work part-time to supplement their work as an evangelist. They may be married with children, but they

---

[41] IBID

realize their gift is in the field of evangelism. If it were the wife, the husband would work toward supporting her work as an evangelist and vice-versa. If it were a single person, he or she would supplement their work by being employed part-time, but also the church would help as well. This person is well trained in every aspect of bringing one to Christ. *Congregation Evangelists* should be very involved in evangelizing their communities and helping the church members play their role at the basic levels of evangelism. There is nothing to say that one church could not have many within, who have the calling of an evangelist, which would and should be cultivated. What are some tools that can use in our effort to persuade others of the truth of God's Word?

Listening Carefully will enable us to understand fully what the unbeliever knows about any subject that we may be discussing with him. For example, if he says that he does not believe in the Bible, it may seem natural to launch into a solid explanation as to why he should believe in the Bible. However, we need to know specifically what it is that has him rejecting the Bible. Is it because he thinks it is just a man's book or does he feel it is full of contradictions and errors, or that it is an ancient book and not practical for today. Therefore, we need to listen carefully to the why of a stated position and not just assume we know what he means.– Proverbs 18:13.

Asking Questions goes right along with listening. Questions can be used to reiterate, making sure we understand what they meant. Questions can be used to get them to explain exactly what it they meant by a statement or a position. Questions can be used to lead a person to the right answer. We might ask the above person that does not believe in the Bible, "have you always felt that way and what is it that contributed to your not believing in the Bible?" After they give us the specifics of why, we can use questions to dig deeper or lead. Suppose they said, 'it is because the Bible is full of contradictions and errors.' We can ask, "Have you ever considered what the difference between errors and contradictions and Bible difficulties is? "Have you ever studied the subject of errors or contradictions within the Scriptures?" After those questions, we might ask, "Do you have a couple examples of those errors and contradictions?" There are literally thousands of Bible difficulties between Genesis 1:1 and Revelation 22:21, which the Bible critic labels as errors and contradictions. Everyone uses common ones as their examples, if we recognize one and know that there is a reasonable explanation, we might offer a brief explanation of what a Bible difficulty is. Then we can demonstrate how that helps us better understand these are not errors and contradictions at all, as we also give him a reasonable explanation of his supposed error or contradiction. Then, we can ask, "would you agree with this explanation?" When we use questions and listen, we are involving the unbeliever to join us in a respectful conversation, giving them a chance to be heard, as opposed to him just hearing us go on and on about a subject.

Using Sound Reasoning will help us reach the heart and mind of our listeners. For example, the above listener said he did not believe in the Bible and we asked why, got the specifics that he was hung up on perceived errors and contradictions, and gave him reasonable and logical answers that they were actually Bible difficulties, followed by a reasonable and logical explanation of his specific error or contradiction. Thus, we close out with the following, "The authors of Bible claim that what they wrote was inspired by God and they were moved along by Holy Spirit as they penned God's Words. (2 Tim 3:16-17; 2 Pet. 1:20-21) Those inspired authors tell us of an opportunity at eternal life, if we trust in the Son of God. (John 3:16) Would you not agree that while this is not evidence that it is, in fact, the Word of God and those things are true, but that it would be sensible nonetheless to investigate it objectively and find out if such claims are true or not?

The person above, who claimed he did not believe in the Bible, gave his reason, saying it is full of errors and contradictions. In our listening and asking questions, he gave us an example, when he says, "If God hardened the Pharaoh's heart, what exactly makes Pharaoh responsible for the decisions he makes?" When we look at the verse below, it does seem to say what our listener has claimed. How can God harden the heart of Pharaoh, so that he says no to all requests from Moses and Aaron and then punish him and his people for his saying no?

Exodus 4:21 Updated American Standard Version (UASV)	**Exodus 4:21** Revised Standard Version (RSV)
21 Jehovah said to Moses, "When you go and return to Egypt see that you perform before Pharaoh all the wonders which I have put in your hand; but I will harden his heart so that he will not let the people go.	21 And the Lord said to Moses, "When you go back to Egypt, see that you do before Pharaoh all the miracles which I have put in your power; but I will harden his heart so that he will not let the people go.

Answer: This is actually a prophecy. God knew that what he was about to do would contribute to a stubborn and obstinate Pharaoh, who was going to be unwilling to change or give up the Israelites so they could go off to worship their God. Therefore, this is not stating what God is going to do; it is prophesying that Pharaoh's heart will harden because of the actions of God. The fact is, Pharaoh allowed his own heart to harden because he was determined not to agree with Moses' wishes or accept Jehovah's request to let the people go. Moses tells us at Exodus 7:13 that "Pharaoh's heart was hardened,[42] and he would not listen to them, as Jehovah had said." Again, at 8:15, we read, "But when Pharaoh saw that there was a relief, he hardened[43] his heart and would not listen to them, as Jehovah had said."

Dealing With the Emotional Beliefs of Others

Everyone has deeply held beliefs that if jabbed emotions may flare. We may be in a conversation with a devout Catholic, who believes that it is proper to address prayers to Mary as intercessor. Even if we were to show Scriptures and respectfully reason with him, he may come back sternly, "I still believe it proper to address prayers to Mary as intercessor." Whether we are witnessing to a Catholic, an atheist, and agnostic, a Muslim, a Hindus, a Buddhist, A Jehovah's Witness, a Mormon and so on, emotions are involved. In some cases, like the Witnesses, it is against their beliefs to be witnessed to, but they can witness to others. If you are aware of their teachings, their background and begin to question these things, even in a respectful manner, they will abandon the conversation quickly.

Many view their beliefs as absolute truths, even relativism,[44] which claims there is no such thing as absolute truth. When relativist's state there is no such thing as absolute truth, this is self-defeating within itself, as they are defeating the very absolute truth claim that they are trying to make, i.e., "all truth is relative." If there is no absolute truth; then, their belief that there are no absolutes cannot be true.[45] However, they would argue their belief vigorously as though it were absolutely true, even get emotional over it. Our beliefs are our worldview. A worldview is "the sum total of answers that a person gives to the most important questions in life." (Dr. Ronald Nash) Dr. Nash goes on to say, "Many people

---

[42] Lit *strong*

[43] Lit *made heavy*

[44] Relativism is the belief that concepts such as right and wrong, goodness and badness, or truth and falsehood are not absolute but change from culture to culture and situation to situation.

[45] "To claim that all moral truths are relative is self-defeating. A statement is self-defeating when what is being affirmed fails to meet its own requirements. An example is the statement, "I can't speak a word in English," to which one might respond, "You just did." The moral relativists' claim commits the same error, since the statement 'All truth is relative' is itself an absolute claim for truth. It is impossible to consistently hold the claims of moral relativism because it denies what it tries to affirm in its very statements."–Hindson, Ed (2008-05-01). The Popular Encyclopedia of Apologetics (p. 354). Harvest House Publishers.

remain blissfully unaware that they have a worldview, even though the sudden change in their life and thought resulted from their exchanging their old worldview for their new one."[46] If we are going to overturn any false reasoning within one's worldview, say that of an atheist, it will take more than mere logic or even Scriptures that would demonstrate their view is erroneous.

We will have to be empathetic and have compassionate hearts, kindness, humility, meekness, and patience, as we use the art of persuasion. (Rom. 12:15; Col. 3:12) We as a teacher, an evangelist, a proclaimer of God's Word, never water down the truth. Moreover, we have strong convictions in what we hold to be true, i.e., our biblical or Christian worldview. For example, Paul stated it this way, "I am convinced that ..." and "I know and am convinced ..." (Rom. 8:38; 14:14, NASB) Even though we know we possess absolute truth, this does not mean we are free to be dogmatic or self-righteous about it, which can come across in our tone. Moreover, we would never use sarcasm or talk down to another when we are sharing our biblical truths, even if this is the way we are being treated in the conversation. We would never want to cause offense or even insult our listener.–Proverbs 12:18.

The apostle Peter tells us that we are to "sanctify Christ as Lord in your hearts, always being ready to make a defense to everyone who asks you to give an account for the hope that is in you, yet with gentleness and reverence." (1 Pet. 3:15, NASB) We will reach far deeper into their mind and heart if we respect their beliefs acknowledging that they have a right to possess them, even though we do not agree with them. This will require humility on our part, for which Paul makes the point that we should "do nothing from selfish ambition or conceit, but in humility count others more significant than yourselves." (Phil 2:3-4, ESV) Jesus in one of his parables said, "For everyone who exalts himself will be humbled, but the one who humbles himself will be exalted." (Luke 18:9-14, ESV) Yes, if we are to persuade others, it will come through our humility, as we truly appreciate God for his helping us to see the truth, and our greatest desire it to share that same truth with others.

Paul wrote to the Corinthians, "For the weapons of our warfare are not of the flesh but have divine power to destroy strongholds. We destroy arguments and every lofty opinion raised against the knowledge of God, and take every thought captive to obey Christ." (2 Cor. 10:4-5) "Paul was certain that he was on a course **to demolish** the **strongholds** or fortifications of **arguments and every**

---

[46] Zondervan (2010-06-19). Life's Ultimate Questions: An Introduction to Philosophy (p. 32). Zondervan.

pretension that anyone set up **against the knowledge of God**. As Paul traveled the world proclaiming the gospel of Christ, he encountered pretentious disbelief supported by clever arguments and powerful personalities. But through the "weakness" of preaching Christ, Paul went about taking **captive every thought to make it obedient to Christ**." (Pratt Jr 2000, p. 417) We as Christians seek to use the Word of God, logic,[47] reason,[48] in our art of persuasion to "destroy arguments and every lofty opinion." We must remember that God has shown us much patience in our early walk in coming to know him. We are over joyed that we have the Word of God, this powerful tool (Heb. 4:12), which will enable us to overturn false reasoning, reaching hearts and minds with the art of persuasion.

Exercise

Someone just said to you, "I don't believe the Bible, as it is full of errors and contradictions." How would you persuade him that this is not the case?

Review Questions

- What does it mean to persuade?
- How can we use persuasion in our evangelism?
- How can we deal with the emotional beliefs others?

---

[47] What is logic? And why in the world would anyone want to study it? Isn't it just a bunch of incomprehensible and arbitrary rules that no one really follows anyway? What good does it do? To most people, logic is an unknown language about an unknown realm, where everything is turned upside down and no one with an IQ below 300 is allowed. You can see it in the panic on their faces when you just mention the word-LOGIC!

Despite all the bad press, logic is not so tough. In fact, it is one of the simplest things to use because you use it all the time, though you may not realize it. We don't mean that you put all of your thoughts into logical form and do a formal analysis of each thought. But when you are at the supermarket and one brand of sugar is 3 cents per ounce but another is 39 cents per pound, it doesn't take long for you to pull out your calculator and settle the issue. Why do you do that? Because you recognize that, those ounces and pounds have to be put in the same category to be compared. That's logic. You use logic to do most everything. When you decide to take your shower after you work out instead of before, you don't necessarily go through all the formal steps it takes to reach that conclusion validly, but your decision rests on logic nonetheless. Logic really means putting your thoughts in order.– Ronald M. Brooks; Norman L. Geisler. Come, Let Us Reason: An Introduction to Logical Thinking (p. 11)

[48] "God is rational, and the principles of good reason do flow from his very nature. Consequently, learning the rules of clear and correct reasoning is more than an academic exercise. For the Christian, it is also a means of spiritual service."–IBID p. 7

CHAPTER 2 Speak the Word of God with Boldness

Acts 4:31 Updated American Standard Version (UASV)

31 And when they had prayed, the place in which they were gathered together was shaken, and they were all filled with the Holy Spirit and began to **speak the word of God with boldness.**

Just three days before Jesus was executed, Jesus told his disciples, "And this gospel of the kingdom will be proclaimed in all the inhabited earth[49] as a testimony to all the nations, and then the end will come." (Matt. 24:14) Jesus would speak on this again just before he ascended to heaven; Jesus said to his disciples, "Go therefore and make disciples of all the nations … teaching them to observe all that I commanded you …" (Matt 28:19-20) Of course, being curious, they were asking him, "Lord, is it at this time you are restoring the kingdom to Israel?" He said to them, "It is not for you to know times or seasons that the Father has fixed by his own authority. But you will receive power when the Holy Spirit has come upon you, and you will be my witnesses in both Jerusalem and in all Judea and Samaria, and to the extremity of the earth."–Acts 1:6-8

It has been and will be mentioned several times in this publication; Christianity has lost its way in the great commission of proclaiming the good news of the kingdom, teaching biblical truths, and making disciples, even in the face of centuries of intensified missionary work this is true. It is the mission of Christian Publishing House and this author that the first-century lifesaving work of evangelism is restored, so that, all Christians may play a role in making disciples. Therefore, it is tools like this publication and others by this author and other authors, which will enable any willing Christian to share biblical truths effectively within their family, their community, their workplace or their school, to make disciples. Within this chapter, we will cover how the Holy Spirit can enable us to be bold when we are sharing biblical truths with others.[50]

The Need to Be Bold

One can only imagine the joy of making a disciple for Christ, who, in turn, goes out to make disciples himself. Congregation Evangelists, be it male or female should be very involved in evangelizing their communities

---

[49] Or *in the whole world*

[50] A recommend read EXPLAINING THE HOLY SPIRIT: Basic Bible Doctrines of the Christian Faith

http://www.christianpublishers.org/apps/webstore/products/show/6565103

and helping the church members play their role at the basic levels of evangelism. There is nothing to say that one church could not have many within, who have the calling of an evangelist, which would and should be cultivated. However, like in the first-century, we in the twenty-first-century have many challenges that get in our way. Generally speaking, few today are eager to hear from God's Word, mostly because the majority have preconceived ideas about it (just a man's book, full of errors and contradictions, and the like); many are of the same mindset as those who were living the days of Noah. "For as in those days before the flood they were eating and drinking, marrying and giving in marriage, until the day that Noah entered the ark." (Matt. 24:38-39, NASB) Then, the apostle Peter warned,

2 Peter 3:3-4 Updated American Standard Version (UASV)

[3] Know this first of all, that in the last days ridiculers will come with their ridicule, following after their own desires, [4] and saying: "Where is this promised coming[51] of his? For ever since the fathers fell asleep, all continues just as it was from the beginning of creation."

On these verses, David Walls writes, "**In the last days** refers to all the days between the first advent of the Messiah and the second advent. Characteristic of that time frame, however long it will be, is the fact that people will make fun of the doctrine of the Second Coming. **Scoffing** toward Christians is to express derision or scorn about a Christian or Christianity, the Bible, or God. It describes the characteristic attitude of the day toward the Second Coming. False teachers argued that the promise of the Second Coming had been delayed so long that we may safely conclude that it would never happen. As far as they could see, the world was going on just as it always had—people lived and died, but nothing really changed." (Walls and Anders 1996, p. 141) Today, we have false teachers on both sides of the second coming fence: (1) ones that scoff at the idea of Jesus' second coming and (2) those that act as though they are prophets of God, knowing the very day and hour.[52] However, we also have those that from liberal and moderate "Christianity" that ridicule, mock and oppose conservative Christianity. All of this, and we have not even gotten to those outside of Christianity, who also ridicule, mock and oppose the Almighty God and his Word, the Bible.

---

[51] Or *presence* (Gr *parousia*), which denotes both an "arrival" and a consequent "presence with."

[52] A recommended read The SECOND COMING of CHRIST: Basic Bible Doctrines of the Christian Faith

http://www.christianpublishers.org/apps/webstore/products/show/5383701

As true Christians, we may face ridicule, mocking and opposition from the governmental officials, the news and entertainment media, other religions, and the agnostics and atheists. However, even more, close to home, it may come from those that our children go to school with, their teachers or it may originate from those we work with, even from close family members. All of these people need to be evangelized to if we are to carry out the Great Commission of proclaiming and teaching God's Word, to make disciples for Christ. We need to evangelize those in false forms of "Christianity," the unbelievers and those in either of these categories, who are closer to us.

However, we face yet more challenges that are in our way. One such challenge is our human imperfection, i.e., our human weaknesses, such as shyness and fear of being ridiculed, mocked and opposed. Lastly, our greatest obstacle is our church leaders, who are failing to train us to be effective evangelizers in our communities. James, Jesus' half-brother, wrote, "One of you says to them [the poor], 'Go in peace, be warmed and filled,'" without giving them the things needed for the body, what good is that? So also faith by itself, if it does not have works, is dead." (Jam. 2:16-17, ESV) This principle can be carried over to pastors, elders, priests, ministers, who say to their congregation, "**You** need to share the gospel in **your** community, so that **you** may help build up the church for Christ." All of this pointing the finger at them by using the second person pronoun, "**you**" repeatedly, and these leaders have not even given them the tools to be effective evangelists within their community. What good is that? Therefore, their supposed faith that the evangelism work will be done, but having no works of training such ones, means they have no genuine faith at all, it is dead. If we are to persist in sharing the Word of God, this will require that we have the tools to help us (i.e., this book and others like it), as well as boldness. In this chapter, we will focus on boldness.

Ephesians 6:19-20 Updated American Standard Version (UASV)

[19] and for me, that a word may be given to me at the opening of my mouth **boldly**, to make known the mystery of the gospel, [20] for which I am an ambassador in chains, that I may proclaim it **boldly**, as I ought to speak.

The Greek word, *parresia*, "boldness" in verse 19 has the sense of in boldness "in an evident or publicly known manner—'publicly, in an evident manner, well known.'"[53] The Greek word, *parresiazomai*, "boldly" in verse 19, is a "(derivative of *parresia* 'boldness,' 25.158) to

---

[53] Johannes P. Louw and Eugene Albert Nida, *Greek-English Lexicon of the New Testament: Based on Semantic Domains* (New York: United Bible Societies, 1996), 337.

speak openly about something and with complete confidence—'to speak boldly, to speak openly.'"[54] However, this boldness, confidence, courage, fearlessness does not give us a license to be blunt or rude to the ones we speak to, even if their demeanor is such. The apostle said to the Christians in Rome, "Never pay back evil for evil to anyone." (Rom. 12:17; See Col. 4:6, NASB) He went on to say, "If possible, so far as it depends on you, be at peace with all men." (Rom. 12:18, NASB) When we go about our evangelism work, sharing God's Word with others, we need to be bold in this hostile world, but it needs to be balanced with tact as well because our objective is not to offend the one we to whom we are witnessing.

To be sure, this sort of boldness calls for personal qualities that involve much effort that needs to be developed over time. We do not just wake up one morning and decide that we are going to be bold from here forward. In addition, we do not just read a couple of Bible verses about being bold, and then, we are all of a sudden able to be bold in our witnessing to others. "But after we [Paul and his companions] had already suffered and been mistreated in Philippi, as you know, **we had the boldness in our God** to speak to you the gospel of God amid much conflict." (1 Thess. 2:2) We today can acquire a similar boldness if we are hesitant, shy or nervous at the idea of speaking to others about the Word of God.

Paul and his traveling companions had boldness, which you can note he said in the above, "we had the boldness in our God." In other words, God removed Paul's fears and gave him boldness. The rulers, elders, and scribes gathered in Jerusalem and commanded Peter and John to no longer witness about Jesus. These Jewish religious leaders had the power of life and death over them. Of course, they could only take their life, not their opportunity at eternal life. However, Peter and John answered them, "Whether it is right in the sight of God to listen to you rather than to God, you must judge, for we cannot but speak of what we have seen and heard." God was well aware of these threats, but he granted his servants to speak his word "*with all boldness*." Ac 4:5, 19-20, 29, ESV) The Father had provided them with Holy Spirit. What about us; Should we expect that the Holy Spirit under this direct and supernatural control will guide, lead, and direct us in the same bold way.

What Was the Reason for the Direct and Supernatural Work of the Holy Spirit in the First Century?

A significant change was in the offing. The Jews had followed the lead of their religious leaders in the last act of rebellion, resulting in their

---

[54] IBID., 398.

rejection as his people. The Mosaic Law was being replaced with the law of Christ. This does not mean that no Jew could be received into the newly founded Christian congregation. To the contrary, the next three and half years would be only the Jewish people, which would make up this new way to God. As was the case with Moses, there was to be a sign, miraculous events, which included the speaking in tongues, this as evidence to those, whose heart was receptive to the truth that the Son of God had come, had given his life for them, and ascended back to heaven. Exodus 19:16-19

However, there was much labor to be done. Beginning in 36 C.E., with the conversion of Cornelius, an uncircumcised Gentile, the gospel got underway in its spread to non-Jewish people of every nation. (Acts, chap. 10) In truth, so swiftly did it spread that by about 60 C.E., the apostle Paul could say that the gospel had been "proclaimed in all creation that is under heaven." (Col. 1:23) Consequently, by the time of the last apostle's death (John c. 100 C.E.), Jesus' faithful followers had made disciples all the way through the Roman Empire—in Asia, Europe, and Africa! By 125 C.E., there were over one million Christians.

If we objectively look at the history of first-century Christianity, the three and a half year ministry of Jesus, founding the Christian congregation, the apostles spreading the good news throughout the whole of the Roman Empire, and the Holy Spirit miraculously guiding, leading and showing the apostles the "things to come," reminding them of all that Jesus had said. The apostles and a select few of others, like Paul, Barnabas, Silas, Apollos, Timothy, Titus, Philip, were under direct and supernatural control as they established Christianity in the first century. While there may have been a few individuals, attempting to cause division in the first century, by 100 C.E. there was but one Christianity, the one Jesus founded, and the apostle grew. The twenty-seven books of the New Testament were to be added to the Old Testament by 200 C.E. The particular work of the Holy Spirit that Jesus spoke of had run its course by the death of the apostle John in 100 C.E., as he was the last apostle. After John, no man has been miraculously guided or directed, in the same manner, and way, because that same specific work of the Holy Spirit was no longer needed. The work of the Holy Spirit from the second century forward has been within the inspired, inerrant Word of God. There was no need for the Holy Spirit to operate the same as in the first century because the work of setting up Christianity and completing the Word of God was completed. The work of the Holy Spirit now takes place through the Spirit-inspired Word of God.

What Were the Gifts of the Holy Spirit in the First Century

What miraculous, supernatural gifts were the apostles and a select few workers to receive, to establish first century Christianity? They would receive a helper, comforter, an instructor, a guide, a supporter, i.e., the Holy Spirit. What did Jesus say about the Holy Spirit, being specifically applied to the apostles and a select few other fellow workers, to accomplish their work of establishing Christianity and completing the Bible? He had much to say on this, as we will discover from the texts below. Italics and underlines are mine.

John 14:15-17 Updated American Standard Version (UASV)

15 "If you love me, you will keep my commandments. 16 And I will ask the Father, and he will give you another Helper, that he may be with you forever; 17 the Spirit of truth, *whom the world cannot receive*, because it does not see him or know him, but you know him because *he dwells with you* and *will be in you.*

John 14:26 Updated American Standard Version (UASV)

26 But the Helper, the Holy Spirit, whom the Father will send in my name, *that one will teach you all things* and *bring to your remembrance all* that I have said to you.

John 15:26 Updated American Standard Version (UASV)

26 "But when the Helper comes, whom I will send to you from the Father, the Spirit of truth, who proceeds from the Father, *that one will bear witness about me.*

This took place with the apostles starting at Pentecost 33 C.E., as well as other Christians throughout the first-century.

John 16:5-8 Updated American Standard Version (UASV)

5 But now I am going to him who sent me, and none of you asks me, 'Where are you going?' 6 But because I have said these things to you, sorrow has filled your heart. 7 Nevertheless, I tell you the truth: it is to your advantage that I go away; for if I do not go away, the Helper will not come to you; but if I go, I will send him to you. 8 And when that one arrives, *he will convict the world concerning sin* and *righteousness* and *judgment*;

John 16:12-15 Updated American Standard Version (UASV)

12 "I still have many things to say to you, but you cannot bear them now. 13 But when that one, the Spirit of truth, comes, *he will guide you*

into all the truth; for he will not speak from himself, but whatever he hears, he will speak; and *he will declare to you the <u>things that are to come</u>.* **14** That one will glorify me, for *he will take what is mine and declare it to you.* **15** All the things that the Father has are mine; therefore I said that he takes what is mine and will declare it to you.

In the above texts, we have some things that the Holy Spirit was to do for the apostles and a select few other fellow workers. While the apostle was not ignorant or illiterate as some commentators suppose, they did not possess training in the Rabbinic study of Scripture, such as the apostle Paul had under Gamaliel. Luke tells us of an account of Peter and John before the Jewish religious leaders, where he writes,

Acts 4:13 Updated American Standard Version (UASV)

13 Now when they saw the boldness of Peter and John, and perceived that they were uneducated and untrained men, **they were astonished**, and they recognized that they had been with Jesus.

All of a sudden, Peter and John, literate fishermen were keeping pace with the Jewish religious leaders, who had training in the Rabbinic study of Scripture. This is the Holy Spirit teaching them, guiding them, instructing them, bringing back to their remembrance all that Jesus had said. Therefore, the apostles and a select few fellow workers needed the Holy Spirit if they were to establish Christianity on the grand scale that it was by the end of the first century and complete the New Testament. There was no way that the apostles alone could have educated themselves to the level of Paul, in such a short period, it was the Holy Spirit, who taught and instructed them miraculously. The Holy Spirit guided them as well. One way was in their writings, as no New Testament author contradicted another; they were all one because there was really one author, God. This is actually true of all forty plus authors of the entire Bible. From the second century forward, this has never repeated. In fact, today we have 41,000 different denominations, all teaching different things on the same doctrines.

Convicting the World Concerning Sin

Nisan 14, 33 C.E., the night of the Passover feast with Jesus, he told the apostles, "When he [the Holy Spirit] comes, he will convict the world concerning sin and righteousness and judgment." (John 16:8, ESV) How did the Holy Spirit do this on Pentecost? The first stage was to baptize the apostle in Holy Spirit, which means that they would have been miraculously endowed with guidance, instruction, teachings, and a remembrance of what Jesus had said. Again, looking at Jesus' words just before his ascension, he said, "for John baptized with water, but you will be baptized with the Holy Spirit not many days from now." (Acts 1:5, ESV) The second stage was the work that these ones would carry out in the first century, namely, putting the world on notice (convicting them concerning their sin and righteousness), which was very similar to what the Mosaic Law had done with the Israelites. Remember the words of the apostle Paul,

Romans 5:20-21 Updated American Standard Version (UASV)

[20] The [Mosaic] Law came in so that the transgression would increase; but where sin increased, grace abounded all the more, [21] so that, as sin reigned in death, even so grace would reign through righteousness to eternal life through Jesus Christ our Lord.

How did the Mosaic Law make sin "increase"? From Adam's rebellion to the Mosaic Law, man was well aware of right and wrong because even in imperfection he had a sense of right and wrong. God had given Adam and Eve a conscience, an internal mechanism, to evidence the difference between right and wrong. In their perfection, they were able to sin still because even if a perfect person entertains bad thoughts, it will lead to sin and death. (Jam 1:14-15) Nevertheless, humankind in imperfection has a measure of that conscience that was given to Adam and Eve, meaning they have always had a sense of good and bad. However, the Mosaic Law laid our more explicitly what sin was and the different aspects of it. The Pentateuch itself contained 613 laws. It was a theocratic government, covering religious obligations, duties of the priesthood, a judicial system, covering business, marriage, family, sexual relations, morality, military, dietary restrictions, sanitary laws and much more. Therefore, the Mosaic Law caused sin to increase. On this Paul wrote,

Romans 7:7-8 Updated American Standard Version (UASV)

[7] What shall we say then? Is the Law sin? May it never be! On the contrary, I would not have come to know sin except through the Law; for I would not have known about coveting if the Law had not said, "You shall not covet." [8] But sin, taking opportunity through the commandment, produced in me coveting of every kind; for apart from the Law sin is dead.

Like the apostle Paul, neither Jewish persons nor us today, would know the full range of sin without the Mosaic Law. Paul gave us the example of coveting. The law exposed the coveting spirit that Paul would never have truly recognized in its fullest sense. This is how Paul could say, "apart from the Law sin *is* dead," specifically, it would not be as recognizable, as exposed, as highlighted. The Law made people more aware of the extent of their sinful nature. We should offer a word of caution, though, the Mosaic Law did not move them toward sin, or make sin more appealing, but rather it exposed sin for what it was. Sin is missing the mark of perfection. Sin is being out of harmony with the Creator, his personality, standards, and ways, which he inculcated in his creation. The Law made it possible to convict more people concerning sin. Now, the apostles, baptized in Holy Spirit were going to take this a step further with the law of Christ. Again, Jesus said to his apostles, "When he [the Holy Spirit] comes, he will convict the world [by way of the apostle workers] concerning sin and righteousness and judgment." (John 16:8, ESV)

What do we mean by 'convicting the world concerning sin'? This is not a reference to sin in general, as though, the Holy Spirit would personally come upon a person who just watched a movie they should not have, or they just told a lie, or they committed any sin. When we feel this inner guilt, a groaning of our inner person, because we know we have just done wrong, this is not the Holy Spirit convicting us of that sin. It is the Holy Spirit working through the Word of God, which convicts us of sin. Sin will cause us to feel guilt, anxiety, insecurity, shame. We get a clearer understanding of this when we consider Paul's words that "the work of the law is written on their hearts, while their conscience also bears witness, and their conflicting thoughts accuse or even excuse them." (Rom 2:15, ESV) In other words, when we fall short of God's standards as they are laid out in Scripture or our God given conscience, we will feel an internal groaning within us, which is our conscience convicting us of wrongdoing.

We are born with the weaker version of the conscience that God had given Adam and Eve. It will prevent most humans from committing the obvious right and wrongs, even if they never read the Word of God their entire life. However, considering that almost all of the teachers and professors in the United States and Especially Europe and Canada, are of a liberal progressive mindset, which is contrary to God's standards, the conscience is greatly weakened by Satan's world. If our conscience is ignored, it will become callused and unfeeling, no longer warning us of our wrongdoing, because it no longer wrongdoing in our heart and mind. On the other hand, if Scripture trains our conscience, it will not allow us to commit the wrongdoing in the first place. Returning to the being made bold by the Holy Spirit, we too can receive the Spirit in our evangelism work, but not in the same way and the same sense as the apostles and their fellow workers.

The Work of the Holy Spirit in the First Century

There was a different level of relationship between fist century Christianity and Christianity over the next 2,000 years. It must be remembered that Christ needed (1) **to train** those that would, (2) **establish Christianity**, and (3) **grow Christianity** to the point that it was **extensive** and **united**. This was needed to withstand the apostasy and false teachers that were to come over the next 2,000 years, who would split Christianity into so many factions, finding the truth and the way of the first century today is nigh impossible. All that Jesus and his apostles were to accomplish took place in a mere one hundred years while also publishing the twenty-seven books of the New Testament that later Christians would bring together as one book. There was a definite need for the Holy Spirit in first century Christianity. Let us look at the gifts of prophesy and speaking in tongues.

As for Tongues, They Will Cease

1 Corinthians 13:8-10 Updated American Standard Version (UASV)

[8] Love never fails. But if there are gifts of prophecy, they will be done away with; if there are tongues,[55] they will cease; if there is knowledge, it will be done away with. [9] For we have partial knowledge and we prophesy partially, [10] but when what is complete comes, what is partial will be done away.

Some may argue that the evidence does not give one any idea of when the gift of tongues was to end. However, they would be mistaken in this case. There are three lines of evidence that present the fact that the gift of tongues would die out shortly after the death of the last apostle, which was the apostle John, who died about 98-100 C.E. **First**, the gift of tongues was always passed on to the person, only by an apostle: either by laying his hands on this one, or at least being present. (Acts 2:4, 14, 17; 10:44-46; 19:6; see also Acts 8:14-18.) **Second**, 1 Corinthians 13:8 informed the Corinthian reader specifically that this gift would "cease." In short, the Greek word for cease [pausontai], means to 'peter out,' or 'to die out,' not to be brought to a halt. We will deal with pausontai more extensively in a moment. **Third**, both one and two are exactly what happened when we look at the history of this gift of tongues. M'Clintock and Strong's Cyclopaedia (Vol. VI, p. 320) says that it is "an uncontested statement that during the first hundred years after the death of the apostles we hear little or nothing of the working of miracles by the early Christians." Therefore, following their passing off the scene and after

---

[55] Namely, miraculous speaking in other languages.

those who in that way had obtained the gift of tongues breathed their last breath; the gift of tongues should have died out with these ones. (Elwell, 2001, 1207-8) This analysis concurs with the intention of those gifts as acknowledged at Hebrews 2:2-4. In other words, The gifts of the Spirit in the first century, which includes speaking in tongues, was evidence that God had abandoned the 1,600 years of the nation of Israel being the way to God to the Christian congregation.

Daniel B. Wallace in his *Greek Grammar Beyond the Basics* helps us to better comprehend how we are to understand *pausontai* of 1 Corinthians 13:8:

> If the voice of the verb here is significant, then Paul is saying either that tongues will cut themselves off (direct middle) or, more likely, cease of their own accord, i.e., 'die out' without an intervening agent (indirect middle). It may be significant with reference to prophecy and knowledge, Paul used a different verb ([*katargeo*]) and out it in the passive voice. In vv 9-10, the argument continues: 'for we *know* in part and we *prophecy* in part; but when the perfect comes, the partial shall be done away with [*katargethesontai*].' Here again, Paul uses the same passive verb he had used with prophecy and knowledge and he speaks of the verbal counterpart to the nominal 'prophecy' and 'knowledge.' Yet he does not speak about *tongues* being done away 'when the perfect comes.' The implication *may* be that tongues were to have 'died out' on their own *before* the perfect comes. (Wallace 1996, 422)

These abilities were only established by the presence or lying on of hands by the apostles. This coincides with 1 Corinthians 13:8 and the history of these phenomena. Our Greek word for "cease" means that the gift of tongues was to 'die out' over time as the last of those who had received this gift passed off the scene of this earth. This is established by the historical fact that the second century saw just that being evidenced. Today, the Christian is moved by Spirit to speak with his heart and mind, defending and establishing the gospel, and destroying false doctrines, snatching some back from the fire. It is these things, which will give credence to the words of the modern-day Christian congregation: "God is really among you."–1 Corinthians 14:24-25.

The special, supernatural gifts, such as speaking in tongues gave impetus to the evangelism work that needed to be done in the first century, into many different lands throughout the Roman Empire. (Matt 28:19-20; Ac 1:8; 2:1-11) In the first century, the ones who spoke in tongues did so in languages that others could understand. (Ac 2:4, 8) If we look at those who claim to do so today, it is some ecstatic explosion of incomprehensible sounds, which only draws attention to them.

1 Corinthians 12:7-11 Updated American Standard Version (UASV)

⁷ But the manifestation of the Spirit is given to each one for a beneficial purpose. ⁸ For to one is given speech of wisdom through the Spirit, to another speech of knowledge according to the same Spirit, ⁹ to another faith by the same Spirit, to another gifts of healing by that one Spirit, ¹⁰ to yet another operations of miraculous powers, to another prophesying, to another the distinguishing of spirits, to another different tongues, and to another interpretation of tongues. ¹¹ But all these operations are performed by the very same Spirit, distributing to each one respectively just as it wills.

What we see here mentioned by Paul, apparently does not take place today in any Christian congregation. He is indicating various direct and supernatural manifestations of the Spirit, which was a direct gift from the Holy Spirit. There was a reason for these miraculous gifts, which Paul mentions in his letter to the Ephesians,

Ephesians 4:11-13 Updated American Standard Version (UASV)

¹¹ And he gave some as apostles, and some as prophets, and some as evangelists, and some as shepherds and teachers, ¹² for the equipping of the holy ones or the work of ministry, to the building up of the body of Christ; ¹³ until we all attain to the unity of the faith, and of the knowledge of the Son of God, to a mature man, to the measure of the stature which belongs to the fullness of Christ.

If we look at the above mention history of the Christian congregation of the first century and what was accomplished, it perfectly fits Paul's reasons here. The reason for the direct gifts of the Holy Spirit was (1) **to train** those that would, (2) **establish Christianity**, and (3) **grow Christianity** to the point that it was **extensive** and **united**. This gift of the Spirit accompanied the baptism of the Spirit on the day of Pentecost. As has been mentioned, the 120 disciples in that upper room, grew to become a united, one denomination of Christianity, which numbered over one million all throughout the Roman Empire, after a mere century. Therefore, when Peter promised the gift of the Holy Spirit on the day of Pentecost, it **was not** to be universally given across the whole of Christianity until the return of Jesus Christ, applying to all who obeyed the Word of God. Rather, it was limited to those of the first century. Even so, it was the apostles and a select few fellow workers, who manifested the Holy Spirit in a supernatural way, by being miraculously taught, instructed, guided, and bringing to their remembrance exactly what Jesus taught for three and a half years, and what Jesus meant by the words that he used. Yes, there were a number, in the first century, who were used as apostles [those caring for many congregations], and some as prophets [those proclaiming God's Word], and some as evangelists [a proclaimer of the gospel or good news],[56] and some as shepherds [elders or overseers in the congregation] and teachers [those who teach within the congregation].

Philip the Evangelist

Philip preached the Word of God to the Samaritans in the city of Samaria after the great persecution arose following the death of Stephen.

Acts 8:12-17 Updated American Standard Version (UASV)

[12] But when they believed Philip as he preached good news about the kingdom of God and the name of Jesus Christ, they were baptized, both men and women. [13] Simon himself also believed, and after being baptized, he continued with Philip; and he was amazed at seeing the signs and great powerful works taking place.

[14] Now when the apostles in Jerusalem heard that Samaria had received the word of God, they sent them Peter and John, [15] who came down and prayed for them that they might receive the Holy Spirit. [16] for he had not yet fallen on any of them, but they had only been baptized in the name of the Lord Jesus. [17] Then they laid their hands on them, and they received the Holy Spirit.

What do we notice here? We have Philip, a very important and prominent evangelist, who took the good news to Samaria. He preached and baptized the Samaritans. Philip was endowed with Holy Spirit with six other men, who were selected for a particular service. "These [seven men] set before the apostles, and they prayed and **laid their hands on them**." (Ac 6:6) We see that Philip was able to perform signs and great miracles. If the gift of the Holy Spirit was to be for all who accepted Jesus and was baptized, why did the Samaritans not receive the Spirit? Philip was not an apostle, meaning he could not confer the gift of the Spirit by laying hands on them, even though he had had hands laid on him, and he could perform signs and great miracles. Therefore, Peter and John were

---

[56] Basic Evangelism is planting seeds of truth and watering any seeds that have been planted. [In the basic sense of this word (*euaggelistes*), this would involve all Christians.] In some cases, it may be that one Christian planted the seeds, which were initially rejected, so he was left in a good way because the planter did not try to force the truth down his throat. However, sometime later he faces something in life that moves him to reconsider those seeds, and some other Christian waters what had already been planted. This evangelism can be carried out in all of the methods that are available: informal, house-to-house, street, and the like. What amount of time is invested in the evangelism work is up to each Christian to decide for themselves.

dispatched to Samaria, to lay hands on the Samaritans, so that "they might receive the Holy Spirit." It should be noted that the gifts of the Holy Spirit were **always** conveyed to others by the apostles of Jesus Christ (1) laying on of hands (2) or in their presence.

The Holy Spirit Falls on the Gentile

Cornelius was a Gentile an army officer (centurion, KJV), who commanded 100 soldiers. He was "a devout man" who "feared God with all his household, gave alms generously to the people, and prayed continually to God," "an upright and God-fearing man, who is well spoken of by the whole Jewish nation." About the ninth hour of the day, he saw clearly in a vision an angel of God come in and say to him, "Cornelius." And he stared at him in terror and said, "What is it, Lord?" And he said to him, "Your prayers and your alms have ascended as a memorial before God." The angel also told Cornelius, "send men to Joppa and bring one Simon who is called Peter." (Acts 10:1-22) Again, the gifts of the Holy Spirit were always conveyed to others by the apostles of Jesus Christ (1) laying on of hands (2) or in their presence.

Acts 10:44-48 Updated American Standard Version (UASV)

44 While Peter was still speaking these words, the Holy Spirit fell upon all who heard the word. **45** All the circumcised believers[57] who came with Peter were amazed, because the gift of the Holy Spirit had been poured out on the Gentiles also. **46** For they were hearing them speaking with tongues and magnifying God. Then Peter answered, **47** "Can anyone withhold water for baptizing these people, who have received the Holy Spirit just as we have?" **48** And he commanded them to be baptized in the name of Jesus Christ. Then they asked him to remain for some days.

Disciples at Ephesus

In Acts chapter 19, we find Paul meeting up with certain disciples that had been baptized by the John the Baptist. Paul explained that John was not aware of the full Gospel before his death. Below you will notice that these disciples of John had not even heard of the Holy Spirit, even though John pointed his disciples toward Jesus. Yet again, the gifts of the Holy Spirit were always conveyed to others by the apostles of Jesus Christ (1) laying on of hands (2) or in their presence.

Acts 19:1-7 English Standard Version (ESV)

1 And it happened that while Apollos was at Corinth, Paul passed through the inland country and came to Ephesus. There he found some disciples. **2** And he said to them, "Did you receive the Holy Spirit

---

[57] I.e., faithful ones

59

when you believed?" And they said, "No, we have not even heard that there is a Holy Spirit." [3] And he said, "Into what then were you baptized?" They said, "Into John's baptism." [4] And Paul said, "John baptized with the baptism of repentance, telling the people to believe in the one who was to come after him, that is, Jesus." [5] On hearing this, they were baptized in the name of the Lord Jesus. [6] And when Paul had laid his hands on them, the Holy Spirit came on them, and they began speaking in tongues and prophesying. [7] There were about twelve men in all.

Young Timothy

Here is yet another experience where someone has received the Holy Spirit by an apostle laying hands on him or her. Once more, the gifts of the Holy Spirit were always conveyed to others by the apostles of Jesus Christ (1) laying on of hands (2) or in their presence.

2 Timothy 1:4-7 Updated American Standard Version (UASV)

[4] longing to see you, even as I recall your tears, so that I may be filled with joy; [5] having been reminded of[58] your unhypocritical faith, which first dwelt in your grandmother Lois and your mother Eunice, and I am sure that it is in you as well. [6] For this reason I remind you to kindle afresh the gift of God which is in you through the laying on of my hands. [7] For God did not give us a spirit of cowardice, but one of power and of love and of soundness of mind.[59]

Christians In Rome

That the gifts of the Holy Spirit were always conveyed to others by the apostles of Jesus Christ (1) laying on of hands (2) or in their presence was clear. Listen to the praise of Paul to these ones in Rome. He writes, "To all those in Rome who are loved by God and called to be holy ones: 'Grace to you and peace from God our Father and the Lord Jesus Christ. First, I thank my God through Jesus Christ for all of you, because your faith is proclaimed in all the world. For God is my witness, whom I serve with my spirit in the gospel of his Son, that without ceasing I mention you always in my prayers, asking that somehow by God's will I may now, at last, succeed in coming to you.'" Paul goes on to tell these Christians.

---

[58] Lit *receiving a remembrance of*

[59] **Sound in Mind:** (Gr. *sophroneo*) This means to be of sound mind or in one's right mind, i.e., to have understanding about practical matters and thus be able to act sensibly, 'to have sound judgment, to be sensible, to use good sense, sound judgment.'–Acts 26:25; Romans 12:3; 2 Timothy 1:7; Titus 2:6; 1 Peter 4:7

Romans 1:11 Updated American Standard Version (UASV)

¹¹ For I long to see you so that I may impart some spiritual gift to you, that you may be established;

Notice that Paul could encourage and counsel them from a distance in the longest letter he had penned. However, it was necessary that he be present to convey gifts of the Spirit by his presence or the laying on of hands.

What have we learned thus far? First, the gift of the Spirit was a miraculous, supernatural gift for helping the first-century believers to be bold, to perform signs and miracles, to speak in foreign languages, to be Jesus' "witnesses in Jerusalem and in all Judea and Samaria, and to the end of the earth." (Ac 1:8) We also notice that the gifts of the Holy Spirit were **always** conveyed to others by the apostles of Jesus Christ (1) laying on of hands (2) or in their presence. Moreover, once the last apostle died, John, in 100 C.E., there was no longer one available to convey the gifts of the Spirit.

Therefore, the Greek word at 1 Corinthians 13:8 for "cease" [pausontai], became a reality in that the gifts that had been given 'petered out,' or 'died out,' namely, they were not brought to a halt, as some were, like prophecy. In other words, they died out as the last ones who were given them died at the beginning of the second century. Second, we can see from the letters of the New Testament authors that in the first century, many of the congregations were filled with members that had the supernatural power of the Spirit. Moreover, when we interpret those letters, this must be a part of the historical setting. Below are a few examples from these letters,

Romans 8:9, 23 Updated American Standard Version (UASV)

⁹ However, you are not in the flesh but in the Spirit, if indeed **the Spirit of God dwells in you**. But if anyone does not have the Spirit of Christ, he does not belong to him. ²³ And not only this, but also we ourselves, having the **first fruits of the Spirit**, even we ourselves groan within ourselves, waiting eagerly for our adoption as sons, the redemption of our body.

Romans 15:30 Updated American Standard Version (UASV)

³⁰ Now I urge you, brothers, through our Lord Jesus Christ and through **the love of the Spirit**, that you exert yourselves with me in prayers to God for me,

2 Corinthians 5:5 Updated American Standard Version (UASV)

⁵ Now the one who prepared us for this very thing is God, who gave us **the Spirit as a down payment** of what is to come.

Ephesians 1:13-14 Updated American Standard Version (UASV)

¹³ In whom also, you having heard the word of truth, the gospel of your salvation, in whom also having trusted, were **sealed with the Holy Spirit** of promise, ¹⁴ who is a down payment of our inheritance for the redemption of the possession, to the praise of his glory.

Ephesians 2:18 Updated American Standard Version (UASV)

¹⁸ for through him we both have our **access in one Spirit** to the Father.

Ephesians 5:18 Updated American Standard Version (UASV)

¹⁸ And do not get drunk with wine, for that is[60] dissipation,[61] but be **filled with the Spirit**,

1 Thessalonians 4:8 Updated American Standard Version (UASV)

⁸ Therefore the one who rejects this is not rejecting man, but God, who also **gives his Holy Spirit to you**.

Titus 3:5 Updated American Standard Version (UASV)

⁵ he saved us, not by deeds of righteousness that we have done, but because of his mercy, through the **washing** of **regeneration** and **renewal by the Holy Spirit**,

Hebrews 2:4 Updated American Standard Version (UASV)

⁴ God also testifying with them, both by **signs** and **wonders** and by various **miracles** and by **gifts of the Holy Spirit** according to His own will.

James 4:5 Updated American Standard Version (UASV)

⁵ Or do you think that the Scripture speaks to no purpose, "The **spirit that dwells in us** strongly desires to envy"?

1 John 2:20, 27 Updated American Standard Version (UASV)

²⁰ But you have been **anointed by the Holy One**, and you all have knowledge. ²⁷ As for you, the **anointing which you received from him**

---

[60] Lit *in which is*

[61] behavior which shows lack of concern or thought for the consequences of an action–'senseless deeds, reckless deeds, recklessness.'–GELNTBSD

remains in you, and you have no need for anyone to teach you; but as his anointing teaches you about all things, and is true and is not a lie, and just as it has taught you, you remain in him.

1 John 4:13 Updated American Standard Version (UASV)

¹³ By this we know that we are remaining in him and he in us, because he has given **his Spirit to us**.

The Holy Spirit and Today's Christians

Can The Holy Spirit do the same for us? No, the Holy Spirit cannot, at least not in the same way and the same sense. How, then, can we receive the Holy Spirit, to be instructed, guide, taught, reminded and to be directed in our witnessing to others in our evangelism work? As an aside, the answer will apply to every other facet of our Christian life as well, we just happen to be focusing on the evangelism aspect. Let us look at the thought of the Holy Spirit instructing and teaching Christians. Today we have over 41,000 different denominations, all teaching different doctrinal positions on the same subject matter. If we choose just one denomination, we find that each of the tens of thousands of pastors in the churches does not have to teach the same thing about the same doctrine. Then, let us take and one church within that denominations, and we will find that the church members do not all believe the same thing as their pastor.

Thus, we have all sorts of men teaching different views on every doctrine. Let us look at a few examples, so we can better understand. In dealing with the inspiration of God's Word, most church leaders teaches The Infallibilist View, meaning that they believe the Bible is infallible only in matters of faith, but that it contains many mistakes, errors, and contradictions in matters when it touches on science, history, and geography. On the other hand, few conservative church leaders still teach The Inerrantist View, meaning that they believe the Bible is without error of any kind. On the doctrine of the atonement, some leaders have The Penal Substitution View, meaning that they believe that Christ died in our place. Others have the Christus Victor View, meaning that they believe Christ destroyed Satan and his works. While others have The Moral Government View, meaning that they believe Christ displayed God's wrath against sin. Concerning the doctrine of Sanctification, there are four main views. We have the Lutheran View, meaning sanctification as a declaration by God. We have the Calvinist view, meaning sanctification as holiness in Christ and personal conduct. Then, we have the Keswick View, meaning sanctification as resting-faith in the sufficiency of Christ. In addition, we have the Wesleyan, View, meaning entire sanctification as perfect love. Even these four beliefs on sanctification are not completely accepted because each church leader can tweak it to fit his understanding of things. These doctrines are just the beginning. We could cover The Providence Debate, i.e., the sovereignty of God. We could talk about different foreknowledge beliefs; the divine image differences the different salvation beliefs, the various beliefs about the human constitution, eternal security, the destiny of the evangelized, baptism, charismatic gifts, hellfire, and numerous others.

These differences in the Christian leader's beliefs are often contradictory. Are we to believe that the Holy Spirit one church leader to teach that sinners are destined to enteral torment in hellfire while other leaders teach eternal destruction for the sinners? Are we to believe that the Holy Spirit teaches different church leaders four different views on sanctification? The belief that the Holy Spirit is still carrying out the same work today as what the Father and the Son assigned in the first century, place the Holy Spirit in a very unenviable position, i.e., teaching different views on the same doctrine, some of which are even contradictory. Can we accept that the Holy Spirit teaches different views on all doctrinal positions, even being contradictory? Remember, it was the Holy Spirit, who taught and instructed the apostles miraculously. The Holy Spirit guided them as well. One way was in their writings, as no New Testament author contradicted another, they were all one because there was really one author, God. This is actually true of all forty plus authors of the entire Bible. Thus, we are to believe that the Holy Spirit moved over forty Bible authors miraculously, over a 1,600 year period, to pen sixty-six Bible books, in all of which there is not one contraction, error or mistake, but now the Holy Spirit is teaching different views and contradictory information? We would not say in the church of and leader, who taught contradictory information, so why would we accept that the Holy Spirit would do such a thing. Supposing that churches evangelized their own communities, which they do not, but let us suppose they did. How should an atheist feel if different churches came to his home to witness to him and they told him contradictory views about the same doctrine?

The problem is the belief that the Holy Spirit is carrying out the same work after that work was completed in the first century. Only the apostles and a select few fellow workers received the Holy Spirit in a direct and supernatural way, teaching them, guiding them, instructing them, bringing back to their remembrance all that Jesus had said. The apostle Paul told Timothy, "The things which you have heard from me in the presence of many witnesses, entrust these to faithful men who will be able to teach others also." (2 Tim. 2:2) We all know that Timothy traveled with Paul for 15 years, being taught by Paul (Paul already being extremely educated by Gamaliel), but more importantly, miraculously taught and instructed by the Holy Spirit. This clearly was not the case with Timothy (his being taught and instructed by the Holy Spirit in the same way and to the same extent), as Timothy was taught by Paul and his study of the Old Testament Scriptures. This text evidences that we are to be taught and instructed by Holy Spirit by way of our study the Holy, Spirit-inspired Scriptures.

If the Holy Spirit were miraculously teaching and instructing Christians today, as took place with the apostles and a select few fellow workers, there would be no need for any sort of Bible study tools, such as Bible dictionaries, encyclopedias, word study dictionaries, commentaries, and the like. Even so, while there are no direct Scriptures to evidence Timothy receiving Holy Spirit in the same way as Paul and the twelve apostles, we know that Holy Spirit led Paul to Timothy on his second missionary tour. We know that Paul saw something in Timothy that brought about a 15-year friendship and bond between the two like no other. Timothy became an extremely valuable co-worker of the apostle Paul, in a time, when the Holy Spirit was building the first-century Christian congregation. Therefore, we cannot discount the possibility that Timothy was guided by the Holy Spirit as Paul had been, maybe not to the same degree, and that he was not taught and instructed in the same way and sense but used more directly by the Holy Spirit than those after the first century, including us today. Let us get back to the apostles for a moment. Let us look at the apostles in the very beginning of Acts, as Jesus tells them,

Acts 1:8 Updated American Standard Version (UASV)

⁸ But you will receive power when **the Holy Spirit has come upon you**; and you will be my witnesses in both Jerusalem and in all Judea and Samaria, and to the extremity of the earth."

Earlier, Jesus had told them that he was going away and that he was sending them a helper, the Holy Spirit. Now, he specifically tells them, "You [namely, the apostles] will receive power when the Holy Spirit has come upon you, and you will be my witnesses in Jerusalem and in all Judea and Samaria, and to the end of the earth." Just after Jesus said these things, as they were watching, he ascended back to heaven to be with the Father. Some days later on Sivan 6, 33 C.E., they would receive the power of the Holy Spirit, where there was an outpouring of Holy Spirit. (Acts 2:1-17, 38) If they had already received the Holy Spirit, they would not have needed to call the brothers together to determine who was going to replace Judas as the twelfth apostle. Moreover, "they cast lots for them [Joseph called Barsabbas, who was also called Justus, and Matthias], and the lot fell on Matthias, and he was numbered with the eleven apostles."–Acts 1:15-26

Obtain Boldness

Jesus told his listeners,

Luke 11:13 Updated American Standard Version (UASV)

[13] If you then, being evil, know how to give good gifts to your children, how much more will your heavenly Father give the Holy Spirit to those who ask Him?"

If we want to receive the Holy Spirit, we just go to the Father in prayer and ask him. If want to be bolder in our sharing of the good news, we can pray to God for the Holy Spirit. However, we must not misunderstand the Scriptures, so as to expect the miraculous, supernatural gifts of the Holy Spirit in the same sense and the same way as the apostle, their fellow workers, and the Christians of the first century. If want to become a better teacher in the Bible class at our churches, we will have to be a better Bible student, take in many Scriptures that deal with the principles of being a more effective teacher, put these into practice, and maybe pick up some good Christian books on being a better teacher. In this way, we would be working in harmony with our prayer, because the Word of God is Spirit inspired, and thus the more we delve into it and apply it in a correct and balanced manner; in essence, we are getting more Holy Spirit. If we want to teach the Bible to the Spanish-speaking people in our community, we may want to learn the Spanish language.

Some might believe that I am suggesting that the Holy Spirit is not active today. This is not the case. It is not the question of whether the Spirit is active, but how the Spirit is active. We can all agree that the Holy Spirit is pleading with the unsaved world, to help them find the path of salvation that leads to accepting Jesus Christ. This is not accomplished in some miraculous, supernatural way, but rather through our work as ambassadors for Christ. New Testament Bible scholar Richard L. Pratt Jr., made the following comment on 1 Corinthians 5:20a,

> Paul's role in the divine plan of reconciliation led him to a remarkable claim. He and his company were **Christ's ambassadors**. "Ambassadors" was a technical political term used in Paul's day that closely parallels our English word "ambassadors." An ambassador represented a nation or kingdom in communication with other nations. Paul had in mind his apostolic call to represent the kingdom of Christ to

the nations of the earth. Ambassadors held positions of great honor in the ancient world because they represented the authority of the kings on whose behalf they spoke.

This was also true for Paul as the ambassador of Christ. When he spoke the message of reconciliation, it was **as though God were making his appeal through** him. Rather than speaking directly to the nations of earth, God ordained that human spokespersons would speak for him. As an apostle, Paul had authority to lead and guide the church (2 Cor. 13:3, 10). Yet, this description applies to all who bear the gospel of Christ to others—even to those who do not bear apostolic authority (1 Pet. 4:11). Though we may not present the gospel as perfectly as Paul did, we do speak on God's behalf when we bring the message of grace to others. But Paul and his company were to be received as mouthpieces of God in the most authoritative sense. (Pratt Jr 2000, p. 359)

2 Corinthians 5:16-20 Updated American Standard Version (UASV)

[16] From now on, therefore, we regard no one according to the flesh. Even though we once regarded Christ according to the flesh, we regard him thus no longer. [17] Therefore if anyone is in Christ, he is a new creation; the old things have passed away; behold, new things have come. [18] And all these things are from God, who has reconciled us to himself through Christ, and who has given us the ministry of reconciliation, [19] namely, that God was in Christ reconciling the world to himself, not counting their trespasses against them, and entrusting to us the message of reconciliation. [20] Therefore, we are ambassadors for Christ, as though God were making an appeal through us; we beg you on behalf of Christ, be reconciled to God.

As ambassadors for Christ, we are not seeking to offer superficial feel-good solutions to the problems of their imperfection, nor the wicked world in which we live. We are not telling them that, if they accept Christ, God will take care of their problems, and they will feel better about life. Sadly, many who first come to a Christian meeting are looking for just that; they want God to help them cope with the imperfection that surrounds their every waking moment. We certainly can counsel them biblically, which will enable them to improve their lot in life, will help them be stronger in dealing with this imperfection we all face, and, generally speaking, if they live a Christlike life, there will be fewer problems that a worldly life. However, our serving as ambassadors for Christ, this is not the goal of our service to the unbelieving world. We are offering them the same gospel that Paul did. In other words, the Father loved the world of humankind so much, he offered the only begotten

Son, and the Father is willing to forgive any of their Adamic, inherited sin, by means of Christ Jesus. Paul wrote,

Romans 5:10-12, 8:32 Updated American Standard Version (UASV)

[10] For if while we were enemies we were reconciled to God through the death of his Son, much more, having been reconciled, we shall be saved by his life. [11] Not only that, but we are also exulting in God through our Lord Jesus Christ, through whom we have now received the reconciliation.

[12] Therefore, just as through one man sin entered into the world, and death through sin, and so death spread to all men, because all sinned,

[32] He who did not spare his own Son, but delivered him over for us all, how will he not also with him freely give us all things?

Exercise

To receive the most from your Bible reading and personal study, see the book INTERPRETING THE BIBLE: Introduction to Biblical Hermeneutics.

Review Questions

• Why is it important that we be bold in out evangelism of the Word of God?

• In what way did the Holy Spirit help the apostles and a handful of fellow workers of the first century, make disciples with boldness?

• How can the Holy Spirit help us to be bold in our evangelism?

• How does attaining boldness help us?

CHAPTER 3 Skillfully Using the Word of God

Ephesians 6:17 Updated American Standard Version (UASV)

[17] And take the **helmet of salvation**, and **the sword of the Spirit**, which is the word of God.

Not long ago, those trying to curb the use of drugs within the American youth had the saying, "the mind is a terrible thing to waste." Our next piece of the armor of God would be a very useful tool for protecting the Christian mind, **the helmet of salvation**. The Apostle Paul said to the Thessalonians, "we must stay sober and let our faith and love be like a suit of armor. Our firm hope that we will be saved is our helmet," because it protects our Christian mind. (1 Thessalonians 5:8) Even though we may have accepted Christ, and have entered onto the path of salvation, we still suffer from imperfect human weaknesses. Even though our foremost desire is to do good, our thinking can be corrupted by this fleshly world that surrounds us. We need not to be like this world, but rather openly allow God to alter the way we think, through his Word the Bible, which will help us fully to grasp everything that is good and pleasing to him. (Romans 7:18; 12:2) You likely recall the test that Jesus faced, where Satan offered him "all the kingdoms of the world and their glory." (Matthew 4:8-10) Jesus response was to refer to Scripture, "Be gone, Satan! For it is written, 'you shall worship the Lord your God and him only shall you serve.'" Paul had this to say about Jesus, "looking to Jesus, the founder and perfecter of our faith, who for the joy that was set before him endured the cross, despising the shame and is seated at the right hand of the throne of God."–Hebrews 12:2.

We need to understand that the examples of faith within Scripture do not come to us automatically. If we are focusing on what this current satanic world that caters to the fallen human flesh and what it has to offer, as opposed to focusing on the hopes that are plainly laid out in Scripture, we will be weak in the face of any severe trial. After a few stumbles, it may be that we suffer spiritual shipwreck and lose our hope altogether. Then again, if we frequently feed our minds or concentrate the mind on the promises of God, we will carry on delighting in the hope that has been offered us.–Romans 12:12.

If we are to keep our Christian mind on the hope that lies ahead, we need to possess the **Sword of the Spirit**. The book that reveals heavenly Father, his will and purposes, i.e., the Bible is stated to be "living and active, sharper than any two-edged sword, piercing to the division of soul and of spirit, of joints and of marrow, and discerning the thoughts and intentions of the heart." This Word, if understood correctly, applied in a balanced manner, can transform our lives, and help us avoid or minimalize the pitfalls of this imperfect life. We can depend on that Word when we are overwhelmed, or temple to give way to the flesh, and when the Bible critics of this world attempt to do away with our faith. (2 Corinthians 10:4-5) We need to heed the words of the Apostle Paul to his spiritual son, Timothy:

2 Timothy 3:15-17 Updated American Standard Version (UASV)

[14] You **[Timothy]**, however, continue in the things you have learned and were persuaded to believe, knowing from whom you have learned them **[Paul, who Timothy traveled with and studied under for 15 years]**, [15] and that from infancy[62] you have known the sacred writings **[the whole Old Testament]**, which are able to make you wise for salvation through trust[63] in Christ Jesus. [16] All Scripture is inspired by God and profitable for teaching, for reproof, for correction, for training in righteousness; [17] so that the man of God may be fully competent, equipped for every good work.

> The goal of all this instruction, discipline, and training is not to keep us busy. God intends **that the man of God may be thoroughly equipped for every good work**. We study the Bible, we rely upon God's Spirit, his revelation, and the community of the faithful to keep us on track—obedient and maturing in faith. Continuing in this commitment will enable us to do whatever God calls us to do. Timothy could withstand the attacks of false teachers, the abandonment of professing believers, and the persecution that surrounded him because God had equipped him for the task. God never calls us to do something without first enabling us through his Spirit and the power of his truth to accomplish the task.

> We neglect the Scriptures at our own peril. Through them we gain the ability to serve God and others. The Scriptures not only point the way; through the mysterious union of God's Word and faith, they give us the ability to serve. (Larson 2000, 307)

After two years of proclaiming the good news, Jesus entered into another campaign throughout Galilee. "Jesus went throughout all the cities and villages, teaching in their synagogues and proclaiming the gospel

---

[62] *Brephos* is "the period of time when one is very young—'childhood (probably implying a time when a child is still nursing), infancy." – GELNTBSD

[63] *Pisteuo* is "to believe to the extent of complete trust and reliance—'to believe in, to have confidence in, to have faith in, to trust, faith, and trust.' – GELNTBSD

of the kingdom and healing every disease and every affliction." Jesus had compassion for the lost sheep of Israel,

Matthew 9:36-38 Updated American Standard Version (UASV)

36 When he saw the crowds, he had compassion for them, because they were harassed and scattered, like sheep without a shepherd. 37 Then he said to his disciples, "The harvest is plentiful, but the workers are few. 38 Therefore, beg the Master of the harvest to send out workers into his harvest."[64]

After stating the above, Jesus "called to him his twelve disciples" and "sent out after instructing them." (Matt. 9:35-38; 10:1, 5) Later, Jesus "appointed seventy[65] others and sent them on ahead of him, two by two, into every town and place where he himself was about to go. Then he was saying to them: 'The harvest, indeed, is great, but the workers are few; therefore beg the Master of the harvest to send out workers into his harvest.'"–Luke 10:1-2

This was true in Jesus' day when there were but about one hundred million people on the planet, how much more true it is today with over seven billion. Moreover, the need for workers is far graver today, as the churches are not sending workers out into their communities to share the good news.

John 4:34-35 Updated American Standard Version (UASV)

34 Jesus said to them, "My food is that I do the will of the one who sent me and complete his work. 35 Do you not say, 'There are yet four months and the harvest comes'? Behold, I say to you, lift up your eyes and look at the fields, that they are white for harvest already.

The areas of humankind alienated from God are, indeed, white for harvesting. Therefore, all should pray that God gathers together workers, preparing them, to go out into the communities of their churches, to sow the good news. When we pray such things, we need to act in harmony with our prayers. One way we can do this is by reading such books as CONVERSATIONAL EVANGELISM, THE EVANGELISM HANDBOOK, and THE CHRISTIAN APOLOGIST, all by Edward D. Andrews. These books will prepare all Christians to share God's Word effectively in their community, in their family, in the workplace or school, and informally.– Matthew 28:19-20; Mark 13:10.

---

[64] **9:37-38 LAC:** All Christians are to request prayerfully that the Father "send out workers into his harvest." Therefore, all Christians must act on behalf of their prayers by zealously participating in proclaiming the Word of God, teaching, and making disciples. (Matt. 24:14; 28:19-20; Act 1:8)

[65] Some mss read seventy-two

The Word of God Is Living and Active

Hebrews 4:12 Updated American Standard Version (UASV)

[12] For the word of God is living and active and sharper than any two-edged sword, and piercing as far as the division of soul and spirit, of both joints and marrow, and able to judge the thoughts and intentions of the heart.

What power the message within the Word of God has! It is so powerful that it can change the entire makeup of anyone's inner person if he is receptive to the truth.

Colossians 3:9-10 Updated American Standard Version (UASV)

[9] Do not lie to one another, seeing that you have put off the old man[66] with its practices [10] and have put on the new man[67] who is being renewed through accurate knowledge[68] according to the image of the one who created him,

The Bible contains so much wisdom; it is almost unfathomable to contemplate it. There are endless amounts of life principles, do's and don'ts, commands, counsel, which can help its reader to have far more success in this wicked world than those who refuse to consider its unrivaled wisdom. Psalm 119:105 makes the point perfectly, 'the Word of God is a lamp to my feet [immediate concerns] and a light to my path [what lies ahead].' The Bible will lead us in the way we ought to go in making everyday decisions, or choosing friends, deciding entertainment, employment choices, just how revealing our clothes will be, and so on. (Ps. 37:25; Prov. 13:20; John 15:14; 1 Tim. 2:9) Living by the principles and counsel of the Word will help us to have better relationships with others. (Matt. 7:12; Phil. 2:3-4) We can make a decision for the day, but we can also plan a life, based on what the future hold, as we have our roadway lit with the Word. (1 Tim. 6:9) Our objective is to live under the umbrella of God's sovereignty, to live according to his will and purposes. (Matt. 6:33; 1 John 2:17-18) Life need not be meaningless to the one living by the Word of God.

Then, there is the fact that the Bible is also a weapon in spiritual warfare. The apostle Paul referred to the Word of God as "the sword of the Spirit." (Eph. 6:12, 17) **The sword of the Spirit** pictures the soldier's

---

[66] Or *old person*

[67] Or *new person*

[68] *Epignosis* is a strengthened or intensified form of *gnosis* (*epi*, meaning "additional"), meaning, "true," "real," "full," "complete" or "accurate," depending upon the context. Paul and Peter alone use *epignosis*.

weapon sheathed to his belt and used both for offensive and defensive purposes. Taking the sword of the Spirit—defined for us as the Word of God—can be understood as using Scripture specifically in life's situations to fend off attacks of the enemy and put him to flight. We see the example of Jesus using the Scripture this way in Matthew 4:1–11."[69] If we are effective in our evangelism, we can be used by God as his ambassador, helping those within Satan's world to be set free from spiritual bondage. Unlike imperfect man sword of carnal warfare, "the sword of the Spirit, which is the word of God," saves lives rather than destroy them. However, this is dependent on just how effective we are at wielding this sword.

Teach the Word of Truth Correctly

Can we imagine the ancient soldier who dared enter into warfare without practicing with his sword? How effective would he be with his weapon? He would likely be killed within minutes. The same holds true with our use of "the sword of the spirit," namely, God's Word, in our spiritual warfare, i.e., we would be beaten down by the critic or opponent in short order. If our faith is genuine, we will be like the prophet Jeremiah. In the beginning, he was hesitant to speak out, saying to God, who had just commissioned him to be his prophet to the nations, "I do not know how to speak, for I am only a youth." However, in time Jeremiah became a force to be reckoned with, so effective a communicator that his enemies viewed him as one that makes gloomy predictions of impending disaster. (Jer. 38:4) After that day of saying, but "I am only a youth," Jeremiah would go on to serve as God's prophet for 65 years, becoming one of the best-known prophets in the history of God's Word. So much so, when Jesus came, the people were discussing who the Son of Man might be, and some thought he was Jeremiah the prophet returned. Thus, we must ask, how did the young, she boy overcome his reluctance to proclaim God's Word? Jeremiah tells us,

Jeremiah 20:9 Updated American Standard Version (UASV)

9 If I say, "I will not mention him,
     or speak any more in his name,"
then it becomes in my heart like a fire burning
     shut up in my bones,
and I am weary of holding it in,
     and I cannot endure it.

---

[69] (Anders, Holman New Testament Commentary: vol. 8, Galatians, Ephesians, Philippians, Colossians 1999, p. 192)

Yes, the truth of God's Word in the heart of man is so very powerful; it will compel, provoke, and encourage him to speak. While we may be shy or reluctant to proclaim God's Word to others, it will become a burning fire within us, to the point we will eventually share it. However, if we have not prepared ourselves to use "the sword of the spirit," namely, God's Word, in our spiritual warfare, we will be beat down by the critic or opponent quickly. Do not believe that every critic is one with a closed heart and mind. Many are critics because they had begun to doubt and started to read books or listen to talks by Bible critics, which only served to reinforce their doubts, and they have never heard anyone overturn these Bible difficulties floating around in their mind and heart. We may recall that the apostle Paul 'reasoned with the unbelievers from the Scriptures, explaining and proving' the truth to those he came across. We may be thinking, "yes, but I am no Jeremiah the prophet nor the apostle Paul." Well, neither were they at one time, and we cannot know who new are until we allow ourselves to be used by God. Paul told young Timothy, "Do your best to present yourself to God as one approved, a worker who has no need to be ashamed, rightly handling the word of truth." (2 Tim. 2:15, ESV) On this, New Testament Bible scholar Knute Larson writes,

> Timothy, by contrast, must do his best to **present [himself] to God as one approved, a workman who does not need to be ashamed.** Timothy, and all who follow Christ, are to consecrate themselves to God, working diligently for his approval. The teacher whom God approves has no need of shame in his presence.

> God bestows his approval on the one who exhibits truth, love, and godliness in daily living, and who **correctly handles the word of truth.** The false teachers were mishandling God's words, using them for their own benefit. Timothy was commissioned to handle the words of God correctly. All preaching should present the truth clearly, cutting through erroneous ideas or inaccurate opinions. (Larson 2000, p. 286)

The English Standard Version renders the participial clause of 2:15 "rightly handling the word of truth," while the Holman Christian Standard Bible renders it "correctly teaching the word of truth," and the New American Standard Bible, "accurately handling the word of truth." The Greek word, *orthotomeo*, means "to give accurate instruction—'to teach correctly, to expound rightly.' ... 'do your best ... to teach the word of truth correctly' 2 Tm 2:15."[70] This is all that can be asked of any Christian, that 'we do our best to teach the word of truth correctly.'

What can help us to teach the word of truth correctly? If we are to teach another, we must correctly and clearly understand the Word ourselves. When we clearly understand something, we are able to give reasons as to why it is so. Moreover, we are able to express it in our own words. If we are to understand the Bible correctly, we must read it within the context of the verses that surround it, the chapter it is within, the Bible book it is within, the Testament that it is in, and the Bible as a whole. According to the Merriam-Webster Dictionary, immediate context (i.e., of a word, phrase, clause or sentence) is "the words that are used with a certain word or phrase and that help to explain its meaning."[71] The meaning of a text is what the author meant by the words that he used. On this Robert H. Stein writes,

> Great confusion can result if we do not pay careful attention to context. For instance, both Paul (Rom. 4:1–25) and James (2:14–26) use the term "faith" (pistis). Yet we will misunderstand both if we assume that by faith they mean "a body of beliefs." We will misunderstand Paul if we assume that he means "a mere mental assent to a fact," and we will misunderstand James if we assume that he means "a wholehearted trust." It is evident from the context that Paul means the latter (cf. Rom. 4:3, 5) and that James means the former (cf. 2:14, 19). (Stein 1994, p. 59)

Stein also wrote, "A context is valuable because it assists the reader in understanding the meaning the author has given the text." Another example would be Paul's statement at Galatians 5:13 (ESV), "For you were called to freedom, brothers. Only do not use your freedom as an opportunity for the flesh, but through love serve one another." If we were looking at this verse alone, not considering what is before and after, we would be asking, what does Paul mean by "freedom"? Was he speaking of freedom from sin and death, freedom from being enslaved to false beliefs, freedom from corruption, or was it something entirely different? If we consider the context, we get our answer. The context tells us the "freedom" that Paul spoke of was our being freed from "the curse of the law," as Christ became the curse for us. (Gal. 3:13, 19-24; 4:1-5) If we look at Galatians 3:10, "Paul quotes Deuteronomy 27:26 to prove that, contrary to what the Judaizers claimed, the law cannot justify and

---

[70] Louw, Johannes P.; Nida, Eugene A. (**Greek-English Lexicon of the New Testament based on Semantic Domains**)

[71] http://www.merriam-webster.com/dictionary/context

save. It can only condemn. The breaking of any aspect of the law brought a curse on the person who broke the law. Since no one can keep the law perfectly, we are all cursed. Paul, with this argument, destroys the Judaizers' belief that a person is saved through the law." [72] Thus, Paul was referring to the freedom that Christians possess. Just because we are not under the Mosaic Law, a law that imperfect man cannot keep perfectly, this is no excuse to use our "freedom as an opportunity for the flesh." Rather, if we truly understand and value our freedom, we will slave for one another because of our love for one another. However, those in the Galatian congregation who lacked that love were engaged in vicious infighting and quarreling.–Galatians 5:15.

There is another meaning of the word "context," i.e., background, conditions, historical setting, and situation. Some call the surrounding text cotext and the historical setting context. Either way, the second meaning here is just as important. The background information that must be considered is, who penned the book, when and where was it written and under what historical setting. Why was the author moved to pen the book, or more realistically, why did God move him to write the book? Within any book on Bible backgrounds, the author will discuss the social, moral, and religious practices of the time Bible book was written. [73]

Correctly handling the word of truth goes deeper than simply explaining a biblical truth accurately. We do not want to use our knowledge of god's Word in an intimidating way. Of course, we want to defend the truth offensively and defensively, following the example of Jesus, who used Scripture to defeat Satan the Devil when under temptation. Nevertheless, figuratively speaking, we do not use the Bible to club others over the head. (Deut. 6:16; 8:3; 10:20; Matt. 4:4, 7, 10) Rather, we want to follow the counsel Peter gave, "in your hearts honor Christ the Lord as holy, **always being prepared to make a defense** to anyone who asks you for a reason for the hope that is in you; **yet do it with gentleness and respect**."–1 Peter 3:15.

New Testament Bible scholar Richard L. Pratt Jr. offered the following on 2 Corinthians 10:3-5,

---

[72] (Anders, Holman New Testament Commentary: vol. 8, Galatians, Ephesians, Philippians, Colossians 1999, p. 37)

[73] An outstanding study tool in getting background information about the New Testament is:

BIBLE BACKGROUNDS OF THE NEW TESTAMENT
Parables, Metaphors, Similes, Gestures and Attitudes
http://www.christianpublishers.org/apps/webstore/products/show/5904404

Paul responded by reminding the Corinthians that his ministry was successful warfare. He had previously described his gospel ministry as a parade of victory in war, and he used similar military analogies elsewhere as well. His apostolic effort was a war he was sure to win.

Paul admitted that he and his company **live[d] in the world**, but insisted that they did not **wage war as the world does**. They did not employ the intimidation, coercion, and violence normally associated with worldly authorities. Instead of employing **the weapons of the world**, Paul relied on **divine power**. These **weapons** appeared weak by worldly standards, but they were actually very powerful. The preaching of the cross brought great displays of God's power in the lives of believers everywhere, including Corinth.

Consequently, Paul was certain that he was on a course **to demolish** the **strongholds** or fortifications of **arguments and every pretension** that anyone set up **against the knowledge of God**. As Paul traveled the world proclaiming the gospel of Christ, he encountered pretentious disbelief supported by clever arguments and powerful personalities. But through the "weakness" of preaching Christ, Paul went about taking **captive every thought to make it obedient to Christ**. (Pratt Jr 2000, p. 417)

2 Corinthians 10:3-5 English Standard Version (ESV)

³ For though we walk in the flesh, we are not waging war according to the flesh. ⁴ For the weapons of our warfare are not of the flesh but have divine power to destroy strongholds. ⁵ We destroy arguments and every lofty opinion raised against the knowledge of God, and take every thought captive to obey Christ,

If we have a sound understanding of the Scriptures and are always working toward growing it, we can accomplish much. Our use of God's Word can "destroy strongholds," namely, expose the false or mistaken beliefs of others, any irreligious practices, as well as all worldviews that are not biblical, but rather are fleshly. In Addition, we will be able to remove "every lofty opinion raised against the knowledge of God." Moreover, we can use our knowledge of Scripture to help unbelievers to bring their thinking in line with a biblical worldview, as we make disciples.

We must keep in mind that our obligation is not just toward the unbeliever, but toward the others who claim to be Christians, who are on a false path. No true conservative, evangelical Christian would consider

Catholicism to be the true way to pure worship of God, and the same would hold true of Pentecostalism, among many other so-called Christian denominations. Both the unbeliever and those claiming to be Christian are holding onto unbiblical beliefs that are deeply embedded in their mind and heart. If we are able to use the Scriptures, logic and reason effectively, we will be able to remove "every lofty opinion raised against the knowledge of God." In the end, then they will understand and find the knowledge of God.

Using Questions Effectively

Why does it matter that we use question effectively when we are witnessing to others about the Word of God? Imagine that you just took your car into the garage because it has been having many different problems. In the first scenario, the mechanic says to throw your keys over on the desk; he can have it fixed as good as new for you, come back Saturday to pick it up. Would you feel comfortable with the mechanic, or would alarms be going off. In a second scenario, you take the car to another garage and the mechanic stops what he is doing; he comes over and asks you some probing questions, like 'what is it doing, what sounds is it making,' and the like. He has you start it; he revs the engine and listens. He asks if he can take it around the block. After that, he asks you some more leading questions based on what he has thus learned. Now, he gives you a preliminary diagnosis but says it would be best to put it on the diagnostics machine to verify his findings. He comforts you with the words; we can get such and such parts in here and have it fixed for you by this Saturday. Why does the second scenario give you much more confidence in the competency of the mechanic? In any field, a person must ask probing and leading questions, to discover symptoms or evidence that can lead them to help find the 'why' or the 'what.' If we are to help an unbeliever, find the truth we must ask effective questions. If we are to help a "Christian" on a false path, find the correct path, we must ask effective questions. Just like the second mechanic, we are trying to discover the cause of what is contributing to the unbelief or the wrong belief. After that, we can use the Word of God to lead them in the way they ought to go.

Jesus was the master teacher, who used questions as he learned more about the student but also allowed the one listening to feel involved in the discussion. For example, when the disciples were in need of a lesson in humility, Jesus started with a question, not a lecture. (Mark 9:33) To teach Peter how to find the principle behind the black and white, Jesus offered him a multiple-choice question. (Matt. 17:24-26) When Jesus sought the disciples understanding of who he was, he asked them viewpoint questions. (Matt 16:13-17) Jesus was about imparting knowledge and understanding, but he did not do this with sermons alone. He also used questions combined with statements, which got down into the hearts of his listeners, moving them to act in harmony with the gospel message he was sent by the Father to deliver to the lost sheep of Israel. We use questions in our ministering to other, because we want to help them to act in harmony with the Word of God. We also want to use questions to overcome their objections that are designed to dismiss us. Moreover, we want to find those with receptive hearts.

What would we do as a parent, if our child came to us, saying, 'I am constantly being challenged about my belief in creation as opposed to evolution?' Certainly, we want our children to be able to have faith in the Word of God as absolute truth and to be able to defend that truth with fellow classmates, even teachers. Rather than stressing the importance of defending God's Word, which may come across as being critical, or offering advice, why not show him how effective viewpoint questions can be.

FIRST EXAMPLE

Father: Say you were to ask your science teacher how DNA is packed with the chromosomes, what would she say?

Son: She would go on and on about it, talking about how efficient that it is. She would say something like, "The most striking property of every chromosome within the eukaryotic cell nucleus is the length of each molecule of DNA incorporated and folded into it. The human genome of 3×10^9 bp would extend over a meter if unraveled and straightened, yet it is compacted into a nucleus only 10^{-5} m in diameter. **It is an astonishing feat of engineering** to organize such a long linear DNA molecule within ordered structures that can reversibly fold and unfold within the chromosome."[74]

Father: What if you were to ask her, "How do we explain that such an astonishing feat of engineering rose by an undirected chance of events; does not a feat of engineering suggest an engineer?

SECOND EXAMPLE

Father: Say you were to ask your science teacher, 'Can you please explain to me about DNA's capacity for stored information,' what would she say?

Son: She would say something like; "The information stored in DNA must by no means be underestimated. So much so, that one human DNA

---

[74] http://what-when-how.com/molecular-biology/chromosomes-molecular-biology/

molecule contains enough information to fill a million-page encyclopedia, or to fill about 1,000 books. Note this fact well: one million encyclopedia pages, or 1,000 books. This is to say that the nucleus of each cell contains as much information as would fill a one-million-page encyclopedia, which is used to control the functions of the human body. To draw an analogy, we can state that even the 23-volume-Encyclopaedia Britannica, one of the greatest mines of information in the world, has 25,000 pages. Therefore, before us lies an incredible picture. In a molecule found in a nucleus, which is far smaller than the microscopic cell wherein it is located, there exists a data warehouse 40 times bigger than the biggest encyclopedia of the world that includes millions of items of information. This means a massive 1000-volume encyclopedia which is unique and has no equal in the world."

"Computers are currently the most advanced form of technology for storing information. A body of information, which, 30 years ago, was routinely stored in a computer the size of a room, can today be stored in small "discs," yet even the latest technology invented by human intelligence, after centuries of accumulated knowledge and years of hard work, is far from reaching the information storage capacity of a single cell nucleus. The following comparison made by the well-known professor of microbiology Michael Denton, will probably suffice to highlight the contrast between the tiny size of DNA and the great amount of information it contains:"

> The information necessary to specify the design of all the species of organisms which have ever existed on the planet, a number according to G.G. Simpson of approximately one thousand million, could be held in a teaspoon and there would still be room left for all the information in every book ever written. (*Michael Denton. Evolution: A Theory in Crisis. London: Burnett Books, 1985, p. 334*)[75]

Father: What if you were to ask her, "How is it that human computer technicians are unable to accomplish these types of results, yet we are to believe that mindless matter can do so alone?"

From a few more examples like this, the son can begin to see how effective viewpoint questions are. Many great publications out there offer strong apologetic reasoning for intelligent design. Some leading authors would be John C. Lennox, William A. Dembski, Jonathan Witt, Stephen C. Meyer, David Klinghoffer, Michael J. Behe, Michael Denton, among many others. How else can we become more effective in our evangelism of others?

---

[75] http://www.dnarefutesevolution.com/human_celli.html

Using God's Word with Persuasion

A confusion that arises over using the Bible effectively when witnessing to others is the belief that is simply boils down to knowing and quoting Scripture. What do we read of the way the apostle Paul went about witnessing to others. It says, "He entered the synagogue and for three months **spoke boldly, reasoning** and **persuading** them." (Ac 19:8-9) On another occasion, "when some became stubborn and continued in unbelief, speaking evil of the Way before the congregation, he withdrew from them and took the disciples with him, **reasoning** daily in the hall of Tyrannus." Persuasion is "attempting to win others over to one's own point of view. It can be either positive, as with preaching the gospel, or it can spring from a malign intent to seduce people from the truth." (Manser 2009) When one is persuaded, he is won over by the ability of the persuader's reasoning, arguments (reasons put forward in support), explaining of the Scriptures, i.e., he is so convinced that he gains confidence in God's Word. When Christians persuade a person to accept the Bible as the inspired, inerrant Word of God, we are winning him over, so that he will place his trust in the Bible. If we are to accomplish this in the skeptical, atheistic, agnostic, humanistic, liberal, progressive world that we live in, we must possess the skills to teach our listeners of the truthfulness of our reasons we put forward in support of the biblical worldview, or rather in opposition to the fleshly worldview of todays' hedonistic society.

We do not want to shy away from using God's Word; because that just demonstrates that, we have a lack of respect for it. The modern day critic of the 20th and 21st centuries has taken over in the driving of the conversation, and it is he who decides what is evidence and what is not. The critic's conclusion is that Bible manuscripts that date back 2,300 years are not historical, archaeological evidence, but rather are biased material and if we cannot offer up secular evidence for what we say; well then, we have no evidence at all. The modern day Bible scholar has chosen to play by the critic's rules of engagement, so they actually run around looking for ways to prove things with secular history alone. First, we do not cower before Satan and his people, leaving them to determine whether we can draw attention to God's Word. It is certainly beneficial and appropriate that our great apologetic arguers, like Norman L. Geisler, William Lane Craig, or Craig Evans defend the truth against the lies of the great minds of Satan's side. However, our primary commission is winning the hearts and minds of those receptive to the truth, not winning arguments against those who will never accept the truth, regardless of the evidence.[76]

Therefore, we need to be quite familiar with the Word of God and know what the authors meant by the words that they used. Whether we open our Bible to share a Scripture or reference it aloud, draw attention to the importance of what God's thinking is on the subject that we may be discussing. After a very brief introduction and our mission of sharing God's Word, we might open with an open-ended question. We might say, fifty percent of marriages in America fail, and then ask, "Why do you think that is?" [Allow for an answer] How do you think this principle from God's Word would help, Paul said, "Let no one seek his own good, but the good of his neighbor." (1 Cor. 10.24, ESV) If both mates were to seek the good of the other, how might we see that playing out, can you think of any examples? [Allow for an answer] If the person is receptive, offer a couple more Bible principles that deal with spouses that seem to be growing apart (Phil 1:10), mates that fail to fulfill their responsibilities (Rom 14:12), the husband that seems to not care where the family is heading (Pro. 14:1) habits that annoy one another (Col. 3:13), and so on.

We need to reason from the Scripture where we leave our listeners with no doubt whatsoever that what they are hearing is the truth. Therefore, we need to use genuine, warm, earnest, profound and honest entreaty, with sound logic. As Jesus and Paul, our objective is to reach the heart of those to whom we witness. This is realized in the words of wise King Solomon, "The purpose in a man's heart is like deep water, but a man of understanding will draw it out." (Pro. 20:5) Yes, we need to draw out what is in the heart of our listener, by using kind, loving and respectful questions that evidence we are personally interested in them. We must avoid being too direct and frank. In other words, we do not want to have a cutting edge to our questions, nor do we want to be too frank or straightforward and showing no delicacy or consideration when using questions. When we are making arguments to substantiate a point, make them clear and logical. We want to offer evidence that will satisfy the listener. Moreover, we want to share what the Bible author meant by the use of his words, not what we think he meant. Time is critical and should be used judiciously. Rather than rush through reading three or four verses that make our point, we should choose the clearest one, use it well by explain, reasoning and illustrating. When we think of using corroborative evidence, again, we turn to Solomon, "From a wise mind

---

[76] Keep in mind that when Geisler, Craig and Evans are debating to on stage against a atheist scientist or the like; they are talking past him, if he is unreceptive to any in the audience that may be receptive. It is evidence that we have answers in the conversation, whether they want to hear them or not, so that unbelievers can see that we do have reasonable, logical answers to the deep questions that plague humanity.

comes wise speech; the words of the wise are persuasive." (Pro. 16:23, NLT) If there is a need for more research on our part, say so, by stating that we will look into this further and get back to them another time.

Carry on Using God's Word Skillfully

The world is ever changing toward being more wicked each and every day. In fact, Paul told Timothy, "Evil people and impostors will go on from bad to worse, deceiving and being deceived." (2 Tim. 3:13) Thus, 2,000 years later this is even truer. Therefore, it is highly significant that "we destroy arguments and every lofty opinion raised against the knowledge of God, and take every thought captive to obey Christ." We do this by using "the sword of the Spirit, which is the word of God."–(Eph. 6:17) As the author of Hebrews tells us, "For the word of God is living and active, sharper than any two-edged sword, piercing to the division of soul and of spirit, of joints and of marrow, and discerning the thoughts and intentions of the heart." (Heb. 4:12, ESV) Jesus words ring true, "For what will it profit a man if he gains the whole world and forfeits his soul? Or what will a man give in exchange for his soul?" – Matthew 16:26, NASB.

Exercise

Someone just said to you, "I don't believe the Bible, as it is just a book by men, not the Word of God." How would you persuade him that this is not the case?

Review Questions

- How powerful is the Word of God?

- How is the Word of God living and active?

- How can we handle the Word of truth aright when we evangelize?

- How can we use the Word of God with persuasion?

- How can we carry on in our skillful use of the Bible?

CHAPTER 4 Always Being Prepared to Make a Defense

1 Peter 3:15 Updated American Standard Version (UASV)

[15] but sanctify Christ as Lord in your hearts, **always being prepared to make a defense**[77] to anyone who asks you for a reason for the hope that is in you; yet do it with gentleness and respect;

When one, who is sincerely interested in our beliefs as a follower of Christ, asks for a reason as to why we believe this or that, we must defend those beliefs with sound biblical answers. When Peter says that we need always to be prepared to make a defense to anyone who asks us for a reason for the hope that is in us, to whom does this apply? Who is supposed to be able to make a defense? Does this apply just to Bible scholars, pastors, elders, priests, church leaders, or all Christians? If we return to the first verse of Peter's letter, he writes, "To those who reside as aliens, scattered throughout Pontus, Galatia, Cappadocia, Asia, and Bithynia, who are chosen." (1 Pet. 1:1, NASB) The ones, who resided as aliens, were Christians living among the Jews and pagan Gentiles of Asia Minor. Thus, the first letter of Peter, especially 1:3 through 4:1 was directed to those who had just recently been baptized. Thus, Peter expected all Christians, even newly baptized ones to be able to defend the hope that lies within all Christians, offering reasonable, logical answers to those who are genuinely interested.

This first letter of Peter was penned about 62-64 C.E., meaning that these early Christians in Asia Minor, like others throughout the Roman Empire, were living under very difficult time, being persecuted on two fronts: by the Jews and the pagan population. The early Christians were mostly converts from Judaism, who now followed Jesus as the way, the truth, and the life. After that, pagans were being converted over to Christianity. The Jewish population viewed the Christians as an apostate form of Judaism, who were stumbling their fellow brothers and sisters. The pagan nations were angered because the Christians had given up their former lifestyle and had now become a new person. To the world, these Christians had undergone a life change that was viewed as apostasy from pagan religion and Judaism, and this was a crime! Because Christians refused to be a part of the world, the world hated them, just as it had hated Jesus. (1 Pet. 1.18; 2:1; 4:4) Even worse, Satan himself became enraged at this new Christian faith. Peter warned, "Be sober-minded; be

---

[77] Or *argument*; or *explanation*

watchful. Your adversary the devil prowls around like a roaring lion, seeking someone to devour."

What counsel within this first letter of Peter would keep these new ones safe, so that they would not return to their former ways? Peter exhorts, "Keep your conduct among the Gentiles honorable, so that when they speak against you as evildoers, they may see your good works and glorify God on the day of visitation."[78] (2:12) Peter goes on to inform them that in those difficult times, they needed to be "be sound in mind[79] and be sober-minded[80] in prayers." (4:7) Again, they needed to be "sober-minded; be watchful" because Satan was 'seeking to devour' them as well. (5:8) Satan uses the enticement of old friends of the world, who were "living in sensuality, lusts, drunkenness, orgies, drinking parties, and lawless idolatry." (4:3) Defending one's hope under normal circumstances is difficult enough, let alone such situations as these. It has even become far more difficult these days and as Paul said that "in the last days difficult times will come," as "evil men and impostors will proceed from bad to worse."–2 Timothy 3:1, 13.

There is one more obligation for these new Christians if they are to maintain their right standing before God and strengthen their faith. Yes, they must also declare and defend their hope. Peter's use of the word "hope" is nearly the same with his use of the word "faith" (1 Pet. 1:3, 13, 21). On this, Thomas R. Schreiner writes, "Believers are to be ready constantly to respond to those who ask about their faith. What Peter emphasized is that they were to be prepared to provide a "defense" (NRSV, apologia–rendered "answer" by NIV) to those who ask about the Christian faith." (Schreiner 2003, p. 175) These new Christians were taught the correct course of conduct by the preaching of the Gospel, through which they had accepted the Christian faith, i.e., "the hope." Peter makes this clear when he writes, "It was revealed to them [the prophets] that they were serving not themselves but you, in the things that have now been announced to you through those who preached the good news to you by the Holy Spirit sent from heaven." (1 Pet 1:12) This now placed what obligation on them. Peter went on to command that they "prepare [their] minds for action." (1:13) What action is Peter talking about? He says, "That [they] may proclaim the excellencies of him who called you out of darkness into his marvelous light." (2:9) When should these ones "proclaim the excellencies"? Peter gives the answer in our main

---

[78] I.e. Christ's second coming to judge

[79] to have understanding about practical matters and thus be able to act sensibly–'to have sound judgment, to be sensible, to use good sense, sound judgment.'– GELNTBSD

[80] to be in control of one's thought processes and thus not be in danger of irrational thinking–'to be sober-minded, to be well composed in mind.'–GELNTBSD

text, "always being prepared to make a defense ... for a reason for the hope that is in you."–1 Peter 3:15

We have far worse conditions today than existed in Asia Minor of 2,000 years ago. Satan is still walking around Christianity like a roaring lion, seeking to devour true Christians. However, he knows his time is far shorter, and he has become desperate in his plight to take as many followers of Jesus Christ with him as possible. The world today under the influence of Satan caters to the fleshly desires of the fallen flesh unlike no other time prior to, because technology has the means of reaching billions in the privacy of their own home. The need to evangelize in our own communities has grown as well because so many are abandoning the faith, and many young ones are not taking up the faith of their parents or grandparents. Christians need to be busy in these last days, sharing the good news, helping a new generation come out of the darkness.

1 Peter 1:13-15 Updated American Standard Version (UASV)

[13] Therefore, gird the loins of your mind,[81] and being sober-minded,[82] set your hope fully on the grace that will be brought to you at the revelation of Jesus Christ. [14] As children of obedience,[83] do not be conformed according to the desires you formerly had in your ignorance, [15] but like the Holy One who called you, you also be holy in all your conduct; [16] because it is written, "You shall be holy, for I am holy."

Defending the Hope That Is In You

We must begin with the fact that we must know accurately what the Bible says on different Bible doctrines and be able to offer substantial reasons for the faith. As to the biblical truths, we do not want to remain a spiritual babe. "For everyone who partakes only of milk is not accustomed to the word of righteousness, for he is an infant. But solid food is for the mature, who because of practice have their senses trained to discern good and evil. Therefore leaving the elementary teaching about the Christ, let us press on to maturity." (Hebrews 5:13-6:1) We can consider a Bible example of one, who lack a deeper knowledge, through no fault of his own, correcting it once it was brought to his attention,

---

[81] I.e., *prepare your minds for action (mental perception)*

[82] **Sober Minded:** (Gr. *nepho*) This denotes being sound in mind, to be in control of one's thought processes and thus not be in danger of irrational thinking, 'to be sober-minded, to be well composed in mind.'–1 Thessalonians 5:6, 8; 2 Timothy 4:5; 1 Peter 1:13; 4:7; 5:8

[83] I.e., *obedient children*

namely, Apollos. The account is below; notice how he can defend the faith much better after he received the way of God more accurately, he eagerly helps others discover this hope.

Acts 18:24-28 Updated American Standard Version (UASV)

24 Now a certain Jew named Apollos, a native of Alexandria, an eloquent man, arrived in Ephesus; and he was well versed in the Scriptures. **25** This man had been orally instructed in the way of the Lord; and being fervent in spirit, he was speaking and teaching accurately the things concerning Jesus, being acquainted only with the baptism of John; **26** and this man began to speak out boldly in the synagogue. But when Priscilla and Aquila heard him, they took him aside and explained to him the way of God more accurately. **27** And when he wanted to go across to Achaia, the brothers encouraged him and wrote to the disciples to welcome him; and when he had arrived, he greatly helped those who had believed through grace, **28** for he powerfully refuted the Jews in public, demonstrating by the Scriptures that Jesus was the Christ.

Just as was true of Priscilla and Aquila, Christian evangelists should be able to share the faith accurately to unbelievers, to those who have started to doubt, and to those in Christian denominations that are not on the true path of salvation. If we are to accomplish these things, we must have an accurate, full, true knowledge of God's Word. Paul wrote to the brothers in Colossae, "For this reason also, since the day we heard of it, we have not ceased to pray for you and to ask that you may be filled with the accurate knowledge[84] of his will in all spiritual wisdom and understanding, so as to walk in a manner worthy of the Lord, fully pleasing to him bearing fruit in every good work and increasing in the accurate knowledge[85] of God." – Colossians 1:9-10

This sharing of the Gospel is not just some basic biblical truth of Jesus's life and ministry, death, resurrection and ascension. Moreover, this is not just being able to string many good sounding words together, but rather words that will lead others to the same hope that we hold so dearly. The principle behind Paul's words to the Corinthians makes this point nicely. He wrote, "I would rather speak five words with my mind in order to instruct others, than ten thousand words in a tongue." – 1 Corinthians 14:19

---

[84] *Epignosis* is a strengthened or intensified form of *gnosis* (*epi*, meaning "additional"), meaning, "true," "real," "full," "complete" or "accurate," depending upon the context. Paul and Peter alone use *epignosis*.

[85] *Epignosis* is a strengthened or intensified form of *gnosis* (*epi*, meaning "additional"), meaning, "true," "real," "full," "complete" or "accurate," depending upon the context. Paul and Peter alone use *epignosis*.

Yes, Christians looking to share biblical truths with others should seek to do so with words of understanding. They should possess an accurate, full and true knowledge about the Father, the Son, The Holy Spirit, the Kingdom of God, and the Father's will and purpose for mankind, as well as the many other laws and principles found in Scripture. Certainly, if we are going to be successful in sharing or defending our beliefs, we must first fully understand them ourselves. Have we bought out the time and applied our mind meditatively in a study of God's Word so that we can effectively share it with others? Paul exhorted his young traveling companion, Timothy, "Do your best to present yourself to God as one approved, a worker who has no need to be ashamed, rightly handling the word of truth." (2 Tim. 2:15) On this, the following commentaries write,

God bestows his approval on the one who exhibits truth, love, and godliness in daily living, and who correctly handles the word of truth. The false teachers were mishandling God's words, using them for their own benefit. Timothy was commissioned to handle the words of God correctly. All preaching should present the truth clearly, cutting through erroneous ideas or inaccurate opinions.[86]

Third, this same workman (specifically, Timothy but by application today all believers) was to be accurate in delivering the message of truth. The truth is the gospel. Paul showed concern that Timothy would present the gospel without perverting or distorting it. He was not to be turned aside by disputes about words or mere empty prattle.[87]

Paul develops this concept in the striking phrase ... Paul's use of [epaischunomai, aischunomai, and aischune] means "unashamed" in the sense that he does not need to be ashamed of his work. The participle orthotomounta qualifies [ergates] and together with the words that follow specifically describes how Timothy may be unashamed: by being a worker who handles accurately the word of truth.

The material that this worker is to handle correctly is "the word of truth" ... Only when he handles it correctly will he be unashamed ... The rendering given in several of the modern translations, using a combination of the verb "handle" and some adverb such as "accurately" (NASB), "rightly" (RSV), or

[86] Knute Larson, I & II Thessalonians, I & II Timothy, Titus, Philemon, vol. 9, Holman New Testament Commentary (Nashville, TN: Broadman & Holman Publishers, 2000), 286.

[87] Thomas D. Lea and Hayne P. Griffin, 1, 2 Timothy, Titus, vol. 34, The New American Commentary (Nashville: Broadman & Holman Publishers, 1992), 215.

"correctly" (NIV), for the compound verb [*orthotomounta*] with the phrase "the word of truth" as the direct object captures this relationship quite well.[88]

If we are going to be "a worker who has no need to be ashamed, rightly handling the word of truth," we must not always rely on others as being more effective, when we are called upon to share or defend our beliefs. Yes, God expects each of us to be capable of supporting our hope with Scripture. We do not want to fall under those who Paul mentioned to Timothy, "always learning and never able to arrive at a knowledge of the truth." (2 Tim. 3:7) We do not want to remain a spiritual babe for our entire Christian life. What do we think of children, who never really grow up and live with their parents off and on for their entire life? When we think of the many different professions in life, such as medicine, law, science, engineer, mechanic and so on, we know that our hands are held throughout our education, but once in the real world, we are expected to be self-reliant. Even Paul said of himself, "When I was a child, I spoke like a child, I thought like a child, I reasoned like a child. When I became a man, I gave up childish ways." – 1 Corinthians 13:11.

If we ever expect to defend our hope effectively, i.e., the faith, we are going to have to study daily. This should not trouble us because it does not take hours every day, but at least 30 minutes or more. The amount that can be accomplished in 30 minutes a day, after 365 days, will be far more than we might have ever expected. A Christian should study the Bible (not just read) a minimum of thirty minutes a day, he should also prepare the lessons assigned for the Bible study at the church and any other service that allows him to prepare ahead of time. A Christian should participate in any comment sessions that are allowed at their particular church, as this gives them practice in effectively sharing biblical truths. Also, A Christian should attend every Christian meeting, as it offers them an opportunity to build others up. A Christian should share every new thing they learn in their personal studies with at least one new friend, which gives them practice at effectively communicating biblical truths. We must have a deep understanding of the biblical truths that we share and defend, which is going to be presented to all kinds of different persons. Our studying daily needs to be a time on the day when we will not be disturbed. We want to turn the phone off, any music, television, and meditatively go through God's Word. The daily study will be our greatest tool for helping us to share and defend the Word of God and out faith effectively. Paul counsels Titus and by extension us as well, "let our

---

[88] George W. Knight, The Pastoral Epistles: a Commentary on the Greek Text, New International Greek Testament Commentary (Grand Rapids, MI; Carlisle, England: W.B. Eerdmans; Paternoster Press, 1992), 411–412.

people learn to devote themselves to good works, so as to help cases of urgent need, and not be unfruitful." (Titus 3:14) If we are studying daily, preparing for meetings, answering at meetings, attending all meetings, sharing a new biblical truth with friends, we will be able to apply Paul's thoughts to the Colossians as well. He wrote, "Let your speech always be gracious, seasoned with salt, so that you may know how you ought to answer each person." – Colossians 4:6

Using the Bible to Defend Our Hope

It should be noted that many today hold back from sharing or defending their Christian faith. Those who do, tend to do so without using the Bible. If we want to defend our hope successfully, we need to have our Bible as the primary evidence of that hope. Our hope lies within God's Word, so we need to use God's Word to defend it. We must persuade with reason from God's Word, not from how we feel, think, or believe. We need to go from 'this is how I **feel**, to, 'this is what I **know**, and here are the Scriptural reasons as to why.' It should be, 'the Word of God says,' Paul wrote,' 'Jesus said,' 'God said,' not 'I feel,' 'I think,' or 'I believe.' It is our effective use of the Bible when we communicated biblical truths to others that are going to convince the right-hearted ones of the truth and the way. One way that we will become more skilled is by our using our Bible at every opportunity: in our personal study of course, in sharing new truths with friends, and especially in looking up every Scripture that is cited in our religious services. Another way is to start paying attention to how commentaries and other study tools, as well as our pastors, elders tie Scriptures together contextually to establish their biblical point. If you were going to share the hope of salvation, could you walk a listener through 5-10 Scriptures that would paint a picture of that hope? Will our listener tell a friend of what they learned, and say, "He straight to his Bible and showed it to me directly!"

If we are sharing or defending biblical truths, we must do so correctly, persuasively, and in such a way that it is easy to grasp. This means that we know it well ourselves, and we have prepared well by communicating in more relaxed moments, which made us better communicators. For example, can we explain the resurrection hope at this very moment to another if they asked? Will our explanation be from the Bible? Will it be what the author meant by the words he used? Will it be persuasive? Will it be easy to follow and understand? If not, then, how can we honestly say we have a resurrection hope? Is there not irony that many young girls can tell you everything about Taylor Swift, but little if anything about their heavenly Father? The same is true of adult males, who can tear a car apart blindfolded, but cannot string along a handful of verses that defend their resurrection hope. And yes, adult females have an immense amount of knowledge about subject matters that interest them, yet likely cannot support their resurrection hope any better. The above are a bit of a stereotype, which is noted, but it makes the point that we prepare for worldly things with far more vigor than we prepare to share and defend the faith.

If we are going to have any success in defending our Christian faith, we must be able to overcome the objections of others. We will find that the same objections are repeatedly used. Therefore, we will eventually, be able to overcome the standard objections easily. However, a couple of words of caution. First, we do not want to become complacent in our response to common objections; because the listener needs to feel as though they are getting an emotionally involved response, not some automatize, robotic response as if we feel like, 'here we go again.' Second, do not be complacent in thinking that every objection is going to be the common ones. If someone has an objection that we have never addressed, just simply say, "you raise a very good point, and the next time we speak, I will give you a logical and reasonable answer." When we research his objection, do so to the point that we know it inside and out. Moreover, be aware that 99 percent of all Bible difficulties have logical, reasonable answers. On this, R. A. Torrey writes, "Humbly. Recognize the limitations of your own mind and knowledge, and do not for a moment imagine that there is no solution just because you have found none. There is, in all probability, a very simple solution, even when you can find no solution at all."[89] In the end, there are answers, so meditate on the objection that has been raised, search through the literature, looking for Scripture and arguments to refute the objection in defense of the faith. Out of many thousands of Bible difficulties that have answers as to why they are, in fact, Bible difficulties and not errors, mistakes or contradictions, there are but a handful that has yet to be answered. This does not mean there is no answer, just that the information needed may be lacking, or it is something we will have to wait on until, a greater mind comes along, or until the second coming of Christ. However, actually, if science had answers to many thousands of issues, but only a few remained unanswered, we would never hear the end of it. It is amazing that we have what we have considering we are dealing with a book where parts of it were penned 2,000 years ago while other parts were written 3,500 years ago.

As a proclaimer and defender of the faith, always be on the alert for points that can be used to overcome objections that we have heard, or what logically sounds like an objection one might raise. Whether we are

---

[89] http://www.christianpublishers.org/handling-bible-difficulties

studying a book, working on the our Bible reading with a commentary or sitting in a pew listening to a talk from our elder or pastor, have our mind attuned to such things. Say, we ae sitting at church, the pastor or elder makes an excellent point that overcomes a particular Bible objection (The Bible is not practical for our day, or there are so many different interpretations, who can know the truth), so we write it down in out notebook, because, yes, we have a notebook and pen. This will further implant the point in our mind. Now, we take it a step further. Find three different people after the meeting and say, "I really enjoyed what the pastor or elder had to say about the objection that the Bible is not practical for our day." Then, we should proceed to reiterate what was said in our own words. This will further embed it in our mind. Our notebook can be used for all kinds of notes at the meetings or during our personal study, but if we take notes on some objection or a Bible difficulty of some sort, highlight it a particular color. Why? We do this because we will also have another notebook that is specifically for Bible difficulties and Bible objections, so we have prepared and refutations. In this special notebook, leave the first few pages blank, as it will serve as out table of content. We can number our pages, so in the front we can write down a phrase that will tell us what the issue is and the page on which it can be found.

Therefore Christian defenders of God's Word and principles,

2 Timothy 2:15 Updated American Standard Version (UASV)

[15] Do your best to present yourself to God as one approved, a workman who does not need to be ashamed, rightly handling[90] the word of truth.

2:15. Timothy, by contrast, must do his best to **present [himself] to God as one approved, a workman who does not need to be ashamed.** Timothy, and all who follow Christ, are to consecrate themselves to God, working diligently for his approval. The teacher whom God approves has no need of shame in his presence.

God bestows his approval on the one who exhibits truth, love, and godliness in daily living, and who **correctly handles the word of truth.** The false teachers were mishandling God's words, using them for their own benefit. Timothy was commissioned to handle the words of God correctly. All preaching should present the truth clearly, cutting through erroneous ideas or inaccurate opinions.

The pastor or teacher must acquaint himself thoroughly with

---

[90] Or *accurately handling* the word of truth; *correctly teaching* the word of truth

Scripture. He should familiarize himself with historical information and the context of the passage, especially when trying to reach back through the centuries to gain an accurate understanding of God's revelation.[91]

Let us have the spirit of Paul,

1 Corinthians 9:16-17 Updated American Standard Version (UASV)

[16] Now if I am proclaiming the good news, it is no reason for me to boast, for necessity is laid upon me. Really, woe to me if I do not proclaim the good news! [17] For if I do this voluntarily, I have a reward; but if against my will, I have a stewardship entrusted to me.

9:16–17. Paul wanted to continue the practice of preaching without pay. He explained that he could not **boast** simply because he preached the gospel. He insisted, **I am compelled to preach.** In other words, he had no choice. God had called him to preach, and he had to fulfill that obligation or fall under divine judgment.

How did Paul enhance his preaching ministry? He preached **voluntarily** so he might receive **a reward.** Paul frequently spoke of himself and of other Christians being motivated to service by a desire for reward and praise (Rom. 2:29; Gal. 6:4–10; Col. 3:24). Eternal reward motivated him as it should all believers. Paul did not want to lose his eternal rewards for preaching willingly and eagerly and without pay. If he preached begrudgingly or received pay, he believed he would be doing nothing more than **simply discharging the trust committed** to him. To raise his preaching above the level of mere obedience, Paul voluntarily gave up his right to remuneration.[92]

Exercise

So that it is easy to understand, sequentially explain:

(1) how the fall of man came about and

(2) the nature of sin

(3) and what hope was offered from Genesis 3:15 forward

---

[91] Knute Larson, *I & II Thessalonians, I & II Timothy, Titus, Philemon,* vol. 9, Holman New Testament Commentary (Nashville, TN: Broadman & Holman Publishers, 2000), 286.

[92] Richard L. Pratt Jr, *I & II Corinthians,* vol. 7, Holman New Testament Commentary (Nashville, TN: Broadman & Holman Publishers, 2000), 148–149.

Review Questions

- When Peter says that we need always to be ready to make a defense of the hope that is in us, to whom does this rule apply?

- What is needed if we are to defend the hope that is in us effectively?

- Why should we use the Bible in proclaiming and defending our hope?

- Why should Christians be able to simplify Bible teachings to make them easy to understand?

CHAPTER 5 Giving Good Answers When We Share God's Word

Colossians 4:6 Updated American Standard Version (UASV)

⁶ Let your speech always be gracious, seasoned with salt, so that you may **know how you ought to answer** each person.

On this New Testament scholar, Max Anders writes, "For the sharing of the message of Christ to be effective, the wise walk must be accompanied with flavorful talk. The believer's talk is to be gracious, rather than gruff, and charming, rather than coarse. The believer's talk is to be **seasoned with salt**. Salt was used for two purposes in Paul's time. It was used as a preservative to keep food from spoiling. This would mean the believer's speech is to be free from corruption, wholesome. Salt was also used as an additive to give flavor to food. If this meaning lies behind the figure, then the believer's speech is to be interesting, witty, tactful, and appealing. Perhaps the best understanding of the reference to **salt** is that the believer's speech is to be both wholesome and appealing. Paul wants believers to **know how to answer everyone**. He tells them to answer with speech which is gracious, wholesome, and appealing." (Anders, Holman New Testament Commentary: vol. 8, Galatians, Ephesians, Philippians, Colossians 1999, p. 346)

Improving Our Answers at Church Bible Studies

As sharers and defenders of God's Word, we need to cultivate our ability to give good answers continuously. Paul wrote that we should "know how [we] ought to answer each person." Certainly, all of us can see the logic in our wanting to endeavor to develop our responses. We can only imagine the heartfelt appreciation that God Himself must feel when we offer a listener a good answer. On this wise King Solomon wrote, "A man has joy in an apt answer, and how delightful is a timely word!" – Proverbs 15:23.

Let us reflect on ourselves for a moment, ask those tough questions, which make us feel uncomfortable. How do we feel about our ability to answer Bible questions? Is our speech "gracious, wholesome, and appealing"? Do we prepare for Christian meetings, so that, we can offer better answers at the meetings? Do we see room for improvement in the answers that we give? Has there ever been a time when talking to a relative, a friend, or a stranger about God's Word that, afterward, we felt that we could have handled that better? This author was engaged in a conversation with four people over 20 years ago, and I was beaten up so bad in that conversation, it caused me to offer the greatest prayer/crying session I had ever had when I got home that night. In short, I prayed that I was very sorry that I let God down that day, and if God could help me afford the books in the years to come, I would make sure this never happened again. It was that night that I became an apologist. Of course, I have been beaten up in conversations since, but when knocked down, I get back up off the mat and continue to fight earnestly for the faith. Therefore, it is true of all of us, we need to continue to grow in our abilities as a communicator, so let us consider what follows.

Giving Answers at Christian Meetings

In most conservative churches across America, all who attend their particular Bible study class know that there are always ones that are ready to give an answer in participation, while the vast majority seldom if ever participate. However, even those who are eager and willing to participate, rarely if at all prepare before the Bible study. We all know what material is going to be covered. We have the book that we are studying through; we have a Bible, and maybe we even have a Bible word dictionary and some other study tools in our home. However, do we ever sit down for an hour and read through the material paragraph by paragraph, looking all the Scriptures up, answering any questions that might be in the book, writing responses in the margins? Even if there are no questions in the book, can we see the important points that we would want to make? It does not matter if we have been going to church for six months on thirty years, we all can give good answers if we prepare beforehand. Wise King Solomon tells us,

Proverbs 15:28 Updated American Standard Version (UASV)

²⁸ The heart of the righteous ponders how to answer,
  but the mouth of the wicked pours out evil things.

Two benefits that come from answering at the Bible study meeting at our church is that we are sinking answers deeper into our long-term memory and it enables us to improve our ability to give good answers when sharing or defending Bible truths. Being the first person to answer the night of the Bible study class can be a bit intimidating for some. However, just prepare well before the evening of the class. When the person reads the paragraph, listen well, thinking of the answer you have written in the margin of your book. When he asks the question, put your hand up and read your answer as clearly as possible. If your nerves are high, you will feel like you are outside of yourself, not even remembering what you said. However, in time you will be able to offer the answer extemporaneously, namely, done unrehearsed, that is, prepared in advance but delivered without notes. If someone has gotten a response that, you really wanted to give before you, do not lose heart, simply expand on the answer, refer to the Scripture in the paragraph supports the answer, or make a personal application to it.

While this author is certainly more longwinded than most when answering, and this is not the best approach. Long answers are not the best. Rather, short answers, say 30-60 seconds, are actually more weightier and will stay with those listening a lot longer. You see, picking one aspect of the paragraph and making a good point about it is best, instead of rambling through all the points in the paragraph where nothing stands out, and the listeners are more lost than ever as to the appropriate answer. Also, answers that are I our own words are best. We can just reiterate or paraphrase what was within the paragraph, even expanding on it a little. When we put it in our own words, we are making the answer our own, and our way of wording things should be common to those in the church, making it easier to understand. This will help us to improve our ability at being a more effective communicator.

If we do not prepare before the Bible study class, we will be sitting there trying to prepare while someone is reading the paragraph and another is offering an answer on the question. We will not comprehend the totality of the paragraph, but will also miss what the other person was saying. We sometimes hear a person give almost the same identical answer as the previous person, and this is likely because they were not fully paying attention to the response that person gave. We need to build a habit of preparing for the meeting before, by reading the paragraph, looking up the Scriptures and writing answers in the margins. We can also use a highlighter to mark the books answer within the paragraph. Remember, when highlighting, do not highlight the whole paragraph, just a few keywords that focus in on the answer, bringing it back to mind. If the book does not have review questions at the end of the chapter, we can still highlight the key points that will help us participate better. We will be able to give spontaneous answers, namely answers that arise from natural impulse or inclination, rather than from planning or in response to prepared questions. This will make the discussion even livelier. It might be our goal at least to give one answer each Bible study meeting, to have something to build on, but we should not hold it at that for too long, or it will become a pattern. We need to feel able to comment freely.

If we are timid at the idea of answering, do not feel alone, as this is common and, in some cases, this stays with us on a small level our entire life. Maybe we have convinced ourselves that other offer better answers than we ever could, so we will just leave it up to them. However, the Bible exhorts us to share, saying, "let us hold fast the confession of our hope without wavering ... and let us consider how to stir up one another to love and good works, not neglecting to meet together, as is the habit of some, but encouraging one another." (Heb. 10:23-25) When we participate in the Bible study, we are 'stirring up one another to love and good works, which encourages them to participate as well. Moreover, there may be times that we come into the Bible study class beat up and worn down by life and after a time of interchange, we leave fully refreshed.

Bible studies classes are usually an atmosphere that is friendly and relaxed. Therefore, if there were an aspect of the study that we did not fully understand, it not being clear in our mind, it would be best to consider the responses to that point and ask some qualifying questions after the meeting of those that may be more qualified at offering a more in-depth, but easy to understand answer. If this is something that is troubling to us, like what the Bible actually says about hellfire. Is eternal torment biblical? Is Hellfire just? Such concerns can be like a burr under a saddle on a horse, over time, it can dig deeper and deeper into us, cause us emotional turmoil. Even after we have discussed it at length with the pastor or elder, we may want to investigate further on our own.

Answering Critics Objections

If we have had

(1) a personal Bible study every day (say 30 minutes),

(2) if we have prepared for all of our meetings

(3) (by reading, looking up Scriptures and highlighting main points, noting how Scriptures apply),

(4) if we have participated in our Bible study classes,

We will find that it is no longer difficult to answer questions of those who are sincerely interested a Biblical response. However, we cannot know everything, so there will be times when the question will be one that we have not addressed before. In that case, we simply say, 'you have raised an excellent point, let me do more research on this, and I will get back with you.' If they actually wanted to know, they will give us this opportunity to investigate it.

While some have questions, others have objections. How are we to deal with complaints? We would not just jump into the answer, as it would be prudent to find out how this objection came about; asking them 'what gave rise to this concern?' For example, a person may misunderstand why God has allowed wickedness, pain, suffering, old age and death for a time. This is because he is confused by those who say everything that has happened and is to happen is how God willed it to be, meaning that free will is not really a reality, and the wicked act of a terrorist cutting the heads off of little children publicly is a part of God's will. This is very unbiblical, and we should empathize with why he is upset and has built up objections. Many objections are the result of a lack of understanding, an unbiblical viewpoint. It is best if we clarify what he has heard, how he understands what he has heard, and then go about rightly explaining what the Bible actually says on the matter.

Another approach is to prevent objections from putting us at odds with each other, as though we were opponents. We can evidence that his objection is of mutual interest. In other words, when we hear an objection, we should not be put off by it, but rather express it as a point the other should be concerned about. For instance, we could say, 'it is good that you brought up wickedness and suffering, it is something that should concern all of us, and we should expect a reasoned answer to such an important issue.' By such an approach, this one may gain a measure of trust and respect for us, opening his mind, where it was closed before, hoping for answers from the Bible.

There will come a time when we are sharing Bible truths with more than one person at a time. At times, the others may not want their friend or family to take an interest in God or what they perceive to be some outdated book that was written by men, so they begin to interrupt. We should not always back away because the newly interested one may perceive his friend or family is correct. If the antagonist raises an objection, he is the one who is really obligated to offer evidence for his remarks so that we can shift the burden of proof back onto the objector. Jesus Christ himself used counter-questions to quiet opposers who tried to hinder with his preaching. Jesus' counter-questions were so effective that Matthew tells us, "And no one was able to answer him a word, nor from that day did anyone dare to ask him any more questions." (Matt. 22:41-46) Therefore, keep in mind that the burden of proof is on the one who is raising the objection, not us. For example, if someone, in a tone that implies disdain, says, "the Bible is a man's book and is full of contradictions and errors." We might respond, "I believe the Bible is written by men, who were inspired by God, moved along by Holy Spirit and the Bible is fully inerrant. Will you please give me a few examples of errors and contradictions in the Bible?" Now, we have placed the burden of proof back on the objector.

The best tool in sharing what the Bible says is the Bible itself. Paul writes, "For the word of God is living and active, sharper than any two-edged sword, piercing to the division of soul and of spirit, of joints and of marrow, and discerning the thoughts and intentions of the heart." (Heb. 4:12) God's word is far more persuasive than we ever could be. Also, when responding to the objection, we need to remain calm and be respectful of other to their beliefs, regardless of whether the objector has a bad attitude or not. Many times, a good answer will turn away his anger or frustration.

After we have had much success in preparing for our Christian meetings and participating in the Bible study class, we will find numerous opportunities to defend and share biblical truths. At work, we may stand out because we do not involve ourselves in their degrading talk, nor do we take smoke breaks, or extra time for breaks and lunch, so they may be curious about why. At school, the same holds true, as students and teachers do not see us as aloof, but rather as being no part of their worldly behaviors. Our neighbors may notice that we never miss our Christian meetings, so they may wonder why such dedication. These are all opportunities to share our faith with others. We can return to the words of Peter from our previous chapter, "but sanctify Christ as Lord in your hearts, always being prepared to make a defense to anyone who asks you for a reason for the hope that is in you; yet do it with gentleness and respect."

Exercise

Someone just said to you, "You Christians claim that Christianity is the only true religion, I find that arrogant when there so many major religions. Why can they not all simply be different roads leading to the same place?" How would you persuade him that it is not arrogant and that all religions are not different roads leading to the same place? In fact, how would you persuade him that not all Christian denominations are leading to the same place?

Review Questions

- How do you personally feel about your ability to answer Bible questions?

- Why is it important to give answers at Christian meetings?

- What must we do if we are to be effective in answering critic's objections?

- Why might it be best to begin giving at answers at church Bible study groups?

- Why is it important to be prepared to give reasons for the hope that lies within us?

- Why is important to reach the heart of our listeners?

CHAPTER 6 Being Skilled at Speaking Without Preparation

Matthew 10:19-20 Updated American Standard Version (UASV)

19 But when they hand you over, do not worry about how or what you are to say; for it will be given you in that hour what you are to say, **20** but the Spirit of your Father **speaking through you.**[93]

Speaking to someone without need of preparation is the most effective way to keep them interested in what you are saying while also moving them accept or act on what is being said. Bear in mind, speaking without rehearsing **does not** mean speaking without being prepared.

We may have studied a particular biblical subject that someone asks about one day. We may have covered it, having had very educational material. The logic and reasoning of the points we expected to make when explaining it one day may very well be sound. Maybe when we were reading it from the book(s), or an internet website, we read it effortlessly and with great confidence. However, now that we are in the midst of explaining the biblical truth, we find that we are stammering, searching for the right way to express ourselves, and it just is not coming across effective. In looking at the individual(s) that we are speaking with, it seems as though they are struggling to follow what is being said. Does it seem likely that we are reaching the heart of these ones?

What lies behind this failure of our being skilled at speaking without the need of preparation? It is likely because we failed to prepare correctly. One wat to improve our recall of what we have read is covered by the website Brainscape. It reads, "When we read, we are using our visual pathways to form memory links. We remember the material because it was something we saw. People who have photographic memory are extraordinarily good at making these kinds of memory connections. For those of us who do not have a photographic memory, relying only on visual memory may leave us with many gaps, and so we have to find other ways to remember things. When reading aloud, we form auditory links in our memory pathways. We remember ourselves saying it out loud, and not only do we form visual links but also auditory links." They go on, "Art Markman, Ph.D. writes in his blog in Psychology Today about the production effect, which explains exactly why reading out loud causes

---

[93] It is not the Holy Spirit miraculously taking over us so that we are able to give the perfect answer. Rather, the Word of God was inspired, where the Holy Spirit moved along men, i.e., the Bible is of the Holy Spirit. If we fail to be studious in the Word of God and have nothing in our head, what can we draw on when it comes time to speak with someone?

us to remember better. Specifically referring to a study in which learners were given a list and asked to read half of it aloud and half of it silently, the learners were able to remember the part of the list they read aloud a lot better than the part of the list they read silently. He adds that while there are memory pathways of visually seeing the words and the auditory pathways of hearing the words, there is also a memory link to the actual production of the word, hence the production effect. Especially if the word or content is different, it makes it easier to remember."[94]

We will actually be reading in an undertone, which reading in a quiet or subdued tone, like muttering something, as it is barely audible. However, some things will be read aloud. While reading a book in an undertone as oppose to self will enhance our ability to recall, but it still falls short of what we need to accomplish. What do we need to do? We need to see the information relationally, how the different points relate to one another; we need to ask questions, organizing what we are reading, so it makes sense to us. We need to highlight the most important points. We need to say it in our own words. If we do not connect with the material in such a way, there is nothing to hold the material in our memory. Moreover, if we do not fully understand what we have read, just reading it aloud to enhance our chances of remembering those most important points later will prove futile. We can explain what we do not fully understand.

When reading a chapter in a book, we will actually be reading aloud, read the title through slowly several times, thinking about we can expect will be covered. Now, move onto the first heading, read it slowly and ponder how it is going to add to what the chapter title gave us, now the next heading and the next until there are no more. Go back and read the headings as well as the paragraph(s) that go with the heading, looking for idea contained in the heading and find it in the paragraph(s). Now, express those thoughts aloud as though you were trying to explain them to another.

We may be reading a book that has many chapters that are interconnected as to the book but are individually subject matters that may come up when talking with others. Maybe some of the chapters run like this, Understanding Christianity, Understanding Faith, Revelation, Inspiration, Inerrancy, and Canonicity, How to Interpret the Bible, and the like. These chapters are relational, but someone might ask us one day, "what exactly is inerrancy of Scripture, my pastor says the only things that are without error are the salvation doctrines, and that the Bible can have errors when it touches on geography, science, history and so on?" When

---

[94] https://www.brainscape.com/blog/2011/10/reading-out-loud-remember/

we read those chapters, we would have read the chapters and headings aloud, pondering as we read the paragraph(s) that go with the headings, what answer is what the author meant by his heading, highlighting those points. As we read the paragraphs, we do so in an undertone, meditatively.

Now, turn those headings into questions and answer the questions aloud as though you were explaining it to someone. In our chapter Inerrancy and Canonicity, we find our first heading is The Inerrancy of the Bible, followed by three paragraphs. Now, make it a question, "what does inerrancy of the Bible mean?" Read the paragraphs, highlighting the answer, but with main words and phrases only. Now, ask the question again and give the answer aloud without looking at the book. Next, we find a subheading, The Bible Teaches Inerrancy, followed by two paragraphs, which we make into the question, "How the does the Bible teach inerrancy?" Again, read the paragraphs, highlighting the answer, but with main words and phrases only. Now, ask the question again and give the answer aloud without looking at the book. Our next subheading is Jesus Testified to Biblical Inerrancy, followed by four paragraphs, which we make into the question, "how did Jesus testify to biblical inerrancy?" Then, follow the same process. Our next subheading is, The Apostles Believed in Inerrancy, followed by three paragraphs, which we make into the question, "What makes us conclude that the apostle believed in inerrancy?" Again, follow the same process. The last subheading before our next heading is The Character of God Demands Inerrancy, followed by two paragraphs, which we make into the question "How does the character of God demand inerrancy?" Our next heading is The Reliability of the Scriptures, which becomes "How can we know the Scriptures are reliable?" Can we imagine how much more we might understand and retain if we followed this process through an entire chapter?

Now, there is more that needs to be done before we can say that we have fully dealt with this chapter, Inerrancy, and Canonicity. We need to take each heading and subheading and one at a time, share this with Christian family and friends. Maybe before a Christian meeting we pull a member aside and say, "you know I was reading on inerrancy the other day and I came across the fact that The Bible Teaches Inerrancy," and then tell the person what we learned. After the meeting, find another member and do the same. We will see that each time we share it, we are expressing it more and more in our words, and we are stammering less in our delivery. Thus, when someone asks us, "how can you say the Bible teaches inerrancy?" We will be skilled at speaking without the need of preparation.

Dealing with the Difficulties of Unrehearsed Speech

Yes, speaking unrehearsed has possible challenges. One is that we might become too wordy, expounding too much, when we are witnessing to others. We may just insert too many points in our explanation, and the person is put off by our long-windedness. We can avoid this by knowing our most important points and reflecting on the situation at hand. If the individual asked us the question, we could use more of our points than if we started talking to him. So, say we are asked, "Did Jesus believe in biblical inerrancy?" Recall that we had four paragraphs, with seven verses, and multiple points that prove he did believe in inerrancy. Since the person asked us, we can likely share most of that. However, if we initially engaged this person in a conversation, and he asked this question, we could take the most important points and use them, closing with "more points could be made, but I want to respect your time." Who know, he may say that he has the time.

Another danger is that eventually, we will get better and better at speaking without the need of preparation, which may result in overconfidence. Eventually, we may not follow the above steps when studying, as we had before, and so, our responses become less and less skillful. Therefore, we must remain humble and show appreciation for the God of the Bible, and it is his message that we are sharing. Therefore, we need to continuous approach our personal study and preparation for our Christian meetings prayerfully and take the time to prepare well. (Isa. 30:20; Rom. 12:6-8) For those that have not gained experience at speaking unrehearsed, do not be put off by attempts that do not turn out as well as we may have hoped. Simply keep preparing well, and look to God for guidance.

What if we are one of those people, who constantly worry about how to word things? Yes, it is true, we are not going to have the same level of wording and grammar and syntax as the chapter in a book, but we must remember that our conversational style with make up the difference. People will be more receptive to our explanations that are easy to understand and are in simple sentences. Moreover, if we study well, the right words will come to us in the end. It should be noted that the more we read, study and communicate, the more our vocabulary will grow as well. However, we do not want to use a conversational style that is high-sounding, just to try to impress others, but rather use good speech that we use in our everyday conversations.

Keeping It Simple

Over time, we will notice that we have acquired just a few main points for many different doctrinal beliefs, as well as a Scripture or two for each belief. We will be able to talk share and defend such beliefs as inerrancy, providence, foreknowledge, the length of the creative days, what the image of God means, atonement, salvation, sanctification, justification, eternal security, the biblical view of baptism, the gifts of the first century, and so on. In time, we will find that these are easily referenced from our long-term memory. In the beginning, if our Bible has a concordance of Bible words or even a small Bible dictionary at the end, we can highlight these terms and there will usually be Scriptures with them. We may even pen in brief notes about context, historical setting or original language words. The more you discuss a belief, the deeper it is embedded in our memory and the more we will attain the ability to speak about it unrehearsed.

Once we have garnered the ability to speak from our memory and can now effectively communicate with others, there is another successful tool in producing an impact. At the beginning of each belief, we might have what I call an impact statement, which is the best and most dramatic evidence that we have, which is to be delivered from a couple memorized sentences for effect. Then, in the end, we have another impact statement, or simply reiterate the one from the beginning. Lastly, if we are using Scriptures and we have our Bible with us, it is best to open it up and have them read from it as we point to the text under consideration, having a significant effect.

Effective impromptu Explanations

In many different parts of a Christian's life, he may be called on to explain his beliefs without an opportunity to prepare. Maybe we are out evangelizing in our community, and someone raises an objection. For example, "I believe in evolution." On the other hand, maybe we are at a family get together, and a family member asks a Bible question. Then, again, we might be at work, and a coworker raises an objection or our child is at school, and a classmate or a teacher criticizes our beliefs. In many parts of the world, it might even be a government official asking us to explain our beliefs. While this is not the case in the United States of America yet, it is heading that way. In this, we refer to a text we used in the previous chapter and will likely mention yet again. Peter urged us, to "sanctify Christ as Lord in your hearts, always being prepared to make a defense to anyone who asks you for a reason for the hope that is in you; yet do it with gentleness and respect. – 1 Peter 3:15.

Early on Peter and John were taken before the Jewish Sanhedrin, which is similar to our Supreme Court here in the United States. The court charged them not to speak or teach at all in the name of Jesus. At Acts 4:19-20, they offered a clear and concise statement. Peter and John answered them, "Whether it is right in the sight of God to listen to you rather than to God, you must judge, for we cannot but speak of what we have seen and heard." When arrested for doing what they were ordered not to do, they were miraculously freed, only to be apprehended doing the same thing yet again, witnessing about Jesus. They were brought and sat before the council. The high priest questioned them, saying, "We strictly charged you not to teach in this name, yet here you have filled Jerusalem with your teaching, and you intend to bring this man's blood upon us." But Peter and the apostles answered, "We must obey God rather than men." (Acts 5:27-29) Some time later, Stephen too was brought before the same court on false charges. We can read his quite lengthy impromptu speech at Acts 7:2-53. In this case, Stephen built a sequential historical case against his accusers, showing centuries of rebellion by the Israelite nation. He concluded his speech by demonstrating that the Sanhedrin was, in fact, evidencing the same rebellious spirit as they had the Son of God executed.

Whether it is an unbeliever in our evangelism work, a family member at a gather, a schoolmate, a coworker, or even a governmental official, how can we make our impromptu explanations effective? We can collect our thoughts by offering God a silent prayer. (Neh. 2:4) Next, we need to think of a mental outline that will explain whatever is being asked of us. We can consider two or three points that need to be in our explanation and the order they should be presented. Then, come up with at least one Scripture per point if possible. Lastly, pause before beginning, as we want to open "with gentleness and respect," so that the one who asked the question will be willing to listen. Then start talking.

If we are under pressure, we should remember Jesus words to his apostles, "When they deliver you over, do not be anxious how you are to speak or what you are to say, for what you are to say will be given to you in that hour. For it is not you who speak, but the Spirit of your Father is speaking through you." Mind you; the context is Jesus promising his apostles miraculous supernatural "word of wisdom through the Spirit, and to another the word of knowledge according to the same Spirit." We can see from the above Scriptures and the whole of the book of Acts that this was the case. However, we should not expect this miraculous gift, as it was something promised to the apostle and the early church.[95]

---

[95] THE HOLY SPIRIT AND THE CHRISTIAN How Are We to Understand the Work of and the Indwelling of the Holy Spirit? by Edward D. Andrews

Nevertheless, if we are regularly having a personal study at home, preparing for the Christian meetings, having a regular sharing in commenting at the Bible study, as well as sharing and defending our faith, our mind will be inundated with Scriptures that were penned as men were moved along by the Holy Spirit.

Exercise

When preparing for our next church Bible study, highlight key phrases that will allow us to answer in our own words instead of reading from the material. Before the night of the meeting, we need to tell at least two people what we learned in those few paragraphs, by simply saying we want to share something new we have learned, and delving into the explanation.

Review Questions

- Why is it important that we be able to give spontaneous answers to Bible questions?

- What are the advantages to being able to give spontaneous answers?

- What are some difficulties that go with giving answers in our own words spontaneously?

- Why is it best to keep it simple?

- How can we have effective impromptu explanations?

CHAPTER 7 Rightly Handling the Word of Truth

2 Timothy 2:15 Updated American Standard Version (UASV)

[15] Do your best to present yourself to God as one approved, a workman who does not need to be ashamed, **rightly handling**[96] **the word of truth**.

One Greek-English Lexicon says of our Greek word orthotomounta (lit., straightly cutting), to give accurate instruction–'to teach correctly, to expound rightly.'[97] Om 2 Timothy 2:15, the *Holman New Testament Commentary* says, "God bestows his approval on the one who exhibits truth, love, and godliness in daily living, and who correctly handles the word of truth. The false teachers were mishandling God's words, using them for their own benefit. Timothy was commissioned to handle the words of God correctly. All preaching should present the truth clearly, cutting through erroneous ideas or inaccurate opinions."[98] *The New American Commentary* says, "Third, this same workman (specifically, Timothy but by application today all believers) was to be accurate in delivering the message of truth. The truth is the gospel. Paul showed concern that Timothy would present the gospel without perverting or distorting it.* He was not to be turned aside by disputes about words or mere empty prattle.

> * Interpreters find a variety of possible sources for the derivation of the term [*orthotomeo*] ("handling aright the word of truth," ASV; "driving a straight furrow, in your proclamation of the truth," NEB). Lock presents the possibilities as a plow cutting a straight furrow, a road engineer's building a straight road, or a mason's squaring and cutting a stone to fit its proper place. He questions whether any one of these were consciously present in Paul's mind (The Pastoral Epistles, ICC [Edinburgh: T & T Clark, 1924], 99).
>
> J. E. Huther properly suggests that the notion of cutting falls quickly into the background so that the meaning is "deal rightly with something so as not to falsify it" (Critical and Exegetical Handbook to the Epistles to Timothy and Titus (1884; reprint, Peabody, Mass.: Hendrickson, 1983], 234). Paul

---

[96] Or *accurately handling* the word of truth; *correctly teaching* the word of truth

[97] Johannes P. Louw and Eugene Albert Nida, *Greek-English Lexicon of the New Testament: Based on Semantic Domains* (New York: United Bible Societies, 1996), 414.

[98] Knute Larson, I & II Thessalonians, I & II Timothy, Titus, Philemon, vol. 9, *Holman New Testament Commentary* (Nashville, TN: Broadman & Holman Publishers, 2000), 286.

wanted Timothy to perform the task opposite that of a peddler of God's word (2 Cor 2:17).

The *New International Greek Testament Commentary* touching on the rendering, says, "The material that this worker is to handle correctly is 'the word of truth' [*ton logon tes aletheias*]. Only when he handles it correctly will he be unashamed [*anepaischunton*]. The rendering given in several of the modern translations, using a combination of the verb 'handle' and some adverb such as 'accurately' (NASB), 'rightly' (RSV), or 'correctly' (NIV), for the compound verb [*orthotomounta*] with the phrase 'the word of truth' as the direct object captures this relationship quite well."

The apostle Paul tells us, "For the word of God is living and active, sharper than any two-edged sword, piercing to the division of soul and of spirit, of joints and of marrow, and discerning the thoughts and intentions of the heart." (Heb. 4:12) "God's Word penetrates the **soul and spirit.** ... God's message is capable of penetrating the impenetrable. It can divide what is indivisible. ... God's message is discerning. **It judges the thoughts and attitudes of the heart.** It passes judgment on our feelings and our thoughts. What we regard as secret and hidden, God brought out for inspection by the discerning power of his Word."[99] As the Word of God is compared to a sword, it only seems reasonable that we would want to have skill in our use of it. This is why Paul told Timothy that he need **not** be ashamed, "rightly handling the word of truth." Whenever we share or defend the Word of God, we want to do it in such a way that we arrive at what the author meant by the words that he used, accurately understanding what it says.

Context is the material surrounding a verse that we are reading, and it is what will help us understand and apply it as it was meant to be understood and applied. We need to keep in mind that the Bible is not just sixty-six books of fragmented, unconnected verses, gathered together haphazardly, and fitting for use under any situations as evidence of a point that we may feel, think or believe to be correct.[100] It is sixty-six books written over about 1,600 years, by forty plus writers, who were moved along by Holy Spirit at the direction of the Father. In other words, it is one book by one author, inspired and fully inerrant. Thus, we need to get the whole picture when we are considering what a verse or set of verses means. We need to consider the setting, who was the book written to, what the reason for writing the book was, and what these particular

---

[99] Thomas D. Lea, Hebrews & James, *Holman New Testament Commentary* (Nashville, TN: Broadman & Holman Publishers, 1999), 72.

[100] We need to go from 'this is how I **feel**, to, 'this is what I **know**, and here are the Scriptural reasons as to why.'

verses were meant to convey, i.e., is it a specific topic different than other parts of the chapter(s). This is important if we are going to "rightly handling the word of truth."

Some Examples

Let us use our main text for this chapter as our example, 2 Timothy 2:15, where Paul writes, "Do your best to present yourself to God as one approved, a workman who does not need to be ashamed, rightly handling[101] the word of truth." These words were written to Timothy in about 65 C.E. after Timothy had been Paul's traveling companion for 15 years. When Paul discovered young Timothy, in his late teens or early twenties in about 50 C.E. in Lystra on his second missionary journey, Timothy "was well spoken of by the brothers." (Acts 16:1-3) Moreover, Timothy was the son of a Jewish woman who was a believer, but his father was a Greek. Paul, in writing this letter, was "reminded of [Timothy's] sincere faith, a faith that dwelt first in [his] grandmother Lois and [his] mother Eunice and now, [Paul was certain, dwelled] in Timothy as well." (2 Tim. 1:1-2, 5) Therefore, the words to Timothy about handling the Word of God aright, were, in fact, written to a person that had been well-grounded in the Word of God and who was caring out the will of the Father in major ways.

Therefore, the words of Paul to Timothy, in this second letter to him, were his telling Timothy how to give instruction to fellow Christians within God's congregations. While it is just as true that we need to 'handle the word of truth aright' when evangelizing unbelievers, Paul was not counseling Timothy on how to convert unbelievers to Christ. This is evidenced by Paul's first letter as well, where he writes to Timothy, "remain at Ephesus so that you may charge certain persons not to teach any different doctrine." (1:3) Later in that same first letter, Paul writes, "Keep a close watch on yourself and on the teaching. Persist in this, for by so doing you will save both yourself and your hearers." (4:16) In addition, Paul's direction at 2 Timothy 2:2, "what you have heard from me in the presence of many witnesses entrust to faithful men who will be able to teach others also." In other words, Timothy's was to use the word of truth rightly to benefit and guide his fellow Christian brothers.

Avoid Distorting God's Word

As Christians, we too, need to be cautious in our interpretation of and applying God's Word so that it is what the author meant by the words that he used, not what we feel, think, or believe it to mean. We

---

[101] *accurately handling* the word of truth; *correctly teaching* the word of truth

need to go from 'this is how I **feel**, to, 'this is what I **know**, and here are the Scriptural reasons as to why.' For example, take the King James Version at Isaiah 14:12-16, where it begins, "How art thou fallen from heaven, O Lucifer, son of the morning! how art thou cut down to the ground, which didst weaken the nations!" In the modern translations, the Hebrew word for Lucifer (*helel*), which means the "shining one," is rendered "day star" or "morning star." (ASV, ESV, LEB, HCSB, while the NASB renders it "star of the morning") Helel in this verse is not a personal name or a title for Satan, but rather a term describes a brilliant position taken the dynasty of kings in Babylon, through the line of Nebuchadnezzar. On this the Baker Encyclopedia writes,

> There are many who believe the expression (and surrounding context) refers to Satan. They believe the similarities between Isaiah 14:12, Luke 10:18, and Revelation 12:7–10 warrant this conclusion. However, although the NT passages do speak of Satan's fall, the context of the Isaiah passage describes the defeated king of Babylon. The Babylonian king had desired to be above God, and so fell from heaven. His doom is pictured as already accomplished. Though defeat is certain for Satan, he yet continues his evil acts against God's people. Not until the final judgment (Rv 12–20) will his fate be sealed and his activity stopped. Isaiah, then, is not speaking of Satan in 14:12 but of the proud, and soon to be humiliated, king of Babylon. (Elwell, Baker Encyclopedia of the Bible 1988, Volume 2, Page 1361)

No, Lucifer in the King James Version is not a title or name for Satan the Devil. Helel is a reference to the King of Babylon as is evidenced from verse 4, which reads, "will take up this taunt against the king of Babylon." In addition, verses 15-16 of chapter 14 says, that this "day star" or "morning star" will be "are brought down to Sheol" i.e. the place where the dead are buried. Moreover, in verse 16, we read, "Those who see you [i.e., "day star" or "morning star." ("Lucifer," KJV)] will stare at you and ponder over you: 'Is this **the man** who made the earth tremble, who shook kingdoms," Clearly, no one would ever suggest that Satan is a man, rather he is a very powerful fallen angel of God. In fact, he is chief of the fallen angels.

Poor Proof Texting

Proof texting is using isolated texts, without regard for context, to establish a doctrinal belief. In many cases, the Scriptures used may not accurately reflect what the original author meant. Please note that this is not saying one cannot use appropriated selected texts from different parts of Scripture to support a doctrinal point. All Bible scholars do this, but each text that is selected has to be used within its original context and with the meaning, the author meant to convey, namely, what the original author intended. In fact, we can turn to Jesus and the apostles and see that they used scattered texts to prove the biblical truth but did this appropriately as mentioned in the above. However, even this needs to be qualified.

On many occasions, a New Testament writer would quote or cite an Old Testament Scripture. Many times the New Testament writer would be using the Old Testament text contextually, according to the setting, and intent of the Old Testament writer (observing the grammatical-historical sense). However, **at times** the New Testament writer would add to or apply the text differently than what was meant by the Old Testament writer (not observing the grammatical-historical sense). This is either a new or a progressive revelation of God, where he has inspired the New Testament writer to go beyond the intended meaning of the Old Testament writer, and carry out what is known as Inspired Sensus Plenior Application (ISPA). In this latter case, the New Testament writer is using the Old Testament text to convey another meaning to another circumstance. This does not violate the principle that all texts have just one single meaning. The Old Testament text has one meaning, and the New Testament writer's adaptation of that text is not the second meaning, but another meaning. The New Testament authors were inspired, moved along by Holy Spirit, so they could skip over historical-grammatical interpretation to give an entirely new meaning, out of context, which is the subjective interpretation. However, what they meant to say with this new meaning is what God meant to say so that they can be subjective. However, we need to stay far from the shores of subjective interpretation, by either penning it or reading it.

Now, proof-texting is only wrong, if we pull the verses out of their context and apply them to a doctrinal position, which is giving them a meaning that the author did not intend. In Romans chapter 9, the Apostle Paul quotes eleven times from other parts of the Bible.[102] However, Paul is not using the verses that he pulls from different books of the Old Testament out of context. They are being used as examples of Israelite history, as it relates to the sovereignty of God: the example of Esau and Jacob, the example of Pharaoh, the example from Hosea, and the example from Isaiah. The concluding two points of Paul were, (1) **"Through faith the Gentiles have found righteousness without even**

---

[102] The quotations are found in Romans chapter 9, verses 7 (Genesis 21:12), 9 (Genesis 18:14), 12 (Genesis 25:23), 13 (Malachi 1:2, 3), 15 (Exodus 33:19), 17 (Exodus 9:16), 25 (Hosea 2:23), 26 (Hosea 1:10), 27, 28 (Isaiah 10:22, 23), 29 (Isaiah 1:9), and 33 (Isaiah 28:16).

seeking it (9:30)." (2) **"Through the law Israel has not found righteousness even after seeking it** (9:31–33)."[103]

The Meaning of a Text Is Often Within the Context

Some Christians have been guilty of misapplying verses within Scripture because many are confused by the *plain sense of the meaning* that is mentioned in some basic biblical interpretation books. For example, Elmer Towns writes that "the Bible should be interpreted literally, which means we should seek the obvious meaning, of words, context, and language."[104] While this is true, phrases like the *plain sense of the meaning* and *obvious meaning* can cause confusion. For example, one might read Proverbs 10:7 in support of the idea that the wicked will not receive a resurrection. It reads, "The memory of the righteous is a blessing, but the name of the wicked will rot." It is true that those guilty of gross wickedness will not receive a resurrection. However, Proverbs 10:7 is not a Scripture that could be used to make a case for the wicked not receiving a resurrection. Some might be asking why, it says, "the name of the wicked will rot," which seems quite *plain* and *obvious* to me. If we look at the context in Proverbs 10, we will take note of a series of contrasts, a wise son contrasted with a foolish son, a slack hand contrasted with the hand of the diligent, the wise of heart contrasted with the babbling fool and so on. However, nothing to do with the resurrection is discussed here. Therefore, it would be wrong to use this text as a proof text that the wicked will not receive a resurrection. Rather the point of verse 7 is that the good people will be remembered as a blessing, but the wicked will soon be forgotten. In other words, the name or reputation of the wicked is not a pleasurable memory, as the name of Adolf Hitler. Nevertheless, there are Scriptures that can be used as evidence that the wicked will not receive a resurrection. (Matt. 23:33; 25:46; Rev. 21:8) Notice that when towns spoke of our seeking the **obvious meaning**, he spoke of words, but he also spoke of context and language.

1 John 4:18 Updated American Standard Version (UASV)

[18] There is no fear in love; but perfect love casts out fear, because fear has to do with punishment,[105] and the one who fears is not perfected in love.

---

[103] http://biblia.com/books/outlnbbl/Ro9.6-29

[104] Towns, Elmer (2011-10-30). AMG Concise Bible Doctrines (AMG Concise Series) (Kindle Locations 1024-1025). AMG Publishers. Kindle Edition.

[105] Gr., Kolasin (Lit., lopping off cutting off), the punishment is the fear of being cut off, i.e., not remaining in God's love on judgment day.

If we were to look at the context of 1 John 4:18, namely, verses 15-21, will help us get at what John meant. Verse 17 reads "By this, love is perfected with us, so that we may have confidence [Gr., *parresia*; Lit., "freedom of speech" "outspokenness"] in the day of judgment; because as he is, so also are we in this world." On this *The Complete Word Study Dictionary* writes, "Especially in Hebrews and 1 John the word denotes confidence which is experienced with such things as faith in communion with God, **fulfilling the duties of the evangelist**, holding fast our hope, and acts which entail a special exercise of faith. *Parresia* is possible as the result of guilt having been removed by the blood of Jesus (Heb. 10:19 [cf. vv. 17, 18]; 1 John 3:21; 4:17) and manifests itself in confident praying and witnessing (Heb. 4:16; 1 John 5:14)."[106] (Bold mine) However, we can see that in verse 18 we are continuing the discussion of having a "freedom of speech" that was spoken of in verse 17. However, John is not speaking about our **fulfilling the duties of the evangelist**.

Rather, our "freedom of speech" is our speech toward God. This is made clear earlier in First John,

1 John 3:19-21 Updated American Standard Version (UASV)

[19] By this we know that we are of the truth and will persuade[107] our heart before him, [20] in whatever our heart condemns us; for God is greater than our heart and knows all things. [21] Beloved, if our heart does not condemn us, we have confidence [Gr., *parresia*; Lit., "freedom of speech" "outspokenness"] toward God;

Therefore, "God is love, and the one who remains in love remains in God, and God remains in him. By this, love is perfected with us" (4:16-17), and we can feel free to come to our heavenly Father in full confidence, i.e., with freedom of speech toward him. Because of Jesus' ransom sacrifice, our imperfection, and inherited sin does not deter us from coming to the Father, asking for help in doing his will. (Matt. 7:21; 1 John 2:1-2, 15-17) Just as a child would feel confident in coming to his loving human father, possessing freedom of speech toward him, knowing his father will help him, even if he has made a mistake. How much more so should this be the case with our heavenly Father? We should feel confident, free to say anything that is in our heart or mind so that we may remain in him, and he remains in us. We should not have some dark fear when it comes to our heavenly Father, thinking that God will seek justice from his imperfect, sinful human, condemning us because our being

---

[106] Spiros Zodhiates, *The Complete Word Study Dictionary: New Testament* (Chattanooga, TN: AMG Publishers, 2000).

[107] Or *assure; convince*

mentally bent toward sin in mind and heart. (Gen 6:5; 8:21; Jer. 17:9) Even so, this does not give us the permission to practice or live in sin, perpetually coming to God for forgiveness, in essence, and taking advantage of his love, mercy, patience and long-suffering. (1 John 3:9-10) Nevertheless, it does mean that if we **commit a sin**, no matter the gravity; we need not have some dreadful fear of going to our heavenly Father, with freedom of speech toward him, seeking correction for the wrongdoing we have committed, be it thoughts or actions. In fact, we know that nothing is hidden from the sight of God. – Psalm 139:1-3, 15-18, 23-24.

Now that we correctly understand 1 John 4:18, we can fully appreciate our remaining in love, meaning we remain in God, and God remains in us. This, love, is perfected with us (4:16-17), because we have the freedom of speech, in prayer, toward God; therefore, we can be confident that he will direct us in the way that we should walk. Our being "perfected in love" means that the love of God is entirely complete in us, in that we are continuously seeking to do his will wholeheartedly. – Ephesians 3:12; Hebrews 4:16; 1 John 5:14

Avoid Abusing Prophetic Scripture

Fulfillment is the result of a prophetic message, prophecies that are fulfilled. Luke 24:27 tells us "And beginning with Moses and all the Prophets, [Jesus] interpreted to them in all the Scriptures the things concerning himself." Matthew especially, referenced many prophecies that were fulfilled in Jesus. Let us look at one from Hosea in Matthew.

Hosea 11:1 Updated American Standard Version (UASV)

1 When Israel was a child, I loved him,
and out of Egypt I called my son.

Matthew 2:15 Updated American Standard Version (UASV)

15 and was there until the death of Herod. This was to complete[108] what had been spoken by the Lord through the prophet, "Out of Egypt I called my son."[109]

Some argue that we need to see Matthew's meaning in Hosea. In other words, Hosea meant to convey the meaning that Matthew expressed. This just is not the case. Did Hosea mean his words to be prophetic, or were they a reference to a historical event, to make a point

---

[108] Gr plēroō

[109] A quotation from Hos. 11:1

to his current readers? His audience would have understood what Hosea meant, by their use of historical-grammatical interpretation. "When Israel was but a boy" is a reference to the nation's early beginnings, when they were young, while they were in Egypt. "I" is Jehovah God speaking through the prophet Hosea, their loving Father, who 'out of Egypt called his son.'

On many occasions, a New Testament writer would quote or cite an Old Testament Scripture. Many times the New Testament writer would be using the Old Testament text contextually, according to the setting, and intent of the Old Testament writer (observing the grammatical-historical sense). However, at times the New Testament writer would add to or apply the text differently than what was meant by the Old Testament writer (**not** observing the grammatical-historical sense). This is either a new or a progressive revelation of God, where he has inspired the New Testament writer to go beyond the intended meaning of the Old Testament writer, and carry out what is known as *Inspired Sensus Plenior Application* (ISPA). In this latter case, the New Testament writer is using the Old Testament text to convey another meaning to another circumstance. This does not violate the principle that all texts have just one single meaning. The Old Testament text has one meaning, and the New Testament writer's adaptation of that text is not a second meaning, but another meaning.

Now, **(1)** was Matthew intending to interpret the message of Hosea, because it was supposedly prophetic, or **(2)** was he using Hosea's meaning of a historical reference, and giving it a *sensus plenior* meaning, by way of inspiration of Holy Spirit? It was the latter, number **(2)**. Hosea's meaning was a historical reference to the Israelite nation when they were in Egypt. Matthew's meaning is to take Hosea's words, and add new additional meaning to them, not suggesting at all that Hosea meant his new meaning.

Dr. John H. Walton's approach in dealing with this sort of circumstance is that we need to grasp the difference between **(1)** message and **(2)** fulfillment. The message of Hosea was not prophetic and was understood by his audience. "Fulfillment is not the message but is the working out of God's plan in history. There are no hermeneutical principles within the grammatical-historical model that enable one to identify a fulfillment by reading and analyzing the prophecy."[110] In other words, we need not concern ourselves with trying to shove a square peg into a round hole. We do not have to fit Matthew's meaning into Hosea,

---

[110] Page(s): 11, Inspired Subjectivity and Hermeneutical Objectivity by John H. Walton Master's Seminary Journal March 01, 2002.pdf

as though Hosea's meaning was prophetic, and this justifies Matthew's conclusions. We are not causing any ripple in Scripture because these two have different meanings from each other. Walton is in harmony with Dr. Robert L. Thomas, with the exception of his seeing Matthew's use of Hosea's words as a **fulfillment**, while Thomas sees them as a **completion**, "some sense the transport of Jesus by His parents from Egypt **completed** the deliverance of Israel from Egypt that had begun during the time of Moses."[111] Bold is mine

It is difficult to see Matthew's use of Hosea's words as a fulfillment, because, Hosea's words were not prophetic. Without an intended prophecy, how can there be a fulfillment? We should see Matthew's use of Hosea's words as completing whatever historical reference Hosea was referring too. What we do know is that if Matthew assigns a different meaning to Hosea's words, it is his meaning and it is subjective. Which if we recall, we are perfectly fine with, because he has the authority to offer subjective sense; he was an inspired Bible writer, who had been moved along by Holy Spirit. Matthew was not interpreting the message Hosea penned, he was giving us a *sensus plenior*, a completion to Hosea's words.

Therefore, we need to look at the Greek word behind fulfillment (*pleroo*). *Pleroo* has a range of meaning, and the context will give us which sense was meant. It can mean, "to fulfill, to complete, carry out to the full, accomplish, and perfect."[112] What is the sense that we find at Matthew 2:15 and other places that New Testament writers use it, when they are referring to an Old Testament Passage? Bible scholar Dr. Robert L. Thomas has this to say on the subject, "Most (if not all) English translations frequently render the Greek verb *pleroo* by the English word fulfill. In some instances, this is unfortunate because the two words do not cover the same semantic domain. In English, fulfill, when used in connection with Old Testament citations, carries the connotation of a historical occurrence of something promised or predicted. The Greek *pleroo*, however, covers more linguistic territory than that."[113] New Testament Scholar Douglas J. Moo adds,

> *Pleroo* cannot be confined to so narrow a focus [as referring to fulfillment of an Old Testament prophecy].... What needs to be emphasized, then, is that the use of pleroo in an

[111] Robert L. Thomas. Evangelical Hermeneutics: The New Versus the Old (p. 263). Kindle Edition.

[112] W. E. Vine, Merrill F. Unger and William White, Jr., vol. 2, Vine's Complete Expository Dictionary of Old and New Testament Words, 8 (Nashville, TN: T. Nelson, 1996).

[113] Robert L. Thomas. Evangelical Hermeneutics: The New Versus the Old (p. 262). Kindle Edition.

introductory formula need not mean that the author regards the Old Testament text he quotes as a direct prophecy; and accusations that a New Testament author misuses the Old Testament by using pleroo to introduce nonprophetic texts are unfounded.'[114]

We can see that the context of Matthew 2:15 leads us to the rendering "This was to **complete** what the Lord had spoken by the prophet, 'Out of Egypt I called my son.'" In other words, "In the Matthew 2:15 citation of Hosea 11:1 Matthew uses [*pleroo*] to indicate the completion of a *sensus plenior* meaning he finds in Hosea 11:1."[115] As we have already said, the single meaning of Hosea 11:1 is not prophetic, but rather a historical reference to the time of Moses, when God called the Israelite nation out of Egypt. Therefore, to use the English rendering fulfill is "misleading." "Matthew's meaning is that in some sense the transport of Jesus by His parents from Egypt completed the deliverance of Israel from Egypt that had begun during the time of Moses."[116]

Now, it is time for a little warning. We should be very cautious of writers who give us interpretations of allegory, typology, and fulfillment that are not explicitly provided by a Bible writer. No human writer at present or that lived after the Apostle John died in 100 C.E., has the authority to give us fulfillment unless a Bible writer stated it. Humans are very curious about what the future holds, especially Christians with the fulfillment of Scripture. This is why books by authors telling us they have unlocked Scripture or that they can explain the fulfillment of things that no Bible writer expressed as a fulfillment, are very dangerous. We cannot reproduce the interpretive skills of the New Testament writers, because they did not always follow the historical-grammatical interpretation (objective), they at times gave a message that was subjective. We do not have the authority to imitate them by our skipping over historical-grammatical interpretation to give revelations about allegory, typology, and fulfillments of Scripture. Therefore, let us stay far from the shores of subjective interpretation, by either penning it or reading it.

New Testament Use of Old Testament

The New Testament writers used Old Testament writers in one of two ways. **(1)** The New Testament writer took the one grammatical-historical interpretation of the Old Testament passage. In this case, we are talking about a fulfillment of the Old Testament passage and we are

---

[114] Moo, Doulas J., "Problems of Sensus Plenior," 191

[115] Thomas. Evangelical Hermeneutics: The New Versus the Old (p. 263).

[116] IBID., p. 263

perfectly fine to word it that way. In other words, the Old Testament passage was written as a prophecy for that future event, not some immediate fulfillment. **(2)** The New Testament writer goes beyond what the Old Testament writer penned, assigning it additional meaning that is applicable to the New Testament context. In other words, the Old Testament writer's grammatical-historical interpretation would have been a fulfillment for him and his audience, not just a hope. The New Testament writer then made the information applicable to his situation, by adding to it, which fit his context. With number **(1)**, we have the New Testament writer staying with the literal sense of the Old Testament writer. With number **(2)**, we have the New Testament writer adding a whole other meaning.

Dr. Robert L. Thomas calls number **(2)** "inspired sensus plenior application" (ISPA), which we will adopt as well.[117] It is inspired because this is an inspired Bible writer adding the additional sense or fuller sense than what had been penned in the Old Testament.

When interpreting the Old Testament and New Testament each in light of the single grammatical-historical meaning of each passage, two kinds of New Testament uses of the Old Testament surface, one in which the New Testament writer observes the grammatical-historical sense of the Old Testament passage and the other in which the New Testament writer goes beyond the grammatical-historical sense in using a passage. Inspired sensus plenior application (ISPA) designates the latter usage. Numerous passages illustrate each type of New Testament use of the Old Testament. The ISPA type of application does not grant contemporary interpreters a license to copy the method of New Testament writers, nor does it violate the principle of single meaning. The ISPA meaning of the Old Testament passage did not exist for humans until the time of the New Testament citation, being occasioned by Israel's rejection of her Messiah at His first advent. The ISPA approach approximates that advocated by John H. Walton more closely than other explanations of the New Testament use of the Old Testament. "Fulfillment" terminology in the New Testament is appropriate only for events that literally fulfill events predicted in the Old Testament.[118]

Most conservative evangelical scholars believe that some biblical prophecies possess more than the initial fulfillment, an extended fulfillment. This writer and many others would also point out that the prophecies in both the Hebrew Old Testament and the Greek New

---

[117] Robert L. Thomas. Evangelical Hermeneutics: The New Versus the Old (p. 242). Kindle Edition

[118] IBID., p. 241

Testament had *meaning* to those who the prophecy was written to; it served as means of guidance for the initial audience, as well as for succeeding generation, down to our day. This is not to say that the prophetic message itself was applicable from then until now, but that its meaning is beneficial to all. In many cases, the *fulfillment* took place within that first generation.

At times, there are New Testament writers that give another fulfillment during the New Testament era, 02 B.C.E. up unto 100 C.E. In addition, there are some cases where a prophecy has a final fulfillment in what the Bible calls the "last days" or "end times," or even during the millennial reign of Christ. Revelation 21:1; Isaiah 65:17; 66:22; 2 Peter 3:13

Here I should qualify what I mean by having *meaning* to the initial audience and being *fulfilled* during the lifetime of the first audience. Isaiah 65:17 informs the initial audience, the contemporaries of Isaiah "I am about to create new heavens and a new earth, and the former things shall not be remembered, and they shall not come to mind." What do "new heavens and a new earth" mean, and when was this to take place?

> **65:17-19**. The new condition of salvation for only a portion of God's people could occur because God had created something entirely new. The new creation would differ greatly from the old one, being dominated by joy instead of mourning and weeping. The joy would be shared by the people and by God. This new creation would share some features with the old. It would still have both heavens and earth. And it would center in the holy city of Jerusalem.[119]

I certainly would agree with Dr. Trent C. Butler's assessment, but is this applicable to the time period of Isaiah's prophesying, c. 780-730 B.C.E.? The words can merely refer to the future in general, as opposed to what we think of as the last days or end times. In other words, the Israelites could place their hope in a bright future, but not knowing the day and the hour. There is nothing in Scripture where another inspired writer took Isaiah words, and gave them meaning of fulfillment. They could have taken place already, but we cannot speak of that in absolute terms, because as was stated earlier, we are not inspired, to be able to speak of fulfillment. However, let us offer a possible time when they could have been fulfilled in the past, but after Isaiah was written.

---

[119] Anders, Max; Butler, Trent (2002-04-01). Holman Old Testament Commentary: Isaiah (p. 374). B&H Publishing.

It could have been fulfilled almost 200 years after Isaiah when the Israelites would come back from the seventy years that they were going to spend in Babylonian captivity. Butler said, "The new condition of salvation [was] for only a portion of God's people." Only a small remnant of Israelites returned home from Babylonian captivity in 537 B.C.E. This would mean that there was no immediate *fulfillment* for the people of Isaiah's day or even the next generation. However, there was *meaning* for the Israelites, because they knew destruction and desolation of Jerusalem was coming, but they also knew that a remnant was going to come through this, and purified worship would be restored to Jerusalem, which offered them hope.

As we grow in our ability to interpret correctly and understand God's Word because we have bought out the time from Satan's world, we will become more and more acquainted with its message of beauty and its meaning in our lives, comforted in the fact we are now sharing and defending what the authors meant to convey. Many times, we have likely looked to the prophecies in the Hebrew Scriptures regarding the blessings coming to what is referred to as the new heavens and the new earth (renewal of the present universe). We know this is the final redemption from the domination of sin (Matt. 19:28; Ac 3:31; Rom. 8:18-21), contemplating the paradise-like conditions that are to come under Christ's kingdom on this new earth.

However, sometimes we are slow to realize that the prophecies of Isaiah and the like had some fulfillment to those who heard it or succeeding generations. Think of the words of Isaiah the prophet at 35:1, 7, "The wilderness and the dry land shall be glad; the desert shall rejoice and blossom like the crocus; the burning sand shall become a pool, and the thirsty ground springs of water; in the haunt of jackals, where they lie down, the grass shall become reeds and rushes." If we look at the context of this Scripture, it is all too clear that it applies to the returned Jews after their seventy years of Captivity in Babylon, under Governor Zerubbabel. In fact, verse 10 specifically says, "and the redeemed of the Lord will return and come to Zion with singing, crowned with unending joy. Joy and gladness will overtake them, and sorrow and sighing will flee." (HCSB) Jehovah saw fit to make the land of Israel a mini paradise for the remnant that was to return from their captivity. In essence, a land that had grown over for seventy years, was restored to paradise-like conditions. Those same miracles, acting on behalf of his people will pale in comparison to the renewed heavens and earth that are to come under the rule of his Son, the Lord Jesus Christ.

Only truly conservative Christianity can completely appreciate that "the word of God is living and active." (Heb. 4:12) Yes, God is very much alive and his speaks to his people today through the page of the living, inspired, inerrant Word of God. In this way, he gives power to his people and understanding of deep biblical truths as to his intentions for his servants. It is for this reason alone that every true Christian should have an internal desire to "handle the word of truth aright." We want to be efficient in our using it to proclaim, to teach, to defend and to make disciples as Jesus had commanded. Paul said to Timothy,

2 Timothy 3:16-17 Updated American Standard Version (UASV)

[16] All Scripture is inspired by God and profitable for teaching, for reproof, for correction, for training in righteousness; [17] so that the man of God may be fully competent, equipped for every good work.

If we are to use the Word of God aright, what must we do? We must read it and study it, seeking the very knowledge of God. (Josh 1-8; Psa. 1:1-3; Deut. 6:4-9; Pro. 2:1-6) Such knowledge and understanding do not come easily, nor should we expect that it would. If we were going to become an attorney, to provide justice for the troubled of this world, would we do this by reading a law book once and a while for a few minutes? If we wanted to be a pediatric heart surgeon, to save the lives of children, would this happen by reading a few medical books here and there and sitting in a few medical classes? If we are to evangelize the Word of God aright, is it going to happen by occasionally picking up the Bible to read and sitting in church services ritualistically? No, we must buy out the time, by having a daily personal study, preparing for meetings, participating in meetings that allow such, and sharing what we learn regularly.

Proverbs 2:1-6 Updated American Standard Version (UASV)

2 My son, if you receive my words
 and treasure up my commandments with you,
[2] making your ear attentive to wisdom
 and inclining your heart to understanding;
[3] For if you cry for discernment
 and raise your voice for understanding,
[4] if you seek it like silver
 and search for it as for hidden treasures,
[5] then you will understand the fear of Jehovah
 and find the knowledge of God.
[6] For Jehovah gives wisdom;
 from his mouth come knowledge and understanding;

Exercise

Did Matthew at 1:23 use a literal treatment of Isaiah 7:14?

Walk through the section on prophetic Scripture as a whole, understand it to the point where you can use your own words to explain it in a brief paragraph to a fellow Christian.

Review Questions

- What background information aids us in properly understanding 2 Timothy 2:15?

- What common explanation of Isaiah 14:12-16 has often been given, but what is the actual Scriptural explanation, and so who truly is the Lucifer of Isaiah 14:12-16, reflecting whose attitude?

- What is proof-texting and how can it be wrong? Whose examples help us to appreciate that you can use texts from different places within Scripture to make a particular point?

- What are some examples of the meaning being within the context?

- How can we avoid abusing Prophetic Scripture?

CHAPTER 8 Effectively Reasoning From the Scriptures

Acts 17:2 Updated American Standard Version (UASV)

[2] And according to Paul's custom, he went to them, and for three Sabbaths **reasoned with them from the Scriptures,**

The value of God's Word is incomprehensible. With it, we are able to answer some of life's most difficult questions. Why are we here? What is the meaning of life? If there is a God and he is good, why so much suffering? What is the purpose of our existence? What is right and wrong and who should determine it? Will world peace ever be achieved? Will poverty ever end? How can we be happy? What is true freedom and does it exist? What happens after we die? Is there such a thing as **absolute truth**? Moreover, I am confident that each of us could add many more life questions to this list. However, the last question above is there such a thing as absolute truth, can be answered with an absolute yes and it is found in the Bible alone. In the Bible, we find answers to the above questions and far more. We discover that we have a Creator and why such a loving Creator would allow sickness, old age and death, with much suffering all throughout our limited lives.[120] We also learn the truth about why we are here, what our Creator expects of us, and how his decisions in our behalf have been for our good. – Psalm 19:7-11; Isaiah 48:17.

As true Christians, we accept the Bible as the inspired, fully inerrant Word of God and that it has the power to change lives for the better, so we defend it and share it with others. (Heb. 4:12) When we share these truths with others, we want to help them to realize that it is not our absolute truths, but rather truths that belong to the God of the heavens and the earth, which he has revealed to us in the Scriptures. Thus, we want to use the Bible, as it is the authority, the absolute truth, when we talk with others, literally reading from it. Like Paul, we want to 'reason with them from the Scriptures.' (Ac 17:2) We want to help them accept the Bible for what it is, the inspired Word of God, and accept what it teaches as absolute truth. – 2 Timothy 2:15.

It is highly important that we share what God's Word says rather than what we feel, think, or believe. This can be exemplified in the prophetic book of Jeremiah. The prophets other than Jeremiah were merely saying what the people wanted to hear, pacifying, i.e., seeking to make the people and rulers less angry, upset, or hostile, saying untrue

---

[120] **Suffering & Evil - Why God?**

http://www.christianpublishers.org/suffering-evil-why-god

things to please them. In other words, they were not telling the people the Word of God.

Jeremiah 23:25-28 Updated American Standard Version (UASV)

[25] I have heard what the prophets have said who prophesy lies in my name, saying, 'I have dreamed, I have dreamed!' [26] How long will this be in the hearts of the prophets who prophesy lies, even these prophets of the deceit of their own heart, [27] who think to make my people forget my name by their dreams that they tell one another, just as their fathers forgot my name for Baal? [28] The prophet who has a dream may relate his dream, but let him who has My word speak My word in truth. What does straw have in common with grain?" declares Jehovah.

On the other hand, Jeremiah did speak God's Word truthfully, even if it was not well received, or it meant his life was in danger. The apostle Paul tells the Corinthians and us that the historical events of the Old Testament were recorded to serve as "examples for us." Thus, like Jeremiah, we too want to feel obligated to teach only what the authors meant when they penned their particular books and not water down the Word of God or impose modern day thinking into the text, deliberately avoiding offense. For example, today we have an undertaking called the feminist movement, belief in the need to secure rights and opportunities for women equal to those of men, or a commitment to securing these. While the idea of attaining the right to vote, equal pay for equal work, among other modern day rights, is perfectly fine, it should not retroactively be applied to the Word of God. Paul clearly states at 2 Timothy 2:12, "I do not permit a woman to teach or to exercise authority over a man; rather, she is to remain quiet." The natural reading of 1 Timothy 2:12 is that Paul in his apostolic authority prohibits women from teaching and exercising authority over a man, which means that women cannot serve as pastors or elders in the Christian congregation. We are not to mold to the pressures of the modern day feminist movement because this position goes back to before the fall, has always been applicable, and will always be applicable. For a detail explanation of this text, see the footnote below.[121]

Even Jesus himself said, "My teaching is not mine, but belongs to him that sent me. If anyone wants to do his will, he will know whether the teaching is from God or whether I am speaking on my own authority. The one who speaks on his own authority seeks his own glory, but the one who seeks the glory of him who sent him, this one is true, and there is no unrighteousness in him." (John 7:16-18) Even the Son of God himself

---

[121] **Women in the Pulpit?**

https://christianpublishinghouse.co/2017/01/03/women-in-the-pulpit/

refused to speak of his own authority, but rather the authority of the Father, who had sent him. Therefore, how much more so should we avoid speaking on our own authority? Like, the elders, all Christians want to be "holding fast to the faithful word which is in accordance with the teaching, so that he will be able both to exhort in sound doctrine and to refute those who contradict." (Titus 1:9) Then, there is the counsel from Paul for Timothy to hand off to the congregations, "preach the word; be ready in season and out of season; reprove, rebuke, exhort, with complete patience and teaching." (2 Tim. 4:2) Whether we are answering questions at a Bible study in the congregation, an elder or pastor is giving a lecture, or we are witnessing to someone outside of the congregation, we want to "preach the word."

However, the Bible is an in-depth, complex book, because it was it was written from 2,000 to 3,500 years ago in many different cultures, the language of biblical Hebrew and Koine (common) Greek, among many other things is it difficult to understand. Therefore, we could never evangelize by just reading the Bible alone, saying no more, especially to this generation that is almost entirely unfamiliar with it. If our listener is to grasp fully what the authors meant and how it applies to us, we are going to have to offer that connection. In the account of the Ethiopian eunuch referred to at Acts 8:26-38, he did not fully understand what was meant in the Book of Isaiah that he was reading in his travels. This Eunuch was familiar with the Hebrew or Greek translation of the Old Testament, as he had come to Jerusalem to worship and was returning to his homeland, and yet he still did not understand Isaiah 53:7-8. How much more help do the unbelievers of today need? Nevertheless, once this eunuch fully understood the importance of the text, seeing how it applied to him personally, he chose to leave the Judaism of the day and become a Christian.

How Jesus Used the Scriptures

Matthew writes, "And when Jesus finished these sayings, the crowds were astonished at his teaching, for he was teaching them as one who had authority, and not as their scribes." (7:28-29) He later writes of Jesus return to his hometown, "He taught them in their synagogue so that they were astonished." (13:54) After that, when Jesus is speaking on a number of subjects, but especially who shall be saved, Matthew says the disciples "were greatly astonished." (19:25) Later still when Jesus dealt with the resurrection belief of the Sadducees, "when the crowd heard it, they were astonished at his teaching." (22:33)

Why were the crowds astonished at Jesus' way of teaching? What does it mean that he was teaching them as one who had authority? How

126

is it that they say no one had ever spoken as Jesus had? The Greek verb used by Matthew about how Jesus' teaching affected others was *ekplessomai*, which meant that they were "so amazed as to be practically overwhelmed–'to be greatly astounded.'[122] In 7:28, the verb is in the imperfect tense, which suggested an ongoing effect. Jesus taught with the authority of the Scriptures, unlike the scribes, who were busy quoting Rabbis as their authority. Jesus, on the other hand, quoted over 120 Hebrew verses in the dialog that is given to us in the Gospel accounts, accounts that would amount to about a three-hour lecture.

Bible Background on the Scribes

In ancient times, the scribes were merely officers whose duties included writing of various kinds; but, on the return of the Jews from Babylonian captivity, the sopherim, as the scribes were called, were organized by Ezra into a distinct body. Among other duties, they copied the Pentateuch, the Phylacteries, and the Mezuzoth. So great was their care in copying that they counted and compared all the letters to be sure that none were left out that belonged to the text, or none inserted wrongly. On stated occasions they read the law in the synagogues. They also lectured to their disciples. Because of the knowledge they obtained through their work, they became natural interpreters of God's law as well as copyists.

The lawyers (Matthew 22:35; Luke 7:30; 11:45; 14:3) and the doctors of the law (Luke 2:46; 5:17; Acts 5:34) were substantially the same as the scribes. Efforts have been made to show that different classes of duties were assigned to lawyers, doctors, and scribes, but without any measurably different results. It may be, as some believe, that the doctors were a higher grade than the ordinary scribes. The scribes were all carefully educated for their work from early life, and at an appropriate age—some say thirty-years-old—they were admitted to office through a solemn ceremony.

The scribes were not only copyists of the law; they were also keepers of the oral traditional comments and additions to the law. Gradually accumulating with the progress of time, these were numerous and were regarded by many as of equal value with the law itself. To this Jesus alludes in Mark 7:5–13. Paul represents himself as having been, before his conversion, "exceedingly zealous of the traditions" of his fathers (Galatians 1:14). The scribes also adopted forced interpretations of the law, endeavoring to find a special meaning in every word, syllable, and

---

[122] Johannes P. Louw and Eugene Albert Nida, *Greek-English Lexicon of the New Testament: Based on Semantic Domains* (New York: United Bible Societies, 1996), 311–312.

letter. Thus the Savior charges them: "Woe to you experts in the law, because you have taken away the key to knowledge. You yourselves have not entered, and you have hindered those who were entering" (Luke 11:52).

At the time of Christ, the people were increasingly dependent on the scribes for a knowledge of their Scriptures. The language of the Jews was passing into the Aramaic dialect, and the majority of the people, being unable to understand their own sacred books, were obliged to accept the interpretation that the scribes put upon them. Hence, their astonishment, as indicated in our text-verse, at the peculiar style of teaching adopted by Jesus, and especially illustrated in His Sermon on the Mount. The scribes repeated traditions, but Jesus spoke with authority: "I tell you." The scribes had little sympathy with the masses, but Jesus mingled with the people, explaining to them in a simple, practical way the requirements of religion.[123]

Hendriksen and Kistemaker asked the question that concerned us as well, "What were some of the reasons for this feeling of wonder and astonishment? Matt. 13:54, 55 may supply part of the answer. Nevertheless, on the basis of the sermon itself and of 7:28 ("not as their scribes") the following items are worthy of consideration:"

a. He spoke the truth (John 14:6; 18:37). Corrupt and evasive reasoning marked the sermons of many of the scribes (Matt. 5:21 ff.).

b. He presented matters of great significance, matters of life, death, and eternity (see the entire sermon). They often wasted their time on trivialities (Matt. 23:23; Luke 11:42).

c. There was system in his preaching. As their Talmud proves, they often rambled on and on.

d. He excited curiosity by making generous use of illustrations (5:13–16; 6:26–30; 7:24–27; etc.) and concrete examples (5:21–6:24; etc.), as the sermon shows from beginning to end. Their speeches were often dry as dust.

e. He spoke as the Lover of men, as One concerned with the everlasting welfare of his listeners, and pointed to the Father and his love (5:44–48). Their lack of love is clear from such passages as 23:4, 13–15; Mark 12:40; etc.

f. Finally, and this is the most important, for it is specifically stated here (verse 28), he spoke "with authority" (Matt. 5:18, 26; etc.), for his

---

[123] James M. Freeman and Harold J. Chadwick, *Manners & Customs of the Bible* (North Brunswick, NJ: Bridge-Logos Publishers, 1998), 420–421.

message came straight from the very heart and mind of the Father (John 8:26), hence also from his own inner being, and from Scripture (5:17; 7:12; cf. 4:4, 7, 10). They were constantly borrowing from fallible sources, one scribe quoting another scribe. They were trying to draw water from broken cisterns. He drew from himself, being "the Fountain of living waters" (Jer. 2:13).[124]

Clearly, Jesus set the example in how one is to use the Scriptures effectively. Let us examine his use of questions.

Luke 10:25 Updated American Standard Version (UASV)

25 And behold, a lawyer[125] [an expert in the Mosaic Law] stood up to put him to the test, saying, "Teacher, what shall I do to inherit eternal life?"

A historical note here, "an expert in the law," or "lawyer" as some translations have it, is not a lawyer as we would think of one today. A lawyer was someone that was an expert in the Mosaic Law. However, this person would have the same level of education on the law as a lawyer would today, many years of study and memorization. Thus, this man would certainly know the answer to such an easy question as the one he asked. Now, if a believer is asked a straightforward Bible question, we might be tempted just to offer an answer. Indeed, as the wisest man ever to live, Jesus could have easily answered the question. Instead, Jesus wanted the man to offer his own thoughts, insights or understanding. However, Jesus knew this man was "an expert in the law," and he recognized the man would have had a certain perspective on his question. In other words, the man was not asked because he did not know. Thus, Jesus asked:

Luke 10:26 Updated American Standard Version (UASV)

26 And he said to him, "What is written in the Law? How do you read it?"

The man answered correctly,

Luke 10:27 Updated American Standard Version (UASV)

27 And he answered, "You shall love the Lord your God with all your heart and with all your soul and with all your strength and with all your mind, and your neighbor as yourself."

---

124 William Hendriksen and Simon J. Kistemaker, Exposition of the Gospel According to Matthew, vol. 9, New Testament Commentary (Grand Rapids: Baker Book House, 1953–2001), 382–383.

125 That is an expert in the Mosaic Law

The conversation could have ended there. Again, the man knew the Mosaic Law but seemingly wanted to see if Jesus would agree with what he knew. Jesus gratified him, letting him feel good, by giving the correct answer. Jesus responded:

Luke 10:28-29 Updated American Standard Version (UASV)

28 And he said to him, "You have answered correctly; do this, and you will live."

29 But he, desiring to justify himself, said to Jesus, "And who is my neighbor?"

Here again, the man looks to prove himself righteous, and Jesus could have just stated the truth, even the Samaritan. However, Jesus having insight into the setting, the Jews detested the Samaritans; so, while he would give the correct answer it would be disputed in a long, back-and-forth conversation, and the Jews who listened would have sided with the man. Thus, Jesus boxed the man into giving an answer by having him reason on an illustration.

The Parable of the Good Samaritan

Luke 10:30-37 Updated American Standard Version (UASV)

30 Jesus replied and said, "A man was going down from Jerusalem to Jericho, and he fell among robbers, who stripped him and laid blows upon and departed, leaving him half dead. 31 Now by coincidence a certain priest was going down on that road, and when he saw him, he passed by on the other side. 32 Likewise a Levite also, when he came to the place and saw him, passed by on the other side. 33 But a Samaritan, who was on a journey, came upon him; and when he saw him, he felt compassion, 34 and came to him and bandaged up his wounds, pouring oil and wine on them; and he put him on his own beast, and brought him to an inn and took care of him. 35 And on the next day, he took out two denarii[126] and gave them to the innkeeper, and said, "Take care of him; and whatever more you spend, when I return I will repay you.' 36 Which of these three, do you think, proved to be a neighbor to the man who fell among the robbers?" 37 And he said, "The one who showed mercy toward him." Then Jesus said to him, "Go and do likewise."

This man had to admit the elite in the Jewish religion, the priest, and the Levite, had not been neighborly, but the Samaritan proved to be a good neighbor. Jesus moved him to reason out a new way of viewing exactly what "neighbor" meant. Instead of letting the man walk him into a long debate, Jesus made the man do all of the reasoning in the

---

[126] The denarius was equivalent to a day's wages for a laborer

conversation and moved him to admit something no Jew would ever utter,[127] as well as grasp a whole new understanding of what it meant to be a neighbor. Jesus took this approach because the circumstances called for it. However, on another occasion, a scribe, another expert in the law, asked him the same question and on that occasion, he chose to give the direct answer. (Mark 12:28-31) Circumstances vary.

What lessons can we take in from the example that Luke provided us? **(1)** Jesus **used Scriptures** initially to answer the man's question. **(2)** Jesus proved **perceptive** enough to **take notice** of the man's agenda. **(3)** Jesus did not just answer the easy Bible question but **shifted the responsibility** to **a question** of his own, by asking the man how he understood the law, giving him a chance to express himself. **(4)** Jesus **complimented** the man for a discerning with the correct answer. **(5)** Jesus made sure the man, and the listeners **made the connection** between the initial question and the Scriptures. **(6)** Jesus **used an illustration** that was able to **reach the heart and mind**, where the answer was kept to the forefront. **(7)** Jesus moved the man **to reason** beyond his basic understanding of a neighbor.

The apostle Paul, as well, was an excellent teacher, one from whom we can learn. His traveling companion, Luke the physician, went with him, and his account of Paul's activity is significant.

Reasoning Adapted to the Listeners

Acts 17:2-3 Updated American Standard Version (UASV)

2 And according to Paul's custom, he went to them, and for three Sabbaths **reasoned** with them **from the Scriptures**, **3 explaining and proving** that it was necessary that the Christ had to suffer and rise again from the dead, and saying, "This Jesus whom I am proclaiming to you is the Christ."

We have already spoken about the fact that Paul reasoned from the Scriptures. However, he did more, as one can see from the above, that he explained, proved, and made application. Many times, we may read a Scripture to someone, and while it seems straightforward, enough to us, yet the listener fails to see the point. We may highlight a word or phrase or a part of the text and then explain the verse. We are doing that with Acts 17:2-3, as we highlight **explaining and proving**. You could also offer to walk them through the context, as we also did previously with

---

[127] Notice the hatred ran so deep between Jews and Samaritans that when asked by Jesus, who was the neighbor I the illustration, he did not say, the Samaritan, but rather, "the one who …"

Acts 17:2-3, when we backed up to verse 1, to show that Paul reasoned from the Scriptures because he talked with Jews in the Synagogue, people, who would be familiar with the Hebrew Scriptures. Another option is offering them additional texts that support the one the evangelist used. If the listener does not grasp the text and the explanation, add an illustration like Jesus did over forty times. Then again, asking the right questions might get the listener to reason on things further. We can learn much by looking at Paul's method of teaching. He did not merely quote a Scripture. Thus, we need to do more than just read a Scripture. Not only did he reason from the Scriptures, but he also adapted his reasoning so that it would fit his audience. He did more than share the gospel with the people; he explained it to them, providing them with proof from the Word of God. Let us consider two examples of how effective Paul's teaching was.

At Acts 13:16-41, we find Paul preaching in the Synagogue at Pisidian Antioch. The first thing Paul did was to attempt to find some common ground with his Jewish audience. (Read 13:16-17) Why take that approach? Well, if he could find some common ground, this would draw his listeners in, making them more willing to reason on a subject that they were not going to agree. Notice too that he did not introduce himself as a Christian, nor did he attempt to bring them the good news of Jesus Christ. He was speaking to Jews, who took issue on both accounts, and he being a former Pharisee, he knew their thinking. Rather he referred to them as 'men of Israel, who fear God, asking them to listen.' He also inferred that he too was like them, a Hebrew from birth. After that, he gave them an important part of Israelite history, which they would have been familiar. Now, here is where the skill comes in, as he held to the common ground he had established when he began to speak about Jesus Christ.

Notice the tie in as Paul moved through the Israelite history, saying God "raised up David to be their king, of whom he testified and said, 'I have found in David the son of Jesse a man after my heart, who will do all my will.' Of this man's offspring God has brought to Israel a Savior, Jesus, as he promised." (13:22-23) Then, he pulled in John the Baptizer as a witness to this fact, a person that these Jews viewed as a prophet of God. (13:24-25; Lu 20:4-6) Knowing that his listeners were well aware that the Jewish leaders in Jerusalem had rejected Jesus, Paul beat them to the punch by mentioning it first; then, establishing that this was fulfilled prophecy. (13:27-29) After that, he drew their attention to the fact that God had not abandoned Jesus, by resurrecting him from the dead, to which there were eyewitnesses among the Jews themselves. (13:30-31) Paul brought this complicated matter home, saying, "We preach to you the good news of the promise made to the fathers." (13:32) From there he went to the Hebrew Old Testament as his evidence of this truth. Paul quoted first from Psalm 2:7 ["'You are my Son, today I have begotten you.'], then Isaiah 55:3 ["'I will give you the holy and sure blessings of David.'], and finally Psalm 16:10 ["'You will not let your Holy One see corruption.']. Paul then went on to reason from those scriptures, "For David, after he had served the purpose of God in his own generation, fell asleep and was laid with his fathers and saw corruption, but he whom God raised up did not see corruption." (13:36-37) Now, Paul closed his argument in a motivating conclusion. Many took serious what he had said. "As they went out, the people begged that these things might be told them the next Sabbath." – Acts 13:38-43.

Now, how did Paul do when he approached a non-Jewish audience? When Paul addressed the Areopagus in Athens, Greece, he used a comparable approach; he essentially adjusted his witness to the new environment and thinking of the Athenians. Here again, he sought a common ground. So Paul, standing in the midst of the Areopagus, said: "Men of Athens, I perceive that in every way you are very religious. For as I passed along and observed the objects of your worship, I also found an altar with this inscription, 'To the unknown god.' For as I passed along and observed the objects of your worship, I also found an altar with this inscription, 'To the unknown god.' What therefore you worship as unknown, this I proclaim to you." (Ac 17:22-23) Rather than get explicit with the Scriptures as he did with the Jews, who would have been familiar with such, he paraphrased portions of God's Word, from which he reason from them, proving and explaining what he was saying. Moreover, since Paul had some knowledge of Greek literature, he quoted two different Greek poets.[128] He did not quote these Greek poets as though they were an authority as the Scriptures are, but the portion he quoted was in harmony with Scripture, and he wanted them to realize the points he was making could be found in their own literature. Because of this approach, "some men joined him and believed, among whom also were Dionysius the Areopagite and a woman named Damaris and others with them." – Acts 17:24-31, 34.

The good news that Paul preached in both Athens and Antioch was the same. The approach he took was very similar but adapted specifically for a particular audience because he wanted to find common ground, to reason with them. His love for God and humanity was so deep that Paul took the time to develop his teaching abilities because he cared. Also, such efforts were fruitful because in both cases he found those, who were receptive to the truths he was sharing. It is hoped this book and others by

---

[128] Verse 28 has a possible quote from Epimenides of Crete, or it could be a traditional Greek formula. The verse also contains a quote from Aratus's poem "Phainomena."

this author will go a long way in helping us to do the same, reasoning from the Scriptures, explaining and proving the points that need to be made, effectively evangelizing our family friends, coworkers, and community.

Exercises

A hypothetical friend loves adventurous sports that are life risking. For example, he likes serious white water rafting, rock climbing up the sides of cliffs and hang-gliding. How would you reason with him that these life-risking sports are unbiblical?

Find someone you know who has strong beliefs that are unbiblical and engage them in a conversation. If you do not know such a person, find them within social media. After the discussion is over, analyze the discussion. What evidence did you present, did you use any illustrations, did you lead him along with questions, and did you evidence concern for his feelings and background.

Review Questions

- When we witness to another, how can we help them to see the importance of the Word of God?

- How did Jesus use the Scriptures?

- What can we learn from the way Paul taught?

- How can we further develop our ability to reason from the Scriptures?

- How can we adapt our reason to our listener?

CHAPTER 9 How Can We Improve Our Evangelism Skills?

1 Corinthians 4:17 Updated American Standard Version (UASV)

¹⁷ That is why I sent you Timothy, who is my beloved and faithful child in the Lord, and he will remind you of my ways which are in Christ, **just as I teach** everywhere in every congregation.

Developing our Evangelism Skills

We are all aware of the outpouring of the Holy Spirit at Pentecost 33 C.E., where Christianity spread and grew rapidly. (Acts 2:40-42; 4:4; 6:7; 11:19-21) Why might our congregation seem to be stagnant, going years with next to no growth, even actually losing ones that we already have? Why did so many Jews and then Samaritans and then Gentiles accept Christ and the kingdom back in the first-century, growing from 120 to over one million in just 10-years? – Acts 8:4-8; 10:44-48.

If one is to accept the good news of the kingdom, certain factors must take place. First, one must obtain an accurate, full, or true knowledge (Gr., epignosis) of biblical truths. (1 Tim. 2:3-4; Rom 10:14) After that, they must put faith in that knowledge of God. (Heb. 11:6) At that point, one will develop an appreciation for the Father's sacrifice of his Son as a ransom sacrifice and his loving-kindness toward humankind. It is like the apostle John expressed it, "In this the love of God was made manifest among us, that God sent his only begotten Son into the world, so that we might live through him. In this is love, not that we loved God, but that he loved us and sent his Son to be the propitiation for our sins." – 1 John 4:9-10.

These are the initial stages of one's accepting Christ. As they are taking in God's Word, putting faith in the things heard, they are also developing spiritual values. Jesus, said, "Blessed are the poor in spirit, for theirs is the kingdom of the heavens." (Matt. 5:3) The phrase "poor in spirit" can be difficult to understand. Let us look at GOD'S WORD Translation, which reads, ""Blessed are those who [are poor in spirit] recognize they are spiritually helpless ..." The Greek word ptochos means "beggar." The "poor in spirit" is an alternative literal rendering. The meaning is that the "beggar/poor in spirit" is aware of his or her spiritual needs as if a beggar or the poor would be aware of their physical needs. Jesus went on to say in verse 6, "Blessed are those who hunger and thirst for righteousness, for they shall be satisfied." One who is self-satisfied and self-righteous is unaware of the need to develop spiritual values and is unreceptive to biblical truths. When this one is first told of the good news of the kingdom, he answers with something like, 'I am not interested. I do not believe in any religion.' Another one who is usually not receptive to biblical truths is the one who is deeply wrapped up in material pursuits. – Matthew 6:33-34; 7:7-8; Luke 12:16-21.

The one's that every Christian proclaimer of the good news is looking for are those that are receptive to biblical truths because they sense a spiritual need that they are lacking. When we are sharing the Word of God with unbelievers, how are we to identify such ones? First, we need to appreciate the fact that the Bible is often misunderstood and even the apostle Peter said the apostle Paul's letters were "hard to understand, which the ignorant and unstable twist to their own destruction, as they do the other Scriptures." (2 Pet. 3:16) Thus, our first concern is to take a book that is admittedly complicated and difficult to understand and make it easy to comprehend. How can we accomplish such things if we do not fully understand God's Word ourselves?

Whose Methods Were Effective?

When the apostle Paul wrote to the Corinthians for the first time, he told them that he was sending them Timothy, the young man that has been traveling with him for a few years, who would go on as his traveling companion for another decade. Paul told the Corinthians that Timothy was his "beloved and faithful child in the Lord, and he will **remind you of my ways** which are in Christ ..." (1 Cor. 4:17) What did Paul mean when he said, "remind you of **my ways**"? Some commentaries take "**my ways**" as referring to Paul's **ways** of living not just his ideas or his doctrinal positions being the same as Jesus Christ. However, we might notice the context, because after Paul told the Corinthians that Timothy would remind them of "my ways" he finishes the sentence by saying, "just as I teach everywhere in every congregation." Therefore, while his personal conduct is certainly a part of "my ways," his methods of teaching are the centerpiece. On this Kistemaker and Hendriksen write, "These ways relate to the work Paul performed while he was with the Corinthians: teaching, preaching, counseling, shaping, nurturing, and praying. They pertain to the work Paul accomplished on behalf of Jesus Christ and the building of the church."[129] It should be mentioned that the verse before these words, Paul wrote, "I exhort you, become imitators of me." (4:16)

Paul like Jesus had methods of teaching and proclaiming. Jesus took the Mosaic Law that can be complex and challenging to understand,

---

[129] Simon J. Kistemaker and William Hendriksen, *Exposition of the First Epistle to the Corinthians*, vol. 18, New Testament Commentary (Grand Rapids: Baker Book House, 1953–2001), 146.

which the ignorant and unstable Jewish religious leaders twisted to their own destruction and taught it to tens of thousands. Jesus conveyed the Hebrew Scriptures with simplicity, unquestionable logic, thought-provoking questions, and striking figures of speech, meaningful illustrations taken from things familiar to his listeners, and his reasoning from more than 120 Old Testament Scriptures recorded in the Gospels. Jesus was thoroughly at ease with God's Word. (Matt. 6:25-30; 7:3-5, 24-27) In other words, Jesus had methods of teaching; he did not just haphazardly go about teaching others. This effective teaching and preaching method he handed down to others, as he taught his apostles and later the seventy others he appointed. These methods will always be the most effective way of reaching the hearts of the receptive ones, who are aware or can be made aware that they have spiritual needs. – Luke 9:1-6; 10:1-11.

The First Obstacle to Our Being an Effective Evangelist

When we enter the pathway of walking with our God, we will certainly come across resistance from three different areas. **Our greatest obstacle** is **ourselves** because we have inherited imperfection from our first parents Adam and Eve. The Scriptures make it quite clear that we are **mentally bent** toward evil, not good. (Gen 6:5; 8:21, AT) In other words, our natural desire is toward wrong. On the other hand, prior to sinning, Adam and Eve were perfect, and they had the natural desire of doing good. This means that they literally had to go against the grain so to speak, like rowing up river, violating their perfect inner person. Returning to our current condition, the Scriptures further tells us of our inner person, i.e., our heart.

Romans 7:21-24 Updated American Standard Version (UASV)

[21] I find then the law in me that when I want to do right, that evil is present in me. [22] For I delight in the law of God according to the inner man, [23] but I see a different law in my members, warring against the law of my mind and taking me captive in the law of sin which is in my members. [24] Wretched man that I am! Who will deliver me from this body of death?

Jeremiah 17:9 Updated American Standard Version (UASV)	**1 Corinthians 9:27** Updated American Standard Version (UASV)
[9] The heart is more deceitful than all else, and desperately sick; who can understand it?	[27] but I discipline my body and make it my slave, so that, after I have preached to others, I myself will not be disqualified.

We are all imperfect with human weaknesses, so we are our greatest obstacle in becoming a competent teacher and proclaimer of biblical truths. Maybe we feel uncomfortable, inadequate and not adequately educated for those whom we may strike up a conversation. While it is true that Jesus did not attend the rabbinical schools of his day, studying under persons such as Gamaliel, as Pau had, as Jesus was the Son of God, a perfect human being. Nevertheless, Jesus was still a student of God's Word.

When Jesus was twelve years old, the family had gone down to celebrate the Feast of the Passover, as they did every year, they accidently left Jesus behind. After a three-day search, they "found him in the temple, sitting in the midst of the teachers and listening to them and questioning them. And all those listening to him were amazed at his understanding and his answers." (Lu 2:46-47) This was a twelve years old. Now, many times in the Gospels, it is said that the people marvels at the way Jesus taught. Matthew tells us, "They were astonished and said, 'Where did this man get this wisdom and these mighty works?'" (Matt. 13:54, ESV) Even though Jesus was very wise as the Son of God and a perfect human, his methods of teaching were very practical and can be learned by anyone. We know the disciples imitated Jesus, so what was said of them. On one occasion, when called before the Jewish Sanhedrin (high court), it was said of Jewish leaders, "Now when they saw the boldness of Peter and John, and perceived that they were uneducated,[130] common men, they were astonished. And they recognized that they had been with Jesus." – Acts 4:13.

Why was Jesus so effective in his evangelism and proclaiming of the good news? Are we to believe that Jesus was like our modern day televangelists, who use exaggerated emotionalism to sway their audiences? No. Jesus was a man who always sought to do the will of the Father, but who also understood the Word of God very well, and taught it in a simple way. If a person failed to understand the simplified explanation, i.e., interpretation of the Old Testament, Jesus would offer even more of a clarification, helping the listeners to grasp what was meant. When Jesus "came to Nazareth, where he had been brought up; and as was his custom, he went to the synagogue on the Sabbath day, and he stood up to read. "And the scroll[131] of the prophet Isaiah was given to him. And he unrolled the scroll[132] and found the place where it was written, 'The Spirit of the Lord is upon me, because he has anointed me

---

[130] This is not suggesting that Peter and John were illiterate, saying they could not read and write. This is saying they were not educated in the Rabbinical schools.

[131] Or a *roll*

[132] Or *roll*

to proclaim good news to the poor. He has sent me **to proclaim release** to the captives and recovering of sight to the blind, to set free those who are oppressed, **to proclaim the favorable year** of the Lord.' And he rolled up the scroll and gave it back to the attendant and sat down ..." This quote was from a prophecy in the book of Isaiah. Jesus then said, "Today this Scripture has been fulfilled in your hearing." – Luke 4:16-21.

The good news that Jesus came to earth to share first, with the Jews, and second, with the rest of humanity, was an offer to release them and us from bondage to sin and death and from the condemnation of Adamic sin.[133] He too was releasing us from our human weaknesses, while also waking us up to Satan's world that caters to the imperfect human flesh. When Jesus taught the Jews the ways of true worship and what was expected of them, they were released from the many twisted interpretations the Pharisees, Sadducees, Scribes, and other Jewish leaders gave to the Scriptures. (Matthew 5:21-48) While the physical cures that Jesus performed were certainly greatly appreciated the being released from the captivity of false worship, the ruler of this world (Satan), and the condemnation to sin and death were of a far greater value. In other words, while Jesus may open the eyes of a blind man, this blind man recognizing Jesus as the truth and the way, leading to an opportunity at eternal life was of far more importance. (John 9:1-34; Deut. 18:18; Matt. 15:1-20) This being released will not be fully evidenced until the second coming of Christ. While our eyes are wide open to all that has been revealed within Scripture, we still live in a fallen world and a fallen condition, but we draw comfort in our hope that Jesus has given us.

1 Peter 3:15 Updated American Standard Version (UASV)

[15] but sanctify Christ as Lord in your hearts, always being prepared to make a defense[134] to anyone who asks you for a reason for the hope that is in you; yet do it with gentleness and respect;

Yes, our imperfect and human weaknesses can be a barrier in our work as an evangelist, but it can be overcome, as we will shortly see.

---

[133] There are three main reasons for Jesus coming to earth. First, he came to bear witness to the truth about God. (John 18:37) Second, he came to suffer for us, leaving us an example, so that you might follow in his steps. (1 Pet. 2:21) Third, he did not come to be served, but to serve, and to give his soul a ransom for many. (Matt. 20:28; Rom. 5:12-21) As is made clear from the above paragraph, Jesus had many sub-accomplishments that went with these three main reasons for coming. For example, while he came to offer his souls as a ransom sacrifice for all, one of the results was a releasing of those who accepted that ransom from condemnation to sin and death.

[134] Or *argument*; or *explanation*

Being aware of our imperfections and all that they entail is the only thing that will save us from the second greatest obstacle.

The Second Obstacle to Our Being an Effective Evangelist

The **second greatest obstacle** is the **world of humankind that is alienated from God**. Its ruler, Satan, designs this world to cater to our fallen flesh. The spirit of this world comes from Satan himself, and if breathed in for too long, we will begin to adopt the same mindset, the same thinking, attitude, conduct, and speech that is opposite of God. This poisonous air will paralyze us quite quickly if we entertain it either by thinking on it, or worse still, engaging in it. – 1 Corinthians 2:11-16

1 Peter 4:3-4 Updated American Standard Version (UASV)

3 For the time that has passed by is sufficient for doing the will of the Gentiles, living in sensuality, lusts, drunkenness, orgies, drinking parties, and lawless idolatry. **4** With respect to this that you do not run with them into the same flood of debauchery, and they malign you;

This spirit of the world or rather the mental disposition of those alienated from God breeds a spirit of disobedience and rebellion that is contrary to God's will and purpose, his standards and values. This spirit is demonic and alienated from our Creator and is under the influence of the ruler of the world, namely, Satan (2 Cor. 4:3-4) Satan's world caters to our fallen flesh, placing these ones at odds with God. As we can see from the desires of the flesh from above (sinful and selfish), it runs counter to the fruitage of the Spirit. Just as being aware of our imperfections and all that they entail is of paramount importance, so too is our being aware of those who are alienated from God. The first two obstacles are what our third obstacle uses against us, hoping that we will fall away, abandon, or tire out, so as to not finish the race of life.

The Third Obstacle to Our Being an Effective Evangelist

The **third greatest obstacle** is **Satan the Devil and his demon army**. Yes, they are so powerful that one demon could kill hundreds of thousands of humans in very short order. That is why true Christians receive a hedge placed around them by God, protecting them from Satan and the demons. Yes, God's servants receive special protection from this powerful force. (Job 1-2) The only way to weaken that protection is to violate your conscience repeatedly, toy with demonic activities, like horror movies, rap and heavy metal music, games like the wigi-board or dungeons and dragons. However, we also weaken our protection from God when we repeatedly involve ourselves in the desires of the flesh.

Below is a list by Paul, which covers the prominent works of the flesh, but it is not exhaustive. However, notice that he ends his list with the phrase, "and things like these." If we are carrying out a work of the flesh not listed and we think all is well because it is not on the list, we are sadly mistaken, because Paul includes all works of the flesh with the phrase, "and things like these."

Our human imperfections and the world that caters to them is with us 24/7. True, we can get control over our vessel by putting on the new personality, gaining the mind of Christ, and the help of Holy Spirit. However, it does not take much to drift away (Heb. 2:1), draw away (Heb. 3:12-13), fall away (Heb. 6:6), become sluggish (Heb. 6:12), shrink back from Christian responsibilities (Heb. 10.39), tire out (Heb. 12:3), refuse (Heb. 12:25), or become hardened through deceptive powers (Gal. 6:9). We just need to entertain the wrong thoughts too long, without dismissing them, and then we are on our way. (James 1:14-15) Now, as far as Satan goes, Peter warns us in the extreme, to "be sober; be on the alert. Your adversary the devil walks around like a roaring lion, looking for someone to devour." (1 Pet. 5:8)

Paul also said that we are to,

Ephesians 6:11-12 Updated American Standard Version (UASV)

[11] Put on the full armor of God, so that you will be able to stand firm against the schemes of the devil. [12] For our struggle[135] is not against flesh and blood, but against the rulers, against the powers, against the world-rulers of this darkness, against the wicked spirit forces in the heavenly places.

Threefold Assistance in Our Being an Effective Evangelist

There is a threefold defense against this threefold opposition to our being an effective evangelist for God. **First**, we have **the Word of God**, which should come in the way of literal translations, like the Updated American Standard Version, the New American Standard Bible, and the English Standard Version. God gave us this special revelation to guide us through this wicked time. It has the power to make us stronger spiritually, as well as fortify us to accomplish his will and purposes. The apostle Paul tells us, "For the word of God is living and active and sharper than any two-edged sword, and piercing as far as the division of soul and spirit, of both joints and marrow, and able to judge the thoughts and intentions of the heart." –Hebrews 4:12.

---

[135] Lit., "wrestling."

The Bible should be read daily, in conjunction with CPH's recommended Bible reading program.[136] We also need to use our Bible in all of our religious meetings. If a Scripture is being read, we need to look it up. We also need to use our Bible in our ministry, meaning that we need to formulate texts that can help us to teach others the good news of the Kingdom.

Deuteronomy 17:19 Updated American Standard Version (UASV)

[19] And you shall come to the Levitical priests and to the judge who is in office in those days, and you shall consult them, and they will declare to you the verdict in the case.

As we work our way through the Bible in our Bible reading program, let us not rush, but make sure we understand the author's intended meaning, and how we can apply that in our lives, as well as share it with others. We should be able to see our walking with God, come to life through the historical accounts found all throughout Scripture.

Joshua 1:7-8 Updated American Standard Version (UASV)

[7] Only be strong and very courageous, being careful to do according to all the law that Moses my servant commanded you; do not turn from it to the right or to the left, so that you may have success wherever you go. [8] This Book of the Law shall not depart from your mouth, but you shall meditate on it day and night, so that you may be careful to do according to all that is written in it; for then you will make your way prosperous, and then you will have good success.

Below in Psalm 1:1-3, you will notice in verse 1 that there is a progression of intimacy through walking in the counsel of the wicked, to standing with sinners, to sitting with scoffers. Each level is a sign of spending more time with, being more deeply involved. We should not be involved with any of these three because this would never be in harmony with a Christian, who is walking with God. After that, the Psalmist in verse 2 helps us to appreciate where our delight is found, the law of Jehovah, to which we read and study in a meditative way, day and night, which simply means on a regular basis. Truly, verse 3 helps us to appreciate the result of avoiding certain ones and cultivating a love for God's Word, endurance and a strong spiritual health. If we follow the counsel of verses 1-2, we will be able to weather any storm that may come upon us. Think, this is but three verses out of over 31,000 verses, which offer us the very knowledge of God.

---

[136] http://www.christianpublishers.org/the-new-bible-study

Psalm 1:1-3 Updated American Standard Version (UASV)

¹ Blessed is the man
    who walks not in the counsel of the wicked,
nor stands in the way of sinners,
    nor sits in the seat of scoffers;
² but his delight is in the law of Jehovah,
    and on his law he meditates day and night.

³ He is like a tree
    planted by streams of water
that yields its fruit in its season,
    and its leaf does not wither.
In all that he does, he prospers.

Second, along with God's Word, are some of the best **Bible study tools** as well as the **Christian congregation**. Paul tells the Ephesians, "Look carefully then how you walk, not as unwise but as wise, making the best use of the time, because the days are evil." (Eph. 5:15-16) Moreover, the Apostle Paul exhorted "let us consider how to stir up one another to love and good works, not neglecting to meet together, as is the habit of some, but encouraging one another, and all the more as you see the Day drawing near." (Heb. 10:24-25) We need to have a personal Bible study for at least thirty minutes a day, every day of the week. Moreover, we need to prepare for the Christian meetings, so as to participate in them, whether it be answering at the Bible study classes or looking up Scripture and taking notes at those with lectures.

Third, we have to be effectively sharing God's Word with others. It is our sharing offensively and defensively that will keep us in battle mode, always prepared to defend the hope that we have, always taking in the very knowledge of God on a more deeper level, the every Word that is Spirit inspired, meaning always taking in and applying Spirit inspired, inerrant Word of God. The apostle Paul told the Galatians that if we can walk by the 'walk by the Spirit, we will not carry out the desire of the flesh.' How are we to walk by the Spirit? We do so by taking the Spirit inspired Word into our minds so that we are inundated mentally by it, so that it becomes our way of thinking, and to do otherwise would trigger a warning from our Christian conscience.

Galatians 5:16-26 Updated American Standard Version (UASV)

¹⁶ But I say, walk by the Spirit, and you will not carry out the desire of the flesh. ¹⁷ For the desires of the flesh are against the Spirit, and the desires of the Spirit are against flesh, for these are opposed to each other, so that you may not do the things you want to do. ¹⁸ But if you are led by the Spirit, you are not under the law. ¹⁹ Now the works of the flesh

143

are evident, which are: sexual immorality, impurity, sensuality, [20] idolatry, sorcery, enmity, strife, jealousy, fits of anger, rivalries, dissensions, divisions, [21] envy, drunkenness, orgies, and things like these. I warn you, as I warned you before, that those who do such things will not inherit the kingdom of God. [22] But the fruit of the Spirit is love, joy, peace, patience, kindness, goodness, faithfulness, [23] gentleness, self-control; against such things there is no law. [24] And those who belong to Christ Jesus have crucified the flesh with its passions and desires.

[25] If we live by the Spirit, let us also walk by the Spirit. [26] Let us not become conceited, provoking one another, envying one another.

Those who follow the flesh will reap the results of such a course by having unattractive fruits. On the other hand, those who follow the lead of the Spirit will have fruitage that is attractive and beneficial for themselves, family, congregation, friends, and neighbors. One thing that we have to realize by looking at other related texts is, these fruits are not the results of our efforts, but rather they are the consequence of having an active faith in Christ, which makes us receptive to them. In addition, it is the fruitage of the Spirit, which is going to sustain us through a lifetime of proclaiming the good news, teaching the Word and making disciples.

While there are many enemies against or in opposition to our walking with God aright, the greatest is our own human imperfection, followed the world of humankind that is alienated from God, as well as Satan the Devil and his demon army. So too, many things can keep us spiritually strong, but the most effective are the Word of God (preparing for Christian meetings and personal study), regular attendance and participation at Christian meetings, followed by effectively sharing our faith.

Therefore, we must trust in God by applying his Word with conviction in our lives, especially in being bold as we go about sharing the Word in these difficult times, just as was true of the apostle Paul and Barnabas in the first century. As these two, brought the Word of God to Iconium, their evangelism created a sharp division of feelings, thoughts and some opposition. On this, Kenneth O. Gangel writes, "As in Pisidian Antioch, the opposition came not from Gentiles but from unbelieving Jews. Luke uses poignant language to describe what happened—stirring up the Gentiles, the Jews **poisoned their minds**, literally 'caused their minds to think evil.' Not only against Paul and Barnabas but against all believers there (**the brothers**). This time, rather than shaking off the dust of the city, Paul and Barnabas evidently decided that the persecution actually gave them a good reason to stay a **considerable time** in Iconium. They spoke boldly for the Lord (Luke surely intends us to understand "Jesus" here), and he confirmed the message through miracles (*semeia kai terata*).

All this took place in Galatia, so we can understand this ministry in light of the Galatian letter. There Paul tells us that these mighty works of the Spirit certified that God approved his gospel (Gal. 3:4–5). Luke uses an interesting phrase–**the message of his grace**–to describe the gospel. The linking of the message with the accompanying miracle reminds us of Hebrews 2:1–4. Signs and wonders in Acts remind us of the transitional nature of this book. Barnhouse puts it well:"

> These signs and wonders were specially given to the apostles and early Christian church workers because there was no written New Testament as yet. Not a line of the New Testament had been written at this point, and there was no solid authority to which the apostles could point and say, "See, we're preaching truth. You can check it in the Word of God!" There was no completed Word of God. So God enabled the apostles to perform wonders and signs to authenticate their ministry, but these wonders and signs would fade as God's Word came into being (Barnhouse, 126).[137]

We must remember as the United States of America, the last bastion of religious freedom on earth fades into an atheistic, socialist country, opposition to our work, as evangelists will grow, as we draw ever closer to the second coming of Christ. Nevertheless, just know that "this gospel of the kingdom will be proclaimed in the whole inhabited earth for a testimony to all the nations, and then the end will come." (Matt. 24:14, LEB) Each of us can do our part by evangelizing our communities, making sure everyone has an opportunity to hear, knowing that as the end draws near almost none will listen.

Rejection Will Be the Norm

Jesus, the greatest evangelist, to have ever live preached to and taught tens of thousands, yet only a few hundred responded. The second greatest evangelist would be the apostle Paul. While it is true he set up congregations all over the then known world; nevertheless, only a fraction of the people he spoke to and taught accepted the truths he shared. For example, what kind of receptions did Paul receive when he preached in Athens? Luke tells us,

Acts 17:18-20 Updated American Standard Version (UASV)

[18] And certain ones of the Epicurean and Stoic philosophers were conversing with him. Some were saying, "What would this idle babbler

---

[137] Kenneth O. Gangel, *Acts*, vol. 5, Holman New Testament Commentary (Nashville, TN: Broadman & Holman Publishers, 1998), 231.

wish to say?" Others, "He seems to be a proclaimer of strange deities," because he was preaching Jesus and the resurrection. [19] And they took him and brought him to the Areopagus, saying, "May we know what this new teaching is that you are presenting? [20] For you are bringing some strange things to our ears; so we want to know what these things mean."

We must understand that true conservative Christianity's greatest enemy is within, namely, liberal and moderate Christianity. We were clearly told by Jesus to be no part of the world, yet liberal Christianity is nine-part world and one-part, Christian. On the other hand, moderate Christian scholars and church leaders are casting doubt on the Scriptures with their historical-critical method of biblical interpretation. The world and liberal Christian views the few remaining conservative Christians as relics of the past, knuckle-dragging Neanderthals, who refuse to adjust their grammatical-historical interpretation of God's Word with the times. It is imperative that we realize that the good news of the kingdom and all other Bible truths is repulsive to the world and so the media are certainly going to be in opposition to us. It seems now that the liberal progressive United States government is following in the footsteps off the liberal European governments as well as Canada and Australia, by suppressing religious freedom for conservative Christianity, while giving more freedom to Islam. As a result, most that we will witness to will have heard a very biased, heretical interpretation of what the Bible says and they will prejudge us and reject God's Word outright, with only a handful listening a little further before making a decision. Even then, that handful who listen a little further, most of them will mock the message in the end. This leaves us but a fraction of that handful, which will be won over by the truth. This is why we must understand well what we are sharing; otherwise, how else will we find those select few? Lastly, keep in mind those who reject the biblical truths are rejecting Christ not us, so let us not personalize it. – Acts 17:32-34; Matthew 12:30

Start Off By Building Rapport

If we are to reach the hearts of those select few that are receptive to biblical truths, we need to start by building rapport. When a complete stranger approaches us, we automatically have subconscious questions or thoughts going through our minds. We sigh, thinking, what do they want? Is this going to be some sales or marketing pitch? What do they want me to buy? Thus, when we begin a conversation with a person that we have never met before, we need to begin by putting their minds to rest by answering who we are and our intentions. How are we to do this? We can follow Jesus example, who said, "As you enter the house, greet it." Of course, we do not greet the house per se, but rather those who live in the house. If the persons there are receptive, our blessing will remain with them, but if they were unreceptive, we leave with our blessing of peace. – Matthew 10:12-13.

What is meant by the translation that is more literal "let your peace come upon it [i.e., the persons of the house]"? It means that as we share the good news with others, our hope is to share the peace that we have found with all with whom we speak. In other words, the moment that we begin speaking, we want them to sense the Christ like personality that we project. Even today, the Jews greet people with "Peace be with you" or "Peace" ("Shalom aleichem" or "Shalom" in Hebrew. Of course, we do not need to follow that example, but our intention should be the same, to put the person at ease, so they will be more receptive the biblical truths that we wish to share. If we introduce ourselves with our personal name, and where we are from, it will evidence that we are local. Therefore, we might say, "hello, I am David and this is John, we are out sharing an important biblical message with our neighbors." We might add that while our biblical message these days is a bit apologetic (defending the Word of God and the Christian faith), we are not apologetic, as though we are embarrassed or ashamed of being out sharing God's message. – Mark 8:38.

Sadly, many are embarrassed to be seen talking with people carrying Bibles, so we need to be respectful of others. Jesus, although being a Jew, witnessed to Samaritans, people who were viewed by Jews as nothing more than dogs in the street. Therefore, most Samaritans would be very hesitant to be caught talking to a Jew. Therefore, Jesus was very discreet in his approach at talking with the Samaritan woman at the well. He made sure the apostles were away before the conversation was to take place, and chose a time of the day when the more prominent people would not be coming to draw water. Jesus was compassionate in his teaching of others. (John 4:5-30) Therefore, if we are witnessing on the streets, we do not want to be like those screaming doomsday comments, shaking their Bible around, trying to shame those who pass by. These ones are doing nothing more than drawing attention to themselves, not God.

Once we have introduced ourselves, made known we too are local, and have stated our purpose, we need to find common ground as quickly as possible. We need to identify with them on some level. We could talk about things that matter. We might start with, "I like to get your insight on something ..." Here we can fill in the blank. First, everyone likes to share what he or she thinks. Make sure it is something in the news.

"I like to get your insight on something, 'what do you think of those who have illegally come into America?"

"I like to get your insight on something, 'what do you think the solution to this ISIS terrorist group?'"

"I like to get your insight on something, 'what do you believe is causing this extreme wickedness in the world today?'"

"I like to get your insight on something, how do you feel about Christian business owners, who refuse to make a wedding cake for same-sex couples?'"

"I like to get your insight on 1 John 4:8, which reads, 'God is love.' "Would you agree that the pain, suffering, old age and death, not to mention the wickedness of today, make it difficult to believe in a loving God?"

"I like to get your insight on something, "it would seem that everyone wants peace, why do you think we still have wars?'"

"I like to get your insight on something, "science has certainly improved our living conditions, but do you think it will ever get to the point of helping humans live forever?'"

"I like to get your insight on something, 'police officers have been called into question of late, do you believe the work they do has been covered well by the media?'"

What has been suggested in the above is only a start. What further can we do to reach those receptive ones before the end comes as Jesus put it? Moreover, what qualities are needed that will make us more effective in our sharing of the good news? The next chapters will address this and more.

Exercise

This week, find three opportunities at introducing yourself to a stranger as a Christian and share just one Scripture, Romans 12:17-18, asking them 'How can the counsel given here be applied in our dealings with neighbors?'

Review Questions

- What are some of the aspects involved in a person's accepting the Good News?

- How can nervousness and embarrassment be conquered in our witnessing to others?

- What should we try to accomplish when we introduce ourselves for the purpose of witnessing to another?

- How can Jesus and Paul's example help us in our approach to others?

CHAPTER 10 Effective Evangelism Leading to More Disciples

Ephesians 4:11-12 Updated American Standard Version (UASV)

¹¹ ["and he gave gifts to men."] ... And he gave some as apostles, and some as prophets, and some as evangelists, and some as shepherds **and teachers**, ¹² for the equipping of the holy ones or the work of ministry, to the building up of the body of Christ;

Jesus was not one who chose to live alone and to have little or no social contact. Rather, his ministry was just the opposite, i.e., his being very involved with the people. If we were to read the four Gospel accounts, we would find Jesus always engaging with the people. As he traveled throughout Judea and Galilee, he observed the state of his people, the Israelites under the supervision of the Jewish leaders, this moving him emotionally, as he felt a deep compassion for them. Do we feel the same for the people we meet in our daily lives or see on the news?

Matthew 9:35-38 Updated American Standard Version (ASV)

³⁵ And Jesus went throughout all the cities and villages, teaching in their synagogues and proclaiming the gospel of the kingdom and healing every disease and every affliction.

³⁶ When he saw the crowds, he had compassion for them, because they were harassed and scattered, like sheep without a shepherd. ³⁷ Then he said to his disciples, "The harvest is plentiful, but the workers are few. ³⁸ Therefore, beg the Master of the harvest to send out workers into his harvest."

Without causing offense, but reflecting honestly, when was the last time our church was involved in evangelizing our community? Does our church have a program that teaches its members how to contend earnestly for the faith? Does our church have a program that teaches its members how to defend God's Word? Does our church have a program that teaches its members how to reason from the Scriptures? Does our church have a program that teaches its members how to explain and prove what is doctrinally accurate? Does our church have a program that teaches its members to be prepared to make a defense to anyone who asks you for a reason for the hope that is in us? Once we have these skills, do our church leaders and members use them to evangelize our community effectively on the streets, door to door, a phone ministry of calling people, and the like? Does any of the churches in our community do any of these things in a major way, or even in a small way?

As was true of Christ, all Christians are responsible for some basic evangelism, i.e., planting seeds of truth and watering any seeds that have been planted. [In the fundamental sense of this word (euaggelistes), this would involve all Christians.] In some cases, it may be that one Christian planted the seed, which was initially rejected, so he was left in a good way because the planter did not try to force the truth down his throat. However, some time later, he faces something in life that moves him to reconsider those seeds and other Christians water what had already been planted. This evangelism can be carried out in all of the methods that are available: informal, house-to-house, street, phone, internet, and the like. What amount of time is invested in our evangelism work is up to each Christian to decide for themselves.

2 Timothy 4:5 Updated American Standard Version (UASV)

⁵ But you, be sober-minded in all things, endure hardship, do the work of an evangelist, fulfill your ministry.

Are the churches of today even slightly carrying out evangelizing work within their communities? Is it enough to have an ad in the phone book, on the radio, or on a website? Is it sufficient to have some special meal occasionally to draw people to the church? Do these special gimmicks really work in the end, or are they momentary and fleeting? The most effective evangelism of a churches own community is that which Jesus and his disciples carry out. They went out into the community, speaking to people face to face, finding those interested in the truth, not a meal. However, we must realize this will take time and effort.

1 Corinthians 3:5-9 Updated American Standard Version (UASV)

⁵ What then is Apollos? And what is Paul? Servants through whom you believed, as the Lord assigned to each. ⁶ I planted, Apollos watered, but God gave the growth. ⁷ So then neither the one who plants nor the one who waters is anything, but only God who gives the growth. ⁸ Now he who plants, and he who waters are one; but each will receive his own reward according to his own labor. ⁹ For we are God's fellow workers; you are God's field, God's building.

What is the process of making disciples, i.e., getting an unbeliever from his unbelief state to the point of accepting Christ as his Savior and being baptized? The above text helps us to appreciate that there are three stages. First, there is the **planting stage**. The unbeliever must initially be introduced to the good news of God's Word. (Matt. 24:14) Second, there is the **watering stage**. If the believer is receptive to biblical truths, it is just a matter of helping him or her to attain an accurate or true knowledge of God's Word. (1 Tim 2:3-4; Rom 10:14) If the unbeliever is skeptical, we must answer questions and resolve doubts. (1 Pet. 3:15; Jude

1:22-23) This can be accomplished by having a one-on-one Bible study with them. Third, there is the **growing stage**. It is God, who grows faith in the unbeliever until he or she becomes a believer. When Paul says, "Neither the one who plants nor the one who waters is anything," does this mean that Stages (1) and (2) are meaningless? Is this suggesting that in the end, it does not matter how we evangelize, to what extent we evangelize, as God is simply going to make it grow regardless? No. The context is within a section of the letter dealing with a split congregation because they were worshipping men like Paul, Barnabas, and Peter. We must not think too much of ourselves, always being humble, but knowing that God uses his servants to facilitate that growth, and he will bless our efforts. Moreover, he is moved at heart that we set aside our mental bent toward evil, our treacherous heart, our fallen flesh, to serve him in this capacity.

In leading a person to salvation, there are about Scriptural five steps, with a couple of sub-steps. These line up well with what Paul had mentioned. **Step one**; they need to obtain an accurate or true knowledge of biblical truth. (1 Tim 2:3-4; Rom 10:14) **Step two**; they must put faith in the biblical truths they have learned, as well as God. (Heb. 11:6) **Step three**; they must repent of their sins. (Ac 17:30-31) **Step four**; they must turn around from their former lifestyle. (Ac 3:19) **Step five**, they must be moved by their love for God, to dedicate their life to him in a personal and private prayer. (Matt. 16:24; 22:37) Finally, they must **(a)** be baptized as a public display of their private dedication (Matt. 28:19-20; Ac 2:38) and **(b)** they must continue to grow in knowledge and live according to those biblical truths. – 1 Peter 2:9; Ephesians 4:22-24; Colossians 3:9-10; Psalm 50:14.

On what Foundation Should Our Evangelism Be Based?

Is our foundation based on the Word of God or on human wisdom? We should consider the counsel that Paul gave his young traveling companion, Timothy. "You, however, continue in the things you have learned and were persuaded to believe, knowing from whom you have learned them, [15] and that from infancy[138] you have known the sacred writings, which are able to make you wise for salvation through trust[139] in Christ Jesus. [16] All Scripture is inspired by God and profitable for teaching,

---

[138] *Brephos* is "the period of time when one is very young–'childhood (probably implying a time when a child is still nursing), infancy." – GELNTBSD

[139] *Pisteuo* is "to believe to the extent of complete trust and reliance—'to believe in, to have confidence in, to have faith in, to trust, faith, trust.' – GELNTBSD

for reproof, for correction, for training in righteousness; **17** so that the man of God may be fully competent, equipped for every good work."

Clearly, when we consider the Gospels, all Jesus said therein comes to about a three to four-hour talk, and he quoted or referred to over 120 Scriptures. Of course, in a three and a half year ministry, Jesus said far more than that, but it gives us insight into how much the Son of God himself depended on Scripture. The apostle Paul is one of the greatest Christian teachers of all time. At a synagogue of the Jews in Thessalonica, "according to Paul's custom, he went to them, and for three Sabbaths **reasoned with them from the Scriptures, explaining and proving** that it was necessary that the Christ had to suffer and rise again from the dead, and saying, 'This Jesus whom I am proclaiming to you is the Christ.'" – Acts 17:1-3.

What was the result of Paul's "reasoned with them from the Scriptures, explaining and proving"? The account says, "Some of them were persuaded and joined Paul and Silas, as did a great many of the devout Greeks and not a few of the leading women." – Acts 17:4.

While we can proclaim and teach anything that is within the Scriptures, what should be our primary message? Since we are to follow in the footsteps of Jesus, we might consider his commission. On one occasion, Jesus "departed and went into a desolate place. And the people sought him and came to him, and they tried to keep him from going away from them. But he said to them, "I must **preach the kingdom of God** to the other cities also, for **I was sent for this purpose**." (Lu 4:43) In fact, in reference to the last days, Jesus said, "And this gospel of the kingdom will be proclaimed in all the inhabited earth[140] as a testimony to all the nations, and then the end will come." – Matthew 24:14.

Returning to the apostle Paul, we see this was an emphasis in his proclaiming and teaching. Here again, Paul "entered the synagogue and for three months **spoke boldly, reasoning** and **persuading** them **about the kingdom of God**. When Paul was in Rome, "they came to him at his lodging in greater numbers; and he **expounded** to them, **testifying about the kingdom of God** and **trying to persuade** them concerning Jesus both from the Law of Moses and from the Prophets, from morning till evening." For two whole years in Rome, Paul was "**proclaiming the kingdom of God** and **teaching** about the Lord Jesus Christ **with all boldness** and without hindrance." – Acts 19:8; 28:23, 31.

---

[140] Or *in the whole world*

We Want to Interest Others in Our Message

Today, the world is very divided by religion, race and nationality just as it was in Jesus' day. (Acts 2:7-11) Even atheism (disbelief in the existence of God) is a religion.[141] Thus, when dealing with the subject of religion, viewpoints vary greatly. Many view religion as a private matter, so they are reluctant to share in such a discussion. We can have a measure of success in engaging such a conversation if we maintain kindness, tact and are adaptable.

On his visit to paganistic, idol-worshiping Athens, Paul set an example of how we can handle such things. Initially, Upon Paul's arriving, "his spirit [mental disposition] was provoked within him as he saw that the city was full of idols." (Ac 17:16) Areopagus is where Paul gave his speech to the Epicurean and Stoic philosophers of Athens. (Acts 17:19, ESV) When he stood up to speak, did Paul begin by attacking their idol worship as being wrong? Note his introduction: "'Men of Athens, **I perceive that in every way you are very religious**. For as I passed along and observed the objects of your worship, I found also an altar with this inscription, 'To the unknown god.' What therefore you worship as unknown, this I proclaim to you.'" (Acts 17:22-23, ESV)

Were these words offensive, so that they would cause his listeners to turn against him or his message? No. He applied the advice he had given the Colossians. He wrote, "Walk in wisdom toward outsiders, making the best use of the time. Let your speech always be gracious, seasoned with salt, so that you may know how you ought to answer each person." (Col. 4:5-6) Peter's words would be applicable as well. He wrote, "But in your hearts honor Christ the Lord as holy, always being prepared to make a defense to anyone who asks you for a reason for the hope that is in you; yet do it with gentleness and respect." (1 Pet 3:15, ESV) Yes, Paul's words were gracious, seasoned with salt, and spoken with gentleness and respect.

The form of worship these Athenians were carrying out was worthless and offensive in God's eyes. Imagine if Paul had started his

---

[141] One might ask, 'how is that possible?' Well, before answering that, here is what atheist.org has to say, "**Atheism** is not a belief system nor is it a **religion**. While there are some **religions** that are atheistic (certain sects of Buddhism, for example), that does not mean that **atheism is a religion**." One can argue that atheism is not a belief system, but that does not make it so. One aspect of a religion is, "a set of strongly-held beliefs, values, and attitudes that somebody lives by." Clearly atheism has strongly-held beliefs, values, and attitudes that they not only live by but they herald throughout the earth on billboards, radio and televisions stations, documentaries, movies, newspapers and anywhere they can be heard. In fact, one could argue that they are more evangelistic than Christianity. Some of their beliefs are humanism, secularism, empiricism, rationalism, and many more.

speech by saying their form of worship was worthless and offensive. While true, he would have alienated them from the start. His objective was to proclaim the kingdom message, which he did by finding common ground. Paul too was very religious, and he used this common ground to transition into what he wanted to say about the one and only true God. In fact, he even quoted a former Greek philosopher and a Greek poet in his address. This is not to say he aligned himself with Greek philosophy, but the few short words that he quoted were correct and bought him even more common ground. After informing them about God, Paul spoke on the resurrection hope. Now when they heard of the resurrection of the dead, some mocked. But others said, "We will hear you again about this." What was the result? "So Paul went out from their midst. But some men joined him and believed, among whom also were Dionysius the Areopagite and a woman named Damaris and others with them." – Acts 17:22-32.

How can we follow the example of the apostle Paul today? First, we should be observant to our surrounding. The way a person dresses, the jewelry that they wear, things in their home, might indicate that they too are religious. Moreover, we want to know what offends certain groups. For example, we had said that even atheism is a religion by definition, which is true. However, they would find such a thought not as common ground, but rather as offensive. Moreover, remember too that our goal is to share the Gospel, as well as other biblical truths, so moments trying to garner rapport should not extend into lengthy social discussions. Therefore, we are looking for noncontroversial introductions, common ground, making a smooth, almost imperceptible transition from common ground to the Word of God. Our intention is not to end up in a theological debate. Nevertheless, if it ends up that the listener takes us into the realms of a doctrinal discussion, there is nothing wrong with talking about what he or she wants to talk about. It may be that they have an unbiblical view of a particular doctrine, which can afford us the opportunity at respectfully, kindly, and lovingly overturning any false reasoning, without turning it into a debate.

Returning to Jesus, we know that he had conviction about carrying out the commission that the Father had given him, in the most simplistic way possible. Anyone or any environment did not trouble him as he spoke on the coming kingdom of God, whether the situation was favorable or unfavorable. He could talk with folks in the privacy of their home, before a few dozen on the streets of a town, or before thousands on the side of a mountain. He was able to do so without notes, without a Bible in hand, yet quote and paraphrase Scripture at will. Even though he was the king of the coming kingdom, the Son of God (perfect human and divine), the people felt as though he was one of them, which made him

154

approachable. He was able to speak on things like fishing, shepherding, farming, so that they knew he was one of them, as a carpenter's son. While his illustrations were very deep subject matter, he would use down to earth language and would explain further to those not understanding, but whose hearts were receptive. We want to possess these same qualities as we go about evangelizing in our communities. – Matthew 4:18-25; 13:1-33; Luke 5:1-3.

How to Reach the Listener's Heart

In the skeptical modern day world, the Bible is seldom readily accepted. The atheism of today is very evangelistic in the spread of their antigod and anti-Christianity message. They publish their message in every forum possible. The schools are filled with unbeliever teachers and professors and have been so for a couple of generations now. Therefore, if the Christian is to read the heart and mind of the modern day unbeliever, he or she will have to defend the Bible and the faith first, through apologetics, also known as preevangelism. As we have already discussed, apologetics is a branch of study that is concerned with proving the truth of God's Word and the Christian faith. This means more time than just one conversation, even a few, as well as careful study if we are to overturn or debunk all of the misinformation these ones have been influenced or affected by from the Bible critic's message, as well as being raised in a liberal-progressive world. One way to accomplish this, is by having a one on one Bible study with them, over an extended period, say one hour on one day a week. This way many subjects and questions can be covered. Right now, this author is working on such a Bible study book that can be used for just this purpose, which should be published by the end of 2015. The title and subtitle are **THE EVANGELISM STUDY TOOL Basic Bible Doctrines of the Christian Faith**. The cover and book description can be found at the end of this publication.

We can turn to Jesus once more, seeking to understand just how he taught one's in his day. Let us take a moment to read the following texts, to see if we can notice the way Jesus is teaching.

Luke 6:9, 32-34, 39-42 Updated American Standard Version (UASV)

⁹ And Jesus said to them, "I ask you, is it lawful on the Sabbath to do good or to do harm, to save life or to destroy it?" ³² If you love those who love you, what credit is that to you? For even sinners love those who love them. ³³ And If you do good to those who do good to you, what credit is that to you? For even sinners do the same. ³⁴ And if you lend to those from whom you expect to receive, what credit is that to

you? Even sinners lend to sinners in order to receive back the same amount. 39 And He also spoke a parable to them: "A blind man cannot guide a blind man, can he? Will they not both fall into a pit? 40 A disciple is not above his teacher, but everyone when he is fully trained will be like his teacher. 41 Why do you look at the speck that is in your brother's eye, but do not notice the log that is in your own eye? 42 Or how can you say to your brother, 'Brother, let me take out the speck that is in your eye,' when you yourself do not see the log that is in your own eye? You hypocrite, first take the log out of your own eye, and then you will see clearly to take out the speck that is in your brother's eye.

You will notice that Jesus asked questions that would enable his listeners to discern the will of God in certain matters, which we can simply refer to them as discerning question. Discerning questions can help our listeners to examine things in light of Scripture. We can use these questions to reach both their minds and hearts. The above discerning questions by Jesus forced his listeners to determine if they truly wanted to be his followers. – Matthew 13:10-17; Mark 8:34-38

The beauty of THE EVANGELISM STUDY TOOL Basic Bible Doctrines of the Christian Faith is that it has review questions at the end of each chapter. These questions are a great teaching tool, which will allow our Bible student to express themselves in their own words. In other words, they would prepare for our visit by highlighting the answers to the question, looking up Scriptures. However, at the study with us, they would not just read the answers off the page; rather, they would give the answers in their own words. This will allow us as the teacher to discern if they fully understood the material. It is important to realize that knowledge of God that directs one to the path of salvation must be based on an accurate understanding of what the Bible authors meant, with our student being able reason and explain the Scriptures, not offer mere speculation.

Person's We Bring to Christ are His Disciples

The apostle Paul viewed the many thousands of people that he brought to Christ as his spiritual children, but never his disciples. An example is that warning that he offered the elders at the congregation in Ephesus. He said, "Pay careful attention to yourselves and to all the flock, in which the Holy Spirit has made you overseers, to care for the congregation of God, which he obtained with the blood of his own Son.[142] I know that after my departure fierce wolves will come in among you, not sparing the flock; and from among your own selves men will

---

[142] Lit with the blood of his Own.

arise, speaking twisted things, to draw away **the disciples** after them. Therefore be alert, remembering that for three years I did not cease night and day to admonish every one with tears." (Ac 20:28-31) Notice that Paul did not have a problem reminding them that it was he, who had slaved night and day as he brought them into and up in the Christian faith. However, he did not say, "to draw away **my** **disciples** after them," but rather "to draw away **the** **disciples** after them," which the disciples is a reference to Jesus' disciples. The same is true today, if we bring people from unbeliever to a believer, they become a disciple of Jesus Christ.

Let us look at how Paul reacted on an earlier occasion when the people of Lystra were seeking to treat them like gods. "They tore their garments and rushed out into the crowd, crying out, and saying, 'Men, why are you doing these things? We are also men of the same nature as you, and proclaim the good news to you that you should turn from these vain things[143] to a living God, who made the heaven and the earth and the sea and all that is in them.'" These men, who were given great powers and authority to accomplish great things, yet knowing very well where they received those great powers and authority, meaning it is only by means of that received power and authority they were able to accomplish those great things. Paul and Barnabas were not seeking credit, as they knew it was only by means of God that these things were accomplished. While it is true that Paul did suggest that Christians imitate him, but only as he imitated Christ. Nevertheless, he was not seeking disciples, but rather to give God the glory, not himself. – 1 Corinthians 3:6, 7; 11:1.

In time, the ones that we have helped to find the path of salvation, they too will seek to share the good news of the kingdom. As Jesus said, "The good person out of the good treasure of his heart produces good ... for out of the abundance of the heart his mouth speaks." (Lu 6:45, ESV) With such good news, it cannot be contained but bubbles forth like a geyser. Just as we used this book and others like it, to enable us to be effective teachers of the good news of the kingdom, we can help Jesus' disciples to acquire those same skills, i.e., disciples making disciples.

Exercise

This week, find three opportunities at introducing yourself to a stranger as a Christian and share just one Scripture, 2 Timothy 4:3-4, asking 'what kind of teachers are churches looking for today?' 'Why do you think that most have lost interest in Christianity today?'

---

[143] I.e. idols

Review Questions

- What must our churches we do if we are to be effective in our preaching and teaching?

- What is the process in making disciples, i.e., getting an unbeliever from his unbelief state to the point of accepting Christ as his Savior and being baptized?

- On what Foundation Should Our Evangelism Be Based?

- How can we interest others in our message?

- How can we reach the listener's heart?

- If we are used by God to bring a person to the road of salvation, whose disciple is he or she?

CHAPTER 11 Helping Others to Accept Biblical Truths

Acts 26:28 Updated American Standard Version (UASV)

[28] And Agrippa said to Paul, "In a short time **you will persuade me** to become a Christian."

Paul before Festus and Agrippa

Let us look at the events surrounding this statement by Agrippa. For this, we will look at *Holman Concise Bible Commentary* by David S. Dockery.

> *Festus Pressured by the Jews (25:1–5).* Felix[144] was removed from office for mismanaging an incident of conflict between the Jews and Gentiles of Caesarea. He was succeeded by Porcius Festus.[145] On his first visit to Jerusalem, the new governor was approached by the Jewish leaders concerning Paul. Planning another ambush, they urged Festus to bring him to Jerusalem for a trial.
>
> *Paul's Appeal to Caesar (25:6–12).* Paul's accusers came to Caesarea and brought unsubstantiated charges against him. Paul denied them all, but Festus wished to pacify the Jews. Unaware of the danger to Paul in Jerusalem, he suggested that they hold a trial there. All too aware of the danger in Jerusalem, Paul resorted to the one legal recourse he had that would insure against his being taken there for trial. He took the matter out of Festus's hands by exercising his rights as a Roman citizen to a trial before Caesar. Festus consulted with his advisers and agreed to process the appeal.
>
> *Festus's Conversation with Agrippa (25:13–22).* Agrippa II ruled over only several small territories, but he had the title "King of the Jews," which gave him several prerogatives, the most significant of which was the appointment of the high priest. He lived with his half-sister Bernice, the source of much scandal. Festus used the opportunity of a visit from Agrippa to

---

[144] **FELIX** was the procurator of the Roman Province of Judea at the time Paul the apostle visited Jerusalem for the last time and was arrested there (Acts 23:24). He held Paul prisoner for two years.

[145] **FESTUS** was the successor of Felix as the Roman Province procurator of Judea (Acts 24:27).

see if the Jewish king might cast some light on the charges against Paul. Festus would need to draw up formal charges against Paul in connection with the appeal to the Roman emperor.

Paul's Address before Agrippa: the Setting (25:23–27). The hearing before Agrippa occurred with great ceremony because of the presence of the king. Festus opened with a brief reference to the Jewish accusations against Paul. He expressed his hope that Agrippa could help him draw up formal charges. He also stated his own opinion about Paul's innocence of any capital offenses.

Paul's Address before Agrippa: The Speech (26:1–23). Agrippa requested Paul to respond. Paul moved quickly to the main issue—the Jewish messianic hope, which was fulfilled in Christ and confirmed by His resurrection. Paul followed with his personal testimony. He pointed to his former zeal as a persecutor of Christians. He told of his conversion in an account very similar to that before the Jewish crowd (22:6–16) and Luke's initial narration (9:1–19). Since his hearers now were primarily Gentile, he dwelt at some length on his call to witness to the Gentiles. Paul concluded with a summary of the gospel for which he was on trial: in accordance with the Scriptures, Christ died and rose to bring light and life to Jew and Gentile alike.

Paul's Appeal to Agrippa (26:24–29). At the mention of the resurrection, Festus interrupted, accusing Paul of madness. Like the Athenian intellectuals, the idea of the resurrection was foolishness to him. Paul did not back off. He turned to Agrippa and asked the king if he were not aware of the Christians. He pointed out that what had happened in Christ was not hidden but occurred fully in the open for all to see. Did Agrippa not believe the prophets? If he did, he too would believe in Christ, for they all pointed to Christ. The king responded tragically, asking Paul if he intended to convert him to Christ with so brief a witness (v. 28). Bold and persistent, Paul insisted that he would wish for *all* those present to become followers of Christ. (Dockery 1998, page 535)

This writer agrees with every word of Dockery until he reached the comments by King Agrippa. Here is Paul standing in the palace of the governor, before a group of men, which included a very important ruler of the Roman Empire. King Agrippa turned to Paul and said, "You are permitted to speak for yourself;" then Paul stretched out his hand and proceeded to make his defense, offering many insight thoughts, to the point that an extraordinary thing takes place. Agrippa says, "In a short time you will persuade me to become a Christian." This was not King Agrippa responding in a provoked way because he was offended that Paul believed he could convert him to Christ in so brief a time. No, rather, it was Paul's skillful defense; the Word of God that is living and active influenced King Agrippa. (Heb. 4:12) We are going to take a moment to evaluate Paul's defense, to see just why he was so effective. (1) We should note that Agrippa said Paul was persuasive. (2) He was skillful in his use of God's Word, using the most significant evangelism tool we have.

Skillfully Persuading Others

In the book of Acts, we find the Greek term (root *peitho*) for persuade or persuasion used many times in reference to the apostle Paul. (Ac 18:4; 19:8; 26:28; 28:23) How does this relate to our sharing of the good news today?

The Greek root of persuade at 18:4 and our theme text 26:28 *peitho* is in the active voice, which "signifies 'to apply persuasion, to prevail upon or win over, to persuade,' bringing about a change of mind by the influence of reason or moral considerations." (Vine 1996, Volume 2, Page 469) Moreover, *peitho* intransitively[146] in the perfect and pluperfect active means, "to have confidence, trust," and is rendered "to trust." (Vine 1996, Volume 2, Page 647) What does all of this mean? If we are to persuade another to accept biblical truths, i.e., to win them over, actually changing their mind, they must have confidence that what we are saying is true, namely, they must trust us and the biblical message that we are sharing is true. With today's unbelievers, it will not be enough to read from the Bible, as most do not believe the Bible to be the Word of God, but rather, they believe it to be the word of infallible men, which to them is full of errors and contradictions.[147] Therefore, the unbeliever is not going to accept and believe biblical truths and then act upon them. That is why we need to be prepared to defend and establish the truth of God's Word as inspired and inerrant. – 2 Timothy 3:14-15.

How are we as Christian apologists supposed to convince a person that does not believe in God that God is a real person, who does not

---

[146] Intransitively describes a verb, or the use of a verb, without a direct object, e.g. the verb "die" in the sentence "He was slowly dying."

[147] OVERCOMING BIBLE DIFFICULTIES: Answers to the So-Called Errors and Contradictions by Edward D. Andrews

http://www.christianpublishers.org/apps/webstore/products/show/6172711

believe the Bible is inspired that the Word of God is the truth, who believes in evolution that God is the Creator of the heavens and the earth, including man? We base our comments on facts, clear, rational thought, sound argument, sensible reasoning, and genuinely sincere appeal. Paul used this approach overturning the false reasoning, to bring about a change of mind in his listeners. Many Christians to make statements of truth but do not provide fact. For example, they might say the Bible was inspired by God, as Holy Spirit moved the men to pen the words, so it is fully inerrant. While all of this is true, it lacks satisfying evidence that it is true. Before delving into how this can be done, let us look at the Bible itself.

While Bible critics, atheists, and agnostics love to take the Bible out of the equation, this is an all too common unfair tactic on their part. The Bible manuscripts are archaeological evidence like any other manuscripts. Let us say that archaeology finds a copy of a manuscript, which the original was clearly penned within 30 – 50 years after the death of Alexander the Great. However, the copy that has been discovered is 200 – 300 years removed from the original. We would never hear of them not using the copy as evidence for the historicity of Alexander. We would never hear of them talking about bias because the author personally knew Alexander. In fact, they would take the information more serious because the author had intimate, first-hand knowledge of Alexander. Lastly, they would never make the argument that the copy being 200 – 300 years removed from the original invalidates its worthiness in establishing the historicity of Alexander. Rather, they would argue that the date is actually very close to the original and is contrary to the normal 400 – 1,000 years of being removed. Now, all of the above possible complaints are what is said about the authors and their four gospels, who wrote about the life and ministry of Jesus Christ. All four authors wrote within 20 – 70 years after the death of Jesus Christ. We have many manuscript copies that date from 30 – 200 years from their originals. The authors were actually disciples of Jesus Christ, who traveled with him for three and a half years. Yet, the Bible critics would say these are not archaeological evidence and should be set aside, and only secular authors can attest to the historicity of Jesus Christ. This is completely unreasonable, and the rule is, we do not attempt to reason with the unreasonable.

Now, the Bible manuscripts are archaeological evidence, and this is where our primary statements should come from. In other words, we use the Bible in making statements and not our personal opinions. In addition, we offer evidence of the truth of Scripture, confirming that it is so. (Pro. 16:23) Of course, initially, we are trying to establish that the Bible is the inspired Word of God and fully inerrant. Many times, the person will have what he or she feels to be Bible errors or contradictions, which supports the contention that the Bible is the word of imperfect man. Therefore, we might simply take them one at a time, asking, "if I can show you facts, clear, rational thought, sound arguments, sensible reasoning that each of your errors and contradictions are not so, will you be willing to accept the truth of Scripture?" Once we have the person to the point of taking the Bible as being the Word of God, we can move onto doctrinal views.

It should also be noted that our job as evangelists is to realize there are many pseudo denominations, which claim to be Christian. Therefore, we are obligated to help them to find the truth within the Scriptures as well. When we are talking about different Bible teachings, that is, on our home territory so to speak, we tend to be more intense in the discussion. We want to avoid such enthusiasm as it may cause us to come off as being unreasonable, as though we are out to mislead the listener. For example, if we are discussing a doctrine that many hold dear, and we make a very frank or straightforward statement, which may very well be true, yet showing no sensitivity or consideration, it is not going to be accepted in the person's mind and heart, regardless if there is much Scriptural support. However, if we show empathy, understanding and concern as we reason with them from the Scriptures, the discussion will be easier to accept, which the person may ponder when alone. Moreover, he or she will likely be open to a future conversation because we have shown him or her respect. – Colossians 4:6.

Persuasion That Reaches the Heart

If we return to the apostle Paul's words in Acts Chapter 26, we will see how he defended himself and the faith. Take note of his introduction. We have to remember that King Agrippa was married to his sister Bernice, an outrage and humiliation among the Jews. Nevertheless, Paul found a way to praise Agrippa. Paul said, "Concerning all the things of which I am accused by the Jews, King Agrippa, I consider myself fortunate that before you I am to make my defense this day; especially because you are an expert in all customs and controversies among the Jews; therefore I beg you to listen to me patiently." – Ac 26:2-3.

First, we notice that Paul respected the office of king, which Agrippa held, calling him "King Agrippa." This demonstrated that Paul respected Agrippa and honored the governing authorities. In fact, two years earlier Paul had written just that to the Roman congregation. He said in his letter, "Let every soul[148] be in subjection to the governing authorities. For there is no authority except by God, and those that exist have been

---

[148] Or *person*

placed[149] by God." In addition, about 3-5 years after Paul's defense before Agrippa, he would write something similar to Timothy. He wrote, "First of all, then, I urge that entreaties and prayers, petitions and thanksgivings, be made on behalf of all men, for kings and all who are in high positions, that we may lead a peaceful and quiet life, godly and dignified in every way." (1 Tim. 2:1-2) Showing the harmony of the Holy Spirit, we add the words of the apostle Peter from his first letter as well. He wrote, "Subject yourselves to every human authority for the sake of the Lord, whether to a king as having supreme authority, or to governors as sent by him to punish those who do wrong and to praise those who do good ... Honor all men. Love the brotherhood. Fear God. Honor the emperor." (1 Pet. 2:13-14, 17) Yes, Paul applied his inspired words himself as he used those words to show respect, giving Agrippa the honor that God had accorded all governing authorities.

Second, we notice that Paul went even further by his noting Agrippa was "an expert in all customs and controversies among the Jews." Paul also stated that he 'considered himself fortunate that before such a wise ruler he was to make his defense.' Paul did not display any smug or superior attitude to his being a Christian, while Agrippa was not. (Phil. 2:3) Just the opposite, Paul begged the king that he might 'listen to him patiently.' What was Paul doing here? He was doing exactly what we need to do in our witnessing to others, namely, establishing an atmosphere in which a critical, possibly hostile, judgmental listener, would be more receptive to the truth. He was developing a base or foundation on which he would build his defense for himself and the faith. We need to follow the example of Paul before Agrippa. No matter who we are speaking with about the Word of God, from the first word to the closing argument, we want to reach the heart of our listener. We can accomplish this by respecting and honoring everyone. This does not mean that we condone any wrongdoing anyone may be involved. We are merely showing sincere interest in his or her individual worldview that can be developed by getting to know their background. – 1 Corinthians 9:20-23.

Using God's Word Skillfully

The apostle Paul sought to motivate those who listened to him so that they would act upon the Gospel. Note his words to the Thessalonians, he writes, "for our gospel did not come to you in word only, but also in power and in the Holy Spirit and with full conviction; just as you know what kind of men we proved to be among you for your sake. And you became imitators of us and of the Lord, for you received

---

[149] Or *established, instituted*

the word in much affliction, with joy inspired by the Holy Spirit, so that you became an example to all the believers in Macedonia and in Achaia." (1 Thess. 1:5-7) Paul not only sought to appeal to the mind, that is, the seat of thought, ideas, and perceptions, but also to heart, namely, the seat of motivation. We return to Paul's defense before King Agrippa, as he handles the Word of God about Moses and the prophets aright. – 2 Timothy 2:15.

Paul was aware the Agrippa was technically a Jew. Therefore, he appealed to Agrippa's knowledge of Judaism. Paul linked his witness in such a way, to deny it was to deny Moses and the prophets. Paul said to all standing there, 'To this day I have had the help that comes from God, and so I stand here testifying both to small and great, saying nothing but what the prophets and Moses said would come to pass. [That is,] the Christ must suffer, and that, by being the first to rise from the dead, he would proclaim light both to the people and to the Gentiles." (Acts 26:22-23) Now, let us look at this exchange to see how Paul not only guides people to the truth but also leads them in such a way, if they reject it, they are rejecting their beliefs or their method of reasoning. Modern day Christian Philosophers and Christian apologists, such as the late Ronald Nash, John M. Frame, John Lennox, Alister McGrath, Sean and Josh McDowell, Ravi Zacharias, Norman L. Geisler and William Lane Craig, among many others, use philosophical arguments to help guide those with college and university degrees into the truth. In logic, reason and philosophy, arguments are used to persuade those who also use logic, reason and philosophy for accepting a conclusion. In other words, they use their own tools against these from higher learning, to reject the logic, reason and philosophical arguments, if sound, is to reject their own tools of the trade.

Acts 26:24 Updated American Standard Version (UASV)

²⁴ And as he was saying these things in his defense, Festus said with a loud voice, "Paul, you are out of your mind; your great learning is turning you to madness."

This statement by Festus really tied the hands of Agrippa. Even still, Paul left him with no means of escape or room to maneuver.

Acts 26:25-26 Updated American Standard Version (UASV)

²⁵ But Paul said, "I am not out of my mind, most excellent Festus, but I am speaking true and rational words. ²⁶ For the king knows about these things, and to him I speak boldly. For I am persuaded that none of these things has escaped his notice, for this has not been done in a corner.

Paul again appeals to Agrippa's vanity, but also his knowledge of Scripture. However, he is also aware that he has just placed Agrippa in a spot. Agrippa was in trouble no matter with whom he sided. If he rejected what Moses and the prophets said, he would be dismissed as a Jewish believer. However, if he said that Paul was correct, he would be viewed as siding with an apostle of Christ Jesus, and making himself a Christian. Moreover, to side with Paul would mean he agreed with the person Festus called, 'out of his mind and had gone mad.' Therefore, Paul did not allow Agrippa to remain in this uncomfortable position for long, so he answered his own question.

Acts 26:27 Updated American Standard Version (UASV)

²⁷ King Agrippa, do you believe the prophets? I know that you believe."

Agrippa saw a great mind at work here, and he could see how effective Paul's reasoning skill was. It moved Agrippa and touched his heart. He did not fear giving Paul a truthful answer, which seems to demonstrate a reciprocation of the same respect and honor that the apostle Paul had shown him.

Acts 26:28 Updated American Standard Version (UASV)

²⁸ And Agrippa said to Paul, "In a short time you will persuade me to become a Christian."

It is true, Agrippa was not moved to become a Christian, but Paul evidenced that "the word of God is living and active and sharper than any two-edged sword, and piercing as far as the division of soul and spirit, of both joints and marrow, and able to judge the thoughts and intentions of the heart." (Heb. 4:12) We should also notice that Paul's defense included both proclamation and persuasion. It is this approach as he "rightly handling the word of truth" which allowed him to bring many congregations of Christians into the fold of Christianity. We see this very thing in his establishing the congregation in Thessalonica.

Acts 17:1-4 Updated American Standard Version (UASV)

¹ Now when they had passed through Amphipolis and Apollonia, they came to Thessalonica, where there was a synagogue of the Jews. ² And according to Paul's custom, he went to them, and for three Sabbaths **reasoned with them from the Scriptures,** ³ **explaining** and **proving** that it was necessary that the Christ had to suffer and rise again from the dead, and saying, "This Jesus whom I am proclaiming to you is the Christ." ⁴ And **some of them were persuaded** and joined Paul and Silas, as did a great many of the devout Greeks and not a few of the leading women.

We can see that Paul was persuasive, as he reasoned with them from the Scriptures, explaining and proving that Jesus was the Christ. In the end, Paul was able to establish one of the earliest Christian congregations. We too must become more skilled in the art of persuasion as we go about sharing the Word of God. If we can, we will find the idea of proclaiming and persuading not so overwhelming, as we too go about adding to the congregation of God.

1 Timothy 2:3-4 Updated American Standard Version (UASV)

³ This is good, and it is acceptable in the sight of God our Savior, ⁴ who desires all men to be saved and to come to an accurate knowledge[150] of truth.

Exercise

This week, find three opportunities at introducing yourself to a stranger as a Christian and share just one Scripture, 1 Peter 5:8, asking them 'How can we know whether Satan really exists?'

Review Questions

- Why was Paul so effective in his defense before King Agrippa?

- How can we skillfully persuade others? (Touch on the Greek word for persuade)

- How can our persuasion appeal to the heart?

- Why is it important that we become effective in using God's Word skillfully?

- What is God's desired toward all men and women?

---

[150] *Epignosis* is a strengthened or intensified form of *gnosis* (*epi*, meaning "additional"), meaning, "true," "real," "full," "complete" or "accurate," depending upon the context. Paul and Peter alone use *epignosis*.

CHAPTER 12 The Reasoning Evangelist

Acts 18:19 Updated American Standard Version (UASV)

¹⁹ And they came to Ephesus, and he left them there, but he himself went into the synagogue and **reasoned with the Jews**.

If someone or a church evangelizes their community, one must be prepared to reason with any culture, and numerous religions, such as the Jewish, Buddhist, Muslim, Hindu, Shinto, Taoism, Confucianism, as well as atheists and agnostics, among others. This can seem overwhelming, but it is not as complicated as it sounds. There are many good Christian books out, which will give you the basics of the major religions in just one book, a chapter on each, and demonstrate how to reason with them.[151]

Reasoning with one means that one uses Scripture, questions and illustrates logically, which causes the listener to think, and get the message in their mind and then in their heart. If someone uses a direct, rigid and unbending approach, one will close off the listener's mind and heart. Meanwhile, a reasoning manner uses logical thinking to get results or draw conclusions, which inspires discussions. The evangelist's desire must be for the conversation to weigh on the mind and heart of the listener, moving them to contemplate the discussion, so they are anxious to engage the evangelist in future discussions.

While it is true that the truth will set one free, it must be received in such a way to do just that. Think of a conversation in terms of two people tossing a ball back and forth. If one tosses the ball so that it is catchable, the odds are better that it will be caught and received well. If one throws a ball like you are trying to take the other person's head off, it will not be received well, and few will catch it. Some people's beliefs remain dear to them, and to have them bluntly disclosed may not be received well.

James 3:17 Updated American Standard Version (UASV)

¹⁷ But the wisdom from above is first pure, then peaceable, gentle, **reasonable**, full of mercy and good fruits, impartial, without hypocrisy.

James says that "the wisdom from above is ... open to reason." The Greek word here *eupeithes* pertaining to being easily persuaded, with the implication of being open to reason or willing to listen—'one who is easily persuaded, open to reason.'"[152] Some translations render it

---

[151] http://astore.amazon.com/bibletranslat-20/detail/0736920846

[152] Johannes P. Louw and Eugene Albert Nida, *Greek-English Lexicon of the New Testament: Based on Semantic Domains* (New York: United Bible Societies, 1996), 422.

"obedient," (LEB) "gentle" (HCSB, NASB). On this verse, the Baker New Testament Commentary says, "Another attribute of wisdom is consideration. The person who is 'considerate' is fair, **reasonable**, gentle in all his deliberations. He quietly gathers all the facts before he gives his opinion. He refrains from placing himself first and always considers others better than himself (Phil. 2:3; 4:5)."[153] (Bold mine.)

Acts 17:1-3 Updated American Standard Version (UASV)

1 Now when they had passed through Amphipolis and Apollonia, they came to Thessalonica, where there was a synagogue of the Jews. 2 And according to Paul's custom, he went to them, and for three Sabbaths **reasoned with them** [the Jews] **from the Scriptures**, 3 explaining and proving that it was necessary that the Christ had to suffer and rise again from the dead, and saying, "This Jesus whom I am proclaiming to you is the Christ."

The Apostle Paul studied under the renowned Pharisee Gamaliel, who was the grandson of Hillel the Elder (110 B.C.E.[154] – 10 C.E.), the founder of one of the two schools within Judaism. Paul describes himself as "circumcised on the eighth day, of the people of Israel, of the tribe of Benjamin, a Hebrew of Hebrews; as to the law, a Pharisee; as to zeal, a persecutor of the church; as to righteousness under the law, blameless." (Phil 3:5-6) He also states, "But whatever gain I had, I counted as loss for the sake of Christ. Indeed, I count everything as loss because of the surpassing worth of knowing Christ Jesus my Lord. For his sake I have suffered the loss of all things and count them as rubbish, in order that I may gain Christ" (Phil. 3:7-8) Thus, we note that Paul "reasoned from the Scriptures" when he talked to the Jews in the Jewish Synagogue. His listeners accepted the Hebrew Scriptures as an authority. Therefore, he began his witness with what they knew and accepted.

However, at Acts 17:22-31, we find Paul witnessing to the Greeks at the Areopagus in Athens; he did not turn to the Scriptures as his source of reasoning. "As in Lystra, so in Athens, it would have been futile to begin with the God of the Old Testament choosing a certain people, sending prophets, and promising a Messiah. That was a message for synagogues or Jews gathering by a river. Paul began with the doctrine of God and launched his message with a local object lesson, the altar to *agnosto theo*.

---

[153] Simon J. Kistemaker and William Hendriksen, Exposition of James and the Epistles of John, vol. 14, New Testament Commentary (Grand Rapids: Baker Book House, 1953–2001), 122.

[154] B.C.E. years ran down toward zero, although the Romans had no zero, and C.E. years ran up from zero. (100, 10, 3, 2, 1 ◀B.C.E. | C.E.▶ 1, 2, 3, 10, and 100)

[unknown god][155] In "Establishing rapport with his Athenian audience, Paul quotes verbatim from two Greek poets. Both writers extol the virtues of the god Zeus ... By quoting these poets, Paul is not intimating that he agrees with the pagan setting in which the citations flourished. Rather, he uses the words to fit his Christian teaching. From the Old Testament, he is able to draw the evidence that man derives his life, activity, and being from God (Job 12:10; Dan. 5:23)."[156] Paul used information familiar to his audience. Then, he took that information and made a case for the Creator, the only true God. On this, Bible scholar John B. Polhill writes,

> As so often in the speeches of Acts, Paul began his discourse with a point of contact with his audience. In this case it was the altars Paul had already observed in the city (v. 16). One in particular caught his attention. It was dedicated "TO AN UNKNOWN GOD." This gave him the perfect launching pad for his presentation of monotheism to the polytheistic and pantheistic Athenians. Piety had no doubt led the Athenians to erect such an altar for fear they might offend some deity of whom they were unaware and had failed to give the proper worship. Paul would now proclaim a God who was unknown to them. In fact, this God, totally unknown to them, was the only true divinity that exists.[157]

In the 1950s and 1960s, almost everyone that someone would talk to on the street possessed some knowledge of the Bible. If one said Old or New Testament, they understood. If an evangelist spoke of the apostles, the person knew what that meant. However, today billions have almost no knowledge of the Bible other than the name "Bible," and it is still regarded as a holy book. People who do not recognize the Bible, nor have any knowledge of the Bible, have **some commonalities** with Christians: they want to hope in something better. They see violence, pain and suffering, sickness, old age, and death every day, the same as any Christian. They too want a better life for themselves and their children. Thus, the ability to reason requires finding common ground such as this. Then, open the Scriptures by explaining how we got here, and how there is hope for something better in Jesus Christ. This reasoning might offer

---

[155] Kenneth O. Gangel, *Acts*, vol. 5, Holman New Testament Commentary (Nashville, TN: Broadman & Holman Publishers, 1998), 289.

[156] Simon J. Kistemaker and William Hendriksen, *Exposition of the Acts of the Apostles*, vol. 17, New Testament Commentary (Grand Rapids: Baker Book House, 1953–2001), 636-7.

[157] John B. Polhill, Acts, vol. 26, The New American Commentary (Nashville: Broadman & Holman Publishers, 1995), 371.

them hope that they have not had, or hope that is more real and legitimate than any they have now.

Even those who have a vast knowledge of the Bible, but who are atheists, agnostics or other critics of the Bible, have as their mission in life to evangelizing their message, "God is dead!" In the last 50-60-years, atheists have made many disciples for themselves. There are millions of Christians and those from other religions who have become atheists because they have succumbed to the misleading propaganda of the books, videos, movies, websites, television shows, and other tools of the atheistic machine. We certainly must reason from the Scriptures, but with these enemies of the faith there must be more.

God is rational, and he has created us as rational beings. The Bible urges us to give the reason for the hope that is in us (1 Pet. 3:15, NIV). Indeed, Jesus declared that the greatest commandment is: "You shall love the Lord your God with all ... your mind" (Matt. 22:37). The Apostle Paul added, "whatever is true, ... think on ...° (Phil. 4:8). Thinking is not an option for a Christian; it is an imperative.[158]

Ephesians 6:17 Updated American Standard Version (UASV)

[17] And take the helmet of salvation, and the sword of the Spirit, which is **the word of God.**

2 Corinthians 10:4-5 Updated American Standard Version (UASV)

[4] For the weapons of our warfare are not of the flesh[159] but powerful to God for destroying strongholds.[160] [5] We are destroying speculations and every lofty thing raised up against the knowledge of God, and we are taking every thought captive to the obedience of Christ,

In Christian spiritual warfare, the mind can help us wield "the sword of the Spirit, which is the word of God." However, a blank mind will do us no good. If we have not taken in knowledge of God, there is nothing to recall that can be used in the battle for the Bible that lies ahead. Do we want to free those brothers and sisters by the tens of millions, who have been taken captive by the world? One could have the absolute best sword ever made, but if he or she does not have the skills to use it, the sword is worthless to use. My prayer is that all Christians will awaken from their stupor and join the fight that some have taken up these last

---

[158] Ronald M. Brooks; Norman L. Geisler. *Come, Let Us Reason: An Introduction to Logical Thinking* (Kindle Locations 12-14). Kindle Edition.

[159] That is *merely human*

[160] That is *tearing down false arguments*

few decades. May they make use of the mind that God gave them, to use their power of reason, to equip themselves to defend the faith?

Believers live in a time when certain critics of Christianity have abandoned all delicacy and decorum in debate. Rather than sticking to rational, carefully reasoned arguments, they have taken off the gloves to launch angry, sarcastic, and sloppily argued attacks. They lob their rhetorical grenades in hopes of creating the (incorrect) impression that belief in God is for intellectual lightweights who believe ridiculous, incoherent doctrines and who also are opposed to all scientific endeavor and discovery. These objectors are writing books—indeed, best sellers—that tend to be more bluster and emotion than substance. New Atheists such as Richard Dawkins, Sam Harris, and Christopher Hitchens characterize this tone of debate. On another front, textual critic Bart Ehrman misleadingly raises doubts about the New Testament text's reliability, while novelist Dan Brown's Da Vinci Code and Jesus Seminar cofounder John Dominic Crossan mislead many into thinking that various Gnostic Gospels give us more reliable information about the historical Jesus than do the canonical Gospels. From various angles the public is being told that we cannot trust what the New Testament, and the Gospels in particular, say about Jesus of Nazareth.[161]

It is no longer a matter of preaching on Sunday and hoping that some new faces show up. It is as though most Christians hide in their fort, the Church, watching as lives are taken one by one, hoping that the enemy will go away or that they can hold out until the return of Christ. The enemy takes one life after the other, and few are lifting themselves to join the fight. There is a need for a knowledge of the deeper things of God's Word, a need to reason with the enemy and his victims, so that they can see that our message is more important, why it involves them as well, and just how they are going to be affected personally. If Christians prove effective in this, we must have the ability to reason with the enemy, defeating him on the battlefield, not hiding in the church waiting for dawn. One of the leading apologists of the 20th and 21st centuries, Dr. William Lane Craig, wrote the following:

This is a war we cannot afford to lose. The great Princeton theologian J. Gresham Machen warned on the eve of the fundamentalist controversy that if the church loses the

---

[161] Craig, William Lane; Copan, Paul (2009-08-01). *Contending with Christianity's Critics: Answering New Atheists and Other Objectors* (Kindle Locations 47-56). B&H Publishing. Kindle Edition.

intellectual battle in one generation, then evangelism would become immeasurably more difficult in the next:

> False ideas are the greatest obstacles to the reception of the gospel. We may preach with all the fervor of a reformer and yet succeed only in winning a straggler here and there, if we permit the whole collective thought of the nation or of the world to be controlled by ideas which, by the resistless force of logic, prevent Christianity from being regarded as anything more than a harmless delusion. Under such circumstances, what God desires us to do is to destroy the obstacle at its root.[162]

The root of the obstacle is to be found in the university, and it is there that it must be attacked. Unfortunately, Machen's warning went unheeded, and biblical Christianity retreated into the intellectual closets of Fundamentalism, from which it has only recently begun to re-emerge. The war is not yet lost, and it is one which we must not lose: souls of men and women hang in the balance. So what are evangelicals doing to win this war?[163]

Biblical and Christian Apologetics

When "false apostles, deceitful workmen, disguising themselves as apostles of Christ" caused trouble in the congregation in Corinth, the Apostle Paul wrote that under such circumstances, we are to *tear down their arguments* and *take every thought captive.* (2 Cor. 10:4, 5; 11:13–15) All who present critical arguments against God's Word, or contrary to it, can have their arguments overturned by the Christian who is able and ready to defend that Word in mildness. (2 Tim. 2:24–26)

1 Peter 3:15 Updated American Standard Version (UASV)

[15] but sanctify Christ as Lord in your hearts, always being prepared to make a defense[164] to anyone who asks you for a reason for the hope that is in you; yet do it with gentleness and respect;

Peter says that we must be prepared to make a *defense.* The Greek word behind the English "defense" is *apologia,* which is actually a legal

---

[162] J. Gresham Machen, *"Christianity and Culture,"* Princeton Theological Review 11 (1913): 7.

.

[163] Craig, William Lane; Copan, Paul (2007-10-01). Passionate Conviction: Modern Discourses on Christian Apologetics (pp. 8-9). B&H Publishing. Kindle Edition.

[164] Or *argument*; or *explanation*

term that refers to the defense of a defendant in court. Our English apologetics is just what Peter spoke of, having the ability to give a reason to any who may challenge us, or to answer those who are not challenging us but who have honest questions that deserve to be answered.

2 Timothy 2:24-26 Updated American Standard Version (UASV)

24 For a slave of the Lord does not need to fight, but needs to be kind to all, qualified to teach, showing restraint when wronged **25** with gentleness correcting those who are in opposition, if perhaps God may grant them repentance leading to accurate knowledge[165] [*epignosis*] of the truth, **26** and they may come to their senses and escape from the snare of the devil, having been held captive by him to do his will.

Look at the Greek word (*epignosis*) behind the English "knowledge" from above. "It is more intensive than *gnosis*, knowledge, because it expresses a more thorough participation in the acquiring of knowledge on the part of the learner."[166] The requirement of all of the Lord's servants is that they be able to teach, but not in a quarrelsome way, but in a way to correct opponents with mildness. Why? The purpose of it all is that by God, yet through the Christian teacher, one may come to repentance and begin taking in an accurate knowledge of the truth.

Whatever its relation to the gospel, apologetics is an extremely important enterprise that can profoundly impact unbelievers and be used as the tool that clears the way to faith in Jesus Christ. (Bold his.)

Some Christians see apologetics as pre-evangelism; it is not the gospel, but it prepares the soil for the gospel.[167] Others make no such distinction, seeing apologetics, theology, philosophy, and evangelism as deeply entwined facets of the gospel.[168] Whatever its relation to the gospel, apologetics **is an extremely important enterprise that can profoundly impact unbelievers** and be used as the tool that clears the way to faith in Jesus Christ. (Bold mine.)

For some, though, apologetics is not discovered until after making a

---

[165] *Epignosis* is a strengthened or intensified form of *gnosis* (*epi*, meaning "additional"), meaning, "true," "real," "full," "complete" or "accurate," depending upon the context. Paul and Peter alone use *epignosis*.

[166] Spiros Zodhiates, *The Complete Word Study Dictionary: New Testament*, Electronic ed. (Chattanooga, TN: AMG Publishers, 2000, c1992, c1993), S. G1922.

[167] Norman Geisler and Ron Brooks, *When Skeptics Ask* (Grand Rapids: Baker Books, 1996), 11.

[168] Greg Bahnsen, *Van Til Apologetic* (Phillipsburg, NJ: Presbyterian and Reformed, 1998), 43.

profession of faith. Many Christians did not come to believe as a result of investigating the Bible's authority, the evidence for the resurrection, or as a response to the philosophical arguments for God's existence. They responded to the proclamation of the gospel. Although these people have reasons for their belief, they are deeply personal reasons that often do not make sense to unbelievers. **They know the truth but are not necessarily equipped to share or articulate the truth in a way that is understandable** to those who have questions about their faith. It is quite possible to believe something is true without having a proper understanding of it or the ability to articulate it. (Bold mine.)

Christians who believe but do not know why are often insecure and comfortable only around other Christians. Defensiveness can quickly surface when challenges arise on issues of faith, morality, and truth because of a lack of information regarding the rational grounds for Christianity. At its worst, this can lead to either a fortress mentality or a belligerent faith, precisely the opposite of the Great Commission Jesus gave in Matthew 28:19–20. The Christian's charge is not to withdraw from the world and lead an insular life. Rather, we must be engaged in the culture, to be salt and light.

The solution to this problem requires believers to become informed in doctrine, the history of their faith, philosophy, logic, and other disciplines as they relate to Christianity. Believers must know the facts, arguments and theology and understand how to employ them in a way that will effectively engage the culture. Believers need Christian apologetics. One of the first tasks of Christian apologetics provides information. A number of widely held assumptions about Christianity can be easily challenged with a little information. This is even true for persons who are generally well-educated.[169]

The ability to reason with others will take time, practice and patience. For example, if someone reasons with others successfully, that person must be reasonable. In a discussion about the historicity about Jesus, a believer knows the other person denying the existence of Jesus is wrong. Moreover, believers possess a truckload of evidence to support this position. However, it is best sometimes to not unload the truck by dumping the entire load at a listener's feet in one conversation, or in one breath. Being reasonable does not mean that a believer compromises the truth because he or she does not unload on the listener.

---

[169] Powell, Doug (2006-07-01). *Holman QuickSource Guide to Christian Apologetics* (Holman Quicksource Guides) (p. 6-7). B&H Publishing. Kindle Edition.

The other person will likely make many wrong statements in the conversation, and we should let most of them go unchallenged; rather, focus on a handful of the most crucial pieces of evidence and do not get lost by refuting every wrong statement. He may make bold condemnatory statements about many Christian beliefs, but remain calm and do not make a big deal of those statements. Listen carefully to the other person, and stay within the boundaries of the evidence in the conversation. For example, in a conversation on the historicity of Jesus when the listener states, "The New Testament manuscripts were completely corrupted in the copying process for a millennium, to the point that we do not even have the supposed Word of God." The evidence for the historicity of Jesus rests in the first and the second century, so it would be a fool's errand to get into an extensive side subject about the restoration of the New Testament text, which took place over the centuries that followed that millennium. There will be another day to talk about the history of the Greek New Testament, but today focus on the historicity of Jesus Christ.

God has given humanity free will, meaning each human has the right to choose, even if that choice is unwise. Believers have the assignment of proclaiming "the good news of the kingdom," as well as "making disciples" of redeemable humankind. Therefore, we must not pressure, coerce, or force people to accept the truth of that "Good News." Christians have an obligation to reason with them by overturning their false reasoning, in the attempt that being used by God to save some.

Joshua 24:15 Updated American Standard Version (UASV)

[15] "And if it is evil in your eyes to serve Jehovah, choose this day whom you will serve, whether the gods your fathers served in the region beyond the River, or the gods of the Amorites in whose land you dwell. But as for me and my house, we will serve Jehovah."

Effective Questions

Luke 10:25 Updated American Standard Version (UASV)

[25] And behold, a lawyer[170] stood up to put him to the test, saying, "Teacher, what shall I do to inherit eternal life?"

A historical note here, "a lawyer" or "an expert in the law," (HCSB), is not a lawyer, as we would think of one today. A lawyer was someone that was an expert in the Mosaic Law. However, this person would have the same level of education on the law as a lawyer would today, many

---

[170] That is an expert in the Mosaic Law

years of study and memorization. Thus, this man would certainly know the answer to such an easy question as the one he asked. Now, if a believer is asked an easy Bible question, we might be tempted to just offer an answer. Certainly, as the wisest man ever to live, Jesus could have easily answered the question. Instead, Jesus wanted the man to offer his own thoughts, insights or understanding. However, Jesus knew this man was "an expert in the law," and he recognized the man would have had a certain perspective on his question. In other words, the man was not asked because he did not know. Thus, Jesus asked,

Luke 10:26 Updated American Standard Version (UASV)

²⁶ And he said to him, "What is written in the Law? How do you read it?"

The man answered correctly,

Luke 10:27 Updated American Standard Version (UASV)

²⁷ He answered: Love the Lord your God with all your heart, with all your soul, with all your strength, and with all your mind; and your neighbor as yourself.

The conversation could have ended there. Again, the man knew the Mosaic Law, but seemingly wanted to see if Jesus would agree with what he knew. Jesus gratified him, letting him feel good, by giving the correct answer. Jesus responded:

Luke 10:28-29 Updated American Standard Version (UASV)

²⁸ "You've answered correctly," He told him. "Do this and you will live."

²⁹ But wanting to justify himself, he asked Jesus, "And who is my neighbor?"

Here again, the man looks to prove himself righteous, and Jesus could have just stated the truth, even the Samaritan. However, Jesus having insight into the setting, the Jews detested the Samaritans; so, while he would give the correct answer it would be disputed in a long, back-and-forth conversation, and the Jews who listened would have sided with the man. Thus Jesus boxed the man into giving an answer by having him reason on an illustration.

Luke 10:30-37 Updated American Standard Version (UASV)

The Parable of the Good Samaritan

³⁰ Jesus replied and said, "A man was going down from Jerusalem to Jericho, and he fell among robbers, who stripped him and laid blows

upon and departed, leaving him half dead. ³¹ Now by coincidence a certain priest was going down on that road, and when he saw him, he passed by on the other side. ³² Likewise a Levite also, when he came to the place and saw him, passed by on the other side. ³³ But a Samaritan, who was on a journey, came upon him; and when he saw him, he felt compassion, ³⁴ and came to him and bandaged up his wounds, pouring oil and wine on them; and he put him on his own beast, and brought him to an inn and took care of him. ³⁵ And on the next day, he took out two denarii[171] and gave them to the innkeeper, and said, "Take care of him; and whatever more you spend, when I return I will repay you.'

³⁶ Which of these three, do you think, proved to be a neighbor to the man who fell among the robbers?"

³⁷ And he said, "The one who showed mercy toward him." Then Jesus said to him, "Go and do likewise."

This man had to admit the elite in the Jewish religion, the priest and the Levite, had not been neighborly, but the Samaritan proved to be a good neighbor. Jesus moved him to reason out a new way of viewing exactly what "neighbor" meant. Instead of letting the man walk him into a long debate, Jesus made the man do all of the reasoning in the conversation, and moved him to admit something no Jew would ever utter,[172] as well as grasp a whole new understanding of what it meant to be a neighbor. Jesus took this approach because the circumstances called for it. However, on another occasion, a scribe, another expert in the law, asked him the same question and on that occasion, he chose to give the direct answer. (Mark 12:28-31) Circumstances vary.

What lessons can we take in from the example that Luke provided us? **(1)** Jesus **used Scriptures** initially to answer the man's question. **(2)** Jesus proved **perceptive** enough to **take notice** of the man's agenda. **(3)** Jesus did not simply answer the easy Bible question, but **shifted the responsibility** through **a question** of his own, by asking the man how he understood the law, giving him a chance to express himself. **(4)** Jesus **complimented** the man for a discerning with the correct answer. **(5)** Jesus made sure the man and the listeners **made the connection** between the initial question and the Scriptures. **(6)** Jesus **used an illustration** that was able to **reach the heart and mind**, where the answer was kept to the forefront. **(7)** Jesus moved the man **to reason** beyond his basic understanding of a neighbor.

---

[171] The denarius was equivalent to a day's wages for a laborer

[172] Notice the hatred ran so deep between Jews and Samaritans that when asked by Jesus, who was the neighbor I the illustration, he did not say, the Samaritan, but rather, "the one who …"

Explaining and Proving

Acts 17:2-3 Updated American Standard Version (UASV)

² And according to Paul's custom, he went to them, and for three Sabbaths reasoned with them from the Scriptures, ³ **explaining and proving** that it was necessary that the Christ had to suffer and rise again from the dead, and saying, "This Jesus whom I am proclaiming to you is the Christ."

We have already spoken about the fact that Paul reasoned from the Scriptures. However, he did more, as one can see from the above, that he explained, proved, and made an application. Many times you may read a Scripture to someone, and while it seems straightforward enough to you, but the listener fails to see the point. You may do as we mentioned previously, highlighting a word or phrase or a part of the text, and then explaining the verse. We are doing that with Acts 17:2-3, as we highlight **explaining and proving**. You could also offer to walk them through the context like we also did previously with Acts 17:2-3, when we backed up to verse 1, to show that Paul reasoned from the Scriptures because he talked with Jews in the Synagogue, people, who would be familiar with the Hebrew Scriptures. Another option is offering them additional texts that support the one the evangelist used. If the listener does not grasp the text and the explanation, add an illustration like Jesus did over forty times. Then again, asking the right questions might get the listener to reason on things further.

The person who makes a claim has the burden of proving it by offering sound arguments. As stated previously, one must give evidence that reasonably satisfies any statements that made. Never be troubled over a listener asking for proof, as they have every right to do so. By thorough arguments, rational reasoning, and serious appeal, you can overturn any faulty reasoning of the one who is listening.

When the person an evangelist talks to makes a claim, he is then responsible to prove it. He may begin with a wrong proposition that forms the basis of his argument or from which a conclusion is drawn. Maybe, the sources he is using are biased, which can be pointed out to him. Additionally, you might note that part of his argument is superficial. Moreover, many times, if you know the issue well enough, one may notice the listener offering evidence, yet failing to mention any facts that support his argument. Then again, one might point out that his evidence is not really evidence at all, but simply appeals to emotion, as opposed to reasons.

For Christians, the Bible is primary evidence, while other sources are secondary. However, as already stated, the majority of people no longer hold the Bible as an authority. Therefore, the evangelist must be versatile by being able to use both in conjunction with each other, or depend on the secondary evidence, until the listener begins to see the value and reasonableness of Scripture. For example, one may use the universe as evidence of a Creator.

> The universe reveals God's existence. It is evident that the things which constituted the universe could not have made themselves (see Cosmological Argument). There must be "a first cause eternally existing, of a nature totally different to any material existence we know of, and by the power of which all things exist; and this first cause, man calls God" (ibid. 26; cf. 28). Paine also argued from motion. Since the universe consists of matter that cannot move itself, the origin of the rotation of the planets is impossible unless there exists an external first cause which set them in motion. This First Cause must be God (Aldridge, 6:17). He also argued from design (*see* Teleological Argument). Since the "work of man's hands is a proof of the existence of man," and since a watch is "positive evidence of the existence of a watch-maker," then "in like manner the creation is evidence to our reason and our senses of the existence of a Creator" (*Complete Works*, 310).[173]

If an evangelist witnesses to someone who sees the Bible as the word of man, not the word of God, how should one respond? Seeing what Bible scholars such as Dr. Norman L. Geisler or Dr. Gleason L. Archer have to say may be helpful. However, the evidence is not the fact that they are saying it is the Word of God, but rather what they provide as evidence. Support from someone that agrees with you, especially the like of the above scholars is evidence, but it is low-level evidence. One could use science by starting with what Scripture says first, and then use science to confirm or give support.

Regardless of whatever one attempt to prove, the level of evidence required will be dependent on the person to whom you are talking. The average person may not need more than Scriptural proof, with some outside sources. Some may require a tremendous amount of evidence. A few people will not be convinced as no amount of evidence is going to persuade them to change their mind. Their heart and mind is closed to the light of truth. They are mentally blind. The evidence that will satisfy this

---

[173] Norman L. Geisler, *Baker Encyclopedia of Christian Apologetics*, Baker Reference Library (Grand Rapids, MI: Baker Books, 1999), 573.

person may not be enough to satisfy another. Therefore, one must pay attention to the listener to meet their needs sufficiently.

One must appreciate that the evangelist seeks redeemable ones, one's who hearts and minds are open to truth or can be opened to the truth. Believers do not seek people with closed minds and hearts. Jesus said, "Do not give dogs what is holy, and do not throw your pearls before pigs, lest they trample them underfoot and turn to attack you." (Matt 7:6) One will recognize these after some experience in witnessing. One sign is they present a claim that that the Bible is the word of man, not God, and is full of errors and contradictions. Ask for one, and they provide one that they feel is the nail in the coffin of the Bible. The evangelist offers them a reasonable answer, which they cannot dispute, so they act as though they never raised that issue and go on to another. The evangelist then gives them a reasonable answer to that one, which they cannot dispute. Instead of showing appreciation that they have received answers to these supposed issues, they act as though they never asked and move on to the next. Therefore, the pattern will continue as they do not seek answers, as they have a closed mind and heart.

How can any Christian obtain or develop more fully the skill to reason from the Scriptures? Several things are important: **(1)** One must have an accurate understanding of what the Scriptures say and mean. One must prepare for Christian meetings that one regularly attends. Regular personal Bible study, every day is necessary. **(2)** One must have a complete picture of the history of the Bible from Genesis 1:1 to Revelation 22:21. This can be accomplished by studying through a book like the *Holman Bible Handbook* by David S. Dockery (Nov 2, 1992). **(3)** One must have an understanding of Bible difficulties, which run from Genesis 1:1 to Revelation 22:21. This can be accomplished by studying through *The Big Book of Bible Difficulties: Clear and Concise Answers from Genesis to Revelation* by Norman L. Geisler and Thomas Howe (Jun 1, 2008). **(4)** One must have an accurate understanding of Bible backgrounds of Bible times. One can accomplish this by studying through *Nelson's New Illustrated Bible Manners And Customs How The People Of The Bible Really Lived* by Vos, Howard (May 15, 1999). **(5)** One definitely must understand how to interpret the Bible correctly. This can be accomplished by studying through *INTERPRETING THE BIBLE Christian Publishing House Bible Study Tool* by Edward D. Andrews (June, 2016). **(6)** One must meditate and ponder the things he or she learns, mentally exploring the information from various perspectives, and appreciating the significance of them. **(7)** While one studies the Bible, look for not only clarifications of Scriptures but also Scriptural whys and wherefores for those clarifications. **(8)** As one studies, consider how to use the verses, to explain biblical truths to different groups of people. **(9)** Contemplate and ponder what kind of illustrations might be used to make biblical points.

Exercise

Using several Scriptures, effectively communicate why _____ is not biblical or is biblical. The director or assistant direct will assign a subject.

Review Questions

• Who must we be prepared to reason with? What does reasoning mean? How is a conversation like tossing a ball? What did James mean by "open to reason?" Explain how Paul reasoned differently, depending on his audience. How did Paul use information differently, depending on his audience? How do we find commonalities with people who have no knowledge of the Bible or those who do not recognize its authority?

• Why is the Christian mind so important in spiritual warfare? Why are Bible critics getting away with offering misleading and false information? If Christians are to be effective in evangelism work, what ability do they need? Where are most Christians hiding today? What ideas are the greatest obstacle to one receiving the gospel?

• What are biblical and Christian apologetics? What does the Greek word (*epignosis*) mean? Christians who come into the faith outside of apologetics usually are unable to do what? Christians who believe but do not know why are often what? The solution to this problem is for believers to do what? When reasoning with others, why should we not unload all of the evidence?

• How did Jesus use questions effectively? What lessons can one take in from the example that Luke provides in 28:25-37? Based on Paul in Acts 17, what more is needed than reasoning from the Scriptures? Who is responsible for providing the evidence? If the Bible critic makes a claim, what weaknesses may the evangelist look for being used? If one witnesses to someone who sees the Bible as the word of man, not the word of God, how should one respond? Why will someone have to provide different levels of evidence? How can any Christian obtain or fully develop the skill to reason from the Scriptures?

CHAPTER 13 Being Prepared to Use God's Word

Colossians 4:17 Updated American Standard Version (UASV)

[17] And say to Archippus, "See that you fulfill the ministry that you have received in the Lord."

Napoleon, *Emperor of the French (1804-1814), 1769-1821*

"The gospel is not a book; it is a living being, with an action, a power, which invades everything that opposes its extension, behold! It is upon this table: This book, surpassing all others. I never omit to read it, and every day with some pleasure."

Isaac Newton, *English mathematician and scientist, 1642-1727*

"We account the scriptures of God to be the most sublime philosophy. I find more sure marks of authenticity in the Bible than in any profane history whatsoever."

President George Washington, *First President of the United States*

"It is impossible to rightly govern the world without God and Bible."

Although many world leaders, powerful men and women, may not have correctly understood much about the Bible, as to correct interpretation, the principles, guidance and direction from our Creator influenced them like no other. What about us as Christians, do we really value the Bible enough that we will buy out the time to understand it better, so as to share it more? Are we able to use the Word of God effectively when sharing it with other? Are we always prepared to talk on the Bible?

Using the Bible to Evangelize

If we are to carry out the great commission of proclaiming, teaching and making disciples (Matt. 24:14; 28:19-20; Ac 1:8), we need to know the Bible well, but also accurately. Let us just briefly touch on the accuracy aspect. The famous, often quoted, frequently misunderstood Philippians 4:13 reads, "I can do all things through Christ who strengthens me." Many take this to mean that through the strengthening of Jesus Christ we can overcome all obstacles or succeed in all things. If we consider it, at the time, Paul penned these words (60-61 C.E.); he had finally made it to Rome. However, this was after he had 'five times received at the hands of the Jews the forty lashes less one. Three times, he was beaten with rods. Once he was stoned. Three times he was shipwrecked, a night and a day he was adrift at sea, and on frequent journeys, in danger from rivers, danger from robbers, danger from my own people, danger from Gentiles, danger in the city, danger in the wilderness, danger at sea, danger from false brothers. Many tames he suffered in toil and hardship, through many a sleepless night, in hunger and thirst, often without food, in cold and exposure.' (2 Cor. 11:24-27) Let us also not forget that he was preparing himself emotionally to be executed for the faith. Does this sound like the strengthening of Jesus Christ he overcame all obstacles or succeed in all things? Hardly, but what Paul is meaning is that through the strengthening of Christ he can steadfastly move forward through and endure through all hardships, even to the point of death by execution. Thus, the verse **does not mean** we overcome obstacles, succeed in all things, but that we steadfastly move forward through, and endure through all hardships.

Sadly, it hurts to pen these words in one book after another, but most Christians by far are biblically illiterate, with most of the fault lying at the feet of the church leadership. Nevertheless, we are just as accountable for any neglect we have shown. Yes, Jesus was the Son of God, divine, and a perfect human, so it is no surprise that he was well acquainted with Scripture. Nevertheless, even at twelve years old, he was able to challenge the Jewish religious leader's erroneous thinking. (Lu 2:40-47) It was not that Jesus, as a baby was just filled with all the knowledge that he had prior to coming to earth, but rather he grew into it. The account says. "The Child continued to grow and become strong, **increasing in wisdom**." (Lu 2:40) Jesus even used the Scriptures to defeat Satan's temptations and lies. (Matt. 4:1-11) We can tell that Jesus had long been reading the Hebrew Old Testament, as he opened a scroll to the exact place he needed to read within the synagogue in Nazareth. (Lu 4:16-21) It was common for him, while speaking to others, to slip easily into using Scripture, as he would say, "It is written," and then he would quote from the Hebrew Scriptures. (Lu 7:27; 19:46; John 2:17) We need to follow his example.

Clearly, the apostle Paul followed Jesus' example, as he quoted and paraphrased hundreds of Scriptures in his fourteen letters, as he went about proclaim and teaching the Word of God. Here again, of course, Paul was inspired, and even his written words are the Word of God as well. When Paul and company "had passed through Amphipolis and Apollonia, they came to Thessalonica, where there was a synagogue of the Jews. And according to Paul's custom, he went to them, and for three Sabbaths **reasoned** with them from the **Scriptures, explaining** and **proving** that it was necessary that the Christ had to suffer and rise again from the dead." (Acts 17:1-3) It seems evident that the Christians in the first-century were able to discuss the Old Testament Scriptures that were available to them. Moreover, as the New Testament books were being penned, the congregations were just as eager to copy and share those books with others, both orally and in written form. This might be why Christians are credited with popularizing the codex if not inventing it because it was easier to find a place within the text.

Apollos Speaks Boldly in Ephesus

The first-century Christian, Apollos, was to talk about God's Word. Each Christian today certainly desires to be able to espouse God and his Word as we are 'always prepared to make a defense[174] to anyone who asks us for a reason for the hope that is in us. (1 Pet. 3:15) We want to always be ready to give an answer from God's Word to sincere questions (Col. 4:6), which is quite rewarding to know we are following in the footsteps of Christ, Paul, Apollos, and the first-century Christians. Our joy grows ever greater as we are able to use God's Word skillfully, efficiently, as we watch the light of understanding grow in the eyes of those with which we speak. Notice Apollos' boldness, how he was fervent in spirit, as he was speaking and teaching the things concerning Jesus accurately.

Acts 18:24-28 Updated American Standard Version (UASV)

24 Now a certain Jew named Apollos, a native of Alexandria, an eloquent man, arrived in Ephesus; and he was well versed in the Scriptures. **25** This man had been orally instructed in the way of the Lord; and being fervent in spirit, he was speaking and teaching accurately the things concerning Jesus, being acquainted only with the baptism of John; **26** and this man began to speak out boldly in the synagogue. But when Priscilla and Aquila heard him, they took him aside and explained to him the way of God more accurately. **27** And when he wanted to go across to Achaia, the brethren encouraged him and wrote to the disciples to welcome him; and when he had arrived, he greatly helped those who had believed through grace, **28** for he powerfully refuted the Jews in public, demonstrating by the Scriptures that Jesus was the Christ.

Helping Spiritually

It is not only our goal to win arguments, to fill heads with knowledge, but also to help people spiritually. Many people that we hope to speak with have had many discussions with Christians over the years. They have read books about God, the Bible, even the Christian faith because they have a spiritual need of which they are unaware. Over these years, they likely have come across aggressive Christians; persons who have beat them with the Bible, and misinformed Christians espousing untruths, not biblical truths. What these now need is a respectful Bible

---

[174] Or *argument*; or *explanation*

discussion where they can get their pent up questions answered by a loving disciple of Christ.

When we come to someone with the Word of God in hand, but also a sincere, loving, Christlike spirit of humility, this adds a persuasive power that he may have never experienced. We want to be sensitive to his experiences with other Christians prior to us, books that they may have read, or relatives they have dealt with, and as we fulfill his spiritual needs by way of God's Word. Even if he is a new Christian, having just come to the faith, he can be prepared to use God's Word as well. At first, he might be shy, timid, or hesitant about sharing God's Word. However, if he regularly prepares for and attends Christian meetings, as well as have a consistent personal Bible study at home daily, it will not be long before he has a deeper knowledge of the Scriptures.

Adapting the Our Message to Our Listeners

Regardless of whom we are speaking to, we can transition to a point of interest, to something they may never have considered.

Maybe we find ourselves talking to a **scientist**.

The Circle of the Earth Hangs on Nothing

Isaiah 40:22 Updated American Standard Version (UASV)

22 It is he who sits above the **circle of the earth**,
    and its inhabitants are like grasshoppers;
who stretches out the heavens like a curtain,
    and spreads them like a tent to dwell in.

More than 2,500 years ago, the prophet Isaiah wrote that the earth is a circle or sphere. First, how would it be possible for Isaiah to know the earth is a circle or sphere, if not from inspiration? Scientific America writes, "As countless photos from space can attest, Earth is round–the "Blue Marble," as astronauts have affectionately dubbed it. Appearances, however, can be deceiving. Planet Earth is not, in fact, perfectly round."[175] Scientifically speaking, the sun is not perfectly, absolutely 100 percent round but in everyday speech, this verse is both acceptable and accurate, when we keep in mind it is written from a human perspective, not from a scientific perspective. Moreover, Isaiah was not discussing astronomy; he was simply making an inspired observation that man came to realize once

---

[175] Charles Q. Choi (April 12, 2007). Scientific America. Strange but True: Earth Is Not Round. Retrieved Monday, August 03, 2015.

http://www.scientificamerican.com/article/earth-is-not-round/

he was in space, looking back at the earth, it is round. See the section about title, "Intended Meaning of Writer."

Job 26:7 Updated American Standard Version (UASV)

7 "He stretches out the north over empty space
and hangs the earth on nothing.

Here the author describes the earth as hanging upon nothing. Many have never heard of the Greek mathematician and astronomer Eratosthenes. He was born in about 276 B.C.E. and received some of his education in Athens, Greece. In 240 B.C., the "Greek astronomer, geographer, mathematician and librarian Eratosthenes calculates the Earth's circumference. His data was rough, but he wasn't far off."[176] While man very early on used their God given intelligence to arrive at some outstanding conclusion that was actually very accurate, we learn two points here. Eratosthenes was a very astute scientist, while Isaiah, who wrote some 500 years earlier, was no scientist at all. Moreover, Moses, who wrote the book of Job over 1,230 years before Eratosthenes, knew that the earth hung upon nothing.

Maybe we find ourselves talking to a **physician**. Today, we know that physical illnesses can be caused by mental factors such as stress, anxiety, anger and so on. The Bible though has long understood this far before modern science. The Bible is all about putting away or getting control over harmful emotions. Certainly, any physician would see that enmities, strife, jealousy, outbursts of anger, disputes, dissensions, factions, envying, and things like these would lead to other health problems. (Gal. 5:20-21, NASB) While, on the other hand, love, joy, peace, patience, kindness, goodness, faithfulness, gentleness, self-control and the like would lead to better health. (Gal. 5:22-23, NASB) Certainly, he would also agree with the proverb, "A joyful heart is good medicine, But a broken spirit dries up the bones." (Pro.17:22, NASB) Moreover, a physician would be intrigued that one of the four Gospel writers, the apostle Paul's close friend and traveling companion, who also penned the historical book of Acts, was spoken of by Paul as, "the beloved physician." – Colossians 4:14.

Maybe we find ourselves talking to a **housewife**. Certainly, she would be interested in how the Word of God views her role as the wife, who manages the home. In fact, the wise man of proverbs knew just how valuable the woman's role is as the caretaker of the home and to find such a one seemed quite difficult in his eyes. He writes, "Who can find a

---

[176] Alfred, Randy (June 19, 2008). "June 19, 240 B.C.E: The Earth Is Round, and It's This Big". Wired. Retrieved Monday, August 03, 2015.

capable wife?" Prov. 31:10, HCSB) A capable wife learns to be skillful at doing a number of different things and cautious and prudent so that her family is well-dressed. (Verses 13, 19, 21, 22) To lessen the family food bill, she may have a garden and shops carefully to keep the costs down. (Verses 14, 16) Clearly, this wife "watches over the activities of her household" and "does not eat the bread of idleness." She works hard, and she capably manages her household's activities. (Verse 27) "She draws on her strength," that is, she has many responsibilities that are physically tasking. (Verse 17) She rises while it is still night and provides food for her household. She sees that her profits are good, and her lamp never goes out at night." (Verses 15, 18) In other words, she has a very long workday, and it is as though her light is always shining the way for her family. Most of all, the capable wife is a spiritual mature. She has reverential fear of displeasing the God she dearly loves, as she radiates deep respect and awe. (Verse 30) Moreover, she also assists her husband in training their children to grow and develop spiritually, morally, mentally and physically. Verse 26 says, "She opens her mouth with wisdom, and the teaching of kindness is on her tongue." Many modern day wives may not even know how God feels about the significant, special and important role the wife plays within the family.

Maybe our Christian children find themselves talking with their **Schoolmates**. Talking about God's Word is not a popular or "cool" thing. Nevertheless, our young ones need to appreciate what an opportunity and privilege they have. First, it should be noted that just being different than most of the school population is speaking volumes. This does not mean that our young ones have to fit the stereotype found in many teen movies or TV shows, where the young Christian teen wears dull clothes, is withdrawn, and infinitely sad. Rather, our teens are bright, happy, fulfilled, outgoing, confident, finding joy in daily life. They are different in that their clothing is fashionable but they do not dress immorally. They are different in that their taste in music is not unwholesome, as they pay careful attention as to their walk with God. They are different in that they honor and respect older ones and people in positions of authority. They are different in that they avoid sexual immorality and other unclean practices of their fellow students. They are different in that their minds are filled with clean, pure thoughts, their conduct is biblically clean. They are different in that they always speak the truth, do not listen to or tell dirty jokes or unclean stories, and do not use bad language. Because of all of these ways that they are clean and pure, our Christian children stand out from other young ones in school and in the neighborhood, and this is one way of sharing the good news. – 1 Peter 1:16; 2:12; 1 Corinthians 6:9-11; 2 Corinthians 6:14-18; Philippians 4:8; Ephesians 4:25, 29, 31; 5:3.

Maybe we find ourselves talking to a **female** working in a male-dominated field or position. Oh, the way women are treated today is as disgraceful in Jesus day. Therefore, females that have had to try to succeed in a male world that has used and abused women of all ages, will likely appreciate how Jesus treated women. Jesus never viewed women as sex objects. The other religious leaders in Jesus' day believed that they could not be in the presence of a woman, as it would only lead to lust. As a result, women were not allowed to talk to men in public, and like Muslim women today, they had to wear a veil in Jesus day. On the contrary, Jesus did not blame the women for the men's inability to control themselves; he advised men to get control over their fleshly desires and to treat women with dignity and respect, as opposed to ostracizing them from society. – Matthew 5:28.

Jesus said to the disciples, "Whoever divorces his wife and marries another commits adultery against her, and if she divorces her husband and marries another, she commits adultery." (Mark 10:11-12) As the *Holman New Testament Commentary: Mark* puts it, "The radicalness is in the words **commits adultery against her**. In Jewish society, a woman could commit adultery against her husband. A man could commit adultery against another man by having relations with that man's wife (Deut. 22:13–29). A man could not, however, commit adultery against his wife. Jesus' proclamation raised the status of women." (Cooper 2000, Page 165) *The Pillar New Testament Commentary: The Gospel according to Mark* says this "is a startling declaration, for in rabbinic understanding a husband's adultery was reckoned against a woman's father or husband, not against the woman herself. Jesus' declaration, however, imputes to women the status of sovereign moral agents." (Edwards 2002, Page 304) What Jesus said about women was so contrary to the Jewish teachings on women that some commentators try to argue that these words by Jesus were not written by Mark, but were added later. This conclusion is absolutely mistaken. Jesus put these Jewish leaders on notice that women were not property, they were not sex objects, but rather they were to be loved, honored and cherished as a compliment to their husbands.

Women in Jesus' day were kept in ignorance, just as is true in Muslim countries today. However, Jesus took the time to teach women. He also encouraged them to offer their thoughts on things. (Luke 10:38-42; John 11:21-27) Jesus cared for women. In the days of Jesus, girls were not valued as much as boys were. On the other hand, Jesus evidenced that the girl's lives were just as important as the boys were. (Mark 5:35, 41, 42; Luke 7:11-15; Luke 13:10-16) In addition, in the days of Jesus, a woman was not viewed as a reliable witness. In fact, in the courts, the woman's testimony was only equal to that of a slave. The first-century Jewish historian, Josephus, advised: "From women let no evidence be accepted, because of the levity and temerity of their sex." Conversely, Jesus had women give the most important testimony in all of human history, to his resurrection. (Matthew 28:1, 8-10) However, because of the long held view of women, their word was not truly taken serious. (Matthew 27:55, 56, 61; Luke 24:10, 11) Nevertheless, by Jesus appearing to the women disciples first, he showed them the great honor and respect that they deserved. – Acts 1:8, 14.

Accurately Handling the Word of Truth

Some will be overwhelmed by the idea of sharing the Word of God with others because they know each person has their own question, concerns worldview, biases, and so on. The Scriptures are so powerful and "is living and active, sharper than any two-edged sword, piercing to the division of soul and of spirit, of joints and of marrow, and discerning the thoughts and intentions of the heart" [of everyone, it touches]. (Heb. 4:12, ESV) Therefore, some realize that it will take time, prolonged efforts to become skillful in using "the sword of the Spirit, which is the word of God." (Eph. 6:17, ESV) This is why the apostle Paul felt that it was necessary to offer young Timothy, who was now in his 30s, who had traveled the then known world with Paul as his traveling companion for 15-years, some parting counsel before his execution. Paul wrote, "Do your best to present yourself to God as one approved, a workman who does not need to be ashamed, rightly handling[177] the word of truth." (2 Tim 2:15) Indeed, we would want to go to our heavenly Father in prayer that we might take in some wisdom.

James 1:5-8 Updated American Standard Version (UASV)

[5] But if any of you lacks wisdom, let him ask of God, who gives to all generously and without reproaching,[178] and it will be given to him. [6] But let him ask in faith, without any doubting, for the one who doubts is like a wave of the sea that is driven and tossed by the wind. [7] For let not that man suppose that he will receive anything from the Lord; [8] he is a double-minded[179] man, unstable in all his ways.

As we can see here, James says that we must "ask in faith, without any doubting." What does he mean? In other words, we must have some evident demonstration that out faith is genuine. If we are praying for more knowledge and wisdom as to sharing the Scriptures; then, we must buy out the time, so we can have some personal Bible study time each

---

[177] Or *accurately handling* the word of truth; *correctly teaching* the word of truth

[178] Without *criticizing*

[179] Or "*indecisive*," i.e., wavering in mind

day, prepare for all the Christian meetings, and develop our communication skills. We will not only find doctrinal truths within the Scriptures, but we will also find truths that help us, as well as those we speak to, cope with every facet of life. As we take in these precious truths, we will be moved to share them with others, to the point that some of our listeners will want to further investigate the Bible for themselves.

Divisions in the Body of Christ

The title of this chapter is Being Prepared to Use God's Word. Let us consider the words of the apostle Paul, followed by the Holman New Testament Commentary on Romans by Kenneth Boa and William Kruidenier.

Romans 10:14-15 Updated American Standard Version (UASV)

[14] How then will they call on him in whom they have not believed? And how are they to believe in him of whom they have never heard? And how will they hear without someone to preach? [15] And how are they to preach unless they are sent? As it is written, "How beautiful are the feet of those who declare good news of good things!"

Calling requires faith. **How ... can they call on the one they have not believed in?** In the Old Testament, calling on the name of the Lord was a metaphor for worship and prayer (Gen. 4:26; 12:8; Ps. 116:4). No one can call out to God who has not believed in him.

Faith requires hearing. **And how can they believe in the one of whom they have not heard?** More than anything else, this question is the crux of all missiological activity since the first century. God has ordained that people have to hear (or read, or otherwise understand the content of) the word of God in order to be saved. One who knows the gospel must communicate it to one who does not know it.

Hearing requires preaching. **And how can they hear without someone preaching to them?** Since no other media except the human voice was of practical value in spreading the gospel in the first century, **preaching** is Paul's method of choice. And yet, in the media-rich day in which we minister, has anything replaced preaching as the most effective way to communicate the gospel? We thank God for the printed page, and even for cutting-edge presentations of the gospel circling the globe on the internet. But it is still the human voice that cracks with passion, the human eye that wells with tears of gratitude, and the human frame that shuffles to the podium, bent from a lifetime of service to the gospel, that reaches the needy human heart most readily. Hearing may not *require* **preaching** in person today, but it always benefits from it. (Boa and Kruidenier 2000, Page 315)

Evangelism is the work of a Christian evangelist, of which all true Christians are obligated to partake to some extent, which seeks to persuade other people to become Christian, especially by sharing the basics of the Gospel, but also the deeper message of biblical truths. Today the Gospel is almost an unknown, so what does the Christian evangelist do? **Preevangelism** is laying a foundation for those who have no knowledge of the Gospel, giving them background information, so that they are able to grasp what they are hearing. The Christian evangelist is preparing their mind and heart so that they will be receptive to the biblical truths. In many ways, this is known as apologetics.

Christian apologetics [Greek: *apologia*, "verbal defense, speech in defense"] is a field of **Christian theology** which endeavors to offer a reasonable and sensible basis for the **Christian faith** , defending the faith against objections. It is reasoning from the Scriptures, explaining and proving, as one instructs in sound doctrine, many times having to overturn false reasoning before he can plant the seeds of truth. It can also be earnestly contending for the faith and saving one from losing their faith, as they have begun to doubt. Moreover, it can involve rebuking those who contradict the truth. It is being prepared to make a defense to anyone who asks the Christian evangelist for a reason for the hope that is in him or her. – Jude 1.3, 21-23; 1 Pet 3.15; Acts 17:2-3; Titus 1:9.

What do we mean by **obligated** and what we mean by **evangelism** are at the heart of the matter and are indeed related to each other.

EVANGELISM: An evangelist is a proclaimer of the gospel or good news, as well as all biblical truths. There are levels of evangelism, which is pictured in first-century Christianity. All Christians evangelized in the first century, but a select few fit the role of a full-time evangelist (Ephesians 4:8, 11-12), like Philip and Timothy.

Both Philip and Timothy are specifically mentioned as evangelizers. (Ac 21:8; 2 Tim. 4:5) Philip was a full-time evangelist after Pentecost, who was sent to the city of Samaria, having great success. An angel even directed Philip to an Ethiopian Eunuch, to share the good news about Christ with him. Because of the Eunuch's already having knowledge of God by way of the Old Testament, Philip was able to help him understand that the Hebrew Scriptures pointed to Christ as the long awaited Messiah. In the end, Philip baptized the Eunuch. Thereafter, the Spirit again sent Philip on a mission, this time to Azotus and all the cities on the way to Caesarea. (Ac 8:5, 12, 14, 26-40) Paul evangelized in many lands, setting up one congregation after another. (2 Cor. 10:13-16) Timothy was an evangelizer or missionary, and Paul placed distinct importance on evangelizing when he gave his parting encouragement to Timothy. – 2 Timothy 4:5; 1 Timothy 1:3.

The office of apostle and evangelist seem to overlap in some areas, but could be distinguished in that apostles traveled and set up congregations, which took evangelizing skills, but also developed the congregations after they were established. The evangelists were more of a missionary, being stationed in certain areas to grow and develop congregations. In addition, if we look at all of the apostles and the evangelists, plus Paul's more than one hundred traveling companions, it seems very unlikely that they could have had Christianity at over one million by the 125 C.E. This was accomplished because all Christians were obligated to carry out some level of evangelism.

OBLIGATED: In the broadest sense of the term for evangelizer, all Christians are obligated to play some role as an evangelist.

- *Basic Evangelism* is planting seeds of truth and watering any seeds that have been planted. [In the basic sense of this word (*euaggelistes*), this would involve all Christians.] In some cases, it may be that one Christian planted the seed, which were initially rejected, so he was left in a good way because the planter did not try to force the truth down his throat. However, later he faces something in life that moves him to reconsider those seeds, and another Christian waters what had already been planted by the first Christian. This evangelism can be carried out in all of the methods that are available: informal, house-to-house, street, phone, internet, and the like. What amount of time is invested in the evangelism work is up to each Christian to decide for themselves.

- *Making Disciples* is having any role in the process of getting an unbeliever from his unbelief state to the point of accepting Christ as his Savior and being baptized. Once the unbeliever has become a believer, he is still developed until he has become strong. Any Christian could potentially carry this one person through all of the developmental stages. On the other hand, it may be that several have some part. It is like a person that specializes in a certain aspect of a job, but all are aware of the other aspects, in case they are called on to carry out that phase. Again, each Christian must decide for themselves what role they are to have, and how much of a role, but should be prepared to fill any role if needed.

- *Part-Time* or Full-Time Evangelist is one who sees this as their calling and chooses to be very involved as an evangelist in their local church and community. They may work part-time to supplement their work as an evangelist. They may be married with children, but they realize their gift is in the field of evangelism. If it were the wife, the husband would work toward supporting her work as an evangelist and vice-versa. If it were a single person, he or she would supplement their work by being employed part-time, but also the church would help as well. This person is well trained in every aspect of bringing one to Christ.

- *Congregation Evangelists* should be very involved in evangelizing their communities and helping the church members play their role at the basic levels of evangelism. There is nothing to say that one church could not have many within, who take on part-time or full-time evangelism within the congregation, which would and should be cultivated.

There is no Christian, who does not need spiritual guidance. As we stand today, Christianity is divided into 41,000 different denominations all claiming to be the truth and the way. Let us take Paul's appeal to the divided Corinthian Church and apply it to our 41,000 different denominations as one body of Christians under Christ. Paul wrote, "I exhort you, brethren, by the name of our Lord Jesus Christ, that you all agree and that there be no divisions among you, but that you be made complete in the same mind and in the same judgment." (1 Cor. 1:10, NASB) On this Richard Oster writes, "Generally speaking it is clear that the issues of uniform thought, judgment and agreement must have pertained to the divisiveness and polarization mentioned in 1:11–17." Let us look at verses 12-13, which read, "Now I mean this, that each one of you is saying, 'I am of Paul,' and 'I of Apollos,' and 'I of Cephas,' and 'I of Christ.' Has Christ been divided? Paul was not crucified for you, was he? Or were you baptized in the name of Paul?"

We have this today on a much grander scale. How many different Christian denominations are based on a man? While this will in no way be exhaustive, it will demonstrate the division.

Thomas Cranmer (1489-1556) begets the Anglican Church, which claim to have their roots in the teachings of Thomas Cranmer and John Calvin.

Martin Luther (1483-1546) begets the Evangelical Lutheran Church, which claim to have their roots in the teachings of Luther.

John Calvin (1509-64) begets the Presbyterian, the Reformed Baptist, and others, which claim to have their roots in the teachings of Calvin.

Ulrich Zwingli (1484-1531) begets the Swiss Reformed Churches and the Evangelical Reformed Church, which claim to have their roots in the teachings of Zwingli and Calvin.

John Wesley (1703-91) begets the Methodists and the Wesleyan Church, both claiming to have their roots in the teachings of John Wesley.

George Fox (1624-91) begets the Society of Friends (Quakers), which claim to have their roots in the teachings of Fox.

Thomas (1763-1854) and Alexander Campbell (1788-1866) beget The Church of Christ, which claim to have their roots in the teachings of Thomas and Alexander Campbell, Walter Scott, and Barton W. Stone.

Thomas Müntzer (c. 1489-1525) begets the Anabaptists, ranking as one of the founders.

Menno Simons (1496-1561) was an Anabaptist religious leader, and his followers became known as Mennonites.

Jakob Hutter (c. 1500-1536) begets the Hutterites.

What lies above is but a few pieces of sand on the beaches earth wide that reflect the division of Christianity because one man disagreed and then abandoned a denomination to form yet another denomination. Every Christian group will tell you that they represent first-century Christianity and their history as a denomination goes back to the first century. In the first century there was but one form of Christianity, that which Jesus founded and the apostles grew. By about 187 C.E. Irenaeus listed 20 varieties of Christianity, and about 384 C.E. Epiphanius listed 80 varieties of Christianity. Let us quote 1 Corinthians 1:12-13 once more but change the names to make our point. "Now I mean this, that each one of you is saying, 'I am of Calvin,' and 'I of Luther,' and 'I of Wesley,' and 'I of Christ.' Has Christ been divided? Calvin, Luther, or Wesley was not crucified for you, were they? Or were you baptized in the name of Calvin, Luther, or Wesley?" If we are going to ever 'all agree and that there be no divisions among us, but that we be made complete in the same mind and in the same judgment." (1 Cor. 1:10), we must be honest with ourselves. When was the last time a Presbyterian, a Lutheran, a Methodist, a Baptist, a Wesleyan or any other came to our home to talk about God's Word, met us on the street to witness about Jesus, or telephoned our home to share some Scriptural truths. Have any of them ever carried out an informal sharing of the good news with us while we waited for the doctor, rode in a taxi, sat at a station, or stood in line at a store?

How could they ever do so when they are so divided amongst themselves. Even within a single denomination, they are fragmented into various denominations. Let us just look at one group, the Baptists, and just the American Baptist organizations.

- **Alliance of Baptists**: 100 congregations, 60,000 members[12]

- **American Baptist Churches USA (ABCUSA)**: 5,800 congregations, 1.4 million members
- **Baptist General Convention of Texas**: 5,700 congregations, 2.3 million members
- **Baptist General Association of Virginia (BGAV)**: 1,400 congregations, 400,000 members
- **Baptist General Conference**: 1,000 congregations, 140,000 members
- **Conservative Baptist Association (CBAmerica)**: 1,200 congregations, 200,000 members
- **Cooperative Baptist Fellowship (CBF)**: 1,900 congregations, 700,000 members
- **General Association of Regular Baptist Churches**: 1,400 congregations, 130,000 members
- **National Association of Free Will Baptists**: 2,000 congregations, 200,000 members
- Old-Line Primitive Baptists
- Progressive Primitive Baptists
- **Southern Baptist Convention (SBC)**: 44,000 congregations, 16.3 million members
- **African-American Baptist groups**:
- **National Baptist Convention of America, Inc.**: 12,000 congregations, 3.1 million members
- **National Baptist Convention**, USA, Inc.: 33,000 congregations, 8.5 million members
- **National Missionary Baptist Convention of America**: 300 congregations, 400,000 members
- **National Primitive Baptist Association**: 1,500 congregations, 250,000 members
- **Progressive National Baptist Convention**: 1,200 congregations, 2.5 million members
- Associations holding to Landmarkism
- **American Baptist Association**: 1,800 congregations, 275,000 members
- **Baptist Missionary Association of America**: 1,300 congregations, 235,000 members
- Interstate & Foreign Landmark Missionary Baptist Association

- Independent (non-aligned) Baptist churches
- **Baptist Bible Fellowship International**: 3,400 congregations, 1.4 million members
- **Independent Baptist Fellowship International**: 540 congregations
- **Southwide Baptist Fellowship**: 900 congregations
- The Spiritual Baptist Archdiocese of New York, Inc.
- **World Baptist Fellowship**: 900 congregations
- In addition, there are many Independent Baptist churches not aligned with any group

All of these are American Baptist groups. Why are they not under just one group name? What is at the root of such divisiveness in the American Baptist movement since the early 17th-century? Simply put, it is doctrinal differences, it is conservative versus liberal, it is the desire for independence. Baptist congregations are what are called autonomous. What does that mean? It means that each individual church is self-governing: doctrinally independent and able to make decisions and act on them as a free and **independent** of any other church. This creates an enormous problem identifying a specific creed. Moreover, the particular set of doctrinal beliefs of Baptists can vary widely. The only thing that all churches can agree on is the local congregation in the governance of church affairs. Being given free will by God, humans have a natural desire for a measure of independence. However, carried too far, this desire gives rise to divisions, a failure to be united in the same mind and the same line of thought. How are we to carry out the evangelism work when we are so divided?

Diligently Studying God's Word

All Christians today are in need of being guided by the inspired Word of God. Certainly, based on the above, we must be concerned with 'there being no divisions among us, but that we be made complete in the same mind and the same judgment.' (1 Cor. 1:10) Therefore, we need to prepare ourselves for the dispensing of biblical truth, knowing that one day; we will find the unity, with true, genuine Christians being brought together as one, as the Father and the Son are one. (John 17:11, 20-23) We have millions of books on every aspect of the Christian faith and a constant flow of books through many different publishing agencies. However, not all books are created equal. We need to be open growing a list of trusted authors, who we know will give us what God said. We are looking for those Christian authors, who use the objective historical-grammatical method of interpretation, as opposed to those who read their meaning into the text by way of their liberal and moderate subjective historical-critical method of interpretation.[180] – Proverbs 2:2-4.

We need to take advantage of the many wonder Bible study tools on the market. We do not want to have our Bible study library simply sitting on the shelf as some form of decoration. If we want to ramp up our research, we can add one book to our library at a time. This author is the CEO and President of Christian Publishing House. While we are new, we are building a library of great books. However, until we have the major resources available for our readers, we recommend Broadman & Holman as a trustworthy place to purchase your Bible study tools.[181]

Exercise

A person says to you, "I do not believe in the Bible, it is an ancient book and has no practical value for us today." How might you respond?

Review Questions

- If we are to be effective in our use of the Bible what must we have?

- What good example did Apollos set for us?

- How are we to help people spiritually?

- How do we adapt our message to our listener and why is this important?

  - How can we go about accurately handling the Word of truth?

  - How extensive are the divisions in the body of Christ?

  - What is the difference between preevangelism and evangelism?

  - According to this author, what is involved in Basic Evangelism, Making Disciples, Part-Time or Full-Time Evangelism, Congregation Evangelism, and who all are obligated to participate and to what extent?

  - Why is it important to study God's Word diligently?

---

[180] See *Evangelical Hermeneutics: The New Versus the Old*, by Robert L. Thomas (Jan 13, 2003)

See also *BASICS OF BIBLICAL CRITICISM: Helpful or Harmful?* [Second Edition] F. David Farnell, Thomas Howe, Thomas Marshall, Benjamin Cocar, Dianna Newman, and Edward D. Andrews (2016)

[181] http://www.bhpublishinggroup.com/category/books/

CHAPTER 14 Developing Our Abilities As a Teacher

2 Timothy 4:2 Updated American Standard Version (ASV)

² **preach** the word; be ready in season and out of season; reprove, rebuke, exhort, with complete patience and **teaching**.

While many today look to Jesus for the miraculous healings and the feeding of thousands, this is actually, not what he was most noted for in his day. He was largely known as a teacher. (Mark 12:19; 13:1) In fact, just after healing many and casting demons out of many, Jesus went into a synagogue to teach. He said to them, "I must preach the good news of the kingdom of God to the other towns as well; for I was sent for this purpose." (Lu 4:38-44) This is our priority today as well. It is our obligation to proclaim the good news throughout the entire inhabited earth, in each of our communities, teaching and making disciples. – Matthew 24:14; 28:19-20; Acts 1:8.

If we are going to carry out what has become known as the Great Commission to make disciples, we have to improve our ability as a teacher. In the above Paul highlights this importance when he tells Timothy to "Pay close attention to yourself and to your teaching; persevere in these things, for as you do this you will ensure salvation both for yourself and for those who hear you." (1 Tim. 4:16) By looking to the previous verse at 1 Timothy 4:1, we find that Paul is counseling Timothy about dealing with the coming apostasy. It reads, "But the Spirit explicitly says that in later times some will fall away from the faith, paying attention to deceitful spirits and doctrines of demons." On this the *Holman New Testament Commentary* states,

> Paul turned from his triumphant hymn of Christ to a stark warning: **the Spirit clearly says that in later times** troublesome things will happen within the church.
>
> The phrase **later times** refers not to some coming event but to the sweep of time from Christ's ascension to his future return. It covers everything in between, from Paul and the early church, to Luther and the Reformation, to Wesley and the Great Awakening, to us. These are the "later times," the last days. This great epoch of the church is the final stage of human history before the triumphal return of Jesus Christ.
>
> These words from Paul are just as relevant to our churches as they were for those in the first century. They will continue to be valid for believers in the future last days. The troubles which Paul describes have been happening throughout history to the present time, at other times with guerrilla tactics and scattered damage, often with frontal assaults and

great devastation to the church.

Paul predicted that **some will abandon the faith**. Apostasy has been around as long as human history. Paul dealt with it in his own day (1 Tim. 1:19; 2 Tim. 2:17–18), and the casualty list is high in our time. Even so, the church will triumph. (Larson 2000, Page 202)

Apostasy ("stand away from") in Greek (*apostasia*) comes from the verb *aphistemi*, which means, "to rise up in open defiance of authority, with the presumed intention to overthrow it or to act in complete opposition to its demands—'to rebel against, to revolt, to engage in insurrection, rebellion.'" (Louw, et al. 1988, 1989, Volume 1, Page 495) In other words, the person is not merely leaving Christianity, but rather he is abandoning the faith. An apostate is one who is **standing off from** the truth in a rebellious spirit and is now turning on the faith he had held at one time. Certainly, this was the case entering the second century of Christianity, shortly after the apostle John died in 98 C.E. This was when Paul had been dead for over 35-years and Timothy was now close to the age of his former friend and apostle. Today, conservative Christianity faces an even greater enemy, who also stands off from the truth, secularism, humanism, relativism, and nihilism. Many so-called "Christian universities" have long gone

Secularism: exclusion of religion from public affairs: the belief that religion and religious bodies should have no part in political or civic affairs or in running public institutions, especially schools

Humanism: belief in human-based morality: a system of thought that is based on the values, characteristics, and behavior that are believed to be best in human beings, rather than on any supernatural authority

Relativism: belief in changeable standards: the belief that concepts such as right and wrong, goodness and badness, or truth and falsehood are not absolute but change from culture to culture and situation to situation

Nihilism: total rejection of social mores: the general rejection of established social conventions and beliefs, especially of morality and religion

the way of secularism, humanism, and relativism. Very few conservative Christian universities remain in the United States.[182] William Lane Craig has the following exhortation to parents, which would also apply to pastors and elders as well,

I think the church is really failing these kids. Rather than provide them training in the defense of Christianity's truth, we focus on emotional worship experiences, felt needs, and entertainment. It's no wonder they become sitting ducks for that teacher or professor who rationally takes aim at their faith. In high school and college, students are intellectually assaulted with every manner of non-Christian philosophy conjoined with an overwhelming relativism and skepticism. We've got to train our kids for war. How dare we send them unarmed into an intellectual war zone? Parents must do more than take their children to church and read them Bible stories. Moms and dads need to be trained in apologetics themselves and so be able to explain to their children simply from an early age and then with increasing depth why we believe as we do. Honestly, I find it hard to understand how Christian couples in our day and age can risk bringing children into the world without being trained in apologetics as part of the art of parenting.[183]

The world has grown unreceptive to even listening to the Gospel let alone accepting it as truth. Thus, we return to the Apostle Paul's words of our need to "Pay close attention to [ourselves] and to **[our] teaching**; persevere in these things, for as [we] do this [we] will ensure salvation both for [ourselves] and for those who hear [us]." (1 Tim. 4:16) The kind of teaching that Paul is revering here is not a simple sharing of the message of Christ, but rather preevangelism, i.e. **Christian apologetics**. As we stand right now, Christians are viewed by the secular world as superstitious, knuckle-dragging Neanderthals, who have refused to join the era of scientific discovery. We can turn this around if we can train the conservative Christians in the way of preevangelism. This Christian apologetics/preevangelism is laying a foundation for those who have no knowledge of the Gospel, giving them background information, so that they are able to grasp what they are hearing. The Christian evangelist is preparing their mind and heart so that they will be receptive to the biblical truths.

---

[182] The top five conservative Christian universities at the time of this book are **1.** Biola University, **2.** Southern Evangelical Seminary, **3.** Veritas Evangelical Seminary, **4.** Westminster Theological Seminary, and **5.** Liberty University

[183] Craig, William Lane (2010-03-01). On Guard: Defending Your Faith with Reason and Precision (Kindle Locations 267-274). David C. Cook. Kindle Edition.

If we become effective Christian apologists, we will reach the heart of those who listen to us and move them to accept Christ. Therefore, the benefits of apologetic studies are that "[we] will ensure salvation both for [ourselves] and for those who hear [us]." Our first goal in Christian apologetics is to know what we believe and why we believe it. If we do this, there will be no fear in facing the secularist. Moreover, if we are an investigative Christian, learning to defend the faith and defend the Word of God, it is highly unlikely that we will stumble into the realms of doubt, and we can assist God in saving those who have. Our Christian children enter into 16-years of education if they go beyond high school into a bachelor degree, 18-years if they achieve a master's degree. This means that they will face dozens of teachers and professors, who are going to inundate them into the world of secularism, humanism, relativism, and nihilism. There is little wonder why so many young Christians go away for a university education and come home after 4-6-years as an agnostic or atheist. We are at war with Satan, the god of this age, demons, and fallen humanity. Therefore, it is imperative that we train our children to enter into battle with those who are going to rain down on them every non-Christian philosophy: secularism, humanism, relativism, and nihilism. However, how are we as parents to remove biblical illiteracy from our children, if we have not first better educated ourselves about God's Word, and trained in the area of Christian apologetics? So how can we cultivate our art of teaching when presenting biblical truths to others?

Developing Our Abilities as a Teacher

First, we need to concern ourselves with a *personal Bible study* and another *study where we prepare* for our Christian meetings. **Second**, we need to *practice explaining the Scriptures* to a friend before we engage the unbeliever, or especially before we share truths with the enemy. We do this by pulling one aside at Christian meetings and sharing points that we learn in our personal studies, as well as commenting at the meetings. **Third**, we need to *observe others* who are effective teachers. We should pay special attention to good teachers when they speak. We can take note of how they defend the faith, reasoning from the Scriptures, explaining and proving, instructing in sound doctrine, and overturning false reasoning. Prayerful study,

Psalm 119:27 (UASV)	Psalm 119:34 (UASV)

27 Make me understand the way of your precepts,
    so I will meditate on your wondrous works.
	34 Give me understanding, that I may keep your law
	    and observe it with my whole heart.

Observing other teachers,

Luke 6:40 (UASV)

⁴⁰ A disciple is not above his teacher, but everyone when he is fully trained will be like his teacher.

Practice to refine our abilities,

---

1 Timothy 4:13-15 (UASV)

¹³ Until I come, devote yourself to the public reading of Scripture, to exhortation, to teaching. ¹⁴ Do not neglect the gift within you, which was given to you through prophecy with the laying on of hands by the elders. ¹⁵ Practice these things, be absorbed in them, so that your progress will be evident to all.

We have but one Almighty Teacher. He has used his human servants to provide us with an infinite library of study tools. We have been fortunate to have guidance throughout these last days of Satan's rulership of the world. However, not every study tool is beneficial for the Christian mind. The apostle Paul spoke of "all wicked deception for those who are perishing because **they did not receive the love of the truth** so as to be saved." (2 Thess. 2:10) Let us just say that not all Christian books contain biblical truths. Therefore, it is highly recommended that the readers find trusted authors and trusted publishing companies, to avoid being misled, as they grow in knowledge and insight, which will enable them to identify what is true from what is false.

Teachings that are Biblical

We are footstep followers of Jesus Christ, and he set the example for grounding the things he taught in the Scriptures. (Matt. 21:13; John 6:45; 8:17) Additionally, even though Jesus was the Son of God, he said, "My teaching is not mine, but belongs to him that sent me." In other words, he taught what the Father taught. (John 7:16-18) We too should be humble and realize that what we teach is not ours, but belongs to the Father, who has sent us out through the Son. Therefore, our teachings should reflect the authority of the Word of God. (2 Tim. 3:16-17) While great apologists like William Lane Craig, Norman L. Geisler, and Ravi Zacharias may be able to reason skillfully with great scientists and philosophers, we need to note that it is always grounded in Scripture. What they know is that "the word of God is living and active and sharper than any two-edged sword, and piercing as far as the division of soul and spirit, of both joints and marrow, and able to judge the thoughts and intentions of the heart." – Hebrews 4:12.

This is not saying that we are not supposed to use our mind, our power of understanding. The Creator gave us the power of understanding and he expected us to use this ability to reason and to teach others about his will and purposes. We need to determine which Scriptures are needed to make our point. We need to ascertain what the author meant by the words that he used. We then need to do as Jesus did, take some complex and profound texts and explain them in our own words. A Bible student carries out what the scholars call **ex**egesis (out of), taking the meaning out of the text, not **eis**egesis (into), reading our meaning into the text. Once we have a sense of what the author meant, this is what we share with others.

Using Questions Effectively

Many times, if we just give our listeners the answer, it does not stimulate their thinking. The readers of this book have likely noticed that many questions have been asked throughout. Using rhetorical questions before, with a slight pause, then giving the answer, will allow the listener to ponder what is coming. In addition, asking a question; then, permitting the listener to offer a reply will help us to see how we might better get into his or her heart, i.e., the seat of understanding. We could share a Scripture, by having the listener read it or we read it ourselves, pause, and then ask him or her to offer what they understand the author to be saying. They may not have the right answer, so, we may need to ask more leading questions that will enable them to arrive at the correct understanding. By involving the listener, we are helping him to reason on the Scriptures, to see how one arrives at the right conclusion, and to make the conclusion his or her own. For example, read 1 Corinthians 6:18, "Flee from sexual immorality. Every other sin that a man commits is outside the body, but the sexually immoral person sins against his own body." Now, ask some tactful open-ended questions. Why do you think God condemns sexual immorality, like sex outside of marriage?" "What do you think of God giving this restriction?" What do you think of God's setting our moral standards?" The person's response will reveal what they truly believe, let us know how better to approach the conversation. Jesus did the same. – Matthew 16:13-17.

Almost everyone loves expressing what their viewpoint is on things. However, people hate being lectured to or argued with. Just how true this is, we need to look no further than a website called Quora,[184] which is a question-and-answer website where questions are asked, answered, edited and organized by its community of users, which was founded in

---

[184] https://www.quora.com/

2009. Many have projected that it will be bigger than Twitter. As of 2014, it was worth about a billion dollars. Proverbs 20:5 states, "The purpose in a man's heart is like deep water, but a man of understanding will draw it out." What did Solomon mean? "People can conceal their real purposes just as deep waters hide objects. But the person who has the understanding offered in Proverbs [or the Bible as a whole] is able to bring even those hidden thoughts to the surface."[185]

When we ask others question it needs to be inviting, not as though we are intimidating them. An great example is an open-ended question, such as, "what do you think needs to be done so that the world is full of peace and security, as opposed to war, insecurity and despair?" After they offer their thoughts, ask, "What in life has made you arrive at that conclusion?" We could then ask about concerns over our children's future. The questions merely need to be asked in such a way that they do not make the listener feel uncomfortable. Each person that we speak with will be different, so we may have to adjust our questions accordingly.

In the above, Proverbs 20:5 helped us to appreciate that we need to **draw people out**. We need to allow those who are willing to listen to us, to speak themselves, sharing their thoughts, while we listen patiently without unnecessarily interrupting. (Jam. 1:19) Once they have shared what is on their mind, we can evidence that we were listening, by reiterating what they said in our responses. We might say, "Your point about _____ is interesting, I would agree with some aspects of it, such as _____. However, let me share a couple Scriptures that might shed some light on it." If they have been ambiguous in their sharing of thoughts, we might ask some clarifying question, as opposed to summing we understood. We might say, "When you use the term _____, what exactly do you mean by that?" Once we understand, we can ask more questions to see why they think, feel, or believe the way they do. Some of what they share may be mostly at odds with the Scriptures, but there may be one part where we find common ground. After we agree with the one aspect; then, gently and respectfully explain why we would disagree with the other points made. We can ask if they have ever considered the Scripture _____, and ask how that affects their position. The one thing we never want to be is dogmatic or argumentative. – 2 Timothy 2:24-25.

The truth is the way people respond to our questions will be based on how well we evidence that we have listened to them. They will know if we are listening with our heart, really seeking to understand what they

---

[185] Anders, Max (2005-07-01). Holman Old Testament Commentary - Proverbs (p. 107). B&H Publishing. Kindle Edition.

mean and why they feel the way, they do. If we unnecessarily interrupt, this will close them down. If we are merely waiting for the moment they stop talking, so we can start talking to share what we want to share, this will be very clear to them. On the other hand, if we do not interrupt, but actively listen, and then acknowledge their comments in our remarks, we will be evidencing a willingness to listen patiently, which will attract the listener to us because they will see that we had warm, personal interest in them. When we actively listen to others, we are showing them honor, which make move them to listen to us in return. – Romans 12:10.

The Significance of Questions

Whether we are going to be successful in helping a critical unbeliever to accept the Bible as the Word of God will depend on *the effectiveness of our questions*. Whether we are going to be successful in helping the skeptical unbeliever to accept a divine Creator will depend on *the effectiveness of our questions*. Whether we are going to be successful in helping the unbeliever to accept the faith will depend on *the effectiveness of our questions*. Whether we are successful in teaching someone in a Bible study to grow in knowledge of God's Word, will depend on *the effectiveness of our questions*. Questions can help us to lead the listener's mind from one point to the next. Questions can help the listener to see how the parts or aspects of something relate to one another, and in the end, arrive at the correct conclusions.

Our use of questions will force our listener or student to think for themselves and to answer in their words. If they are explaining things, as they understand them, this will help us discover if they fully grasp what is being said. Note in this book that at the end of each chapter, there are review questions, which are designed to help the reader get the overall point. These questions make sure the reader understands the material and sees how to make practical application of it. Below are different types of questions that we can use in our teaching.

(1) **Closed Ended Questions**: These are designed for a one word or a short phrase answer. They can be used to begin conversations, which allow the listeners to be involved without contributing too much. However, closed questions that require simple short answers, yes or no answers can also be used to control the conversation and to lead.

- Do you think the Bible is actually the Word of God?
- Have you always felt that way about the Bible?
- Do you believe that this is all there is to life?

(2) **Open Ended Questions**: These are designed for longer answers. They require our listener to think and ponder. We will better understand their beliefs and feelings, their wants, needs, and problems. They allow the listener to have some control in the conversation. We can use an open ended question after we have a few brief answers from our closed ended questions.

- What is it that leads you to believe the Bible is not the Word of God?

- What about the world today that troubles you the most?

(3) **Leading Questions**: These infer that there is but one correct answer and it guides the listener to that answer.

- **Q**: After reading Matthew 7:13-14, does this not suggest there are two courses in life, one that leads to destruction, which many are on and on that leads to life, which few are finding?

- **A**: Yes

- **Q**: After reading Matthew 7:15, does this not suggest there will be some who appear as innocent as sheep, but really are false prophets to the point of being ravenous wolves?

- **A**: Yes

- **Q**: After reading Matthew 7:16-20, what is it that will help us identify these false prophets?

- **A**: Their fruit

- **Q**: After reading Matthew 7:21, who does Jesus say are the only ones who will enter into the kingdom.

- **A**: Jesus said only those doing the will of the Father.

- **Q**: After reading Matthew 7:22, will there be those who believe that are doing the will of the Father?

- **A**: Yes

- **Q**: After reading Matthew 7:23, will Jesus accept their excuses for failing to do the will of the Father?

- **A**: No

(4) **Clarifying Questions**: These questions can be used in one of two ways. First, they can be used to clear up something that the

listener said. Second, they can be used to clarify that the listener fully understands what something means.

- **NOTE/Q**: The term prophet has two basic meanings. First, it means one who proclaims a message. Second, it means one who foretells the future. What does the term "prophet" mean here?
- **A**: It means one who proclaims a message.
- **Q**: What did Jesus mean by many being on the path of destruction? Was Jesus referring to his disciples (i.e., Christians) and those of religions other than Christianity, or was he referring to his disciples?
- **A**: The many Jesus referred to was his disciples, coming Christians.
- **Q**: How do you know that the many who are on the path to destruction are the disciples of Jesus Christ?
- **A**: Just after Jesus talks about the two paths, Jesus said 'be careful of false prophets.' Then, a few verses later he says "Not everyone who says to me, 'Lord, Lord,' will enter the kingdom of heaven ..."
- **Q**: Are these false teachers found within Christianity and why are they so hard to recognize?
- **A**: If it is the many Christian disciples, who are on the path to destruction; then, the teachers who taught them must have been Christian teachers. They are hard to recognize because Jesus compared them to sheep. In other words, they come across as innocent appearing.
- **Q**: What did Jesus mean by the term "fruit"?
- **A**: In other words, we would recognize them by their words and deeds.
- **Q**: Based on who you said could enter into the kingdom, 'those doing the will of the Father,' what should we know?
- **A**: What the will of the Father is?
- **Q**: Did the many on the path to destruction believe they were doing the will of the Father?
- **A**: Yes
- **Q**: Jesus started out by talking about two paths and false teachers, correct.
- **A**: Yes

- **Q**: False teachers imply false teachings, correct.

- **A**: Yes

- **Q**: What did Jesus say he would say to those who thought they were doing the right thing or thought they were teaching the right thing but were not?

- **A**: 'I never knew you; depart from me, you workers of lawlessness.'

- **Q**: We have false teachers, who are difficult to recognize, as they appear as innocent as sheep. Recognizing them can only be accomplished by recognizing their fruit (words and deeds), as well as knowing the true will of the Father. Does it not then seem prudent on our behalf that we should apply 2 Thessalonians 2:10 and 2 Corinthians 13:5?

- **A**: Yes, the ones, who are deceived by these false teachers, will perish because refused to be receptive to the truth. Therefore, we need to be in a constant mode of examining ourselves, as well as our beliefs, to see whether we are really in the truth.

2 Thessalonians 2:10 Updated American Standard Version (UASV)

[10] and with all wicked deception for those who are perishing, because they did not receive the love of the truth so as to be saved.

2 Corinthians 13:5 Updated American Standard Version (UASV)

[5] Examine yourselves, to see whether you are in the faith. Test yourselves. Or do you not realize this about yourselves, that Jesus Christ is in you?—unless indeed you fail to meet the test!

(5) **Refocusing Questions**: These questions can be used to get back on track. In talking to people about the Bible, they tend to jump from topic to topic. It is best to stay on one topic, resolve those issues and then move on to the next topic. We can use questions to refocus people back on topic.

- Yes, but how does Jesus' words relate to _____?

(6) **Viewpoint Questions**: These questions can be used to find out how our listener feels about a particular biblical truth.

- Does this sound reasonable?

- Would it not be helpful if you applied these things in your life?

- Do you think God wanted the world to be like this?

The questions that we use can help the listener to better reason on the information before him. For example, what is a ransom? What ransom price did Jesus pay? Why was Jesus' ransom price needed? It was Adam who sinned, so how is it just that his descendants must also pay the price of death? Why did it have to be Jesus, who paid the ransom with his life? What has the ransom made possible for every human?

Our questions as a teacher are asking who, what, when, where, why and how. It is our goal that our listener grows in Bible knowledge and gains a correct understanding of God's Word. This is the case whether it is the first time we have talked with him, or we are doing a regular Bible study. What he says in response to our questions will help us to gauge how well we are accomplishing our goals. Many in the world have a callused unfeeling conscience because they have regularly violated it. Our questions can be used to sensitize the listener's conscience, enabling him to sense the difference between good and bad. (Gal. 3:1-6; 1 Cor. 9:1-14.) In addition, our questions can get into the heart attitude of the listener so that he sees the practical benefits of God's Word. – Isaiah 25:9.

Keeping it Simple

Much of God's Word is deep and quite complex, as it is filled with poetry, idioms, hyperbole, and apocalyptic language, figurative and symbolic language, religious terms, many different genres, and so much more. Therefore, as a teacher, an evangelist, we need to simplify it, so that it is easy to understand. Once we explain a meaning behind a complex text and walk through how we got there, the truth is relatively simple. What we face in talking with people, are those who have read literature that misrepresents the biblical truth. Therefore, it is our goal as a teacher, to make the Bible easy to understand. If we are skillful at our task, we can take that complex and deep information and convey it simply, clearly, and accurately. Our goal as a teacher is never to make the information more complicated than it has to be. We need not add any more details than is necessary to convey the intended meaning. When we read a Scripture, we should ignore the urge to comment on every aspect of the text. For example, Matthew 24:14 reads, "And this gospel of the kingdom will be proclaimed in all the inhabited earth as a testimony to all the nations, and then the end will come." Are we using the verse because we are focusing on the gospel being proclaimed, or the fact that it is to be proclaimed in all the inhabited earth, or that it needs to be proclaimed before the end will come?

Using Persuasion

If we **listen carefully**, we can identify what our listener already believes about different things. For example, if they say, "I do not believe the Bible is the Word of God." If we just jump into a conversation of why the Bible is the Word of God, we have ignored the "why" does he not believe the Bible is the Word of God. It could be certain things, which may have pushed him into that belief. What if it all stems from his childhood of having Christian parents, who abused the Bible as they abused him? What if his disbelief in the Bible is a result of the hypocrisy he has seen in organized religion? What if it is because he has read some books by Bible critics? Lastly, what if his disbelief in the Bible is because he does not believe there is a God. Thus, we should never make assumptions as to why someone believes as he does. – Proverbs 18:13.

Therefore, it is important that we **ask questions** so that we can determine the why of his beliefs. The first question if based on the above declaration that he does not believe the Bible is the Word of God, might be, "do you believe there is a God?" If he answers "no," we still need to press on, by asking, "What has led you to this belief?" Once we have the *why* he does not believe in the Bible, we can ask yet another question, such as, "Have you had the time to investigate the Bible thoroughly for yourself?" If he says "no," we press on with, "Since the Bible says of itself that it is the Word of God, and its author offers its readers eternal life if we believe and obey, does it not seem prudent that we investigate it ourselves, to see whether its claims are true." If he agrees that this would be a wise course, we could offer to aid him in his investigation.

If we are going to reach the person's heart, who does not believe in the bible, we will have to use **sound reasoning**. We could wet his appetite by suggesting that we share a few evidences of inspiration now, and that we might study through a book with him one on one.[186] If he agrees, we could talk to him about fulfilled prophecies, which are evidence of foreknowledge, something humans do not possess. (2 Peter 1:20-21) We could take him to the detailed prophecy found at Isaiah 44:24, 27, 28; 45:1-4. We could explain that this prophecy was written between 778 and 732 B.C.E., and the person who carried it out was the Cyrus the Great, who lived some 200 years later. We could walk him through how Cyrus conquered the Babylonian empire. It is mind boggling that when Isaiah uttered that prophecy, Babylon was nothing; Assyria was the world power of that period. After that prophecy, we could touch on

---

[186] IS THE BIBLE REALLY THE WORD OF GOD? Myths? Errors? Contradictions? Scientifically Inaccurate? [Second Edition]

http://www.christianpublishers.org/apps/webstore/products/show/7138936

Jeremiah's prophecy, which had been penned by 590 B.C.E. that told of the destruction of Edom. Then, we share the historical fact that it was the Maccabean leaders Judas Maccabeus and John Hyrcanus, along with the Roman Empire that fulfilled this prophecy in the second and first centuries B.C.E. We could then share Jesus prophecy of the destruction of Jerusalem. (Luke 19:41-44; 21:20, 21) We can look at the places where the Bible touches on science, saying things longer before science ever knew. (Isa. 40:22; Lev. 11:6) We could close this initial evidence out with the fact that the Bible was written throughout a 1,600-year period, with over forty writers, and it is in complete harmony from Genesis to Revelation.

Using Discernment

Discernment is keenly selective judgment. In other words, we have the ability to judge well, and our ability to determine is finely tuned and able to sense minor differences, distinctions, or details, to obtain spiritual direction and understanding. A Christian who has both knowledge and *discernment* is able to make decisions that if Jesus were in our place, and in our imperfect human condition, he would have made the exact same decision. One way that we can use discernment is in our sharing of the biblical truths with others who possess different worldviews[187] and backgrounds,[188] so as to save some. The apostle Paul said,

1 Corinthians 9:19-23 Updated American Standard Version (UASV)

[19] For though I am free from all men, I have made myself a slave to all, so that I may gain more. [20] And so to the Jews I became as a Jew, that I might gain Jews; to those under the law I became as under the law, though I myself am not under the law, that I might gain those under the law. [21] To those without law I became as without law, although I am not without law toward God but under the law toward Christ, that I might gain those without law. [22] To the weak I became weak, that I might gain

---

[187] A worldview is the sum total of our beliefs about the most important things in life.

[188] Keep in mind that, even though Paul said, "I became as," so that he might become all things to all men, so as to save them, he never became anything that would be contrary to God's will and purposes. A bad example of this would be the modern day Christian heavy metal bands, who by all appearances, are just like the worldly ones. Such bands are nine parts world to one part, Christian. Can we imagine young Timothy, Paul's student and traveling companion, being a member of Stryper, Vengeance Rising, Deliverance, Believer, Tourniquet and P.O.D? Much of modern day Christianity, has become like the world in their misguided attempt to evangelize the world. They are nine parts world to one part, Christian. This so-called evangelism is an excuse for loose conduct, i.e., an and excuse to be worldly under the guise of 'saving some.' While we are using a hyperbolic extreme example here of being like the world, to save some out of the world, which is complete foolishness, there are many other minor to major examples within modern day Christianity. Jesus used hyperbole, which is to over exaggerate to emphasize a point, but sadly, in our day, we do not need to over exaggerate because our example found in these so-called Christian metal bands is a reality.

the weak. I have become all things to all men, that I might by all means save some. [23] But I do all things for the sake of the gospel, that I may become a fellow partaker of it.

The appropriate, sensible, and efficient use of discernment in our witnessing to others encompasses the ability to adjust our part of the conversation with the listener, to involve his or her interests. This means that we must be prepared to discuss anything. If we are new to the Christian faith, we will have a limited number Bible subjects that we can discuss. However, if we study well over time that will quickly improve, but in the meantime, this should not dissuade us from engaging ones at every opportunity. How do we prepare to the point where we are deeply familiar with the Bible in an apologetic sense, which will enable us to engage almost any topic that may come up? First, we have a personal Bible study, where we are studying through the Bible chapter-by-chapter with the Holman Old and New Testament Volumes, combined with Norman L. Geisler's Big Book of Bible Difficulties. Second, we prepare well for each Christian meeting, so that we may participate when opportunity affords itself. Third, we share what we learn with fellow Christians, family, and friends. Fourth, we take opportunities to share biblical truths with others outside of our circle when an opportunity presents itself. Fifth, we must discern **what** to share, **how much** to share, with **whom**, and consider the **circumstances** and **setting** of our conversation. Certainly, if in line at Wal-Mart, we would not share as much as we would with a person in the waiting room at the doctor's office. We would not talk about the inappropriateness of Christian metal bands with a senior citizen, nor would we discuss world affairs with a young adult unless they bring it up. Are we talking to a "Christian" from a denomination that is not true Christianity? We would certainly not approach this person, in the same way, we would an unbeliever. With an unbeliever, we have many foundational matters to establish first. If we kept dealing with foundational issues, defining and explaining to a person of another denomination, false or not, they may get offended out our regularly treating them as though they know nothing. Again, we need to take into account their personal circumstances and use discernment.

Helping Those Who Evade Bible Conversations

Proverbs 19:8 Updated American Standard Version (UASV)

[8] He who acquires heart[189] loves his own soul;
he who keeps discernment[190] will find good.

---

[189] Or *aquires good sense* or *aquires wisdom*

Proverbs 19:8 offers us wise words when it comes to our sharing biblical truths with others. There is a greater likelihood of success if we come to a person who generally evades Bible conversations with tact and discernment. If not that time, our approach will have laid a fine foundation for another occasion by either another or ourselves.

At times, when we attempt to engage a person in a conversation about the Bible, all of a sudden they do not have time and must go. In all likelihood, it is not that they do not have time, it is that they do not have time for a lengthy drawn out conversation. If we discern that this is the case, we can try to get around this excuse. We say, "I certainly understand and respect a busy schedule, so I will be brief." If we wanted to delve into a particularly profound point with this person, we can now hit the high points, and stick to our word about being brief, and then close out the conversation. This will leave the person with a newfound respect that some need not have drawn out conversations. Moreover, there may even be a couple cases where this moved them to want to hear more, so they offer to go on in the conversation.

What if we discern that the person is short on time? If we misread and try to go on, he may see us as being pushy, which results in a negative impression. If we are visiting people's homes to share the gospel, what might be indicators that they are not prepared to have a discussion? What if they come to the door with a cooking utensil in hand? What if we can smell food that has or is being cooked? What if the moment we introduce ourselves, they look at their watch? If these or any others indicate they are busy, we can simply hand them a Bible tract, apologize for interrupting and say we will stop back another time. This will impress on them that we have respected the fact that they were too busy to talk, making them more receptive the next time.

Proverbs 17:27 Updated American Standard Version (UASV)

²⁷ He who restrains his words has knowledge,
and he who has a cool spirit is a man of discernment.[191]

Proverbs 17:27 offers us wise words when it comes to our sharing biblical truths with those who are short, brusque, terse, rude, snappy even sharp with us. If our voice is soothing, showing that we are concerned about the person, it can ease any tension he may be feeling toward us. Also, if we can get him on a topic that he is interested in, so that he is sharing his thoughts, he may not be so defensive. If not, our tone and our willingness to respect his time and circumstances will leave him appreciating Christians far more than when we engaged him. A warning is

---

[190] The Hebrew word rendered here as "discernment" (*tevunah*) is related to the word *binah*, translated "understanding." Both appear at Proverbs 2:3.

[191] IBID.

offered here as well. If someone appears to be angry, we should just beg off from the conversation and move on, as he might be in a different state of mind later. Furthermore, a female should never witness outside of the public with any male, unless they have another female with them.

Some may appear to be argumentative. Here again, we must discern if he is closed-minded or simple sincere in what he believes to be true. If we decide that he is sincere, it will be a real test of our long-suffering because we should not elevate our tone in the conversation. We should never immediately discern that a person is insincere simply because they have a different view. We may want to use our questions, to draw out exactly what he believes and then use the authority of Scripture instead of our reasoning. (Prov. 20:5) When one hears a Bible verse, he can be more receptive than if we were to say the same thing in our own words. If I say that we are imperfect humans, and we cannot go without sinning, it is my words saying this. If I let him read 1 John 1:8, it is God saying this, "If we say we have no sin, we deceive ourselves, and the truth is not in us." How he reacts to the text, will determine if we continue the conversation, is it beneficial for him, or are we trying to win a discussion. We should leave with an air of mutual respect, and come back another time because he may respond differently. It is no easy task in deciding how much to converse, or should we continue or wait for another occasion. However, over time we will better discern these things, but only if we are out there sharing God's Word in the first place. – 1 Corinthians 3:6; Titus 1:9.

Exercise

Choose about four different Bible topics. For each subject, pick at least four verses that establish this doctrinal position, selecting and adjusting the verses as though you were building a court case. Now, determine how to use leading questions or rhetorical questions to walk someone through these verses. Go out and share one topic with fellow Christians before or after meetings, family and friends, which will give you the practice of sharing God's Word. Do one subject at a time. Do each subject enough times, so that you move through the texts with easy. If you seem to lose focus or stammer, try it another day with someone else. In addition, participate more at the Christian meetings that allow comments.

Review Questions

- How might we develop our abilities as a teacher?
- How can we use questions effectively?
- Why are questions significant to our sharing of the gospel?
- What is persuasion and why is it important?
- What is discernment and how might we use it?
- How can we use discernment in our approach of ones who seem to be evading Bible conversations?

CHAPTER 15 Using Illustrations (Parables)

Matthew 13:34 Updated American English Standard Version (UASV)

34 All these things Jesus spoke to the crowds in **parables**, and without a **parable**, he would not speak to them.

Who Is The Rich Man?

One day a wealthy father took his son on a trip to the country so that the son could see how the poor lived. They spent a day and a night at the farm of a very poor family. When they got back from their trip, the father asked his son, "How was the trip?" "Very good, Dad!" "Did you see how poor people can be?" "Yeah!" "And what did you learn?" The son answered, "I saw that we have a dog at home, and they have four. We have a pool that reaches to the middle of the garden; they have a creek that has no end. We have imported lamps in the house; they have the stars. Our patio reaches to the front yard; they have the whole horizon." When the little boy was finished, the father was speechless. His son then added, "Thanks Dad for showing me how poor we are!"[192]

This was a modern day parable. We have like heard many such stories from parents, grandparents, or schoolteachers. Parables or illustrations are easy to remember because they are light a picture book that might be read to a young child, they stay with you for life. In order to appreciate them, our ears and eyes are not the main tools we must open our minds. Most are not aware but humans process things with images, as this helps them to better process the information and fully understand. Jesus' use of illustrations was of a great variety, such as examples, comparisons, similes, metaphors, and parables.

The parable is a comparison or similitude, a short simple, usually fictitious, story from which a moral or spiritual truth is drawn. The parable as a teaching tool is effective in at least five ways: **(1)** They capture and grip our attention. **(2)** They stimulate the thinking ability. **(3)** They stimulate feelings and reach the sense of right and wrong of the heart. **(4)** They assist in our ability to recall. **(5)** They are always applicable to human life, in every generation. The primary reason the Bible writers use parable is to teach. However, they assist in other ways as well.

---

[192] http://www.parablesite.com/

(7) Understanding a parable, will sometimes force the student not willing to buy out the time, to abandon the pursuit of an answer. Their interest is mere surface and not a matter of the heart. – Matthew 13:13-1.

(8) Parables have the capacity to give the hearer a warning and a reprimand, yet there is no room to retaliate against the speaker, because the hearer is left to discern the application himself. "And when they saw it, the Pharisees began to say to his disciples, "Why does your teacher eat with tax collectors and sinners?" And when he heard it, he said, "Those who are healthy do not have need of a physician, but those [who are sick]. But go and learn what it means, "I want mercy and not sacrifice." For I did not come to call the righteous, but sinners." – Matthew 9:11-13.[193]

(9) The parable can be useful in giving correction to another, helping to sidestep prejudice. This was the case when the prophet Nathan had to counsel King David on his adulterous affair with Bathsheba and the murder of her husband Uriah. – 2 Samuel 12:1-14.

(10)   Parables have the ability to expose a person as to whether he or she is truly servants of God. Jesus said, "Whoever feeds on my flesh and drinks my blood has eternal life, and I will raise him up on the last day." (John 6:54, ESV) By this, Jesus was able to remove those who were not there because of their love for him. – John 6:60-66

Step One in Understanding Parables

Read the context of the parable. We need to find out the setting of the parable, looking for the conditions and the circumstances. Why was the parable told? What prompted its being told? Below, we see the people of Israel being addressed as "rulers of Sodom!" and "people of Gomorrah!" What does that bring to mind? It reminds us of the people of Canaan who were gross sinners again Jehovah God. Gen 13:13; 19:13, 24.

The two debtors (Lu 7:41-43): The reason as to **the why** of the parable of the two debtors, one of whom owed ten times as much as the other, and the parable's implications for us are found in what prompted its telling. (Lu 7:36-40, 44-50) We have to look at the attitude of Simon, the one who was entertaining the guests if we are to find the why of the parable. It was his attitude toward the woman who came in and anointed Jesus' feet with oil.

---

[193] W. Hall Harris, III, The Lexham English Bible (Logos Research Systems, Inc., 2010), Mt 9:10–13.

Step Two in Understanding Parables

Consider the cultural backgrounds, such as the laws and customs of the setting, as well as the idioms that were spoken of earlier.

Building on The two debtors (Lu 7:41-43): The reason as to *the why* of the parable of the two debtors, one of whom owed ten times as much as the other, and the parable's implications for us are found in what prompted its telling, Luke 7:36-40, 44-50.

To have an uninvited person arrive was not out of the ordinary, but they would enter the meal and take a seat along the wall, conversing with those who were invited as well as those who were reclining at the table in the center of the room.

Jesus' parable of the two debtors was quite applicable to the situation. Jesus was pointing out that Simon, the host, did not provide water for Jesus' feet, nor did he greet him with a holy kiss, not counting the fact that he did not grease his head with oil. These were common customs in the first-century culture. However, this woman, who had sinned greatly, she sought Jesus out and showed him greater love and hospitality than Simon had, the host.

Below is the parable of the dragnet (Matt 13:47-50). A knowledge of Levitical law deepens the understanding here. Leviticus 11:9 defines what the Israelites might eat "of all that are in the waters ... any that has fins and scales." Verse 12 of that chapter holds out what God said was unclean and therefore detestable to the Jewish people.

Matthew 13:47-50 Updated American Standard Version (UASV)

⁴⁷ "Again, the kingdom of heaven is like a dragnet cast into the sea, and gathering fish of every kind; ⁴⁸ and when it was filled, they drew it up on the beach; and they sat down and gathered the good fish into containers, but the bad they threw away. ⁴⁹ So it will be at the end of the age; the angels will go out and separate the wicked from among the righteous, ⁵⁰ and throw them into the fiery furnace; in that place there will be weeping and gnashing of teeth.

Below Jesus curses an unproductive fruit tree. Why, what purpose did it serve? An understanding of the historical setting gives us the answer. Fruit trees in first-century Palestine were taxed, with unproductive trees being cut down; therefore, Jesus used this as an opportunity to make an illustrative point. On his return to Jerusalem, Jesus grew hungry. As was the right of any Jew under Mosaic Law, Jesus chose to have figs for breakfast; he noticed the fig tree by the road. Seeing the leaves on it, Jesus assumed it had fruit. Nevertheless, the leaves had sent a false message. The tree had no fruit; the promise of fruit was an empty one.

Remember step one? Find the context. In the section before this, Jesus had judged Israel and its religious leaders, and found them wanting for their idolatrous behavior. (21:12-17) Using the fig tree in an illustrative way, he used it as a small parable, exposing the fruitlessness of Israel and its awaited doom. In similar manner, the religious leaders falsely advertised the fruit of doing God's will and purposes, but like the tree they were sending out a false message. Beneath the leaves of their show display, lie the unfruitful hearts of unbelievers.

Matthew 21:18-22 Updated American Standard Version (UASV)

[18] Now early in the morning, as he was returning to the city, he became hungry. [19] And having seen a certain fig-tree on the way, he came to it, and found nothing in it except leaves only; and he said to it, "Let no fruit come from you ever again." And at once the fig tree withered.

[20] And the disciples having seen this, wondered, saying, "How did the fig tree wither at once?" [21] And Jesus answered and said to them, "Truly I say to you, if you have faith and do not doubt, you will not only do what was done to the fig tree, but even if you say to this mountain, 'Be taken up and cast into the sea,' it will happen. [22] And all the things you ask in prayer, having faith, you will receive."

Step Three in Understanding Parables

This is a two-point step. The first point is to **look to the author of the parable for the upcoming meaning of the parable**. An interpreter of a parable by Jesus would see what he meant in the context it was spoken, and then consider his teaching as a whole. The second point is, **do not assign subjective meanings to the elements of a parable**. Generally, a parable teaches one basic point. We do not want to follow in the path of allegorical interpreters that find significance in every tiny aspect of parable, like Augustine in his interpretation of the Good Samaritan. No, we need to look for the main point. Discovering the main point of a parable can be achieved using the following four stages.[194]

---

[194] The stages to discovering the main point are based on Dr. Robert Stein's book, the Basic Guide to Biblical Interpretation, specifically pages 147-148.

Stage One: Discovering the Main Characters

In any given parable, it is highly important to find the main 2-3 characters. Throughout these stages, let us examine the parable of the Good Samaritan. For a better understanding of the significance of the characters and the impact of this parable to its original audience, we need to look back at step two of understanding parables, the cultural background. Our modern mind thinks of the Samaritans as good because of this parable, but this is not how Jesus' audience would have viewed them. Jews considered them a detestable enemy of God. The Samaritan's history was marked with idol worship and defiance of God's law. This combined with hundreds of years of betrayal and conniving, served to fuel the Jewish fires of hatred toward them. Commenting on the attitude of Jews toward Samaritans, the Talmud no doubt expressed the feeling of many Jews: "May I never set eyes on a Samaritan." In addition, the Talmud taught, "a piece of bread given by a Samaritan is more unclean than swine's flesh." So intense was anti-Samaritan feeling that some Jews even cursed Samaritans publicly in the synagogues and prayed daily that the Samaritans would not be granted everlasting life.

Luke 10:29-37 Updated American Standard Version (UASV)

[29] But he, desiring to justify himself, said to Jesus, "And who is my neighbor?" [30] Jesus replied and said, "A man was going down from Jerusalem to Jericho, and he fell among robbers, who stripped him and laid blows upon and departed, leaving him half dead. [31] Now by coincidence a certain priest was going down on that road, and when he saw him, he passed by on the other side. [32] Likewise a Levite also, when he came to the place and saw him, passed by on the other side. [33] But a Samaritan, who was on a journey, came upon him; and when he saw him, he felt compassion, [34] and came to him and bandaged up his wounds, pouring oil and wine on them; and he put him on his own beast, and brought him to an inn and took care of him. [35] And on the next day, he took out two denarii[195] and gave them to the innkeeper, and said, "Take care of him; and whatever more you spend, when I return I will repay you.' [36] Which of these three, do you think, proved to be a neighbor to the man who fell among the robbers?" [37] And he said, "The one who showed mercy toward him." Then Jesus said to him, "Go and do likewise."

---

[195] The denarius was equivalent to a day's wages for a laborer

Characters

(1) The man going down to Jericho

(2) The Robbers

(3) The Priest

(4) The Levite

(5) The Good Samaritan

(6) The Innkeeper

(7) The lawyer

The three main characters are the priest, the Levite and the good Samaritan. Think about it, does it really matter who the man is? Jesus told the story of one man, who is a victim without making known the man by race, occupation, or reason for traveling. What about the robbers and the innkeeper? They only serve the function of getting us to that main point. They are like the extra in a movie. Their only role is to move the movie along.

Stage Two: Looking to the End

As is true with any kind of story, the end of the story carries the weight of importance. This is no different with parables. The ending is where the answers lie. Look at the end of the story one more time; take note of Jesus' question to the lawyer. Jesus removed the attention from the term "neighbor." Essentially the lawyer had asked, 'who is the one that I should show my neighborly love to?' Notice his attention is on the one receiving the kindness. However, Jesus asked, "which of these three, do you think, proved to be a neighbor to the man who fell among the robbers?" Notice that Jesus' focus was not on the recipient of the love, but the one who showed the love, the Samaritan.

Stage Three: Who Carries the Conversation

We may have noticed that there is no conversation between the man going down to Jericho and anyone else. There is no conversation between the robbers and the man, the priest and the man, the Levite and the man, the Samaritan and the man. The only direct conversation is between the Samaritan and the innkeeper. The focus of conversation is between the Samaritan and the innkeeper, which highlights the Samaritan's motive and heart attitude.

Stage Four: Who Gets the Most Press

Generally, whoever gets the most coverage in a story is the primary character, followed by the secondary person that must exist to facilitate the story and its main point. In the parable of the Good Samaritan, there is little doubt that the Samaritan gets the most coverage throughout the parable, as he gets six verses, while everyone else received one verse. However, the man who went down to Jericho receives just as much coverage, with seven verses actually. Yet, his role is secondary to the active role of the Samaritan.

Thus, our two primary characters are the Samaritan and the man going down to Jericho. It might be added that the "man" who went down to Jericho and fell victim to robbers, was a Jew, as the context of the story shows. The lawyer asking the question is also a Jew, likely with many other Jewish listeners. The priest and Levite in the parable were Jewish religious leaders, who 'when they saw him [their own Jewish countryman lying there dying from a robbery] they passed by on the other side.' However, we have a Samaritan willing to help a Jewish victim. Thus, the primary point involves both characters (they who received the most press). Remember Jesus focus was on the person showing the love, not the victim needing loving act of kindness. A **true neighbor** [the Samaritan] takes the initiative to show love to **others** [the man going down to Jericho] regardless of their ethnic background.

He Did Not Speak to Them without a Parable

Many would rightly argue that Jesus Christ was the greatest teacher who ever lived. His use of parables contributes to his being considered as such. It has been 2,000 years, but if asked what Jesus said about the sower, the weeds among the wheat, the mustard seed, the merchant seeking pearls, or any of the other three dozen parables, some Christians would know the accounts. Why did Jesus use parables so much in his teachings? Moreover, why were they so effective?

The apostle Matthew offers a reason for using parables, when he writes, "He did not speak to them without a parable. This was to fulfill what was spoken through the prophet." (Matt 13:34-35, NASB) Matthew was referring to Psalm 78:2, which reads in part, prophetically speaking of Jesus, "I will open my mouth in a parable." The idea that hundreds of years earlier, it would be prophesied that the Son of God would use parables as one of his main methods of teaching, certainly evidences their value.

However, Jesus offered another reason for his use of parables. He had just given the crowds the parable of the sower, And the disciples came and said to Him, "Why do You speak to them in parables?" Jesus answered them, "To you it has been granted to know the mysteries of the kingdom of heaven, but to them it has not been granted ... I speak to them in parables; because while seeing they do not see and while hearing they do not hear, nor do they understand. In their case the prophecy of Isaiah is being fulfilled, which says, 'You will keep on hearing, but will not understand; You will keep on seeing, but will not perceive; For the heart of this people has become dull, With their ears they scarcely hear, And they have closed their eyes, Otherwise they would see with their eyes, Hear with their ears, And understand with their heart and return, And I would heal them.'" – Matthew 13:2-15; Isaiah 6:9-10.

In other words, Jesus used parable to sift out those who were not going to be receptive to the truths he wished to share. How did the parables accomplish this? Well, we just saw in the beginning of this chapter that interpreting parables is not as easy as one might thing, as there are rules and principles of interpretation that must be followed. Therefore, if one were humble and admitted they did not fully understand, they would be moved to ask for the answer of what was meant. (Matt. 13:36; Mark 4:34) Those with proud hearts would have the truths hid from them, not be Jesus, but by their own pride. What though made them so effective?

Careful Use of Details

Jesus carefully selected the details. If there was a need to provide specifics in a story that he was relating, he made sure that they were there. For example, in the parable of the lost Sheep, Jesus stated exactly that there were a hundred sheep, one went astray, and leaving ninety-nine behind, with the owner going out to search for the one. In the parable of the lost sheep, the details mattered, to stress the importance of the one, i.e., each one of us count as much as the whole. (Matt. 18:12-14) How many laborers were in the parable of the workers in the vineyard? (Matt. 20:1-16) How many talents were given in the parable of the talents to make the point about being entrusted? – Matthew 25:14-30.

On the other hand, if adding details were unnecessary, he left them out, as it may prevent ones from arriving at what he meant to convey. If we think about the Parable of the Unforgiving Slave, Jesus never gave us just how that slave managed to run up a debt of ten thousand talents (a talent = 6,000 denarii), so we are talking 60,000,000 denarii, and a single denarius was equal to a day's wages for a typical worker. Let me put it another way; a talent was worth about twenty years' wages of a laborer, which makes Jesus hyperbolic point that it was a sum of money that could never be repaid. Note how I have given enormous details on this one point because it makes my point. Jesus using such an astronomical number meant it was not necessary that he give how the slave got there because it made his point that we need to forgive. Moreover, it showed just how much God could forgive while imperfect humans tended to forgive far less. (Matt. 18:23-35) When we look at the

Prodigal Son Parable, we see that Jesus never said why the younger son demanded that he has his inheritance early, or why he wasted it. However, in that same parable, Jesus went into details on the part that matter, once the younger son returned in a humble, repentant manner. The details of the Father's response was what was needed for Jesus to convey his point of just how much God can forgive while imperfect humans (the older son) tended to forgive far less. – Isaiah 55:7; Luke 15:11-32.

Think too, of how wise Jesus was in the way he depicted the characters in his parables. When Jesus gave us a character, he was not bogged down in what he looked like, but rather he focused on what the character said or how he acted in the story. When we think of the Parable of the Samaritan, we are not given what he looked like, how old he was, but rather how he dealt with an injured Jew, who were enemies with Samaritans, lying in the road. Jesus gave what details were necessary for us to arrive at the point of loving our neighbor, regardless of race or nationality. – Luke 10:29, 33-37.

Jesus knew that his parables impact would be far great if it were not muddled with unnecessary details, but had some details peppered in the right place. Therefore, he was able to make it easier for those listening to him, as well as millions of future readers, to recall and retell these same lessons with his parables.

Take Information from Daily Life

Jesus had a prehuman existence in heaven, so he would have been aware of everything every society had ever done, in every single person's life. Thus, he had a storehouse of material to draw on for his parables. What did he do, though? He did not take the life experience of a Pharaoh and incorporate it into a parable for the poor Jewish person in the first century. No, rather, he used the information that related to their lives, and things that he experienced as he grew up in Nazareth. An example was his observations of his watching his mother take a piece of fermented dough saved from a previous baking and using it to prepare leavened bread. (Matt. 13:33) What about his observations of the fishermen on the Sea of Galilee (Matt. 13:47) Then, although Jesus was a perfect human, as a child he likely placed with other children in the marketplace. (Matt. 11:16) Certainly, he must have saw seeds being sown by farmers, he must have gone to some marriage feasts, and he grain fields at harvest time. (Matt. 13:3-8; 25:1-12; Mark 4:26-29) This is why we see things from his daily life scattered throughout his parables. Jesus' parables also drew on things from creation, like plants, animals, and nature. (Matt. 6:26, 28-30; 16:2-3) In the parable of the Good Shepherd, John Chapter 10, Jesus uses sheep, which were common in first-century Israel, and how they follow their shepherd. Jesus also used current events that his listeners would have been aware of, such as those eighteen on whom the tower in Siloam fell and killed them. – Luke 13:4.

Exercise

As you learn several new things from the Bible, come up with an illustration that would best convey what the author meant. Then, share this illustration with some at the Christian meetings.

Review Questions

- What is a parable?
- In what five ways is the parable as a teaching tool effective?
- In what other ways do parables assist as effective teaching tools?
- What barriers are there to understanding parables?
- How is the allegory of the Good Samaritan a perfect example of excess and demonstrates the interpreter's ability to make a text say whatever he wants?
- Explain step one in understanding parables.
- Explain step two in understanding parables.
- Explain step three in understanding parables.
- Explain the importance of discovering the main character.
- Why should we look to the end of a parable?
- Why should we focus in on, who carries the conversation?
- Why is important to discover, who gets the most press?
- Why did Jesus teach with parables?
- How do we know that Jesus used parables, to which his first-century listeners could relate?
- Why is it important that we be careful with the details when we use illustrations?
- On what can we draw when using illustrations?

CHAPTER 16 Reaching the Heart of Our Listener

Acts 18:1-4 Updated American Standard Version (UASV)

¹After these things he departed from Athens and went to Corinth. ²And he found a Jew named Aquila, a native of Pontus, having recently come from Italy with his wife Priscilla, because Claudius had commanded all the Jews to leave Rome. He came to them, ³and because he was of the same trade he stayed with them and worked, for they were tentmakers by trade. ⁴And **he reasoned** in the synagogue every Sabbath, **trying to persuade** Jews and Greeks.

If we were to read all four Gospel accounts, focusing on Jesus' way of teaching, we would find that he was all about reaching the heart of his listeners. Looking at the Parable of the Sower, Jesus starts with simply telling them the parable. (Matt 13:1-9) He then tells them the purpose of his use of parables. (Matt. 13:10-17) He then closes with explaining the Parable of the Sowers. (Matt. 13:18-23) The setting here was Jesus telling the parable to great crowds gathered about him by the sea. Almost all just thought he was sharing stories with principles behind them, nothing more. It is in this section that Jesus lets us know that his parables are deeper than that, and that is why his explanation of the parable to his disciples was as follows, "You, therefore, listen to the parable of the sower." (Matt. 13:8, LEB) Others read, "Hear then the parable of the sower." The seed was the message of the kingdom and for us on a grander scale it is the Word of God as a whole. This seed was being thrown on four *different* kinds of soil, i.e., *differing* conditions of the heart. The thing to keep in mind is this; all four *different* types of heart conditions heard the Word.

Hearing the Word

The first type of soil is hard, the second did not have much soil, and the third fell among the thorns. The fourth type of soil, nothing like the other three, the seeds fell on good soil. The **seed** was *sown beside the road* **[first soil]**. This is packed soil, meaning that this one was too much involved in Satan's world and the fallen flesh for the seed of the Word to take root in his shallow heart. While the Word of God may sound attractive, he is sidetracked before, he can grow to love God's Word, so *"the evil one comes and snatches away* what has been sown in his heart." The **seed** *"was sown on the rocky places* **[second soil]**, this is the man who hears the word and immediately receives it with joy." This is referring to a person who likes what the Bible has to say, as they will listen to the Christian message and by all intent and purposes appear to be a Christian, but the Word in no way affects his heart. When he faces the difficulties of life or opposition to his faith or the Word, he fails to apply the Word of God because he had never actually taken it seriously. Jesus says of this one, "he has no firm root in himself but is only temporary, and when affliction or persecution arises because of the word, immediately *he falls away*."

The **seed** "was *sown among the thorns* **[third soil]**, this is the man who hears the word, and the worry of the world and the deceitfulness of wealth choke the word, and it *becomes unfruitful*." This refers to the one who hears the word but his anxieties over his love of money and love of the world cause him anxiety, and he is overcome and becomes unfruitful. "And the one on whom **seed** was *sown on the good soil* **[fourth soil]**, this is the man who hears the word and understands it; who indeed bears fruit and brings forth, some a hundredfold, some sixty, and some thirty." This refers to the one who hears the Word with a receptive heart. James, Jesus' half-brother in his letter, was very straightforward with the advice that fits with what Jesus is saying here about the good soil or the good heart. James wrote, "But prove yourselves doers of the word, and not merely hearers who delude themselves." (Jam. 1:22) He also said, "Faith without works is dead." (Jam. 2:14-26) Works do not save us. However, we cannot have a genuine faith without an evident demonstration of that faith in Christian works. Indeed, each of us wants to believe that the Word of God is falling on our heart of good soil. Nevertheless, in the end, it will be God, who makes that determination. (Pro. 17:3; 1 Cor. 4:4, 5) Notice that the man with the good soil, i.e., heart, produces fruit and brings forth different levels of yield depending on his circumstances. The yield is our Christian works that evidence our faith as being genuine and our soil (heart) as being good.

As we can see from the Parable of the Sower, Jesus was about sowing the Word of God on good soil. We want those to whom we speak to understand it and to act on it. Therefore, as we witness and teach, we need to focus on getting to the heart of our listeners. We want them to love the Word of God and its Author. Thus, we want to imitate Jesus in our evangelizing and teaching. This means that we will take the time out of the world to study, grow in a knowledge of God's Word, to help others find the path to salvation. Certainly, the apostle Peter followed in the footsteps of Christ right at Pentecost 33 C.E., just after Jesus ascension back to heaven. Peter was able to reach the hearts of 3,000 who were then baptized. He explained the prophecy of Joel, helping his listeners to reason from the Scriptures as it related to the death and resurrection of Jesus Christ, and how this was the will and purposes of the Father. (Acts 2:1-36) "Now when they heard this they were **cut to the heart**, and said to Peter and the rest of the apostles, 'Brothers, what shall we do?'" (Acts 2:37) We learn in verse 41 that "Those who received his word were baptized, and there were added that day about three thousand souls." As Christian teachers, we also want to reach people's hearts and help them to grow to love the Word of God.

Buying Out the Time to Reach the Heart

This next two heading sections will go beyond the conversation with someone and enter the realms of having a personal one-on-one Bible study. First, we need to study a book with him that will enable him to understand the basic Bible beliefs fully. I am recommending a book of mine that will be out by January 2016. *THE EVANGELISM STUDY TOOL Basic Bible Doctrines of the Christian Faith* by Edward D. Andrews[196] Once we begin our study with a Bible student, we must of course help them to acquire the knowledge that they need, but they also must feel something about this knowledge. Jesus said at John 17:3, "And this is eternal life, **that they know you** the only true God, and Jesus Christ whom you have sent." The clause "that they may know you," indicates a relationship between the person knowing and God. It is so, in this respect, God is of value or importance to the one who knows, hence a relationship. This will take its course naturally, as we get the Bible student to reason on what they learn. – Acts 17:2-3.

(1) How does the account of Abraham offering up his son Isaac help us to appreciate the sacrifice the Father made with the Son? ((John 3:16; Gen. 22:1-18) Note how Isaac is described in Genesis 22:2.

- How does this help us with the hope that we hold? Rom. 8:32, 38-39)

- Is there anything required on our part, if so, what? (Gen. 22:18; John 3:36)

(2) When Peter at Pentecost identifies Jesus as a prophet like Moses, what accountability and responsibility comes with it? (Acts 3:22, 23; Deut. 18:15-19)

- What is the greatest thing that Jesus has spoken to us, and why are they very appropriate at present? (Matt. 24:14; 28:18-20; Acts 1:8)

(3) The author of Hebrews explains what the priesthood of Aaron foreshadowed. How does this help us draw closer to Jesus in know his qualities, which are? (Heb. 4:15–5:3; 7:26-28)

---

[196] http://www.christianpublishers.org/apps/webstore/products/show/6102323

- How should we feel about going to the Father in prayer in the name of Jesus, so we can overcome our human weaknesses?

(4) Jesus ransom Sacrifice was far superior to anything under the Mosaic Law, yet why is it important that we pay special attention to the our sinning in a willful ongoing way? (Hebrews 10:26-27)

- If we are moved by a love, an appreciation, for an opportunity at eternal life and the hope of such, what things will we be thorough in doing? (Heb. 10:19-25)

Be Prepared to Study – Student and Teacher

If we are studying with a Bible student, say one day a week for an hour, both the student and the teacher should prepare for each study. Before the study, both should know how much material is going to be covered in the following session. Both teacher and student should have read the material, looked up and researched any cited texts, and answered any questions within the material. The answer should be highlighted, with any extra thoughts written in the margins of the book. The teacher should prepare with the student's needs in mind. As we grow to know our students, we can spend extra time on areas that they may need help.

Overcoming Objections

We now return to conversation evangelism (i.e., preevangelism), which seeks to persuade other people to become Christian, especially by sharing the basics of the Gospel, but also the deeper message of biblical truths. Each time we speak with anyone, we need to make the most of our opportunity to share God's Word in the best, most efficient, way possible. Even in the difficult times of these last days, we are reminded, "... let us continually offer up a sacrifice of praise to God, that is, the fruit of lips that acknowledge his name." (Heb. 13:15, ESV) We need to 'always be prepared to make a defense to anyone who asks us for a reason for the hope that is in us.' (1 Pet. 3:15) This is true even to the point of being able to overcome what may seem like legitimate objections by those with a sincere interest in an answer.

Objections can come about for any number of reasons. There will be people who honestly believe that they have a legitimate reason for not accepting God or his Word. We simply have to be prepared without even knowing what the objection may be. Over time, we will begin to have ready responses because objections will be the same for many people. They may say, "I reject Christianity because of the blood spilled by Christianity throughout the medieval times and the Reformation." Many individuals are well aware of the religious record of hypocrisy, oppression, and inquisitions.

Moreover, televangelist, living a lifestyle of luxury off the back of their flock, manipulating their people in a cultish way is very prevalent today. Some struggle with the concept of hellfire, while others struggle with a loving God, who is all-powerful, yet fails to prevent pain, suffering and death. As these objections come our way, the best thing is to answer them if we can.

However, not with some weak solution where we are stammering to make sense of things, as this will only make things worse. If we do not have a reasonable response, we say, "You have raised an excellent point, while I cannot give you an answer today, I can come back with a reasonable, logical response later." Then, we spend a week researching the issue and return with the response that will be well received by a person with an open mind.

If a person tries to dismiss us out of hand with "I am not interested," we can ask them some tactful questions. We might say, "if I may respectfully ask, why you are not interested?' You could go on, "there is always the possibility that I may have an answer to something that might have been troubling you." You could even be frank by saying, "I mean there are things that have troubled me in the past." Yes, there are times when we are being cut short; we can take one last opportunity by asking some tactful, direct, and thought-provoking questions. The most important piece of advice here comes from the last part of Peter's words at 3:15, that is, we are to "do it with gentleness and respect."

Exercise

Someone said to you, "I do not believe the Bible is the Word of God. Yes, it offers good advice but so did many ancient books. Moreover, there is no such thing as absolute truth anyway." How would you respond?

Review Questions

- Why do Christians need to reach the heart of their listeners?
- Explain Jesus' Parable of the Sower. How does it apply to us today?
- How might we reach the heart of a Bible student that we are studying with one-on-one?
- How should the teacher and the student prepare for their study?
- How can we overcome objections?

CHAPTER 17 Using the Bible When Evangelizing

Acts 17:1-4 Updated American Standard Version (UASV)

¹ Now when they had passed through Amphipolis and Apollonia, they came to Thessalonica, where there was a synagogue of the Jews. ² And according to Paul's custom, he went to them, and for three Sabbaths **reasoned with them from the Scriptures,** ³ **explaining and proving** that it was necessary that the Christ had to suffer and rise again from the dead, and saying, "This Jesus whom I am **proclaiming** to you is the Christ." ⁴ And some of them were **persuaded** and joined Paul and Silas, as did a great many of the devout Greeks and not a few of the leading women.

What kind of success have we had in our communities when we have attempted to share the good news with others? If we are net getting the response that we might hope for, could it be that we are not using our Bibles when we evangelize. As we can see from the above, Paul's success came about from his reasoning from the Scriptures. Yes, the Bible is primarily viewed as a relic today, and even most are not familiar with it, some even detesting it. However, "the word of God is living and active and sharper than any two-edged sword, and piercing as far as the division of soul and spirit, of both joints and marrow, and able to judge the thoughts and intentions of the heart." (Heb. 4:12) Yes, the Bible will expose to us, who have a receptive heart. True enough, we are obligated to do our fair share of reasoning, explaining and proving, as we attempt to persuade them that the Bible is the Word of God, but if we run into an unreasonable mind that fails to accept our reasoning, we now know we can move on to another.

If we and others are not out in our communities, making the Word of God known, it will not be long before it is a relic in some museum. Therefore, our evangelism and especially our evangelism with our primary tool, the Bible, are of greater importance today than in any other. We do not want to adopt the attitude that others can do the work we were assigned or that God will find the ones who are his. As we have clearly seen, God has given us the privilege of serving as his ambassadors of the good news to the world. Moreover, such an attitude would not be in harmony with Scripture. Romans 10:14 pointedly asked, "How then will they call on him in whom they have not believed? And how are they to believe in him of whom they have never heard? And how will they hear without someone to preach?" To use the Bible efficiently necessitates preparation.

Using the Bible to Introduce Ourselves

When we engage people about the Bible, how will they view us after the conversation? Do we want them to identify us clearly as a disciple of Jesus Christ, who is very efficient with our Bible? Would it not be great if they told their friends, "I ran into a Christian yesterday, and while I may not agree with everything he said, he sure was able to find whatever he wanted from the Bible and made pretty good arguments as well." If we are to be known in such a way, clearly, we must be able to use the Bible when we are witnessing.

We can begin a conversation by using the Scriptures themselves, touching on the common desires and current events. We might say, "Hello, my name is _____; I am sharing a Scripture that offers hope from Revelation 21:4, which reads, 'and he [God] will wipe away every tear from their eyes, and death shall be no more, neither shall there be mourning, nor crying, nor pain anymore, for the former things have passed away.' Do you think that this is ever possible?" Therefore, we have offered a Scriptural Introduction and a thought provoking question.

"Hello, my name is _____; I am sharing a Scripture that offers comfort in these difficult times from Proverbs 29:2 (ESV). It says, 'When the righteous increase, the people rejoice, but when the wicked rule, the people groan.' Do you believe that we will ever see a day when there will be no more wickedness?" In both of these Scriptural introductions, there is an opportunity to build on a conversation of what turmoil our planet is in and its need for a solution, but imperfect humans have failed miserably. This will lead to the only true hope, which is Jesus Christ and his Kingdom. For all who want to shut us down and not engage, simply have a Bible tract read, to see if they will at least take that.

Thinking of the immigration issue that is all over the media today, how might we use that in out introduction? "Hello, my name is _____; I am out sharing some thoughts on situations that impact communities around the world, but especially here at home. Would you not agree if people of different backgrounds and cultures could live together in unity, life would be far better?" [Allow an answer] "Would this not also make life more secure for everyone?" [Allow an answer] Look at Acts 10:34-35 (ESV), "Truly I understand that God shows no partiality, but in every nation anyone who fears him and does what is right is acceptable to him." What would this require of us? [Allow an answer] This hot topic can go in many different ways, as polls have shown a variety of different views on the matter. We simply need to prepare ourselves and start making use of the Bible.

Psalm 119:130 Updated Standard Version (UASV)

[130] The unfolding of your words gives light;
it gives understanding to the simple.

Making Use of the Bible

Jesus referred to the Hebrew Scriptures as his authority over 120 times, from direct quotations to references, allusions, and paraphrases. There are over 960 from the other authors outside of the Gospels. (John 7:16; Acts 17:2) We all should want to copy their example, as we go about sharing the Scriptures. The question we want to ask ourselves is, are we able to use the Scriptures as efficiently as we would like? One of the best ways we can improve our abilities in this matter is through Bible study, personal and family. However, there are other ways as well.

One way to improve our abilities to use the Bible is when we are at the Christian meetings. Many churches today put the Scriptures up on a big screen by way of a computer and a projector. We should not allow the church to take away the one tool that will enhance and maintain our skill of using the Scriptures. Every time a Scripture is mentioned or even fully quoted, we need to look it up in our Bibles. Remember the days before the technology of the cell phone, how we had many phone numbers memorized, because we actually had to dial the numbers when we called. Now, if our cell phone dies, we have no clue what other people's numbers are. Technology in the churches is doing the same to our skills of using our Bibles effectively because of their use of computers and projectors.

Another way is that we stop reading Christian books, and we start studying them. We need to be at a desk or a table with a tablet, pen, pencil, highlighter, and a Bible. Every time a Scripture is referred to, we look it up. We want to begin to build cases for biblical augments in the process. As we start turning to all of these scriptures, we need to start underline key words, phrases, and clauses that are relevant to making a biblical point. We need to remember the points that are made and eventually we will have a stream of them that tell us something, evidence for a particular teaching.

What we can also do is use those blank pages in our Bible, making a list of topics for Bible discussion. Once we have a lengthy list of subjects, it is only a matter of adding Scriptures as we come to them in our studies. If we make good use of the Bible in every facet of our Christian life, such as personal study preparing for meetings, and at the meeting, we will be able to make proper use of the Bible when witnessing to others. – 1 Timothy 4:16.

Using Good Judgment

The Bible is under attack today, and it is as hated as much any person has been. Thus, we must be careful in our use of it because the mere sight of it can cause some to get angry. Our goal is not to provoke others, but rather to build rapport, so they are receptive to our message. Therefore, if we see any body language from the listener that would indicate the mere mention of the Bible cause frustration, we would want to change our tactics, such as talking around the Bible until the mood lightens. Then, there are those, who are not troubled by the Bible but are of a new generation that knows absolutely nothing about the Bible or theological terms like a ransom sacrifice or a propitiatory cover. We may overwhelm them if we overly use the Bible or do not define and qualify some words that we use.

The apostle Paul told young Timothy to "rightly handling the word of truth." The same would hold true for us today. We certainly want to copy the good example of Jesus and the New Testament authors, as we too make good use of the Bible in our evangelism. We can do so by opening it and reading from it directly, or merely quoting it, or even paraphrasing what the author penned.

Exercise

This week, find three opportunities at introducing yourself to a stranger as a Christian and share just one Scripture, John 5:28-29, asking them 'what them what do you think, is the resurrection that Jesus spoke of possible?' Another exercise for this week is looking up every Scripture that comes before your eyes. Once it is looked up, ponder why the speaker or book used that particular text. Once that is realized, underline the word, phrase, or clause within the text. If the text is a good fit for any of our Bible topics, we should add it. You might want to read a few verses before and after our text if time permits, just so you are aware of the context.

Review Questions

- Why is it highly important that we use the Bible in our evangelism?

- How can we using the Bible to introduce ourselves?

- What are some ways we can improve our abilities to use the Bible?

- Why is it important that we use good judgment in our use of the Bible when evangelizing?

CHAPTER 18 Witnesses to Those from Other Religions

1 Timothy 2:3-4 Updated American Standard Version (UASV)

³ This is good, and it is acceptable in the sight of God our Savior, ⁴ who desires all men to be saved and to come to an accurate knowledge[197] of truth.

Witnessing to a Muslim

Many have not had many opportunities to witness to a Muslim. Most of us because of radical Islam (e.g., ISIS and Al Qaeda) over the past 15-years have gotten to know that they have a fervent belief in Allah, the Islamic name of God. However, most Muslims are not that familiar with what the Bible truly teaches. It is our hope that we can share our faith with Muslims when the opportunity presents itself. (1 Tim. 2:3-4) The following is a simple introduction to that process. For more on this subject, please see the following book that will be out late 2015. A CHRISTIAN'S GUIDE TO ISLAM: What Every Christian Needs to Know About Islam and the Rise of Radical Islam by Daniel Janosik[198]

Islamic Worldview

A worldview in the simplest terms is "the sum total of a person's answers to the most important questions in life."[199] Ironically, in today's world, while everyone has a worldview, most are unaware of what it is and how it may affect their life. For this reason, most worldviews are deficient, contradictory, and seldom are they united in thought with their many different pieces. (Nash 1999, 13)

While most of the earth's seven billion residents are walking around unaware of the fact that they are carrying an insufficient worldview; it actually affects every facet of their life. Moreover, it is actually a matter of life and death that one not only become better aware of their worldview. However, it must be brought into alignment with the only worldview

---

[197] *Epignosis* is a strengthened or intensified form of *gnosis* (*epi*, meaning "additional"), meaning, "true," "real," "full," "complete" or "accurate," depending upon the context. Paul and Peter alone use *epignosis*.

[198] http://www.christianpublishers.org/apps/webstore/products/show/5749263

[199] Zondervan (2010-06-19). Life's Ultimate Questions: An Introduction to Philosophy . Zondervan. Kindle Edition.

that matter, the thinking of the Creator of humankind himself as he has revealed to us through his loving revelation, the Bible.

What is of supreme importance then, is that the Christians continuously evaluate their own worldview, making sure that it is in harmony with God's Word. Nevertheless, it is just as important to familiarize ourselves with the worldview of others: Buddhism, Hinduism, Shintoism, and Islam, to mention a few. "Converts and immigrant [of Islamic] communities are found in almost every part of the world. With about 1.62 billion followers or 23% of the global population, Islam is the second-largest religion by number of adherents and, according to many sources, the fastest-growing major religion in the world."[200]

Evangelism is the obligation of every Christian, to teach and preach the gospel to the ends of the earth. (Matt 24:14; 28:19-20; Ac 1:8) It is for this reason that we will look at the worldview of Islam and contrast it with the Christian belief system. Initially, we will offer a brief overview of how Islam got its start and explain some terms that should help us better understand the Islamic mindset. Next, we will look at a short overview of five facets that every worldview possesses: Islam's view of God, view reality, knowledge, moral code, and religious character. Finally, we will contrast the beliefs systems of Islam with Christianity before ending with a brief overview of what has been said herein.

Short Overview of Islam[201]

Muhammad bin [son of] Abdullah, was born about 570 C.E., in the prosperous trade city of Mecca. Young Muhammad was very much dissatisfied with the religious system of his day, it becoming known as the 'time of ignorance.' His people were steeped in idolatry and the worship of hundreds of local deities. Muhammad through his interactions with local Christian and Jewish traders had becomes just as disappointed with their approach to God as well. As far as he was concerned, both Judaism and Christianity had abandoned Allah,[202] and for this reason, the God of the Bible was raising up one last prophet to restore the pure religion of Abraham.

According to *A Christian's Pocket Guide to Islam* "the Jews, the Arabs gained a superficial knowledge of the Old Testament stories and Jewish

---

[200] Islam - Wikipedia, the free encyclopedia, http://en.wikipedia.org/wiki/Islam (accessed September 14, 2015).

[201] [Ar *islām* submission (to the will of God)] 1817.—*Merriam-Webster's Collegiate Dictionary*. Eleventh ed. Springfield, Mass.: Merriam-Webster, Inc., 2003

[202] (Arab. *Allāh*, a contraction of *al-Ilāh*, "the God")—*The Encyclopedia of Christianity*, 749

folklore, which is seen in the pages of the Quran. The Christianity that Muhammad encountered was brought to Arabia chiefly by Christians who had fled from the Byzantine Empire, victims of the intricate Christological controversies of those days, who had been condemned as heretics. Muhammad's very imperfect understanding of Christian doctrine was probably due to the nature of these informants." (Sookhdeo 2001, 10)

Muhammad's marriage into a wealthy family afforded him the opportunity to engage in meditative thought as to his religious environment. It was on one of these occasioned trips that Allah or Gabriel began to come to him while he was in his trance. The inhabitants of Mecca were not receptive to these visions, believing Muhammad to be "demon-possessed." It is at this point, about 622 C.E.; Muhammad made his flight to Medina. This also corresponds with the start of the Muslim[203] calendar. As a result, dates are known as A.H.[204] (Sookhdeo 2001, 12, 80)

The Arabic word jihad[205] was given birth to in about 624 C.E. after the battle of Badr, in which it was decided that the Muslim had an obligation to perform a jihad whenever they perceived a threat of any sort. Further, it was here in Medina that the Quran, a sacred textbook, was further developed into the final revelation from Allah. It is here too that many of the traditions of Islam had their beginning: prayer toward Jerusalem, Friday as the day of worship, and the fast of Ramadan.[206] In Muhammad's lifetime, he managed to conquer all of Arabia, being the first to unite all Muslims as one, into the religion of Islam. Muhammad died in 632 C.E. and was succeeded by Caliph[207] Abu Bakr in 634 C.E. and Caliph Umar in 644 C.E. Throughout this initial period of unity, Syria, Iraq, Persia, and Egypt fell to the newly founded Islamic empire. (Sookhdeo 2001, 13)

There are the two major divisions of Islam, the Sunni and the Shiah. This came apart back at the time of Muhammad's successors and is based on a discrepancy of understanding as to who are his lawful religious heirs. Does the procession come after Muhammad's lineage as the Shiite Muslims assert or is it based on elective office as the majority Sunni claim?

---

[203] [Ar muslim, lit., one who submits (to God)] ca.1615—Merriam-Webster's Collegiate Dictionary. Eleventh ed. Springfield, Mass.: Merriam-Webster, Inc., 2003

[204] Anno Hegirae, year of the flight

[205] [Ar jihād] 1869: a holy war waged on behalf of Islam as a religious duty also: a personal struggle in devotion to Islam esp. involving spiritual discipline—ibid.

[206] [Ar Ramaḍān] ca. 1595: the ninth month of the Islamic year observed as sacred with fasting practiced daily from dawn to sunset—ibid.

[207] [caliphe, Ar khalīfa successor] 14c: a successor of Muhammad as temporal and spiritual head of Islam —ibid.

The argument continues to this day, with no resolution in sight. The Sunni Muslims are in the majority by about ninety percent, with most of the ten percent of Shiah being found in Iran. Of course, with the Shiah being in the minority, they are under constant persecution by the Sunnis. (Sookhdeo 2001, 65)

Five Facets of the Islamic Worldview[208]

Unlike most of the religious systems that exist today, Islam has accomplished a way of life that many other institutions only dream of, a unity to the point that the Quran and the hadith[209] govern their religious system, state laws, and all social settings, Shariah law.[210] It is sacrilege to violate any of the religious norms, and one Muslim will correct another, and in many cases, it can mean death in Islamic countries.

View of God

Allah is the God of Islam. The Quran states: "So believe in God and His apostles. Say not 'Trinity': desist: it will be better for you: for God is One God." (Surah 4:171, AYA) The Quran does not dispute the reality of God's existence, like the Bible, it simply speaks as though he is. For the Muslim, Allah is almighty, all powerful, all knowing, and has no equal. Allah is the God of judgment and is to be feared in the sense of dread, not a reverential fear. As Abraham was God's friend, the concept of a Muslim being the friend of Allah would be foreign to his mindset.

View of Reality

Islam believes Allah, "Almighty God" is the One who created the universe. They believe that the universe we are living in is not eternal as on the Day of Judgment there will be new Heaven and new earth. "On the Day when the earth will be changed to another earth and so will be the heavens and they (all creatures) will appear before Allah, the One, the Irresistible." (Quran 14:48) Further, they believe the universe to be material, as the earth is under your feet, and is directed by God.

---

[208] As the Sunni are in the vast majority, this worldview will largely reflect their belief system. The hadith is the narrative record of the sayings or customs of Muhammad and his companions; and the collective body of traditions relating to Muhammad and his companions.—*Merriam-Webster's Collegiate Dictionary*. Eleventh ed. Springfield, Mass.: Merriam-Webster, Inc., 2003

[209] The hadith is the narrative record of the sayings or customs of Muhammad and his companions; and the collective body of traditions relating to Muhammad and his companions.—*Merriam-Webster's Collegiate Dictionary*. Eleventh ed. Springfield, Mass.: Merriam-Webster, Inc., 2003

[210] Shariah law is the immensely detailed body of rules and regulations, instructions for religious practice and daily life.—*A Christian's Pocket Guide to Islam*. Pewsey, Wiltshire: Isaac Publishing, 2001, p. 19.

Knowledge

Aristotle's work greatly influenced the Arab world. Arabic scholars, such as Avicenna and Averroes, expanded on and built on Aristotelian thinking in their attempts to bring into line Greek thought with the Muslim teaching. Setting aside the philosophical aspect of epistemology, and looking at the knowledge of Islam as it pertains to their religious institution, one will find that it has predominately been borrowed from late Judaism and Christianity and fused into Muhammad's understanding, as later interpreted by the Arabian scholars. For example:

- **Quran**: "Allah receiveth (men's) souls at the time of their death, and that (soul) which dieth not (yet) in its sleep. He keepeth that (soul) for which He hath ordained death."

- **Quran**: "I do call to witness the Resurrection Day . . . Does man think that We cannot assemble his bones? . . . He questions: 'When is the Day of Resurrection?' . . . Has not He [Allāh] the power to give life to the dead?" (75:1, 3, 6, 40)

- **Quran**: "They ask: When is the Day of Judgement? (It is) the day when they will be tormented at the Fire, (and it will be said unto them): Taste your torment (which ye inflicted)." (51:12-14)

- **Quran**: "And as for those who believe and do good works, We shall make them enter Gardens underneath which rivers flow to dwell therein forever." (4:57) "On that day the dwellers of Paradise shall think of nothing but their bliss. Together with their wives, they shall recline in shady groves upon soft couches." (36:55, 56)

- **Quran**: "And if ye fear that ye will not deal fairly by the orphans, marry of the women, who seem good to you, two or three or four; and if ye fear that ye cannot do justice (to so many) then one (only) or (the captives) that your right hands possess." (Surah 4:3)

Christian Moral Code vs Islam

Each human that has descended from Adam and Eve have a moral code (conscience) that is inherent in them from birth, which corresponds to the words found at Genesis when God said, "Let us make man in our image." This moral code is an internal awareness that enables one to choose between what is right and what is wrong, "and their conflicting thoughts accuse or even excuse them." – Romans 2:15.

This inner moral code, while inherent from birth must be trained; if not, it can be deceptive. It can serve as a guide to one's life. However, it can become dangerous or even treacherous if it has not been enlightened under the correct standards, being in harmony with its maker. As this moral code develops over time it can be influenced for the good or bad by one's environment, worship, and behavior. It is the correct understanding of the Word of God, which trains the moral code.

On the surface, it may appear that the moral values of the Muslim are humane and selfless in nature. Even many similarities further the misbelief that the Christian and the Muslim are worshiping the same God, similarly, but just by different names. Islam believes that faith is dead without evidence of good works; God will punish any worship that is not directed at him, rights against crime against your fellow man, adultery and fornication are wrong, similar abhorrence to the seven deadly sins, the obeying of the law of the land, drunkenness, suicide and homosexuality are forbidden.

This section does not contain the space to look at all facets of the Islamic moral code; therefore, we will briefly consider how the women of Islam are treated. Unlike the West, it is the woman, who brings honor to the family. Thus there are many restrictions on the women of Islam, in order to protect the family honor. There is an equation within Islam: the greater the restriction, the greater the honor. For example, without exception, a girl must retain her virginity for marriage. The woman must have someone, even a child, who accompanies and supervises her everywhere she goes. The woman's role in the house is to be the caretaker, and no Muslim husband would dare lift a hand, even if the wife has a fulltime job outside the home. In the name of modesty, the woman is to be covered from the 'neck to wrist and ankle, as well as her hair.' The marriage is arranged, and while the female may refuse, the pressure is usually insurmountable. While it is permissible for a man to marry a Christian or a Jew (as they would then be Muslim), a Muslim woman can only marry a Muslim man. Divorce in the Islamic community is very similar to the Jewish religious leaders of Jesus day: the man can divorce the woman for any reason by simply saying three times, in front of witnesses: "I divorce you." The woman, on the hand, is largely unable to divorce the husband. The rape of Christian women within Islamic countries, while being a dishonor to the woman, it is a means for a Muslim man to proliferate the Muslim population because a child is Muslim if born of a Muslim man. While many today are attempting a progressive liberal approach in looking at similarities between Islam and Christianity, it has its dark side, and any syncretism attempts are severely misplaced. (Sookhdeo 2001, 59-64)

Religious Character

As opposed to delving into Islam's highly developed religious rituals and traditions; we will take a brief look at how Islam's tolerance, or lack thereof for other religious institutions. Actually, Islamic scholars who are behind the footnotes in the Quran and articles dealing with Islam's view of Christianity and Judaism have begun a campaign to conceal their hatred for these religious institutions, viewing them as infidels.[211] For example, while the word *fight* may be found in the writings, it actually means *kill*. The end game for Islam is to convert the world to Islam and to rule from Jerusalem, under Shariah law. This can be done by preaching, or by terrorism and killing the infidel. The words of the infamous Osama bin Laden bring this point home with a chilling effect: "I was ordered to fight the people until they say there is no god but Allah, and his prophet Muhammad."

Islam versus Christianity

ISLAM	CHRISTIANITY
View of God: Islam considers the Trinity to blasphemous. (Q: 4:171, 5:17, 5:72-75)	**View of God**: Trinity—one God on three persons—separate in person, equal in nature and subordinate in duty. (John 1:1; Isa 44:8)
View of Man: While man may be may be weak, he is capable of righteousness before God.	**View of Man**: Man is fallen and sinful by nature, as inherited from Adam. (Rom 5:15)
View of Salvation: Islamic belief is that we can attain a righteous standing before God by works, and the denial of Christ's ransom sacrifice. (Q: 4:157)	**View of Salvation**: Man, who is fallen cannot save himself, and is in need of a savior, and salvation is by faith alone. (John 3:16; Matt 20:28)
View of Heaven: The Islamic perception of heaven is very carnal as they will drink wine and have	**View of Heaven**: The Christian perception of heaven is that we are no longer troubled with

---

[211] Suras 2:190-193, 2:216, 2:244, 3:56, 3:151, 4:56, 4:74, 4:76, 4:89, 4:91, 4:95, 4:104, 5:51, 5:32-38, 7:96-99, 8:12-14, 8:39, 8:60, 8:65, 9:5, 9:14, 9:23-30, 9:38-41, 9:111, 9:123, 22:18-22, 25:52, 47:4, 47:35, 48:16, 48:29, 61:4, and 66:8-10.

sexual relations with dozens of virgins. (Q: 2:25, 4:57, 13:35, 36:55-57, 37:39-48, 47:15, 52:20-23, 55:46-78, 56:12-40)

the concern of eating and drinking, there being no one getting married, for we will be like angels and drinking and with our new bodies, pain and suffering will be no more. (Rom 14:17; Matt 22:30; Rev 21:4)

View of Predestination: Ironically, while Islam believes that man cannot be held responsible for his actions; Shariah law is very quick to exact justice for certain actions, many of which result in death. (Q: 35:8)

View of Predestination: This term is really dealt with under doctrines, such as: foreknowledge, salvation, eternal security, the destiny of the unevangelized. Under these doctrinal positions, you have numerous views, but the majority consensus is that man is to be held responsible for his actions.

View of the Qur'an: Islam believes that the Qur'an is the very word of God through Muhammad and inerrant, never attaining copying errors. (Q: 61:6)

View of the Bible: Conservative Christianity believes the Bible to be the inspired, inerrant Word of God. (2 Tim 3:16; 2 Pet 1:21)

View of the Bible: Islam believes the Bible to have been the inspired Word of God, but has been corrupted beyond all trustworthiness.

View of the Qur'an: Early collections of Muhammad's writings came in several different variations because they were retrieved from memory. Around 650-656 there was an attempt to deal with this by creating a standard edition.

(Sookhdeo 2001, 25-48)

While it is paramount that the Christian, who attempts to engage the Muslim in his ministry, be very much aware of the belief system of Islam, it is best to accept that, it is very difficult to disprove Islam based on knowledge alone. It is God alone, who will help the message grown within the Muslim heart. (1 Cor. 3:5-9) However, this knowledge of Islam will enable the evangelizer to counter, explain, and overturn the wrong beliefs that may be raised by the Muslim. It should be understood that most Muslims are like most Christians, in that; they are not that familiar with their Quran, like the Christian with his Bible.

To the Muslim, Muhammad is the greatest prophet that has ever lived, and it will bring the conversation to a complete stop, if it should be perceived that the Christian is criticizing him in any way. While the Christian cannot honor Muhammad in a conversation with such honorifics as 'the blessed Muhammad,' it is fine to say 'the prophet Muhammad.' Instead of attempting to dethrone Muhammad, it is the wisest course to educate them about Christ, which they do not view as being the Son of God, but rather a great prophet like Muhammad.

Islam has circled the earth with its presence, and it would be a mistake, to assume that every Muslim is the same. Many Muslims are only Muslim in a very basic sense: prayer, Ramadan, and occasioned visits to the mask. They may have been westernized and feel ousted by the conservative Islamic community. However, Islamic extremist is just as prevalent, and caution is the word of the day. Until one has come to realize whom they are speaking with, it is best to be very cautious about what is said, and how it is said. It must also be kept in mind that his objective is to evangelize his visitor, as much as it is the Christian's objective to evangelize him.

A white Christian attempting to evangelize a non-white Muslim is at a disadvantage from the start because they are lumped in with the immoral western world. It is best to address this immediately with, "I know that the western world is immoral in the extreme, and even within the Christian community, there are such cases, but would you agree that all major religions have those who do not represent themselves well?' (Sookhdeo 2001, 73-75)

Some final suggestions are to be friendly and tactful. (Pro. 25:15) Keep in mind that while Most Muslims do not know their Quran well, what they do know is deeply entrenched has been learned by rote. Part of the Muslim development is hearing the fundamental Muslim teachings repeatedly, which is part of their spiritual development. If we are to reach the heart of a Muslim, it will be through patience and understanding. Arguing with a Muslim will serve us no better than arguing with any other person over religious matters. Instead of using the word "Bible," refer to it as the book of God. Muslims also do not like the phrase "Son of God," but they have great regard for Jesus as a prophet or messenger, so avoid the phrase "Son of God" until you have a long record of rapport. It is best to witness to just one person and avoid talking with a group. Most importantly, women should witness to women and men to men. If a female Muslim were caught talking with a westerner for an extended time, her life could be in danger, as honor killings are becoming the norm even in the West. In addition, keep in mind modestly dressed in the West is not necessarily modestly dressed in the Muslim world. Some things to build rapport on are the greatness of God and the love of God. We could speak on the wrongness of idol worship, the wickedness found in the world today, wars, uprisings, racial hatred, as well as the hypocrisy of religion. If we sense any anger, it is best to excuse ourselves from the conversation as soon as possible.

Each of us is affected by the diversity of the world we live in, and it has come to almost every neighborhood. With this variety of beliefs, it is no longer the case of a Christian attempting to share his gospel with unbelievers. Thus, we need to educate ourselves and broaden our understanding of what others worldviews are, which may very well open up the opportunity of one receiving life. As Islam makes up 23 percent of the earth's population (1.62 billion followers), we have given more space to them, which will not be the case with other groups below.

Witnessing to an Atheist

First, it should be recognized that today's atheist is not the same as the atheist of 30-50 years ago. The atheists of the 1950s to the 1980s simply did not believe in creation or a Creator and were not eager to share that belief with others. Today, the atheists movement is more involved in sharing their beliefs than Christians are. Their messages are on billboards, the radio and television, and they have actually written many apologetic books defending their faith, i.e., secularism, humanism, relativism, and nihilism. We have now entered the era of the New Atheism.

New Atheism is a social and political movement that began in the early 2000s in favor of atheism and secularism promoted by a collection of modern atheist writers who have advocated the view that "religion should not simply be tolerated but should be countered, criticized, and exposed by rational argument wherever its influence arises."[212] There is uncertainty about how much influence the movement has had on religious demographics worldwide. In England and Wales, as of 2011 the increase in atheist groups, student societies, publications and public appearances coincided with the non-religious being the largest growing demographic, followed by Islam and Evangelicalism.[213] New Atheism lends itself to and often overlaps with secular humanism and antitheism, particularly in

---

[212] Hooper, Simon. "The rise of the New Atheists". CNN. Retrieved 16 March 2010.

[213] "Census 2011: religion, race and qualifications - see how England & Wales have changed". The Guardian.

its criticism of what many New Atheists regard as the indoctrination of children and the perpetuation of ideologies.[214]

While the New Atheists authors write mainly from a scientific perspective, we should not assume that every atheist is a scientist. Many atheists have read the bestselling books by such authors as Christopher Eric Hitchens (1949–2011),[215] Richard Dawkins,[216] Sam Harris,[217] and Daniel Dennett.[218] Christopher Hitchens said that a person "could be an atheist and wish that belief in god were correct," but that "an antitheist, a term I'm trying to get into circulation, is someone who is relieved that there's no evidence for such an assertion."[219] Another thing that we should not assume about all atheists is that they are super intelligent and there is no way that we could ever compete with them in a conversation about science. Most atheists only know what they have read from the atheist books listed in the footnotes, which are not science textbooks.

Well, it should be noted that we have some Christian apologists who have done the work for us, giving us the material so that if we choose to have a better understanding and wish to at least hold our own in such a conversation, we can. The Christian apologists highlighted below are not given extra space because they are all around the best apologists. Christian apologist can have a vast knowledge of many subject areas but they cannot be an expert on everything. While one may be an expert on textual criticism, defending the trustworthiness of Scripture, another may be a Christian philosopher and theologian, while others may be a physicist, mathematician, or scientist, studying the philosophy of science, it is the latter, who are focused on here because of the subject matter.

---

[214] New Atheism - Wikipedia, the free encyclopedia, http://en.wikipedia.org/wiki/New_atheism (accessed September 15, 2015).

[215] Christopher Hitchens was the author of God Is Not Great and was named among the "Top 100 Public Intellectuals" by Foreign Policy and Prospect magazine. In addition, Hitchens served on the advisory board of the Secular Coalition for America.

[216] Richard Dawkins is the author of The God Delusion, which was preceded by a Channel 4 television documentary titled The Root of all Evil? He is also the founder of the Richard Dawkins Foundation for Reason and Science.

[217] Harris is the author of the bestselling non-fiction books, The End of Faith, Letter to a Christian Nation, The Moral Landscape, and Waking Up: A Guide to Spirituality Without Religion, as well as two shorter works initially published as e-Books, Free Will and Lying. Harris is a co-founder of the Reason Project.

[218] Daniel Dennett, author of Darwin's Dangerous Idea, Breaking the Spell and many others, has also been a vocal supporter of The Clergy Project, an organization that provides support for clergy in the US who no longer believe in God, and cannot fully participate in their communities any longer.

[219] Christopher Hitchens' Religion and Political Views | The .., http://hollowverse.com/christopher-hitchens/ (accessed September 15, 2015).

The leading Christian apologist is **William Lane Craig**. He is a Research Professor of Philosophy at Talbot School of Theology and Professor of Philosophy at Houston Baptist University. He is an American Christian apologist, analytic Christian philosopher, and theologian. Craig's philosophical work focuses primarily on philosophy of religion, but also on metaphysics and philosophy of time. His theological interests are in historical Jesus studies and philosophical theology. He is known for his debates on the existence of God with public figures such as Christopher Hitchens and Lawrence Krauss. Craig established an online apologetics ministry, Reasonable Faith. His current research deals with divine aseity and the challenge posed by Platonist accounts of abstract objects. Craig is also an author of several books, including Reasonable Faith, which began as a set of lectures for his apologetics classes.[220]

John C. Lennox is an Irish mathematician, philosopher of science, Christian apologist, and Professor of Mathematics at the University of Oxford. He is a Fellow in Mathematics and Philosophy of Science at Green Templeton College, Oxford University. He is also Pastoral Advisor of Green Templeton College and Fellow of Wycliffe Hall. He is a leading voice defending the notion of the relationship between science and religion. Lennox is a leading figure in the evangelical intelligentsia movement.[221]

Christian apologist **Stephen C. Meyer** received his Ph.D. from the University of Cambridge in the philosophy of science. A former geophysicist and college professor, he now directs the Center for Science and Culture at the Discovery Institute in Seattle.[222] Christian Apologist **William A. Dembski** is a mathematician and philosopher. He is a Research Professor in Philosophy at Southwestern Seminary in Ft. Worth, where he directs its Center for Cultural Engagement. He is also a senior fellow with Discovery Institute's Center for Science and Culture in Seattle. Previously he was the Carl F. H. Henry Professor of Theology and Science

---

[220] *On Guard: Defending Your Faith with Reason and Precision* (Mar 1, 2010) by William Lane Craig and Lee Strobel; *Reasonable Faith (3rd edition): Christian Truth and Apologetics* (Jun 15, 2008) by William Lane Craig; *Contending with Christianity's Critics: Answering New Atheists and Other Objectors* (Aug 1, 2009) by William Lane Craig and Paul Copan; *Come Let Us Reason: New Essays in Christian Apologetics* (Mar 1, 2012) by William Lane Craig and Paul Copan

[221] *God's Undertaker* (Feb 18, 2011) by John Lennox; *Seven Days That Divide the World: The Beginning According to Genesis and Science* (Aug 23, 2011) by John Lennox; *God and Stephen Hawking* (Feb 18, 2011) by John Lennox; *Gunning for God* (Oct 21, 2011) by JOHN C. LENNOX

[222] Darwin's Doubt: The Explosive Origin of Animal Life and the Case for Intelligent Design (Jun 3, 2014) by Stephen C. Meyer; *Signature in the Cell* (Jun 23, 2009) by Stephen C. Meyer

at The Southern Baptist Theological Seminary in Louisville, where he founded its Center for Theology and Science. Before that, he was Associate Research Professor in the Conceptual Foundations of Science at Baylor University, where he headed the first intelligent design think-tank at a major research university: The Michael Polanyi Center.

Christian Apologist **Norman L. Geisler** (Ph.D., Loyola University) has taught theology, philosophy, and apologetics on the college or graduate level for over 50 years. He has served as a professor at Trinity Evangelical Seminary, Dallas Theological Seminary, and Liberty University. He was the co-founder of both Southern Evangelical Seminary and Veritas Evangelical Seminary. He currently is the Chancellor of Veritas Evangelical Seminary, the Distinguished Professor of Apologetics at Veritas Evangelical Seminary, and a Visiting Professor of Apologetics at Southern Evangelical Seminary.[223]

The list of Christian apologists could go on for some time, as we have so many, to name just a few more, Ravi Zacharias (RZIM.org), Greg Koukl (STR.org), Paul Copan (PaulCopan.com), Gary Habermas (GaryHabermas.com), Richard Howe (Richardghowe.com), Hugh Ross (Reasons.org), and (Tim Keller (TimothyKeller.com). Many may be unaware that we now have some very prominent female Christian apologists, such as Judy Salisbury (logospresentations.com),[224] Dianna Newman (ses.edu),[225] Sarah Renee,[226] Nancy Pearcey,[227] Melissa Cain-Travis,[228] Holly Ordway,[229] Leslie Keeney[230] Kristen Davis,[231] Lori Peters,[232]

---

[223] I Don't Have Enough Faith to Be an Atheist (Mar 15, 2004) by Norman L. Geisler and Frank Turek; Christian Apologetics (May 15, 2013) by Norman L. Geisler; Christian Ethics: Contemporary Issues and Options (Jan 1, 2010) by Norman L. Geisler; The Big Book of Bible Difficulties: Clear and Concise Answers from Genesis to Revelation (Jun 1, 2008) by Norman L. Geisler and Thomas Howe

[224] A TIME TO SPEAK: PRACTICAL TRAINING for the CHRISTIAN PRESENTER Authored by Judy Salisbury, Foreword by Josh McDowell

http://www.christianpublishers.org/apps/webstore/products/show/5943504

[225] BASICS OF BIBLICAL CRITICISM: Helpful or Harmful? [Second Edition] F. David Farnell, Thomas Howe, Thomas Marshall, Benjamin Cocar, Dianna Newman

http://www.christianpublishers.org/apps/webstore/products/show/5346435

[226] http://thevalleygirlapologist.blogspot.com/

[227] http://www.pearceyreport.com/about.php

[228] http://sciencereasonfaith.com/

[229] http://www.hieropraxis.com/

[230] http://www.lesliekeeney.com/

[231] http://www.doubtlessfaith.com/learning-center.html

[232] http://graniteapologists.com/

Pamela Christian,[233] and Sarah Geis.[234] These women are taking the apologetic world by storm. They are setting a fine example for young girls, who can relish in the fact that they can prepare to defend the faith and the Word of God just as well as a William Lane Craig or a Norman L. Geisler. Why have I given you so many names and links? These are indispensable resources if we are going to defend the faith against the New Atheism. While many of the above Christian apologists, both male and female, possess some of the greatest minds, which would seem to prevent the average Christian from partaking of their knowledge, it just is not so. Their books, their websites, their blogs and their videos are designed for the churchgoer, written on about a 9th-11th grade level. Below, I will offer the reader the basics of what we can do to succeed in giving a witness to the New Atheist, but first we must consider the various reasons as to why they may not believe in the first place.

Reasons for Disbelief

Not all atheists were born to atheist parents. Many were a part of some religion or another, believing in God, but over time abandoned their faith. Their faith was weakened by severe health problems in the family, a death of a loved one, or some great injustice befell them. With others, it was one agnostic or atheist professor after another once they reached schools of higher learning, which eroded their belief in the Bible or God.

A man was born with a debilitating illness. As an infant, he had been baptized into Catholicism; he had long felt there was no God. The end came one day when he asked the priest, "Why did God make give me this illness?" The priest replied, "Because he loves you." The answer was so insane, so he walked out, never looking back. Consider a young woman who was diagnosed as having cancer at the age of thirteen, who spent most of her youth in and out of hospitals. The mother of this child was so desperate; she brought a Pentecostal into the hospital to pray for the young girl because the word was he could heal the sick. Sadly, though, there was no cure, there was no miraculous healing. After her daughter's death, the most swore that she would never believe in some God, becoming an atheist.

- "I have seen many friends that I went to high school with just completely abandon their faith, and I was in

---

[233] http://pamelachristianministries.com/

[234] http://justifiedfaith.com/

danger of doing the same when I first went to college."
– Chad, college junior

- "No matter what background you come from, the transition from high school to college will try your faith." – Vanessa, college sophomore[235]

- A pastor's kid tells his father, "I'm not a Christian anymore. I don't know what happened. I just left it."[236]

Again, we turn to William Lane Craig's words, as he offers the following exhortation to parents, which would also apply to pastors and elders as well,

> I think the church is really failing these kids. Rather than provide them training in the defense of Christianity's truth, we focus on emotional worship experiences, felt needs, and entertainment. It's no wonder they become sitting ducks for that teacher or professor who rationally takes aim at their faith. In high school and college, students are intellectually assaulted with every manner of non-Christian philosophy conjoined with an overwhelming relativism and skepticism. We've got to train our kids for war. How dare we send them unarmed into an intellectual war zone? Parents must do more than take their children to church and read them Bible stories. Moms and dads need to be trained in apologetics themselves and so be able to explain to their children simply from an early age and then with increasing depth why we believe as we do. Honestly, I find it hard to understand how Christian couples in our day and age can risk bringing children into the world without being trained in apologetics as part of the art of parenting.[237]

Reaching the Heart of an Atheist

Many are like the above example, or have other reasons as to why they abandoned the faith. The key ingredient is their reason, which they have dwelled on to the point they have hardened their hearts. If we

---

[235] Top 10 Challenges Christian Students Face in College | eNews .., http://www.cedarville.edu/eNews/ParentPrep/2012/Challenges-Christian-Students-Fa (accessed September 15, 2015).

[236] The Leavers: Young Doubters Exit the Church | Christianity Today, http://www.christianitytoday.com/ct/2010/november/27.40.html (accessed September 15, 2015).

[237] Craig, William Lane (2010-03-01). On Guard: Defending Your Faith with Reason and Precision (Kindle Locations 267-274). David C. Cook. Kindle Edition.

repeatedly violate the Christian conscience that has been trained to distinguish between good and bad, it will become callused, unfeeling. To violate the conscience is to ignore it, when it is tugging at you to do the right thing. While this applies largely to sinning and ignoring the Christian conscience, it can just as easily apply to irrational thinking as well. If we have an issue with God, with his Word, with the faith, with someone in the faith, with injustices of the world and we ignore these, failing to find an answer, we will eventually fall away from the faith. Paul called this a spiritual shipwreck. Paul told young Timothy "some have rejected and suffered shipwreck in regard to their faith." (1 Tim 1:19, NASB) If we entertain our false reasons, our confidence in God and his Word of truth, the Bible, can grow weak and our faith can die. Just as we have reasons for the hope that dwells in us, we can also have reasons if they go unanswered or at least addressed, they can kill the hope that dwells in us.

Many of these ones, not all, simply need a solution to their reason for abandoning the faith. 'Why does evil exist?' 'Why does an all-powerful God of love allow evil to exist?'[238] Why do bad things happen to good people?' 'Why is life so unfair?'[239] 'What is the meaning of life?' 'Why is there so much religious hypocrisy?' If we lack understanding of an issue that is eating at us, we begin to drift away, become sluggish, become hardened by the not knowing, so that we shrink back to destruction. Just as we entered the path of life, we can also reenter the path of death.

Our first goal when someone says, 'I am an atheist,' is to ask why. If he is open to talking further, we need to try to find out what led his reason and his falling away. As we listen to his story, we need to do so with empathy because this could be us, or it could be a loved one, and we would want an empathetic ear if that were the case. After we have what we need to make a spiritual diagnosis, we can look for a solution. We can start by saying, it has been our experience that there is a reasonable and logical answer to every Bible difficulty that we have encountered. We can show even more empathy if we have struggled with something that made us pause for a moment. After this rapport, ask something like, "What if I can find you a reasonable, logical answer to this issue that has plagued you for so long. Even if you still choose to remain an atheist, would it not be a relief to have that answer?" If he answers yes, we now have a serious job ahead of ourselves. Undoubtedly, there is much information on the issue. We must find it and the answer that we promised. Undeniably, not all atheists are going to accept the truth. However, there are many who are willing to find a response to the issue that tore them from their faith. Use reason, logic, persuasion and, above

---

[238] http://www.christianpublishers.org/suffering-evil-why-god

[239] http://www.christianpublishers.org/why-is-life-so-unfair

all, the power of God's Word, to lead them into the truth or back to the truth.[240] – Acts 28:23-24; Heb. 4:12.

Witnessing to a Jewish Person

The sons of Israel in the first-century responded positively to the preaching of Jesus and his apostles. (Acts 10:36) The same holds true for today. However, you have **Messianic Judaism**, is a movement that combines Christianity, most importantly, the Christian belief that Jesus is the Messiah, with elements of **Judaism** and **Jewish** tradition. This is not going to be acceptable, though, as Jesus told them we are not trying to put new wine in an old wineskin. First, we must deal with the fact of whether the Jews are still God's chosen people.

Are the Natural Jews Today Still God's Chosen People?

To the twelve tribes in the Dispersion: (James 1:1c)

The **twelve tribes in the dispersion** that James mentions are not actual the 12 tribes of Israel. We note in verse 2 James says, "Consider it all joy, my brothers," and the tribes of Jewish Israel were not James' brother, 'who were holding their faith in their glorious Lord Jesus Christ, as natural Israel rejected Jesus Christ vehemently. (Jam. 1:2; 2:1, 5) During the last days of Jesus' ministry, he explicitly stated what was to happen to natural Israel. Jesus said, "I tell you, the kingdom of God will be taken away from you and given to a people producing its fruits." (Matt. 21:43) A short time later, he said,

Matthew 23:37-39 Updated American Standard Version (UASV)

Lament over Jerusalem

37 "Jerusalem, Jerusalem, who kills the prophets and stones those who are sent to her! How often I wanted to gather your children together, the way a hen gathers her chicks under her wings, and you were unwilling.

38 Behold, your house is being left to you desolate!

39 For I say to you, from now on you will not see me until you say, 'Blessed is he who comes in the name of the Lord.'"

In looking at verse 37 of Matthew 23, we see that Jesus' words are not those of a harsh judge, who is looking readily to punish the Jewish

---

[240] This author has accomplished this several times with ones who have left the faith. They bought out the time and over an extended period, they finally saw their way out of the long years of darkness, and the light of God's Word was eventually a welcome sight.

people for their 1,500 years of rebelling and sinning horrendously against the Father. Rather, he has tried to be patient with them throughout his last three and half year ministry. When Jesus began his ministry, all Jesus wanted was nothing more than what his Father wanted, i.e., repentance for centuries of willful sinning, so that they could avoid the judgment that was coming. Well, over five hundred natural Israel responded to Jesus' words, with thousands upon thousands more listening to the apostle Paul and other evangelists. They escaped the judgment that came upon Jerusalem in 70 C.E. (Lu 21:20-22) In verse 38, Jesus indicated that very soon God was not going to accept the worship of the Israelites, at the typical temple in Jerusalem. (Matt 24:1-2) In verse 39, Jesus is saying, they will never see him with eyes of faith unless they accept him and his Father.

In other words, natural Israel lost its favored position as God's chosen people, and this was to be given to another. Who? This new nation proved to be a spiritual Israel, which the apostle Paul referred to as "the Israel of God." It would be made up of Jews, who accepted Jesus Christ and non-Jews. Entry into this "Israel of God" was not dependent on natural descent, but rather on one coming to "know you the only true God, and Jesus Christ whom you have sent." (John 17:3), In other words, it was a matter of 'trusting in Jesus Christ.' (John 3:16) Nevertheless, natural Israel was made up of 12 tribes, so James was simply drawing on the number 12, which carries the connotation of completeness. If a natural Jew or a non-Jew were to become a part of this spiritual Israel, the Israel of God, they would have to acknowledge, "Circumcision is a matter of the heart, by the Spirit, not by the letter." (Rom. 2:29) He must further understand "it depends on faith, in order that the promise may rest on grace and be guaranteed to all …" (Rom. 4:16) There are many verses, which qualify what it means to be a part of this Israel of God. See also, Rom. 4:17; 9:6-8; Gal. 3:7, 29; 4:21-31; Phil. 3:3

These spiritual Israelites were dispersed throughout the Roman Empire. Shortly after Pentecost 33 C.E., there were arrests, threats, and beatings. (Ac 4:1-3, 21; 5:17, 18) At that time, Stephen was seized and stoned to death. " (Ac 7:52-60) The murder of Stephen was only the beginning, as Saul of Tarsus was to bring great persecution on the Christians in the Jerusalem area, which led to the dispersing of Christians throughout the then known world. (Ac 8:1-4; 9:1, 2) However, this really failed, as it was not long before Christian congregations were found everywhere, by the evangelism of none other than the very persecutor turned Christian, namely, the apostle Paul (formerly known as Saul). In fact, about 62-64 C.E., Peter writes, "To those who are elect exiles of the Dispersion in Pontus, Galatia, Cappadocia, Asia, and Bithynia."--1 Peter 1:1

Written for Our Instruction

We can learn some object lessons from what God has disclosed to us in his Word. Paul told the Corinthians "these things happened to those people as an example but are written for our instruction." (1 Cor. 10:11) He also told the congregation in Rome, "For whatever was written beforehand was written for our instruction, in order that through patient endurance and through the encouragement of the scriptures we may have hope." (Rom. 15:4) The Israelites are a perfect example for us to learn. God personally chose Abraham, Isaac and Jacob, because they were walking with him, while others chose to abandon him. The nation of Israel was the descendants of Jacob's 12 sons. They became God's chosen people, of whom he made a covenant, to which they agreed to follow. If they walked in the truth, they would be blessed by Jehovah's presence. If they abandoned that walk like the pagan nations, they would lose his presence, resulting in the difficulties that came with living in this fallen world. Whilst they maintained their loyalty, they never became victims to enemy nations. (Deut. 28:7) Furthermore, they could depend on crop growth that was exceptional year after year, as well as their flocks of animals. (Ex. 22:1-15) Moreover, they had no reason to build jails to house criminals, because they had the perfect social system. (Ex. 22:1-15) In addition, they did not suffer from diseases like other nations (Deut. 7:15). Jehovah promised them that they would "be blessed more than all of the peoples," and when they walked in the truth, this proved to be true.

Deuteronomy 7:14 Updated American Standard Version (UASV)

[14] You shall be blessed above all peoples; there will be no male or female barren among you or among your cattle.

We all have the history before of how Israel **refused** to walk in the truth. They would walk in the truth for a number of years, and then they would abandon that truth until life was impossibly difficult, moving them to return to Jehovah. This walking in the truth, abandoning the truth, and repenting to return to the truth, went on for 1,500 years. The final difficulty in this back and forth was their rejection of the Son of God. His words to them were quite clear, and needs to be repeated again:

Matthew 21:43 Updated American Standard Version (UASV)

[43] Therefore I say to you, the kingdom of God will be taken away from you and **given to a nation,**[241] **producing the fruit** of it.

Again,

---

[241] Or *people*

Matthew 23:37-39 Updated American Standard Version (UASV)

37 "Jerusalem, Jerusalem, who kills the prophets and stones those who are sent to her! How often I wanted to gather your children together, the way a hen gathers her chicks under her wings, and you were unwilling.

38 Behold, your house is being left to you desolate!

39 For I say to you, from now on you will not see me until you say, 'Blessed is he who comes in the name of the Lord.'"

Just who are **the people** that the Kingdom was to be given to after the Israelites fell out of favor with Jehovah God? God chose for himself a new spiritual nation, which became the Christian congregation that Jesus established between 29 and 33 C.E. He no longer had the descendants of Abraham, Isaac and Jacob as his chosen people, by which other nations would bless themselves. Keep in mind again, only Jews were brought into the Christian congregation from 29 C.E. (Jesus started ministry) up unto 36 C.E. (first Gentile Baptized, i.e., Cornelius). This is explained in greater detail below.

Acts 10:34-35 Updated American Standard Version (UASV)

34 So Peter opened his mouth and said: "Truly I understand that God shows no partiality, **35** but in every nation anyone who fears[242] him and works righteousness[243] is acceptable to him.

Acts 13:46 Updated American Standard Version (UASV)

46 And Paul and Barnabas spoke out boldly and said, "It was necessary that the word of God be spoken to you first; since you thrust it aside and judge yourselves unworthy of eternal life, behold, we are turning to the Gentiles.

Did this mean that no Jewish person could be a part of the Kingdom? Hardly! The first disciples of that Kingdom for seven years, 29 C.E. to 36 C.E. were only Jewish people. After 36 C.E., and the baptism of the first Gentile, Cornelius, anyone, including the Jews, could be a part of this Kingdom, as long as they accepted the King, Jesus Christ. Jesus said, "I am the way, and the truth, and the life. No one comes to the Father except through me." (John 14:6) At Jesus' Baptism, there was a voice from heaven saying, "This is my beloved Son, with whom I am well pleased." (Matt.3:16-17) Jesus' teaching, miraculous signs, his ransom

---

[242] This is a reverential fear of displeasing God because of one's great love for him. It is not a dreadful fear.

[243] I.e., *does what is right*

sacrifice and resurrection, established him as the truth, having the authority and power of the Father.[244] The Christians in the first century were given the position of being God's chosen people. (Acts 1:8; 2:1-4, 43) It would be through Jesus to the Christian congregation that the truth would now flow. As Paul told the Corinthians, "For to us God has revealed them through the Spirit. For the Spirit searches all things, even the depths of God." (1 Cor. 2:10) It happened just as Jesus had said it would, "I praise you, Father, Lord of heaven and earth, because you have hidden these things from the wise and intelligent, and have revealed them to young children." – Matthew 11:25

However, more truth was on the horizon with the birth of the Christian congregation. There had been 39 books written by the Jewish writers of the Hebrew Old Testament (2 Tim. 3:16-17), and now there was to be added an additional 27 books by Jewish Christians, making up the Greek New Testament (2 Peter 2:15-16). Thus, there were 66 small books, written over a 1,600-year period that would make one book, which we hold today in our modern-day translations. Yes, some 40 plus Bible writers were, as Peter put it, "men carried along by the Holy Spirit spoke from God." (2 Peter 1:21) The above view is Scriptural, but it is also the minority view. Most believe as Dr. Elmer Towns,

> Israel's hardness of heart. The Bible speaks of a partial and temporary insensibility of the nation of Israel. The Jews, who had the Scriptures and should have welcomed their Messiah, rejected him and called for his crucifixion. "He (Jesus) came unto his own (the Jews), and his own received him not" (John 1:11). Paul spoke of "blindness (hardness)" as happening to Israel (Rom. 11:25). Israel's rejection is temporary. The time is coming when many Jews will turn to Christ (Rom. 11:26; 2 Cor. 3:14, 15). God's temporarily setting aside the nation he loves so much ought to be a warning to Christians not to reject the teaching of the Scriptures.[245]

Elmer Towns says, "Israel's rejection is temporary. The time is coming when many Jews will turn to Christ." They had 1,500 years as God's chosen people, favored in every way, and they abandoned God at every turn, to the point of sacrificing their own children to false gods, culminating in the rejection of the Son of God, who said he had come specifically for them. Moreover, John himself says that anyone or group

---

[244] Matt. 15:30-31; 20:28; John 4:34; 5:19, 27, 30; 6:38, 40; 7:16-17; 17:1-2; Acts 2:22

[245] Towns, Elmer (2011-10-30). AMG Concise Bible Doctrines (AMG Concise Series) (Kindle Locations 960-965). AMG Publishers. Kindle Edition.

who rejects Jesus Christ is the antichrist (i.e., instead of or against Christ). The Messianic Jews do accept Christ, so most would think they are fine. However, that just is not the case because it is the **combining it** with elements of **Judaism** and **Jewish** tradition. What did Jesus say about Jewish tradition? He said you are "making void the word of God by your tradition that you have handed down." (Mark 13:7) Let us look at Jesus words at Luke 5:38, "But new wine must be put into fresh wineskins." What did Jesus mean?

> The conclusion of the second picture is stated positively: new wine must have new skins; new ways must have new containers. Jesus' teaching will not survive by making it conform to old ways. A new form, a new spirit, and a new approach are required. Old questions are irrelevant. Such a message had relevance beyond the time of Jesus' ministry. In the early church and throughout the new age, to re-Judaize Christianity would have missed the newness of what Jesus brings. The issue raised here is one of the major concerns in the Book of Acts, as the church wrestles with the proper limits of the influence of its Jewish heritage. The focus is not on a return to something old and ancient, but on the presence of something new. This does not mean that some forms of the old worship, like fasting, cannot continue; but it does mean that they are seen differently. The remarks fit the situation in Jesus' ministry, but the significance became timeless for the church's perspective.[246] (Bock 1994, p. 521)

Will the Jews in the last days, or during the great tribulation, finally be moved to accept Jesus Christ?

Romans 11:25-26 Good News Translation (GNT)

[25] There is a secret truth, my friends, which I want you to know, for it will keep you from thinking how wise you are. It is that the stubbornness of the people of Israel is not permanent, but will last only until the complete number of Gentiles comes to God. [26] And **this is how** all Israel will be saved. As the scripture says,

"The Savior will come from Zion
and remove all wickedness from the descendants of Jacob."

Notice the GNT says, "this is how (ESV, HCSB, "and in this way") Greek, *houtos*] all Israel will be saved." In addition, notice that this "**all Israel** will be saved" is not accomplished by the some conversion of

---

[246] Paul raises such issues in 1 Cor. 7:17–24; 8–11; and Rom. 14–15. While not rejecting Jewish worship forms, he did not regard them as required. His approach parallels Jesus'.

all the Jews, but rather "the complete number of Gentiles comes to God." A Manual Greek Lexicon of the New Testament [Edinburgh, 1937, G. Abbott-Smith, p. 329] defines houtos as meaning "in this way, so, thus."). In addition, A TRANSLATOR'S HANDBOOK ON PAUL'S LETTER TO THE ROMANS [New York, 1973, United Bible Societies, p. 227], says, "This is how relates back to what Paul has previously said."

If we are to understand Romans 11:25-26 correctly, it must be in the context of the book of Romans as a whole, and the rest of the New Testament. What did Paul say at Romans 2:28-28, "For no one is a Jew who is merely one outwardly, nor is circumcision outward and physical. But a Jew is one inwardly, and circumcision is a matter of the heart, by the Spirit, not by the letter. His praise is not from man but from God." At Romans 9:26 Paul says, "For not all those who are descended from Israel are truly Israel."

What about the argument that the Abrahamic covenant assures that the Jews will always be God's chosen people.

Galatians 3:27-29 New American Standard Bible (NASB)

27 For all of you who were baptized into Christ have clothed yourselves with Christ. 28 There is neither Jew nor Greek, there is neither slave nor free man, there is neither male nor female; for you are all one in Christ Jesus. 29 And if you belong to Christ, then you are Abraham's descendants, heirs according to promise. (Italics mine)

Here we see things from God's perspective, it is not a matter of being a natural descendant of Abraham that makes one a part of Abraham's seed. Are the things going on in Israel today and un unto Christ's return a part of Bible prophecy?

Ezekiel 37:21-22 Updated American Standard Version (UASV)

21 then say to them, Thus says the Lord Jehovah: Behold, I will take the sons of Israel from the nations among which they have gone, and I will gather them from every side and bring them into their own land 22 and I will make them one nation in the land, on the mountains of Israel; and one king will be king for all of them; and they will no longer be two nations and no longer be divided into two kingdoms.

Israel has not been under one king of the line of David for well over 2,300 years. The state of Israel today is a republic.

Isaiah 2:2-4 Updated American Standard Version (UASV)

2 It will come to pass in the latter days
   that the mountain of the house of Jehovah
will be established on the top of the mountains,

and will be lifted up above the hills;
and all the nations will stream to it,
³   and many peoples will come, and say:
"Come, let us go up to the mountain of Jehovah,
   to **the house of the God of Jacob**,
that he may teach us concerning his ways
   and that we may walk in his paths."
For the law[247] will go forth from Zion,
   and the word of Jehovah from Jerusalem.
⁴ He will judge between the nations,
   and will correct matters for many peoples;
and they shall beat their swords into plowshares,
   and their spears into pruning hooks;
nation shall not lift up sword against nation,
   neither shall they learn war anymore.

What do we find when we look at the city of Jerusalem today? Do we find "the house of the God of Jacob"? No, we do not; rather we find an Islamic shrine. Certainly, living within the heart of Islamic nations, they would not ever dream of "beat[ing] their swords into plowshares."

Zechariah 8:23 English Standard Version (ESV)

²³ Thus says **the Lord** of hosts: In those days ten men from the nations of every tongue shall take hold of the robe of a Jew, saying, 'Let us go with you, for we have heard that God is with you.'"

Zechariah 8:23 American Standard Version (ASV)

²³ Thus says **Jehovah** of hosts: In those days it shall come to pass, that ten men shall take hold, out of all the languages of the nations, they shall take hold of the skirt of him that is a Jew, saying, We will go with you, for we have heard that God is with you.

Zechariah 8:23 Young's Literal Translation (YLT)

²³ Thus said **Jehovah** of Hosts: In those days take hold do ten men of all languages of the nations, Yea, they have taken hold on the skirt of a man, a Jew, saying: We go with you, for we heard God [is] with you!

Within the book of Zechariah alone the personal name of God (Jehovah JHVH, or Yahweh YHWH) appears 130 times. If you are ever around an orthodox Jew, say Jehovah or Yahweh, and he will jump back and say something like, "we do not say the blessed name." Jews, because of traditions and superstitions have not said the personal name of God for about 2,000 years. It is to the point that it has even been removed from

---

[247] Or *instruction* or *teaching*

almost all English translations, replacing it with the title "the Lord" or "LORD." These prophecies of a restored Israel, who do they apply to, natural Israel?

Galatians 6:15-16 Updated American Standard Version (UASV)

¹⁵ For neither circumcision counts for anything, nor uncircumcision, but a new creation.¹⁶ And as for all who walk by this rule, peace and mercy be upon them, and upon **the Israel of God**.

This "Israel of God" is not based on the requirements that Abraham had received from God, i.e., all males having to be circumcised. Instead, as was stated in 3:26-29, "there are neither Jew nor Greek, ... for you are all one in Christ Jesus. **29** And *if you belong to Christ, then you are Abraham's descendants*, heirs according to promise."

The Average Jewish Person

It should be noted that the average Jew we might run into is generally a faithful follower of the traditions of Rabbis, and doctrinal view are likely not be of interest. Somewhat like the Catholic Church viewing the word of the pope to be equal to Scripture, this would be true of the average Jew and Rabbi traditions. Therefore, while we might have thought we could have had some deep Bible discussion to build rapport, this is unlikely. In addition, the word "Bible" is generally viewed as a Christian book. It is for this reason; it is best to talk of the Hebrew Scriptures, even the "Torah." If anyone can read biblical Hebrew, which I know there are a limited number, his or her success of reading from the Hebrew Scriptures directly would be very success with the Orthodox Jews, who will seldom give a Christian the time of day.

Well, we might be wondering just what can we talk about with the average Jewish person. They hold to the fact that there is one God, monotheism, who is interested in the welfare of his creation. However, it is best not to use the personal name of God ("Jehovah" or "Yahweh"), as one of their traditions is that the divine name should not be pronounced. They, like Christians, believe that God has involved himself in human history and continued to do so. Some Jewish people struggle with why God would allow the atrocities of six million Jews being slaughtered during the Holocaust of World War II.[248] Most are aware of the history within the Hebrew Scriptures, which makes for many talking points.

Of course, it is best to stay away from Jesus being divine but many Jews do see Jesus as a prophet. It might be best not to refer to him as the

---

[248] http://www.christianpublishers.org/suffering-evil-why-god

Messiah, even though that is the Hebrew transliteration and preferable to "Christ." The reason is the Jewish people are still awaiting the Messiah. This deep discussion would have to wait until we have talked with someone many times and have built up much rapport and trust. It would be better, to begin with such ones as Noah, Abraham and Moses, and their role in Jewish history and how it affects us today.

When the time comes to address Jesus as the Messiah, we would want, to begin with, Deuteronomy 18:15 (UASV), which reads, "Jehovah your God will raise up for you a prophet like me from among you, from your brothers to him you shall listen." Then, ask the person, "Who was it that Moses was thinking of when he spoke of a prophet like himself?" "How should this prophecy be understood?" [Allow for an answer] Ask/state, "You would agree that Moses was speaking of a specific, special individual, right?" [Allow for an answer] I know some Jewish scholars have held that Moses was just making a general comment about God's intention to rise up many coming prophets, but the Hebrew word for prophet (navi) is in the singular is it not?" [Allow for an answer] "This coming one is being compared to Moses in what way?" [Allow for an answer] Then, have him read the closing words of Deuteronomy,

Deuteronomy 34:10-12 Updated American Standard Version (UASV)

¹⁰ Since that time no prophet has risen in Israel like Moses, whom Jehovah knew face to face, ¹¹ for all the signs and wonders which Jehovah sent him to perform in the land of Egypt against Pharaoh, all his servants, and all his land, ¹² and for the mighty hand[249] and for all the great wonders which Moses performed in the sight of all Israel.

Ask him if he would agree that is was like the Joshua, the son of Nun, who recorded these words about Moses. [Allow for an answer] Ask, if he feels that Joshua, who too was a great leader in Israel, viewed himself as the coming prophet like Moses. [Allow for an answer] Ask again, "what do you think Moses meant that God would raise up a prophet like Moses?" "In other words, what was it about Moses that this coming one would resemble?" [Allow for an answer]

We could then delve into how Moses was a great leader; he was a representative of God, "a prophet, a miracle worker, a teacher, and a

---

[249] I.e., *mighty power*

judge."[250] We could ask as series of leading question. What did Jeremiah promise at 31:31-34? (Read)

Jeremiah 31:31-34 Updated American Standard Version (UASV)

[31] "Behold, days are coming," declares Jehovah, "when I will make a new covenant with the house of Israel and with the house of Judah, [32] not like the covenant which I made with their fathers in the day I took them by the hand to bring them out of the land of Egypt, My covenant which they broke, although I was a husband to them," declares Jehovah. [33] For this is the covenant that I will make with the house of Israel after those days, declares Jehovah: I will put my law within them, and I will write it on their hearts. And I will be their God, and they shall be my people. [34] And no longer shall each one teach his neighbor and each his brother, saying, 'Know Jehovah,' for they shall all know me, from the least of them to the greatest, declares Jehovah. For I will forgive their iniquity, and I will remember their sin no more."

"What was this new covenant and what was its purpose?" [Allow for an answer] "When was the new covenant to come into effect?" [Allow for an answer] "Consequently, what would happen to the Mosaic Law?"

What is promised in Jeremiah 31:31-34? What was the new covenant's stated purpose? Consequently, what would become of the Law covenant? [Allow for an answer] How was this new covenant going to affect the nations?" (Read Gen. 22:18) [Allow for an answer] This type of building and leading will evidence your familiarity with the Hebrew Scripture and give him something to ponder.

Witnessing to a Jehovah's Witness

This is no easy task for most Christians. The Jehovah's Witnesses are well trained to defend their beliefs. They spend five meetings a week, much personal study and meeting preparation in taking in what they believe and learning how to defend their version of the faith. This is not said to scare anyone off from trying to approach the Witnesses, but rather to encourage you to prepare well. The irony is; we do not have to go out and find the Witnesses, as they come to us because they go house-to-house. The objective is not to be confrontational, as Witnesses are trained to abandon such conversations.

The best thing we can do is know what we believe very well and be accomplished at defending it. It is best to know what they believe as well

---

[250] Crucifixion or Cruci-Fiction ? (genesis, quotes, baptize .., http://www.city-data.com/forum/religion-spirituality/507377-crucifixion-cruci-fi (accessed September 16, 2015).

and what Scriptures they use to defend such views. However, it is not that simple because they will know what we believe and what verses we use and they will be prepared to undermine those verses. As I said, it is not going to be easy. It gets worse still, if the average Witness cannot deal with our preparedness, but they believe we are sincerely interested, they will bring a pioneer[251] with them the next time they visit us. These ones have far more experience and knowledge. If that fails, they will bring the most qualified congregation elder. Do not be fooled; some Witnesses study secular books; they learn Hebrew and Greek, among many other academic fields. These latter ones are few in number, but I thought I would mention it in case they happen to be in your area.

If we want the Witnesses to visit us, all we have to do is write or call the main branch of Jehovah's Witnesses[252] and ask for one of their books, which will give us the basic beliefs they hold too. They will not mail us the publication; they will have someone from the local Kingdom Hall (their church) deliver it. When they come, they will walk us through the book and look to start a study with us. If we want to win them over to our side, this is the best way, as we would have them all to ourselves in our home, going over doctrinal positions. It is best to make this stipulation, though, "I will study your book with you, but as you know, I believe differently, so along the way, I may raise objections, ask for more proof, as well as share how I see whatever we may be discussing." They will agree to this stipulation because they always believe they have the upper hand.

The best approach is to agree where there is an agreement because believe it or not; there will be more agreement than one might imagine. When we come to points of disagreement, have them make their case, letting them get through the entire presentation and then undermine it with Scripture from their New World Translation. We can be prepared because they will give us a copy of the book to prepare for the study; they will also provide us with a New World Translation if we ask for one. As we prepare for the study, be prepared to be surprised because the Witness literature is excellent at using verses based on isolated reading

---

[251] An auxiliary pioneer is a Witness, who spends 50-hours a month out evangelizing. A regular pioneer is a Witness, who spends 70-hours a month out evangelizing. It used to be 70-hours for the auxiliary and 90 hours for the regular pioneer. They also have a special pioneer that spends 120 hours a month.

[252] Jehovah's Witnesses

25 Columbia Heights

BROOKLYN NY 11201-2483

UNITED STATES

+1 718-560-5000

sound as though they do support what is being said in their publications. Thus, we need to look the verses up three literal translations (NASB, ESV, and HCSB), we need to read the section of Scripture that the text is found in and look it up in a commentary volume. A superb, easy to read commentary volume set is Holman Old and New Testament Commentary Volumes. If there are translation issues, we need to investigate these. If there are textual issues, we need to examine these.

Once they arrive for the study, we should have our legal pad or our tablet right beside us with our information. Once we complete the study, let the Witness know that we take issue with some of the verses that they had used to support their position. Then, go through them one by one. It is as simple as that. If we share this information without asking them to defend against it, over the course of their study book (4-6 months), they will begin to doubt their position. One cannot sit through one correction after another over so many months and not begin to wonder about whether they are in the right religion. One thing that we do not want to do is what many of the cult books that undermine the Witnesses beliefs recommend, i.e., shock and awe. They want us to sit there, take a Witness belief, and methodically undermine it. This will not work; the Witness will not open, look in, or be a part of such a book. Even if we do not show them the book, they will walk out if the situation looks like an assault on their faith. I apologize for this analogy, but one can cook an animal alive if they turn up the heat slow enough. If we walk through a couple of their books over an extended period, it will be so slow of an undermining that it will not be an affront, an assault.

Exercise

Biblical Interpretation: After reading **Romans 12:19**, The student will explain the results of the steps that he followed:

Step 1: What is the historical setting and background for the author of the book and his audience? Who wrote the book? When and under what circumstances was the book written? Where was the book written? Who were the recipients of the book? Was there anything noteworthy about the place of the recipients? What is the theme of the book? What was the purpose for writing the book?

Step 2a: What would this text mean to the original audience? (The meaning of a text is what the author meant by the words that he used, as should have been understood by his readers.)

Step 2b: If there are any words in this section that one does not understand, or that stand out as interesting words that may shed some insight on the meaning, look them up in a word dictionary, such as

Mounce's Complete Expository Dictionary of Old and New Testament Words.

Step 2c: After reading the section from the three Bible translations, doing a word study, write down what you think the author meant. Then, pick up a trustworthy commentary, like the Holman Old or New Testament commentary volume, and see if you have it correct.

Step 3: Explain the original meaning in one or two sentences, preferably one. Then, take the sentence or two and place it in a short phrase.

Step 4: Now, consider their circumstances, the reason for it being written, what it meant to them, and consider examples from today that would be similar to that time, which would fit the pattern of meaning. What **implications** can be drawn from the original meaning?

Step 5: Find the pattern of meaning, the "thing like these," and consider how it could apply in our modern day life. How should individual Christians today live out the implications and principles?

Review Questions

- What is the approach for witnessing to Muslims?
- What is the approach for witnessing to atheists?
- What is the approach for witnessing to Jews?
- What is the approach for witnessing to Jehovah's Witnesses?

CHAPTER 19 Pay Attention to How You Listen

Luke 8:18 Updated American Standard Version (UASV)

¹⁸ Therefore, **take care how you listen**; for whoever has, to him more shall be given; and whoever does not have, even what he thinks he has shall be taken away from him."

Jesus' caution to his audience about how they listen proves just as relevant today as it was 2,000 years ago. If one only hears the words, but not what lies behind those words, he will find himself in trouble with his spouse, children, employer, and everyone else he communicates with daily. More importantly, it could jeopardize one's hope of eternal life. We need to consider more than the words themselves.

We must hear the words that are spoken, as well as the way it is said, the tone and the body language, to get the sense of what someone means. A common complaint of wives to husbands is that they passively listen to them, blocking out much of what they do not want to hear because they oppose or are not interested in what she is saying. Sadly, we tend to be less appreciative of those who are closest to us than total strangers. Active listening is a form of listening that results in the speaker and listener having a full understanding of what is meant. There are seven points to active listening:

(1) Pay close attention to what is being said; listen for the ideas behind the words. Do not just hear, but also feel the words. Let the speaker know that you are listening, by leaning forward a little, looking at him, not staring, but having sufficient eye contact.

(2) Look at a facial expression, the tone of the voice, the inflection of the voice, the mood and body language. Get at the feelings behind the words. People generally do not say all that is on their mind or convey their true feelings at times, so the listener must pay close attention to the non-verbal signs.

(3) Turn off your internal thinking as much as possible. In other words, do not be thinking of how to respond to certain points while he is still talking, because you are going to miss the whole of what he has said.

(4) Let the speaker know you are paying attention by **nodding from time to time**, as well as acknowledging with verbal gestures.

(5) Reiterate is not a common word, but it means to repeat what you think the person meant by what they said, but in your own words, to see if you understood them correctly. "So, you mean ... right?"

(6) The person you are speaking with will acknowledge that you are correct, or he will correct you, and will restate what they meant, and likely in a more comprehensive way since you misunderstood. **Pay even closer attention** as they explain again, what they meant.

(7) When they have explained their message again, you must **repeat your reiteration**.

Considering how to listen proves vital if we are going to be an effective evangelizer. There has been no greater teacher than Jesus Christ because he was an effective communicator, as well as an active listener. While some may be effective speakers, very motivational and moving, they lack teaching skills. Every time we open our mouths to share the Good News with another person, be it five minutes, or an ongoing study with them, we must build a relationship with them.

Jesus in the Temple at Twelve Years Old

Luke 2:41-47 Updated American Standard Version (UASV)

[41] Now His parents went to Jerusalem every year at the Feast of the Passover. [42] And **when he was twelve years old**, they went up according to the custom of the feast. [43] And after the days were completed, while they were returning, the boy Jesus stayed behind in Jerusalem. And his parents did not know it, [44] but supposing him to be in the company, they went a day's journey; and they began looking for him among their relatives and acquaintances. [45] and when they did not find him, they returned to Jerusalem, looking for him. [46] Then, it occurred, after three days they found him in the temple, sitting in the midst of the teachers and **listening to them** and **questioning them**. [47] And all those listening to him were **amazed at his understanding and his answers**.

This incident develops into something far more magnificent than one might first realize. Kittel's *Theological Dictionary of the New Testament* helps the reader appreciate that the Greek word *eperotao*, which means to ask, to question, to demand of, for "questioning" was far more than the Greek word *erotao* to ask, to request, to entreat, for a boy's inquisitiveness. *Eperotao* can refer to questioning, which one might hear in a judicial hearing, such as a scrutiny, inquiry, counter questioning, even the "probing and cunning questions of the Pharisees and Sadducees," for instance those we find in Mark 10:2 and 12:18-23.

The same dictionary continues: "In [the] face of this usage it may be asked whether ... [Luke] 2:46 denotes, not so much the questioning curiosity of the boy, but rather His successful disputing. [Verse] 47 would fit in well with the latter view." Rotherham's translation of verse 47 presents it as a dramatic confrontation: "Now all who heard him were beside themselves, because of his understanding and his answers." Robertson's Word Pictures in the New Testament says that their constant amazement means, "They stood out of themselves as if their eyes were bulging out."

After returning to Jerusalem, and three days of searching, they found young Jesus in the Temple, questioning the Jewish religious leaders, to which "they were astounded." (Luke 2:48) Robertson said of this, "(The) second aorist passive indicative of an old Greek word [ekplesso]), to strike out, drive out by a blow. Joseph and Mary 'were struck out' by what they saw and heard. Even they had not fully realized the power in this wonderful boy."[253] Thus, at twelve years old, Jesus, but a boy, is already demonstrating he is a great teacher and defender of truth. BDAG says, "To cause to be filled with amazement to the point of being overwhelmed, amaze, astound, overwhelm (lit., strike out of one's senses)."[254]

The Jewish culture, and especially Jesus' Jewish family, displayed an effective ability to listen. The Jewish religious leaders, on the other hand, seemed eager to speak, not listen. Jesus was not in the temple to win conversations with the greatest teachers of Jewish Law, but rather to listen. It says in verse 46 that the twelve-year-old Jesus was "listening to them." Once he listened to them, he then knew what they meant, their motives for what they said, and it was at that time, he proceeded in **"asking them questions."** Good listening leads to good questions.

Verse 47 says, "All who heard him were amazed at his insight and his answers," which means that Jesus' questions were intensely insightful, and even penetrating. If one finds himself in a conversation with a Bible critic in a public setting, where others are listening, we must listen. If one discerns that the Bible critic does not have a receptive heart, and nothing we say will open his eyes to the truth of God's Word, we must consider others who may be listening. Because of that larger audience one will then do as Jesus did, use effective questions to put the Bible critic on defense, so that those around know we do have answers for the criticisms, giving them faith in the message they heard.

---

[253] A.T. Robertson, Word Pictures in the New Testament (Nashville, TN: Broadman Press, 1933), Lk 2:48.

[254] William Arndt, Frederick W. Danker and Walter Bauer, A Greek-English Lexicon of the New Testament and Other Early Christian Literature, 3rd ed. (Chicago: University of Chicago Press, 2000), 308.

Do Not Allow Yourself to Get in the Way

Passive involvement in a discussion can lead to getting in the way of our own objective. One must be aware that not everyone has taken the time to read a book on effective communication. Therefore, a person in the conversation may be someone who goes on for some time and gets lost or side tracked with other subjects not relevant to the discussion. If that occurs, respectfully stop them, and briefly explain that it would be best to stay on topic, and offer that person the point that they were making.

Overzealousness also proves another way that we get in the way of our own objective. A trap that one can fall into with a very active mind is anticipating what the speaker will say. It can be rude to interrupt them by finishing their thoughts, or worse, to assume what they will say, and then offer feedback on one's assumption. Many times that leads to the response, "I was not going to say that at all, what I was going to say was ...." Each time one interrupts the other speaker unnecessarily, that person withdraws further and further from being an active participant in the conversation. Rather, let the person finish their thoughts and hold off for a few seconds to see if they will start again before you respond.

The person, who may seem like a Bible critic, can make a believer defensive, which can unnerve most evangelists. If someone approaches a believer with an alleged error or contradiction, what should we do? We should be frank and honest. If we do not have an answer, we should admit such. If the text in question gives the appearance of difficulty, we should admit this as well. If a believer remains unsure how to answer, simply say that you will look into it and get back to them, returning with a reasonable response.

However, do not express disbelief and doubt to people who have legitimate concerns about the Bible, because they will be moved even further in their disbelief. Moreover, it will put them on offense and place the believer on defense. With great confidence, tell them there is an answer. The Bible has withstood the test of 2,000 years of persecution and is the most printed book of all time, currently being translated into 2,287 languages. If these critical questions threatened its credibility, the Bible would not be the book that it is.

The evangelist must keep Paul's words "knowledge puffs up" at the fore of his thinking, because as one grows in knowledge and understanding, it is too easy to fall prey to a haughty spirit. After the evangelist has spent hundreds of hours listening to unbelievers talk about the Bible, one will hear the same thing many times. This is like watching the same uninteresting movie dozens of times. This can cause the evangelist to start speaking in a disdainful tone to the person who is speaking. It may be blatant, or even subtle, but the unbeliever will notice it, and while they may respectfully finish the conversation with the evangelist, they will not care what the believer said before the end of the conversation.

Proverbs 16:18 Updated American Standard Version (UASV)

[18] Pride goes before destruction,
and a haughty spirit before a fall.

In the end, God has given each of us the right to make our own decisions. The evangelist that respects another person's right to their views may win the day in the end. If a Bible critic goes through a conversation with both speakers having an equal time, they will feel were respected. They will be open to speaking to another Christian at another time. We must keep in mind that we are planting seeds of truth. Life experiences have a way of altering heart conditions. One unbeliever may have something happen in their life, which makes them more receptive to Bible truths, and the next Christian they engage will have success in watering those seeds.

Getting Beneath the Surface

In witnessing to others, there will come times when one feels the other person is holding back. The unbeliever really does not want to go deeper into the conversation because perhaps she does not wish to offend. Maybe she views the Bible or God as foolish, and anyone that holds them as truth, just as foolish. Therefore, they just give surface answers to finish the conversation. Gently and respectfully ask some questions that will probe beneath the surface answers that she has been supplying. One could ask, "Can you tell me more about ...? What is it that has brought you to this conclusion?"

In some cases, people hold back because of past hurts. Maybe their child died, and this has only reinforced to them that there cannot be a loving God. They may not feel like sharing the hurt, so he attempts to get out of the conversation. If a couple of tactful questions might get them to open up, go ahead. However, if it seems that additional questions will do more damage than good, let it go because they will respect the believer for handling the conservation that way. On the other hand, if the searching questions prove effective, and the person becomes emotional in explaining why they have not been able to accept God, do not get analytical; rather, be a comforter who is an empathetic and understanding listener.

How questions are asked can make all the difference. If one seeks answers that lie beneath the surface, we should avoid the "why" questions because they come across in more like an interrogation. This may make the other person close down even further. You can use qualifiers to get deeper. Thus, it would not be, "Why do you not believe in God?" Rather it would be, "What has contributed to your understanding of God?" Another way might be to ask, "How have you have come to your current position on God?" Searching questions at the right time comes about because a believer has been an active listener.

Exercise

Spend one week doing nothing but listening and asking questions of people. You can offer some thoughts, but focus on drawing out everyone you meet: family, friends, coworkers, fellow Christians and anyone you evangelize. Let your questions draw out their inner thoughts and use their answers, to enable you to ask more questions and acknowledge that you were listening in some way.

Biblical Interpretation: After reading **James 4:7**, The student will explain the results of the steps that he followed:

Step 1: What is the historical setting and background for the author of the book and his audience? Who wrote the book? When and under what circumstances was the book written? Where was the book written? Who were the recipients of the book? Was there anything noteworthy about the place of the recipients? What is the theme of the book? What was the purpose for writing the book?

Step 2a: What would this text have meant to the original audience? (The meaning of a text is what the author meant by the words that he used, as should have been understood by his readers.)

Step 2b: If there are any words in this section that one does not understand, or that stand out as interesting words that may shed insight on its meaning, look them up in a word dictionary, such as *Mounce's Complete Expository Dictionary of Old and New Testament Words.*

Step 2c: After reading your section from the three Bible translations, doing a word study, write down what you think the author meant. Then, pick up a trustworthy commentary, such as Holman Old or New Testament commentary volume, and see if you have it correct.

Step 3: Explain the original meaning in one or two sentences, preferably one. Then, take the sentence or two; place it in a short phrase.

Step 4: Now, consider their circumstances, the reason for it being written, what it meant to them, and consider examples from our day that would be similar to theirs, which would fit the pattern of meaning. What **implications** can be drawn from the original meaning?

Step 5: Find the pattern of meaning, the "thing like these," and consider how it could apply in our modern day life. How should individual Christians today live out the implications and principles?

Review Questions

- Why should we "consider how we listen?" What are the five points to active listening?

- Why might we address a Bible critic's questions in a public setting?

- Why is it best, respectfully, to stop a person, who is jumping from subject to subject? What is the result of being too active in the conversation, unnecessarily interrupting? How should we handle a question on the Bible when we do not know the answer? Why can we express confidence in the trustworthiness of the Bible, even if we do not have an answer to the current question? Even though we may have heard it all before, why should we approach a person's concerns as though it were the first time? Even though we may not overturn false reasoning, what might a respectful attitude accomplish in the end?

CHAPTER 20 Methods of Evangelism

1 John 4:10, 19; 5:3 Updated American Standard Version (UASV)

[10] Herein is love, not that we have loved God but that he loved us and sent his Son to be the propitiation [covering] for our sins. [19] We love because he first loved us. [3] For this is the love of God, that we keep his commandments. And his commandments are not burdensome.

Jesus gave us the greatest commanded that Christianity has ever received, which was "go therefore and make disciples of all nations, baptizing them" and "teaching them to observe all that I have commanded you." (Matt. 28:19-20) A Christian can make the claim that he has faith in the Good News within God's Word. However, if that person never shares that Good News with others, it would hardly be considered a genuine faith. If one failed to be obedient to the Greatest Commission ever given, it could hardly be a real faith.

1 John 4:20 Updated American Standard Version (UASV)

If anyone says, "I love God," and hates his brother, he is a liar; for he who does not love his brother whom he has seen cannot love God whom he has not seen.

When it comes to expressing love, there is no better example than Jesus. He has always worked on behalf of the Father's best interests. When he was here on earth, he always did the will of the Father it was his highest concern. After he left us a perfect example to follow, he then offered his human life as a ransom sacrifice so that all trusting in him might live. He was modest, caring and sympathetic, and understanding, helping those weighed down and troubled. His words offered those who listened and obeyed eternal life. (John 6:68) Love of God and neighbor, in fact, are inseparably tied to one another. Jesus is the very embodiment of love. Everything he does is a result of his love. Being made in the image and likeness of God humans have a measure of that love, which can be cultivated to an even greater degree. (Gen. 1:27) By demonstrating love to our neighbor, we show love for God.

When we consider the sacrifice made by the Father and the Son, we should be moved to demonstrate our profound gratefulness in return. It was Jesus, who set the example, when he said, "But so that the world may know that I love the Father, and just as the Father has commanded me, thus I am doing." (John 14:31) What are some of the different ways we can evidence our love for neighbor, faith in Jesus, and obedience to the will of the Father? At the end of this handbook will be appendices for each of these forms of evangelism mentioned below, offering practical suggestions on how effectively to carry out that particular form.

Bible Studies with Bible Students

Below we will discuss several different forms of evangelizing friends, family, and our local community. The goal of every witnessing opportunity is to start a one-on-one Bible study with the person, preferably in their home, once a week for an hour. All congregation members, who are active in the evangelism of their community, should be able to carry on a Bible study program with a new one. There should be a basic theology book, like THE EVANGELISM STUDY TOOL Basic Bible Doctrines of the Christian Faith by Edward D. Andrews (Jan., 2016), which could be used as a study tool. You do not want people becoming a member of your congregation based on emotionalism. Rather, you want then joining because they are able to make an informed decision based on knowledge of the Scriptures.

These studies can be carried out in their home, or in your home, even in the congregation if it is open and available. It is a one-on-one study with you and him or her. Your objective is to go through two books. The first book would be on doctrinal beliefs. The second book would be on the basics of how to interpret Scripture. This book highly recommends, *Basic Bible Interpretation* by Roy B. Zuck (Jan 1991).[255] Of course, you want to invite them to church, offering them transportation, if needed. Throughout this study process of several months, the objective is more involved than taking in knowledge (while this is important), but also includes helping them as they transition from the world, to the Christian faith, putting on that new Christ-like person. (Eph. 4:23-24; Col. 3:8-10) They should be treated as if they are your spiritual child. (1 Cor. 4:17)

If a congregation chooses to use Edward Andrews' book, *THE EVANGELISM STUDY TOOL Basic Bible Doctrines of the Christian Faith*, it should be noted that this book does have any study questions at the end of its chapters. Therefore, the person in charge of the Evangelism program must study through the book himself first, covering the questions as he goes. This study process would be used thereafter as people in the church study this book as well. Then, the study process would be given to the Bible student of the congregation member, along with his or her copy of the book. It would be explained to the Bible student, that he or she is to prepare for the study beforehand, by going through the section the teacher assigns, reading, looking up the Scriptures, and underlining or

---

[255] ISBN-13: 978-0781438773

highlighting the answers to the questions. When the study is conducted, the student should save any question they may have written down, until they have covered the assignment first.

Witnessing from House to House

Two groups are known the world over for this form of evangelism, Jehovah's Witnesses and Mormons. However, I have had a few Baptist pastors come to my door, which was a surprise. This form of evangelism should not be shied away from because one does not want to be affiliated with Witnesses and Mormons. The early Christians carried out a house-to-house evangelistic work (Luke 9:1-6; 10:1-7; Acts 5:42;[256] 20:20), and there has never proven to be a more foundational way of reaching your neighbor.

This is a difficult work, as most people are not receptive to God's Word, seeing it as a book by man, foolish and outdated. Therefore, it takes a true love for God and neighbor to be out in our community repeatedly, year after year, engaged in a world that is uninterested, and in opposition to the work, which Jesus assigned.

2 Corinthians 2:14-17 Updated American Standard Version

[14] But thanks be to God, who always leads us in triumph in Christ, and manifests through us the sweet aroma of the knowledge of Him in every place. [15] For we are the aroma of Christ to God among those who are being saved and among those who are perishing; [16] to the one an aroma from death to death, to the other an aroma from life to life. And who is adequate for these things? [17] For we are not, like so many, peddlers of God's word, but as men of sincerity, as commissioned by God, in the sight of God we speak in Christ.

Holman New Testament Commentary

2:14a. Paul had been disappointed in Troas and Macedonia, but through it all God had been good to him. He began this acknowledgment of divine goodness with thanksgiving: **But thanks be to God**.

2:14b–16a. Paul delighted in God's care for him. He expressed this joy with the metaphor of a victory parade. Paul was convinced that God

---

[256] R. C. H. Lenski, in his work The Interpretation of The Acts of the Apostles, Minneapolis (1961), made the following comment on Ac 5:42: "Never for a moment did the apostles cease their blessed work. 'Every day' they continued, and this openly 'in the Temple' where the Sanhedrin and the Temple police could see and hear them, and, of course, also *kat oikon*, which is distributive, 'from house to house,' and not merely adverbial, 'at home.'"

always leads believers **in triumphal procession in Christ**. Paul drew upon the triumphal parades that were known throughout the Roman world. Prisoners of war were marched through the streets as fragrant perfumes filled the air. At the end of each parade, many prisoners were executed. For this reason, the smells of the parade were sweet to the victors, but they were the **smell of death** to the defeated.

Paul saw several similarities between these victory parades and his own ministry. (1) He and those with him were members of the victorious army led by **Christ**, as were the rest of the apostles. (2) Their gospel preaching spread **everywhere ... the knowledge** or acknowledgment **of God** as the victor. Similarly, Roman victory parades spread knowledge about victories and caused people to acknowledge the victors. (3) Paul said that he and the apostles were like the perfumes of the victory parades. They became **to** (the honor of) **God** like **the aroma of Christ**, or more specifically, like **the aroma** accompanying Christ's victory. Both the victors of this spiritual gospel war (**those who are being saved**) and the defeated (**those who are perishing**) smelled their **aroma**. (4) This **aroma of Christ**, however, affected each group differently. To Christ's enemies, Paul and those with him were **the smell of death**, but to those following Christ they were **the fragrance of life**.

This metaphor contrasted Christian and non-Christian reactions to evangelists. To Christians, Paul and his company presented reminders of the wonders of salvation. For non-Christians, they raised the terror of divine judgment. No one could ignore them because their fragrance was spreading throughout the world.

2:16b. As Paul contemplated his analogy between Roman victory parades and his gospel ministry, he was overwhelmed. He exclaimed, **Who is equal to such a task?** The answer he implied was that no one was worthy of playing such an important role in human history and in the kingdom of God. It was astounding that God appointed humans to this role.

2:17. Paul wanted the Corinthians to know that he did not view his ministry as an ordinary job. He did not **peddle the word of God for profit**. He distinguished himself and those who worked with him from **so many** others who had reduced their ministries to mere occupations. Unlike the gospel peddlers, Paul and his company spoke **before God with sincerity**. Paul still lingered on the accusation of insincerity and duplicity he had addressed in the preceding section. He could not have been insincere because he looked upon his ministry so highly. Instead, he served as one **sent from God**, considering his task a sacred privilege. The fact that he did not accept payment for his preaching further demonstrated his sincerity.[257]

Zondervan Illustrated Bible Backgrounds Commentary

And through us spreads everywhere the fragrance of the knowledge of him (2:14). One of the standard features of religious or civic rituals in antiquity was the use of incense and other fragrant materials. Religious processions, the arrival of an important dignitary, the triumphal return of a Roman general, and so on, were all occasions on which such aromatics might be used. In describing the triumphal procession of Aemelius Paulus, Plutarch tells us that "every temple was open and filled with garlands and incense."[258] Continuing the image of the Roman triumph, Paul portrays his crushed and vanquished apostolic existence as the means through which the aroma of the crucified Christ is mediated to those around him. Paradoxically, God's strength is most potently displayed through Paul's weakness. Already the apostle is preparing the ground for his startling declaration in 12:10, "For when I am weak, then I am strong."

For we are to God the aroma of Christ among those who are being saved and those who are perishing (2:15). Embedded within the imagery of the triumphal procession is an allusion to the Levitical sacrifices of the Old Testament, where the terms *euōdia* (niv "fragrance") and *osmē* (niv "aroma") combine to refer to a sacrificial "aroma pleasing to the Lord" (Lev. 2:2, 12; 6:14, etc.). As elsewhere (e.g., Col. 1:24), Paul portrays his apostolic suffering as an extension of the suffering of Christ, and he will make this point more explicitly in 4:10: "We always carry around in our body the death of Jesus."

To the one we are the smell of death; to the other, the fragrance of life (2:16). Although the transitions between metaphors is abrupt, Paul returns to the spectacle of the triumph and notes the differing effects the aroma-filled parade route would have on those involved. For the cheering crowds, the victorious soldiers, and the gloating general, this was the sweet fragrance of victory. But to the unfortunate captives destined for the auctioneer's block or execution in the forum, this was the scent of death itself.

Unlike so many, we do not peddle the word of God for profit (2:17). Preaching the gospel for mere financial gain has been a problem from the earliest days of the Christian movement. Already by the time of the *Didache* (ca. a.d. 80–150) Christian communities were exhorted to

---

[257] Richard L. Pratt, Jr, vol. 7, I & II Corinthians, Holman New Testament Commentary, 320-21 (Nashville, TN: Broadman & Holman Publishers, 2000).

[258] Aemelius Paulus 32.

judge itinerant Christian teachers with reference to their desire for monetary gain: "And when the apostle leaves, he is to take nothing except bread until he finds his next night's lodging. But if he asks for money he is a false prophet."[259] ...

Paul's point is that unlike so many who proclaim their "religion" for a price, he and his companions preach Christ for altruistic reasons.[260]

While it is true that this sort of evangelism, house to house, can be very trying, it also brings the greatest joys at the same time as well. Imagine that you are in a desert, walking, staggering alone, dehydrated, parched, gasping for air, and you come up a source of water over the next dune that you cross. The relief, the joy, the gratitude, the thoughts that you had for miles of walking, where you had considered, "I will just lie down, and never wake again," are all gone, as you fall to the ground in tears, grateful that you never gave up! One may be out in this evangelistic work for months, growing ever tired of coming across the ungrateful, the critics, the sarcastic, the short tempered, the uninterested, and the opposer, when they finally come upon the smiling face that invites them in their home. They get you something cold to drink, and they then sit and listen to the message that you have brought, and you can see the light in their eyes, the hunger and thirst to know more.

The same difficult time as is found in the above plays out, but this time, it is the Bible critic, who lets you in and offers you a drink. They let you share the Good News that you have brought, patiently waiting their turn to communicate. Unknown to you, they have been reading one Bible critic book after another. You pause after leaving them with a question, and then they pounce on you like a lion after his prey, with one question after another. You can be one of two people: either **(1)** the prepared or **(2)** the unprepared.

As the **unprepared**, you are struck by the fact that you have been carrying a Bible for many years, and are unable to defend the very book you call the Word of God. You are hurt by the fact that you have learned how to share your faith, but have never considered how you might defend your faith. As the **prepared**, you hold up your hand, the young mind in front of you comes to a halt, and you say, "I see that you have been doing much reading. I am very pleased that you have some interest in the Bible." You go on, saying, "We can address every one of your concerns, one at a time, and this approach will work best as we resolve

---

[259] Did. 11:6.

[260] Clinton E. Arnold, Zondervan Illustrated Bible Backgrounds Commentary Volume 3: Romans to Philemon., 207-08 (Grand Rapids, MI: Zondervan, 2002).

one, and then move onto the next." He agrees that this is the best approach.

He leans in, eyes as bright from the start, and argues that "**if there was** an Adam and Eve, and an Abel who was now dead, so, where did Cain get his wife?"

You respond with, "If one were to read a little further along, they would come to the realization that Adam had a son named Seth; it further adds that Adam "became father to sons *and daughters*." (Genesis 5:4) Adam lived for a total of 800 years after fathering Seth, giving him ample opportunity to father many more sons and daughters. Therefore, it could be that Cain married one of his sisters. If he waited until one of his brothers and sisters had a daughter, he could have married one of his nieces once she was old enough."

You continue, saying that "In the beginning, humans were closer to perfection; this explains why they lived longer and why at that time there was little health risk of genetic defects in the case of children born to closely related parents, in contrast to how it is today. As time passed, genetic defects increased and life spans decreased. Adam lived to see 930 years. Yet Shem, who lived after the Flood, died at 600 years, while Shem's son Arpachshad only lived 438 years, dying before his father died. Abraham saw an even greater decrease in that he only lived 175 years, while his grandson Jacob was 147 years when he died. Thus, due to increasing imperfection, God prohibited the marriage of closely related people under the Mosaic Law because of the likelihood of genetic defects. (Lev. 18:9.)"

Undaunted by your response, he realizes you have offered him a reasonable answer, but he moves on. He asks, "If we read at Exodus 4:21 that God is here **hardening Pharaoh's heart**, what exactly makes Pharaoh responsible for the decisions he makes?"

You respond with saying, "This is actually a prophecy. God knew that what he was about to do would contribute to a stubborn and obstinate Pharaoh, who was going to be unwilling to change or give up the Israelites so they could go off to worship their God. Therefore, this is not stating what God is going to do; it is prophesying that Pharaoh's heart will harden because of the actions of God. The fact is, Pharaoh allowed his own heart to harden because he was determined not to agree with Moses' wishes or accept Jehovah's request to let the people go. Moses tells us in Exodus 7:13 (UASV) that 'Pharaoh's heart was hardened, and he would not listen to them, as Jehovah had said.' Again, at 8:15 we read, 'When Pharaoh saw that there was a respite, he hardened his heart and would not listen to them, as Jehovah had said.' "

This goes on for some time, one question after the other. Over time though, you could feel that he was losing steam, and he was slowing with less and less eagerness. Soon, he was leaning in, because he wanted to hear what you had to say, and was no longer dismissive of your reasonable, logical responses. Before you left, he was now asking you, "Can you come back, as I want to hear more about your message?" Yes, you were **used by God**, as you defended the Word; you defended the faith, and you were used by God to open the eyes of the blind, because you listened to the inspired Word of God. (Prov. 2:1-6; Josh. 1:8; Ps. 1:1-3; 1 Pet. 3:15; Jude 1:3, 22-23) You may feel that it takes too much time to be this **prepared** as opposed to the shameful embarrassment of being **unprepared**. This could not be further from the truth, as it only takes one hour a day of personal Bible study, six days a week, Monday through Saturday.

Now, what other ways can we share our faith with our community?

Street Witnessing

The primary method of sharing the Good News in the community is by going house-to-house. However, maybe you are unable to find certain ones at home because they work a shift at the time you are able to go out. Then, some people live in gated communities, which you cannot get access to because there is a restriction against the house-to-house work. In addition, some high-rise apartment buildings do not allow entry but to those that live, or if you are invited, meaning that you are cut off from sharing the message with these as well. This is why witnessing on the street can be quite effective, as we must reach everyone. The most important thing to keep in mind is that this should be carried out in the most respectful way possible, never being aggressive, or have any showy display, such as loud talk, or especially yelling and screaming.

Informal Witnessing

This is sharing the Good News with people as you come across them in the community: the store, doctor's office, public transportation, and so on. We are actively to seek out these ones in our everyday activities, such as a fellow employee, a fellow student at school, being served by a waitress at a restaurant, visiting a friend, and so on. All of these are acts of what is known as an informal evangelism. (John 4:7-15) These are unplanned but not unprepared occasions where we have an opportunity to share some form of Christian teaching with another person.

This is an effective tool in your evangelism toolbox, in helping them to hear the Good News of God's kingdom. As this facet of witnessing is usually quite brief, one must be prepared with what they might say, and have a Bible tract with them, getting something into their hands before parting ways. On that tract should be a way for them to get back with you if they so desire. If you feel things went well enough in this short exchange, you may ask them for some contact information. It takes a lot of courage to approach complete strangers, but it is our love for them, which moves us to buy out the time in this sort of evangelism. It is God, who gives "us a spirit not of fear but of power and love and self-control. Therefore, do not be ashamed of the testimony about our Lord." –2 Timothy 1:7-8.

Telephone Witnessing

Small groups of congregation members put to use a reverse phone directory (lists phone numbers by addresses), and go to a small call center that has been set up in the congregation. This is great for getting to people that live in gated communities, or in high-rise apartments that you do not have access to otherwise. Just because we are not face-to-face, does not mean that it is any less effective. In fact, it may be easier on both of you, because there seems to be less stress. The Christian making the call can have notes in front of him, as well as any kind of research tool, enabling him to field questions. It could be set up so that it works off a desktop computer, with a headset that also has a microphone, leaving the hands free. This is certainly an effective tool.

Remember, this is not the primary way to reach people but is only a tool for those that you cannot find at home in your community (i.e., the reverse phone directory). The headset should be set up on the computer so that you can have a splitter plugged in, and multiple people can listen. This way you can train ones, who have done this form of witnessing. However, it would be best if two people at a time take a call (Luke 10:1). One is the person, who is trying to reach the person, they could not find at home, and the other is the helper, who looks up information or takes notes based on the conversation.

Telemarketing has caused people to shy away from taking calls from anyone they do not know. Therefore, it is best to show feelings of kindness, pleasantness, and tactfulness with your voice. Do not speak too loud, and do not speak too low. You may mention at the outset that you are not selling anything. Use your name, letting them know that you live in their community, and were sharing one Scripture with them and their neighbors. Rather than ask if you can read a Scripture, after stating that is why you have called, just jump to the Scripture, fully citing it and reading it. After reading it, ask a very short open-ended question about the Scripture. If he or she shares their thoughts, keep your word by offering a short comment and closing out the call. Before hanging up, ask if you may call back this time next week, so you can briefly share another Scripture. On the third or fourth week of doing this, you can begin to engage in more of a conversation. Remember, you will eventually want to visit them in their home, and start a Bible study with them.

Witnessing by Writing Letters

Again, this would be perfect for getting to people that live in gated communities, or in high-rise apartments that you do not have access to otherwise. Moreover, this would be the approach for one who has a physical disability that keeps them from going out into their community. You can write letters to people within your community, sharing a short biblical thought with them, and enclosing a tract as well. This is an easier form of evangelism, because to can take your time, to get your words just right, and there is no pressure.

Returning to Evangelize Again

You have made the initial contact with a new believer. In the initial conversation, you have planted a couple of biblical truths, so you need to return to water these, enabling them to grow. (1 Cor. 3:6-8) You now need to get some kind of contact information: phone number, email, or address. You can leave them with a biblical question to ponder, stating what would be the best way to get back with them. Keep in mind that while it may not seem like there is much interest; life is always influencing a person's worldview. Moreover, it is your job to cultivate interest as well.

Remember, your end objective is to start a Bible study with ones who are interested. You are always in search of those, who will be receptive to a Bible study. (Matt. 10:11) If you do have one who gives you their contact information, make sure that you get back with them in about a week, because you do not want their interest to fade. In planning your phone call if it was a phone number, or your email, or a visit to their home, make sure you prepare well. Before leaving the first time, you may have left her or him with a thought provoking question, which you will be addressing this second time. You should have written their name down, and some interesting information that you gleaned from your initial conversation. Use that to show interest in the return.

Your love of God and neighbor keeps this person on your mind until your next contact with them. Once you are on the line with them, or at their home, use their name; try to make the same connection you had the first time around, by spending some time, showing a genuine interest in them. Make them the center of attention by asking open-ended questions that they can answer at length, and be an **active listener** (more on active listening later). In other words, do not be thinking about your next comment or question when the person is talking. An active listener will look at the person while they are talking (not a constant stare, but periodic), and they will move their head in agreement or in word, to let the speaker know that you are listening. If possible, show that you are empathetic to what they are saying, by responding with something like, "I have felt that way before, too." It is permissible to ask short clarifying questions as well, which is another way to help the speaker know you are interested.

Remember that your second contact is all about them, with your interjecting some Scripture in, so they remember, it is God's Word that brought you to them. On the second visit, share at least one Scripture, getting their insights as to what they think, tactfully offering the correct interpretation if they are off the mark. With each visit, keep in mind that you are working toward starting a Bible study with them, and inviting them to a congregation meeting. On the visit where you bring up the possibility of a Bible study, pull out the book you intend to use and hand it to them. Explain to them that the study is free of charge, something that takes place once a week, in the convenience of their home if they like, for 30-60 minutes. Have them turn to the Table of Contents in the book and walk through some of the things you would be covering. Again, it is our job to cultivate interest in others. Conversation skills are not something that can be taken in by reading some rules and principles. No, they are learned by implementing those rules and principles repeatedly, until you become skillful. The first time you find an uninterested person, and you develop interest by way of your conversation skills, it will bring you real joy that you have never felt in your life.

Witnessing to Strangers at Meetings

You should be alert to noticing any new faces at the meetings, going up to them and introducing yourself. You should get to know them as you express that you genuinely hope to see them again, befriending yourself to them. Keep in mind that, if everyone assumes that someone else will carry out this form of witnessing, no one will end up doing it, leaving a new believer feeling unwanted.

Witnessing by Our Conduct

Either our conduct can help us to shine light on the truth of God's Word, or we can bring reproach on it. (Titus 2:10) If others outside of your congregation have something good to say about your work in the community, this brings honor and glory to God. (1 Pet. 2:12) This can bring new ones to your congregation, because of what they have heard.

Effective Use of Bible Tracts

If you are to engage another in an effective conversation, you have to get the conversation started. Like a good book, or a great magazine article, the beginning will determine if you keep going. What you want to do is get the person's attention immediately. You introduce yourself, and a very brief statement that you are talking to people in your community about the Bible, and then offer a tract visually. Most Bible tracts have two things in common: (1) the titles are designed to peak interest, and (2) the cover image is designed to leap off the page at you, making you want to read it.

Another facet of offering tracts is their size. In a world where it seems that no one has time for anyone else, these short Bible tools can have an impact. When you offer something with a title and image that will capture the interest of the listener, your success is bound to increase. The best way to offer the tracts is to pick out about 4-6 of your best ones, with eye-opening titles and images. Either spread them out as you would a hand of cards, and show them, or preferably place them in the hands of the person, and ask, "Which one would you like?" Now, they are in his hands, he is looking through them, settles on one, and says, "This one."

Now, of course, you will have read every tract you offer yourself very studiously. Therefore, you will have a question lined up that highlights the substance of the tract he chose. After asking for it, open the tract, read that paragraph that answers the question, and the Scripture that is cited in it from your Bible. If the listener is very conversational, discuss more of the tract, giving him many opportunities to share in the conversation. Before closing the conversation, let him know that you would love to talk again, and write your contact information on the back of the tract, and ask him for his email or phone number.

Exercise

Read 1 Peter 1:3-25. This assignment is to help improve our reading skills. When practicing before the meeting, read slowly to enunciate every word meticulously, as well as adequate volume, and moving along at the appropriate pace. We must read and speak words clearly, to not only be understood, but also leave an impression. In addition, read with precision, stopping or pausing for punctuations, as well as changing the tone of your voice, or adding the inflections that are required. It would be best if you had someone follow along, letting you know if you to make the appropriate pauses or inflections.

Read Galatians 6:1-10. This assignment is to help improve our reading skills. When practicing before the meeting, read slowly enunciating every word meticulously, as well as sufficient volume, and moving along at the appropriate pace. We must read and speak words clearly, to not only be understood but also leave an impression. In addition, read with precision, stopping or pausing for punctuations, as well as changing the tone of your voice, or adding the inflections that are required. It would be best if you had someone follow along, letting you know if you to make the appropriate pauses or inflections.

Review Questions

- What sacrifice was made for each person, which was based on what from the Father and the Son, and why should this motivate us in our evangelism of others?

- How is the Bible study to be carried out with the Bible student?

- According to 2 Corinthians 2:14, how is God leading Christians today, and to what custom from ancient times does Paul's words refer? What took place at ancient Roman victory parades, and what did the aroma suggest to different ones? What is the application of the metaphor at 2 Corinthians 2:14-16?

- What will someone likely face in house-to-house evangelism work, but why should believers be steadfast? What do you want to be, the prepared or the unprepared, and why?

- What is an effective way of finding people that you may not get in their home, and how should you carry out this form of evangelism?

- How can someone effectively carry out informal witnessing?

- How can someone effectively carry out telephone witnessing?

- Why should someone not overlook letter writing as a form of witnessing?

- Whose responsibility is it to generate interest, and what is the goal of witnessing to others no matter what method one uses? What is active listening, and why should we make the listener the center of attention? How might someone use a second visit with an unbeliever to demonstrate what a Bible study would be like?

- Why is it important to befriend new people at any of these meetings?

- Why is someone's personal conduct outside of the congregation so important?

- Why are Bible tracts an important tool in our evangelism, and how can we effectively use them.

CHAPTER 21 Fulfilling Our Role as an Evangelizer

A Christian Evangelizer is one who proclaims the gospel or sharing the Word of God about a particular doctrine or set of beliefs to others with the intention of converting them to the **Christian** faith. In many ways, angels could by extension be labeled evangelizers as well. They certainly have passed the good news on throughout the last 6,000+ years and have helped in the work of converting unbelievers into believers. (Luke 1:19; 2:10; Acts 8:26, 27, 35; Rev. 14:6)

Certainly, if we learned one thing in this publication, Jesus commanded all of his disciples to be evangelizers. (Matthew 28:19, 20; Acts 1:8) The apostle Paul told Timothy, "But you, be sober-minded[261] in all things, endure hardship, **do the work of an evangelist**, fulfill your ministry." (2 Timothy 4:5) What is the good news that we are to proclaim to others? First and foremost, we inform them that the Creator of heaven and earth is our heavenly Father, and he loves us. (John 3:16; 1 Peter 5:7) We can inform them of what it is that one needs to do to have a righteous standing before our heavenly Father, although we are imperfect at this time. (Psalm 15:1-5; Romans 5:12) We can offer them the hope that one day soon God will remove sin, old age, and death, and they will be no more. (Isaiah 65:17; Revelation 21:3-4) As genuine Christians, we have two questions that we must ask ourselves. **(1)** Why is it that people need to hear the good news? **(2)** How can we do all that is expected of us as evangelizers?

Why Do People Need to Hear the Good News?

Just imagine that we are the Creator and we allowed sin to enter into the World. Imagine, as God we have tolerated evil, sickness, pain, suffering and death until our day in order to resolve all the issues raised by Satan in the Garden of Eden (by way of the serpent as a mouthpiece) and at the time of Job. We are self-centered in thinking that this has only pained us. Imagine that you are holding a rope on a sinking ship that 20 other men, women, and children are clinging to, when your child loses her grip and falls into the ocean. You can hold the rope, saving 20 people, or you can let go and attempt to rescue your daughter. God has been watching the suffering of billions from the day of Adam and Eve's sin. Moreover, it has been His great love for us, which causes Him to cling

---

[261] **Sober Minded**: (Gr. *nepho*) This denotes being sound in mind, to be in control of one's thought processes and thus not be in danger of irrational thinking, 'to be sober-minded, to be well composed in mind.'–1 Thessalonians 5:6, 8; 2 Timothy 4:5; 1 Peter 1:13; 4:7; 5:8

to the rope of issues, saving us from a future of repeated issues. Nevertheless, he will not allow this evil to remain forever. He has set a fixed time when He will end this wicked system of Satan's rule.

Why did God not destroy the Satan, Adam, and Eve right away?

I would follow up with what would have happened if God had chosen that path. Hundreds of billions of angels with free will were watching, and they knew of the issues raised. What would their love of God have been like if God did not address the issues raised? Was Satan right? Was God lying? Would free will creatures, spirit, and humans, be better off? Will God just destroy us over anything? First, the spirit creatures would have followed God out of dreadful fear, rather than fear of displeasing the one they loved so much up to that point, like a child to a parent. Second, what happens if the issue is raised a hundred thousand years after a restart and there are 30 billion perfect humans on the planet? Would God simply destroy everyone again and start over. Do we think it wise that he does this reboot every time or was it not better that he settled the issue once and for all?

POINT: Satan raised Issues of sovereignty in the Garden of Eden.

POINT: Can humans walk on their own; do they really need their Creator? Are they better off without God?

POINT: Was God lying and withholding?

The Issues at Hand

(1) Satan called God a liar and said he was not to be trusted, as to the life or death issue.

(2) Satan's challenge, therefore, took into question the right and legitimacy of God's rightful place as the Universal Sovereign.

(3) Satan also suggested that people would remain obedient to God only as long as their submitting to God was to their benefit.

(4) Satan all but said that humankind was able to walk on his own, there being no need for dependence on God.

(5) Satan argued that man could be like God, choosing for himself what is right and wrong.

(6) Satan claimed that God's way of ruling was not in the best interests of humans, and they could do better without God.

If God had destroyed the rebellious three: Satan, Adam, and Eve; he would not have resolved the issues of

(1) Whether man could walk on his own,

(2) if he would be better off without his Creator,

(3) if God's rulership were not best, and

(4) if God were hiding good from man.

(5) In addition, there was an audience of untold billions of angelic spirit creatures looking on.

If God destroyed without settling things, these spirit persons would be following God out of dreadful fear, not love, fear of displeasing God. Moreover, say He did kill them and start over, and ten thousand years down the road (with billions of humans now on earth), the issues were raised again, He would have to destroy billions of people again, and again, and again all throughout time, until these issues were laid to rest.

What God has done is, allow time to pass, and the issues to be resolved. Man thought he was better off without God, and could walk on his own. In addition, man has attempted every kind of rulership imaginable, and one must ask, 'have they proven themselves better than rulership under the sovereignty of their Creator?' (Proverbs 1:30-33; Isaiah 59:4, 8) Sadly, the issues must be taken up to the brink of destroying man. (Rev 11:18) Otherwise, the argument would be that if given enough time, they could have turned things around. If man goes up to the point of destroying himself and Armageddon comes at the last minute, it will have set a case law, solved the issue, and the Bible can serve as the example forever. If the issues of God's sovereignty or the loyalty of His created creatures, angelic or human, is ever questioned again, we would have the Holy Bible that will serve as a law established based on previous verdicts of not guilty, please see below.

What Have the Results Been?

(1) God does not cause evil and suffering. Romans 9:14.

(2) The fact that God has allowed evil, pain and suffering have shown that independence from God has not brought about a better world. Jeremiah 8:5, 6, 9.

(3) God's permission of evil, pain, and suffering has also proved that Satan has not been able to turn all humans away from God. Exodus 9:16; 1 Samuel 12:22; Hebrews 12:1.

(4) The fact that God has permitted evil, pain, and suffering to continue has provided proof that only God, the Creator, has the capability and the right to rule over humankind for their eternal blessing and happiness. Ecclesiastes 8:9.

(5) Satan has been the god of this world since the sin in Eden (over 6,000 years), and how has that worked out for man, and what has been the result of man's course of independence from God and his rule? Matthew 4:8-9; John 16:11; 2 Corinthians 4:3-4; 1 John 5:19; Psalm 127:1.

Satan's impact on the earth's activities has carried with it conflict, evil and death, and his rulership has been by means of deception, power and his own self-interest. He has demonstrated himself an unfit ruler of everything. Therefore, God is now completely vindicated in putting an end to this corrupted rebel along with all who have shared in his evil deeds.—Romans 16:20.

When a teenager becomes a rebel in our house, we have a choice: **(1)** severe punishment or **(2)** teach them an object lesson.

HUMANS AND ANGELS are a created product no different than a car coming off of an assembly line, i.e., (1) they owe their existence to their creator and (2) they were created to function based on the design of the creator. If we take a ford escort and treat it like a heavy duty four-wheel drive truck and go off roading (not what the car was designed to do), what will happen?

God wisely chose to teach both angels and humans an object lesson. Neither was designed to walk on their own. Both angel and human were given relative freedom (under the sovereignty of God), not absolute freedom. They were not designed to choose what is right and what is wrong on their own. They were given God's moral standards by way of an internal conscience. How can we tell a rebel that we do not have absolute freedom, we are better off under the umbrella of our creator's sovereignty, we cannot walk on our own? They will just reject it as a rebel teenager would.

OBJECT LESSON: We let them learn from their choice, no matter how painful it is, and hard love means that we do not step in until the lesson is fully learned. Humankind was essentially told, "Oh, you think you can walk on your own, well go ahead, we will see how that works out." After six-thousand-years, God could actually use a common saying among young people today: "How is that absolute freedom working out for you?"

When will the lesson fully be learned? Humankind will walk right up to the very edge of the cliff of killing themselves, actually falling over, when God will step in and stop the object lesson. To stop it anytime before, will cause doubts. If it had been stopped a century ago, the argument would have been; God simply stepped in before we got to the scientific age because he knew we were going to find true peace and security, along with something to give us eternal life. However, if

289

humanity has actually fallen over the edge of the cliff and the destruction of us is definite, and God steps in, no argument can be raised, the object lesson is learned.

Why Was Satan Not Kicked Out of Heaven Right Away?

Satan stayed in his realm, just as humans stayed in theirs. God changed nothing right away because he would have been accused of adjusting the pieces on the chessboard to get the desired outcome, i.e., cheating. When will Satan be kicked out of heaven? Satan and the Demons lost access to the person of God long age, and they lost some of their powers, such as being able to materialize in human form, like they did when they took human women for themselves at the flood, producing the Nephilim.

Satan would be thrown to the earth very shortly before the end of his age of rulership, when "he knows that his time is short." (Rev 12:9-12) This, then, means that Satan will be thrown from heaven likely sometime before the Great Tribulation and Christ's return. Revelation 12:12 says, "'Therefore, rejoice, O heavens and you who dwell in them! But woe to you, O earth and sea, for the devil has come down to you in great wrath because he knows that his time is short!'"

Notice that it is at a time, when "Satan knows that his time is short!" What comes next for Satan? He will be abyssed, thrown into a super-maximum-security prison for a thousand years (for lack of a better way to explain it) while Jesus fixes all that Satan done. After the thousand years, he will be let loose for a little while, and he will tempt perfect humans, and sadly some will fall away. In the end, Satan and those humans will be destroyed, and Jesus will hand the kingdom back over to the father. We know these things because we have a deep knowledge of God's Word. The unbelievers today are so unfamiliar with the Bible that they say things like, I don't believe in the Bible.' 'The Bible contradicts itself.' Men wrote the Bible not God.' 'There are thousands of Christian denominations and every one of them has his own interpretation of the Bible, each saying they are the truth.' 'There is no such thing as the truth, i.e., absolute truth.' 'The Bible is not practical for our day.' 'Even if there was some Creator, we cannot possibly know God.' This ignorance about God and the Scriptures is why we need to evangelize.

How Can We Do Our Best as Evangelizers?

We may be struggling with gathering and holding the interest of prospective disciples. Do we find that we are struggling even to get a few words into the conversation? Are we being dismissed in the middle of our introduction or right afterward? If so, let us look to our exemplar, Jesus Christ,

Luke 10:5 Updated American Standard Version (UASV)

⁵ Whatever house you enter, first say, 'Peace be to this house!'

Most are thinking, 'this comment will not go over too well today,' and that would be correct. Nevertheless, it gives us the foundation for an introduction, getting us into the Bible discussion we so much desire. They need to see us as their friend, who comes with information that will be encouraging and bring them peace of mind in this wicked world. We could begin with, "I am very pleased that I found you at home. I have brought you a gift today, which I believe will make this day, the best day of your year." This is a friendly opening, which is encouraging regardless of the person. Of course, whatever brief Scriptural message we have, must come across as being beneficial, not superficial. Below are more introductions that may get us into a good conversation.

Many Christians are struggling to capture and hold the interest of an unbeliever when starting a conversation. They need to have an effective introduction, which will enable them to arouse interest.

Jesus said that whatever house [or conversation] you enter, first say, 'Peace be to this house!' (Lu 10:5) This is not a common way of greeting someone in the Western world; rather, it is more the Eastern way. However, let us consider the principle behind it, which may give us introductions into a conversation. What we are looking to do is introduce ourselves in a very friendly and respectful way, with the sense of something that may bring them a measure of peace now.

We might have a Bible tract with us that deals with what Christian life can be like in a wicked world, or what life will be like under Christ, or how living a Christian way can bring joy even now. If we cannot find such a Bible tract, have 3-4 verses ready to be read. We might say, "Hello, my name is _____, and I am sharing some very good news with my neighbors. What if I could read you a message in 90 seconds that would give you peace of mind today, tomorrow and the rest of your life?" This message is warm, friendly, and has two aspects that the unbeliever will appreciate: (1) we mention how short our comments will be, (2) a question that is so intriguing that few would walk away without the answer. Below are some other introductions that may work for us.

Warm Introductions

We might start by introducing ourselves, and say, "I have a gift for you that is certainly going to make life far more interest, it is encouraging, to say the least, do you have 90 seconds?

291

If we shake their hand and introduce ourselves by giving our name, and as we are doing so, we see they **are smiling**, we might say,

"It certainly is nice to see someone smiling in these difficult times; you must have found a measure of happiness. This is what I am sharing with others, may I add to the happiness you apparently already have, it will take but a minute or two."

If we shake their hand and introduce ourselves by giving our name, and as we are doing so, we see they **are not smiling**, we might say,

I know life in this world of evil, lack of love, crime, and violence, not to mention selfishness can be overwhelming, may I take 1-2 minutes, to offer you hope that can bring joy and happiness now."

These are warm; they are thought provoking, very short ways of introducing unbelievers to the Word of God.

Hello, I am _____, have you ever wondered why Christians such as myself, risk themselves to share Bible messages with such persons as yourself?" Allow a response, and building from there. If they say yes they have wondered why tell them why. If they respond with a sarcastic remark, treat it like a joke, and smile as you reason your way out of his trying to end your conversation. If more sarcasm is repeated, simply offer a Bible tract and move on, as we cannot reason with the unreasonable.

Subject Introductions

An excellent way to break the ice is by introducing a topic that may be of interest to the unbeliever. We have to be cautious here because we do not know their worldview. Are the liberal, moderate, or conservative? These titles are not just a political position, but also relate one's worldview as well. If we interject a topic by immediately take a Christian worldview, and the unbeliever is liberal, we will have ended the conversation before it has begun. Topics can be local, national, or even the world over, but they must be something that the unbeliever would have likely heard. One thing is sure about human nature; people love to share their views with others, even strangers. Therefore, introduce the subject as a question.

Another way to generate interest is to ask the unbeliever questions that we might not want to hear the answers to but will give us an opportunity at a lengthy conversation.

- "Why do you think that so many people no longer believe the Bible to be the Word of God?"

- We would like to get your view on, "Is the Bible inspired of God or is it just 66 books written by men?"

- "What do you think about Christianity today?

- "Do you think Armageddon is a real thing that we need to worry about."

- "Do you believe the Bible is really the Word of God?"

Whatever way we decide to start a conversation, we must be prepared for the responses. Are we able to defend the Word of God as inspired and fully inerrant?[262] Are we ably to defend the faith? Are we able to defend the Christian worldview? Are we able to effective communicate without losing our temper, or letting it get into a debate?

Jumpstarting with a Subject

We might say, "We all thought that technology would give us more time, but would you not agree that our lives are even busier than ever, wishing we had more time?" Allow for a response, and then say, "Well, I do have some good news for you, did you know that the Bible actually has counsel on how we can buy out more time? May I share it with you?"

Another approach is to mention a local problem that is affecting their community. We might say, "We would love to hear your insights on _____, it is greatly impacting our community." People love to offer advice, and letting them speak at length is a way to build rapport. However, if their insights are not even close to being rational, do not attack their thoughts. Simply find an ounce of common ground within them, and move on into the biblical message we prepared. The objective of starting with the local problem was to jumpstart our biblical message, not debate.

Another conversation starter might be, "have you ever contemplated what it might be like to live forever in a perfect world, with a perfect body and mind?"

Work with other Christians in your church, and generate some great conversation starters, based on the biblical message that you are seeking to convey. Then, create a Bible insert, so that it is handy when members are out evangelizing in the community.

Keep in mind that a well-prepared introduction does not mean that a person of interest will not go off in another direction. Do not be so prepared that we are thrown off our mission, because they are not interested in what we came to talk about. Simply be happy that they are

---

[262] We recommend, IS THE BIBLE REALLY THE WORD OF GOD? Myths? Errors? Contradictions? Scientifically Inaccurate? [Second Edition] by Edward D. Andrews

http://www.christianpublishers.org/apps/webstore/products/show/7138936

willing to talk, and take advantage of whatever subject they want to discuss.

Simple Introductions

We could simply start out with asking them, 'how is your day going, I have brought something that will undoubtedly make it even better.'

If we notice at the very beginning that he or she is a friendly person, because they are smiling and offering their hand, we might say, "It is so nice to meet someone with a pleasant disposition, which means you are making the best of this stressful world we live in. Would you not agree that there is little in the world where we can find true happiness?" Allow a response, and then share "I have come to bring you, even more, happiness."

On the other hand, if you clearly see the other that you are about to engage is not I a good mood, say, "I have stopped you today because we are offering encouraging information, hope for a better future. As you read or listen to the news, there is not much to encourage us into believing life is going to be better for our children or grandchildren. Do you have a very brief moment, so that I might share some good news with you?"

Introductions need to be simple, short, and encouraging. They are designed as a stepping-stone into the biblical message that we want to share. We might simply say, "I am a Christian, and we are speaking with our neighbors about some good news. We do this because we love and care for our neighbors."

Make Every Effort to See Them Again

We live in a world of skepticism, agnostics, atheists, who carry hopelessness around with them 24/7. Thus, one cannot just bring someone into Christianity overnight. Thus, when we engage someone in our evangelism work within our community, we need to make every effort to see them again. At first, it may be by sharing emails, or cell phone numbers, and hopefully, their address, so we can may a personal visit. Once we are regularly visiting them at their homes, we need to buy out the time to see them at least weekly, even for a just a few minutes; otherwise, all was for not. We **(1)** look for interested ones, and then, **(2)** we cultivate the interest of those we have already found.

We might ask ourselves, 'am I open to developing disciples, or have I only been stuck in the mode of initiating interest?' Once we discover one, who has a love for righteousness, ones who are upset over world conditions, who are receptive to biblical truths, we need to grow that one into a disciple. Simply because a person is dismissive in an initial

294

discussion, this does not mean they are not open to biblical truths. We have to learn how to overcome those dismissive thoughts, which takes skill and practice. (Luke 19:3-5) How can we do this?

We have to be as skilled with our Bible, as one is with and tool from a professional trade. We can be in awe if we are able to see a skilled worker at work, thinking 'it must have taken a very long time to develop them skills.' In some cases, maybe so, but we can draw comfort in the fact that the human body and mind is very receptive to learning new skills. One way to begin is to have a regular Bible study program at home, studying (1) the Bible from cover to cover with commentary volumes, (2) how to interpret Scripture, (3) foundational doctrines, and (4) effective evangelism.

The more we know, the better we know, the more we practice, the more confident we will be, and the more effective we will be. There are many good books out there on how to become a better evangelist, how to communicate effectively with others, and how to reason from the Scripture, to overcome false reasoning, and to explain truths. Yes the head knowledge of how is very important, but it must be followed up by practice and repetition. We can begin by having a full share in commenting at any Christian meeting that is designed for such. We can also share things that we learn with our spiritual brothers and sisters. We can also invite fellow spiritual brothers and sisters over, to role-play and work on better communication. Like any skilled person, it takes dedication, patience, and love to become good, or better yet, effective.

Whenever we do have an opportunity to spend some quality time with one who truly wants to talk about the Bible, how should we approach it? First, the first few times, let him do most of the talking if he is so inclined, and be an active listener, discovering how he feels, thinks, and believes. We also are building rapport, because he feels as though we are truly interested in him. In this stage, he is likely to make many statements that are unbiblical, dismiss the urge to correct him constantly. If you are commenting to help him move along, find some aspect of what is said to agree with, making a brief statement. Once things are developed, it is time to be more structured.

It is always best to use ourselves in this next approach of helping him appreciate that things must be biblically correct. Start with, "'when I first started showing interest in the Bible, I would say things like, 'I think, I feel, or I believe.'" I was shown Matthew 7:21, which reads, "Not everyone who says to me, 'Lord, Lord,' will enter the kingdom of heaven, but the one who does the will of my Father who is in heaven." State, 'clearly, you would agree, it is not our will, what we think, what we believe, or how we feel, but the will of the father, what he thinks, believes and feels that is important?' If we read on in verse 23, it makes the point that we must always keep in mind. If we are only doing our will, Jesus will say to us, "'I never knew you; depart from me, you workers of lawlessness.'" Then say, "You would agree that our thinking must be biblically correct, right?"

This mindset of being biblical will be our guiding force until he has made it his own. We will have to keep sharing that point as we help him understand some of his beliefs are unbiblical. It is best to move a person into seeing the need of getting the correct understanding by having them see that is what the Bible requires, as the Bible carries the authority and power.

Hebrews 4:12 Updated American Standard Version (UASV)

[12] For the word of God is living and active and sharper than any two-edged sword, and piercing as far as the division of soul and spirit, of both joints and marrow, and able to judge the thoughts and intentions of the heart.

However, when it comes down to it, we have to be realistic, the world we live in has little interest, so we must address how we are to cope with such an environment.

Evangelizing in a World of Little Interest

How can we respectfully bow out of a conversation when we conclude that an unbeliever is not genuinely interested? (Pro. 15:23; 25:11) Should we try to overcome their attempts a rejecting the message until they out-and-out tell us to leave them alone? Would it not be better to end the conversation with them still having a measure of respect for us, a representative of Christianity? Ecclesiastes 3:7

We need to be able to discern between sharing biblical truths in a clear and understandable manner, giving the unbeliever the ability to make a choice, as opposed to forcing our truths on another. We are not some worldly salesperson. God never forced us to be his servants; rather he allowed us the freedom to whom or what we wanted to serve. (Josh. 24:15) We can feel good that we have carried out the Great Commission that Jesus gave all of us (Matt. 28:19-20), as long as we gave the unbeliever a clear and understandable message, even if he rejects that message.

Moreover, if someone rejects our message, he is not rejecting us he is rejecting God. If he merely rejects us for personal reasons, or out of hand, we should not view him as an enemy of the truth; he may be reached somewhere down the road. However, if this one seems well prepared with antichrist type answers, with anti-biblical, with anti-Christian answers, he may very well be an enemy of the truth, who actually proactively evangelizes against the truth. We should respect both of them, and we should move on either way. However, with the latter, even though he seems interested in dialoguing, his goal is to stumble us, so we should not continue, but rather respectfully bow out of the conversation.

For the one that is simply not interested, we can simply say, "I am grateful for the opportunity of speaking with you. Maybe a future conversation will go a little longer; nevertheless, I appreciate your time that you have given today. "May I simply leave you with this Bible tract?" If he says not, respect that too. Why should we take this approach?

The unbeliever will have gained respect for Christianity where it might have been lacking before. He will be impressed with the fact that you respected his right to choose. With the reasonableness that we showed him, it may mean the next Christian he talks to will get a better response. Thus, we watered, cultivated and God will use another to make the seeds of truth grow.

In instances where we are shut down before we ever get started, we need to have a Bible tract that we can offer. "Sir, may I at least leave you with this tract that takes but 1-2 minutes to read." On the back of that tract should be some kind of contact information that will help the unbeliever to get back in touch with us. We have to be balanced, both having the ability to win over those not wanting to talk, and the ability to know when not to try out of respect.

We do not know why some are not interested. They simply may have had somewhere to be, or he was too busy. Another may be his experiences of Christians arguing with him, not respecting him, even insulting him. Alternatively, it could simply be he is available or even wanting to get into a lengthy conversation. The last reason is why it is important to always quality our conversation openers with some kind of adjective: brief, short, or a couple of minutes. If we do say such a thing, we need to honor what we said and be brief.

Our doing any of the above does not mean that we never may an effort to overcome objections, or that we do not do as the apostle Paul, persuading ones to listen to the truth. (Ac 18:4; 26:28; 2 Cor. 5:20) We make allowances for those who show little or no interest, as they may be affected by time or circumstances, so we should not judge them as an enemy of the truth. If we get any indication that, we are trying to reason with the unreasonable, i.e., persuade a closed mind, we do not push ahead until we cause offense. Rather, we must use our God-given discernment, to warmly and respectful bow out of the conversation, leaving the unbeliever with one morsel of rapport.

We must also keep in mind that our ministry is more than winning souls for Christ. Another aspect of our ministry is warning the wicked, even though almost none will accept the truth because they have a closed heart and mind. Nevertheless, even though this chapter started out quite optimistically, we must also be realistic as to the other side of our evangelism job. If I have made one point clear in the entirety of this book, may, it be this. We are not doomsayers, like the Westboro Baptist Church. We do not get loud and yell, nor do we threaten them with eternal torment. This type of rhetoric wins no souls that last. They end up serving God out of fear, not love.

God's people willing offer themselves to their heavenly Father just before the return of Jesus Christ.

Psalm 110:3 Updated American Standard Version (UASV)

³ Your people will offer themselves willingly
  on the day of your power,
  in holy array;
from the womb of the dawn,
  the dew of Your youth belongs to you.

Our heavenly Father and his Son, Jesus Christ will be well pleased with those who offer themselves willingly, evangelizing with their whole soul, mind, heart and spirit.

2 Corinthians 9:7 Updated American Standard Version (UASV)

⁷ Each one must give as he has decided in his heart, not reluctantly or under compulsion, for God loves a cheerful giver.

If God loves a cheerful giver, one that is not under compulsion, or reluctant, why did Paul say in his previous letter to the Corinthians, "For if I preach the gospel, that gives me no ground for boasting. For necessity is laid upon me. Woe to me if I do not preach the gospel!" Here Paul is saying, "Necessity is laid upon" him, and 'Woe to me if I do not preach the gospel!' Which is it? On the other hand, did Paul change his mind in the few months between First and Second Corinthians? It is not a contradiction, or change of mind, as they both agree. A necessity is laid upon us, but God wants us to do it willingly, not under compulsion. The "woe" that Paul felt was not out of some fear of reprisal, if he did not carry out his ministry of evangelism. Rather, it was a feeling of "woe," because he felt the same as God, the love for the people fear that they would miss the hope of "life." Paul was well aware of and empathetic to the Hebrew Old Testament texts, such as

Ezekiel 3:18 Updated American Standard Version (UASV)

¹⁸ When I say to the wicked, 'You shall surely die,' and you give him no warning, nor speak to warn the wicked from his wicked way, in order to save his life, that wicked person shall die in his iniquity, but his blood I will require at your hand.

Warning the Wicked

It is our responsibility to give a warning to the wicked people, just as it was Ezekiel's responsibility to give a warning to Judah. Ezekiel, Paul and us realize that God's love for humanity, who suffers from imperfection and the desire to do wicked things; need to be warned as well. Yes, Paul loved the people he witnessed to, and so should we. If we go ahead and look at the next verse, we will see that Paul willingly carried out his ministry, making personal sacrifice in order to do so.

1 Corinthians 9:17 English Standard Version (ESV)

¹⁷ For if I do this voluntarily, I have a reward; but if against my will, I have a stewardship entrusted to me.

It should sadden all of us that so many out of so-called conservative Christianity are not arranging their lives around an evangelism program because their church is not carrying out the work. Nevertheless, an author on evangelism cannot judge the hearts its readers. However, Paul himself clearly said, "each one tests his own work, and then his reason to boast will be in himself alone and not in his neighbor." (Gal. 6:4) We are well aware of the fact that many of us have families, and Paul was quite clear about our need to care for them too. He wrote, "But if anyone does not provide for his relatives, and especially for members of his household, he has denied the faith and is worse than an unbeliever." (1 Tim. 5:8) Regardless, our love of our neighbor and even our enemy (Matt. 5:43-44), should move us to have some share in the evangelism work, we simply need to buy out the time. If our church has nothing along these lines, we may want to inquire as to why.

If we find joy in the fact we have offered a used coat to a homeless person or a meal to a hungry family at a shelter; imagine what our joy will be if we play a role in getting another person on the path to eternal life. Imagine how our inner person will shine as we see this unbeliever become a believer. Imagine each time they learn something new, or finally, grasp something that they have been struggling with, we will have a continued joy as they grow in the truth, and make it their own.

Exercise

Find someone you do not know this week and share this. Some have asked this question, 'How can we know for sure that Jesus was resurrected?' Have you ever wondered about that? *Give them a moment to respond.* Then briefly share with them 1 Corinthians 15:14, emphasizing the importance of why Jesus' resurrection matters. If we could speak again, I can show you how we know that the resurrection was not a deception or some fraud.

Find someone you do not know this week and share this. The world of the 21 century has been nothing but chaos since it began. Has this ever made you stop and wonder about the meaning of life? Why are we here? Is there something more? Give them a moment to respond. What would you say is the biggest problem standing in the way of worldwide peace and happiness today? *Give them a moment to respond.* What if I could show you from the Bible, just how God is going to remove that problem and all other, could we talk again?

Review Questions

- What is an evangelizer?
- Why is it vital that we share and the people hear the good news?
- How can we effectively and efficiently sharing the Word of God?
- How does the principle behind Luke 10:5 help us with introductions?
- Why are warm introductions so effective?
- What are subject introductions, and why are they so effective?
- Why are simple introductions effective?
- Why is it important that we make every effort to see them again?
- How are we to evangelize in a world with little interest?
- What are some reasons why some may not engage us I a conversation?
- We win souls for Christ, but what else are we doing while evangelizing?

Bibliography

Akin, Daniel L. *The New American Commentary: 1, 2, 3 John.* Nashville, TN: Broadman & Holman , 2001.

Aldrich, C Joseph. *Lifestyle Evangelism.* Portland, OR: Multnoma Press, 1981.

Anders, Max. *Holman New Testament Commentary: vol. 8, Galatians, Ephesians, Philippians, Colossians.* Nashville, TN: Broadman & Holman Publishers, 1999.

—. *Holman Old Testament Commentary - Proverbs .* Nashville: B&H Publishing, 2005.

Anders, Max, and Doug McIntosh. *Holman Old Testament Commentary - Deuteronomy.* Nashville: B&H Publishing, 2009.

Anders, Max, and Steven Lawson. *Holman Old Testament Commentary - Psalms: 11.* Grand Rapids: B&H Publishing, 2004.

Anders, Max, and Trent Butler. *Holman Old Testament Commentary: Isaiah.* Nashiville, TN: B&H Publishing, 2002.

Andrews, Edward D. *THE EVANGELISM HANDBOOK: How All Christians Can Effectively Share God's Word in Their Community.* Cambridge: Christian Publishing House, 2013.

Andrews, Edward D. *THE CHRISTIAN APOLOGIST: Always Being Prepared to Make a Defense .* Cambridge: Christian Publishing House, 2014.

Andrews, Stephen J, and Robert D Bergen. *Holman Old Testament Commentary: 1-2 Samuel.* Nashville: Broadman & Holman, 2009.

Bercot, David W. *A Dictionary of Early Christian Beliefs.* Peabody: Hendrickson, 1998.

Boa, Kenneth, and William Kruidenier. *Holman New Testament Commentary: Romans.* Nashville: Broadman & Holman, 2000.

Brand, Chad, Charles Draper, and England Archie. *Holman Illustrated Bible Dictionary: Revised, Updated and Expanded.* Nashville, TN: Holman, 2003.

Bromiley, Geoffrey W., and Gerhard Friedrich. *Theological Dictionary of the New Testament, ed. Gerhard Kittel, vol. 4.* Grand Rapids, MI: Eerdmans, 1964-.

Brooks, Ronald M, and Norman L Geisler. *Come, Let Us Reason: An Introduction to Logical Thinking.* Grand Rapids: Baker Books, 1990.

Butler, Trent C. *Holman New Testament Commentary: Luke.* Nashville, TN: Broadman & Holman Publishers, 2000.

Butler, Trent C. *Holman Old Testament Commentary - Hosea, Joel, Amos, Obadiah, Jonah, Micah* . Nashville: Broadman & Holman Publishers, 2005.

Carpenter, Eugene E., and Philip W Comfort. *The Holman Treasury of Key Bible Words: 200 Greek and 200 Hebrew Words Defined and Explained.* Nashville: Broadman & Holman Publishers, 2000.

Carson, D. A. *New Bible Commentary: 21st Century Edition. 4th ed.* Downers Grove: Inter-Varisity Press, 1994.

Coleman, E. Robert. *The Master Plan of Evangelism.* Westwood, NJ: Fleming H. Revell Company, 1964.

Cooper, Rodney. *Holman New Testament Commentary: Mark.* Nashville: Broadman & Holman Publishers, 2000.

Craig, William Lane. *On Guard: Defending Your Faith with Reason and Precision.* Ontario: David C. Cook, 2010.

Dockery, David S. *HOLMAN CONCISE BIBLE COMMENTARY Simple, straightforward commentary on every book of the Bible.* Nashville: Broadman & Holman, 1998.

Easley, Kendell H. *Holman New Testament Commentary, vol. 12, Revelation.* (Nashville, TN: Broadman & Holman Publishers, 1998.

Easton, M. G. *Easton's Bible Dictionary.* Oak Harbor, WA: Logos Research Systems, 1996, c1897.

Edwards, James R. *The Pillar New Testament Commentary: The Gospel according to Mark.* Grand Rapids: Wm. B. Eerdmans Publishing Co., 2002.

Eims, LeRoy. *One to One Evangelism.* Wheaton, IL: Victor Books, 1974, 1990.

Elwell, Walter A. *Baker Encyclopedia of the Bible.* Grand Rapids: Baker Book House, 1988.

—. *Evangelical Dictionary of Theology (Second Edition).* Grand Rapids: Baker Academic, 2001.

Elwell, Walter A, and Philip Wesley Comfort. *Tyndale Bible Dictionary.* Wheaton, Ill: Tyndale House Publishers, 2001.

Freedman, David Noel, Allen C. Myers, and Astrid B. Beck. *Eerdmans Dictionary of the Bible* . Grand Rapids, Mich.: W.B. Eerdmans , 2000.

Gangel, Kenneth O. *Holman New Testament Commentary: Acts.* Nashville, TN: Broadman & Holman Publishers, 1998.

Gangel, Kenneth O. *Holman New Testament Commentary, vol. 4, John* . Nashville, TN: Broadman & Holman Publishers, 2000.

—. *Holman Old Testament Commentary: Daniel.* Nashville: Broadman & Holman Publishers, 2001.

Geisler, Norman, and David Geisler. *CONVERSATION EVANGELISM: How to Listen and Speak So You Can Be Heard.* Eugene: Harvest House Publishers, 2014.

Green, Joel B, Scot McKnight, and Howard Marshall. *Dictionary of Jesus and the Gospels.* Downers Grove, IL: InterVarsity Press, 1992.

Guder, Darrell L. *Missional Church: A Vision for the Sending of the Church in North America.* Grand Rapids: Wm. B Eerdmans Publishing Co., 1998.

Hastings, James, John A Selbie, and John C Lambert. *A Dictionary of Christ and the Gospels.* New York, NY: Charles Scribner's Sons, 1907.

Hindson, Ed, and Ergun Caner. *The Popular Encyclopedia of Apologetics: Surveying the Evidence for the Truth of Christianity.* Eugene: Harvest House, 2008.

Kennedy, D. James. *Evangelism Explosion.* Wheaton, IL: Tyndale House Publishers, 1977.

Kistemaker, Simon J., and William Hendriksen. *Exposition of the First Epistle to the Corinthians, vol. 18, New Testament Commentary.* Grand Rapids, MI: Baker Book House, 1953–2001.

Knight, George W. *The Pastoral Epistles: A Commentary on the Greek Text, New International Greek Testament Commentary.* Grand Rapids, MI; Carlisle, England: W.B. Eerdmans; Paternoster Press, 1992.

Larsen, L. David. *The Evangelism Mandate.* Wheaton: Crossway Books, 1992.

Larson, Knute. *Holman New Testament Commentary, vol. 9, I & II Thessalonians, I & II Timothy, Titus, Philemon.* Nashville, TN: Broadman & Holman Publishers, 2000.

Lea, Thomas D. *Holman New Testament Commentary: Vol. 10, Hebrews, James.* Nashville, TN: Broadman & Holman Publishers, 1999.

Lea, Thomas D., and Hayne P. Griffin. *The New American Commentary, vol. 34, 1, 2 Timothy, Titus.* Nashville: Broadman & Holman Publishers, 1992.

Louw, Johannes P, Eugene A Nida, Smith. Rondal B, and Karen A Munson. *GREEK-ENGLISH NEW TESTAMENT Based on Semantic Domains (Vol. 1, Second Edition).* New York: United Bible Societies, 1988, 1989.

Manser, Martin H. (Managing Editor) McGrath, Alister E. (General Editor) Packer, J. I. (Consultant Editor). *DICTIONARY OF BIBLE THEMES: The Accessible and Comprehenssive Tool for Topical Studies.* Grand Rapids: Zondervan Publishing Company, 2009.

Martin, Glen S. *Holman Old Testament Commentary: Numbers.* Nashville: Broadman & Holman Publishers, 2002.

Mayers, Mark K. *Christianity Confronts Culture: A Strategy for Crosscultural Evangelism.* Grand Rapids : Zondervan, 1987.

McCue, Rolland. *Promises Unfulfilled: The Failed Strategy of Modern Evangelism.* Greenville, SC: Ambassador Group, 2004.

McRaney, William. *The Art of Personal Evangelism.* Nashville: Broadman & Holman, 2003.

Mirriam-Webster, Inc. *Mirriam-Webster's Collegiate Dictionary. Eleventh Edition.* Springfield: Mirriam-Webster, Inc., 2003.

Mitchell, Michael R. "The Conditions of Discipleship." *Liberty University.* 2004. http://bb7.liberty.edu/webapps/portal/frameset.jsp?tab_tab_group_id=_2_1&url=%2Fwebapps%2Fblackboard%2Fexecute%2Flauncher%3Ftype%3DCourse%26id%3D_998944_ (accessed September 29, 2010).

Mitchell, Michael R. *Leading, Teaching, and Making Disciples: World-Class Education in the Church, School, and Home.* Bloomington: Crossbooks, 2010.

Morgenthaler, Sally. *Worship Evangelism.* Grand Rapids: Zondervan Publishing House, 1995.

Mounce, William D. *Mounce's Complete Expository Dictionary of Old & New Testament Words*. Grand Rapids, MI: Zondervan, 2006.

Myers, Allen C. *The Eerdmans Bible Dictionary* . Grand Rapids, Mich: Eerdmans, 1987.

Nash, Ronald H. *Life's Ultimate Questions: An Introduction to Philosophy*. Grand Rapids, MI: Zondervan, 1999.

Packer, J. I. *Evangelism and the Sovereignty of God*. Downers Grove, IL: InterVarsity Press, 1979.

Posterski, C. Donald. *Reinventing Evangelism*. Downers Grove, IL: InterVarsity Press, 1989.

Pratt Jr, Richard L. *Holman New Testament Commentary: I & II Corinthians, vol. 7*. Nashville: Broadman & Holman Publishers, 2000.

Rainer, S. Thomas. *Evangelism in the Twenty-First Century*. Wheaton, IL: Harold Shaw Publishers, 1989.

Reid, Alvin. *Introduction to Evangelism*. Nashville: Boardman & Holmes , 1998.

Rooker, Mark. *Holman Old Testament Commentary: Ezekiel*. Nashville: Broadman & Holman Publishers, 2005.

Schreiner, Thomas R. *The New American Commentary: 1, 2 Peter, Jude*. Nashville: Broadman & Holman, 2003.

Sisson, Dick. *Evangelism Encounter*. Chicago, IL: Victor Books, 1988.

Stein, Robert H. *A Basic Guide to Interpreting the Bible: Playing by the Rules*. Grand Rapids: Baker Books, 1994.

Stetzer, Ed, and David Putman. *Breaking the Missional Code: Your Church Can Become a Missionary in Your Community*. Nashville: Broadman & Holman, 2006.

Stott, John. *The Art of Preaching in the Twentieth Century: Between Two Worlds*. Grand Rapids, MI: Wm. B. Eerdmans, 1994.

Sutton, Jerry. *A Primer on Biblical Preaching*. Bloomington, IN: CrossBooks, 2011.

Vine, W E. *Vine's Expository Dictionary of Old and New Testament Words*. Nashville: Thomas Nelson, 1996.

Wallace, Daniel. *Greek Grammar Beyond the Basics*. Grad Rapids: Zondervan, 1996.

Walls, David, and Max Anders. *Holman New Testament Commentary: I & II Peter, I, II & III John, Jude.* Nashville: Broadman & Holman Publishers, 1996.

Weber, Stuart K. *Holman New Testament Commentary, vol. 1, Matthew.* Nashville, TN: Broadman & Holman Publishers, 2000.

Wood, D R W. *New Bible Dictionary (Third Edition).* Downers Grove: InterVarsity Press, 1996.

Zodhiates, Spiros. *The Complete Word Study Dictionary: New Testament.* Chattanooga: AMG Publishers, 2000, c1992, c1993.

Subject Index

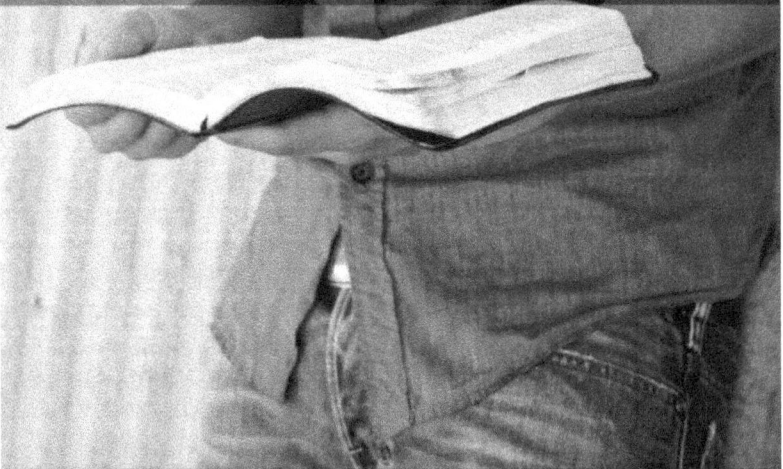

SECOND EDITION

THE CHRISTIAN
APOLOGIST
Always Being Prepared to
Make a Defense

Andrews provides an excellent apologetic tool for
Christians seeking to better understand & defend
the Word of God."—Christian Publishing House

EDWARD D. ANDREWS

THE EVANGELISM HANDBOOK

How All Christians Can Effectively Share God's
Word in Their Community

EDWARD D. ANDREWS

I rejoiced greatly to find some of your children
walking in the truth, just as we received
commandment from the Father.—2 John 1:4

Edward D. Andrews

YOUR WORD
IS TRUTH

Being Sanctified in the Truth

EVIDENCE THAT YOU ARE TRULY CHRISTIAN

Keep Testing Yourselves to See If You Are In the Faith—Keep Examining Yourselves

EDWARD D. ANDREWS

"SAVING Those Who DOUBT"

CRISIS OF
FAITH

EDWARD D. ANDREWS

OVERCOMING BIBLE DIFFICULTIES

Answers to the So-Called Errors and Contradictions

EDWARD D. ANDREWS

www.ingramcontent.com/pod-product-compliance
Lightning Source LLC
Chambersburg PA
CBHW021501090426
42739CB00007B/408